Shojo Beat

Baby & Me

Vol. 14

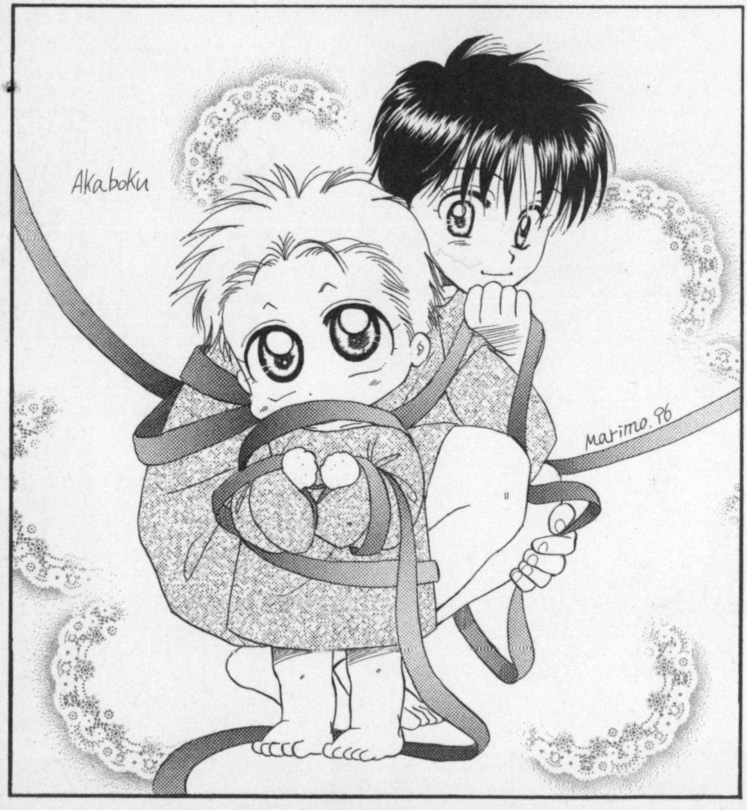
Akaboku
Marimo.96

Story & Art by **Marimo Ragawa**

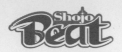

BABY & ME, Vol. 14
The Shojo Beat Manga Edition

Story & Art by
MARIMO RAGAWA

English Adaptation/Lance Caselman
Translation/JN Productions
Touch-up Art & Lettering/HudsonYards
Design/Yuki Ameda
Editor/Shaenon K. Garrity

Editor in Chief, Books/Alvin Lu
Editor in Chief, Magazines/Marc Weidenbaum
VP, Publishing Licensing/Rika Inouye
VP, Sales & Product Marketing/Gonzalo Ferreyra
VP, Creative/Linda Espinosa
Publisher/Hyoe Narita

Printed in Canada

Published by VIZ Media, LLC
P.O. Box 77010
San Francisco, CA 94107

Shojo Beat Manga Edition
10 9 8 7 6 5 4 3 2 1
First printing, June 2009

PARENTAL ADVISORY
BABY & ME is rated T for Teen and is recommended for ages 13 and up. This volume contains adult situations.
ratings.viz.com

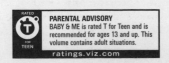

store.viz.com

BABY & Me

Creator: Marimo Ragawa

SBM Title: *Baby & Me*

Date of Birth: September 21

Blood Type: B

Major Works: *Time Limit,
Baby & Me*, *N.Y. N.Y.*, and
Shanimuni-Go (Desperately—Go)

M arimo Ragawa first started submitting manga to a comic magazine when she was 12 years old. She kept up her submissions
for four years, but to no avail. She decided to submit her work
to the magazine *Hana to Yume*, where she received Top Prize in
the Monthly Manga Contest as well as an honorable mention (Kasaku) in the
magazine's Big Challenge contest. Her first manga was titled *Time Limit*. *Baby
& Me* was honored with a Shogakukan Manga Award in 1995 and was spun
off into an anime.

Ragawa's work showcases some very cute and expressive line work along with
an incredible ability to depict complex emotions and relationships. Some of
her other works include *N.Y. N.Y.* and the tennis manga *Shanimuni-Go*.

Ragawa has two brothers and two sisters.

BABY & ME — Table of Contents

Chapter 75   5

Chapter 76   35

Chapter 77   65

Chapter 78   99

Chapter 79   129

Chapter 80   159

Selected Illustrations
from My Old Notebooks   189

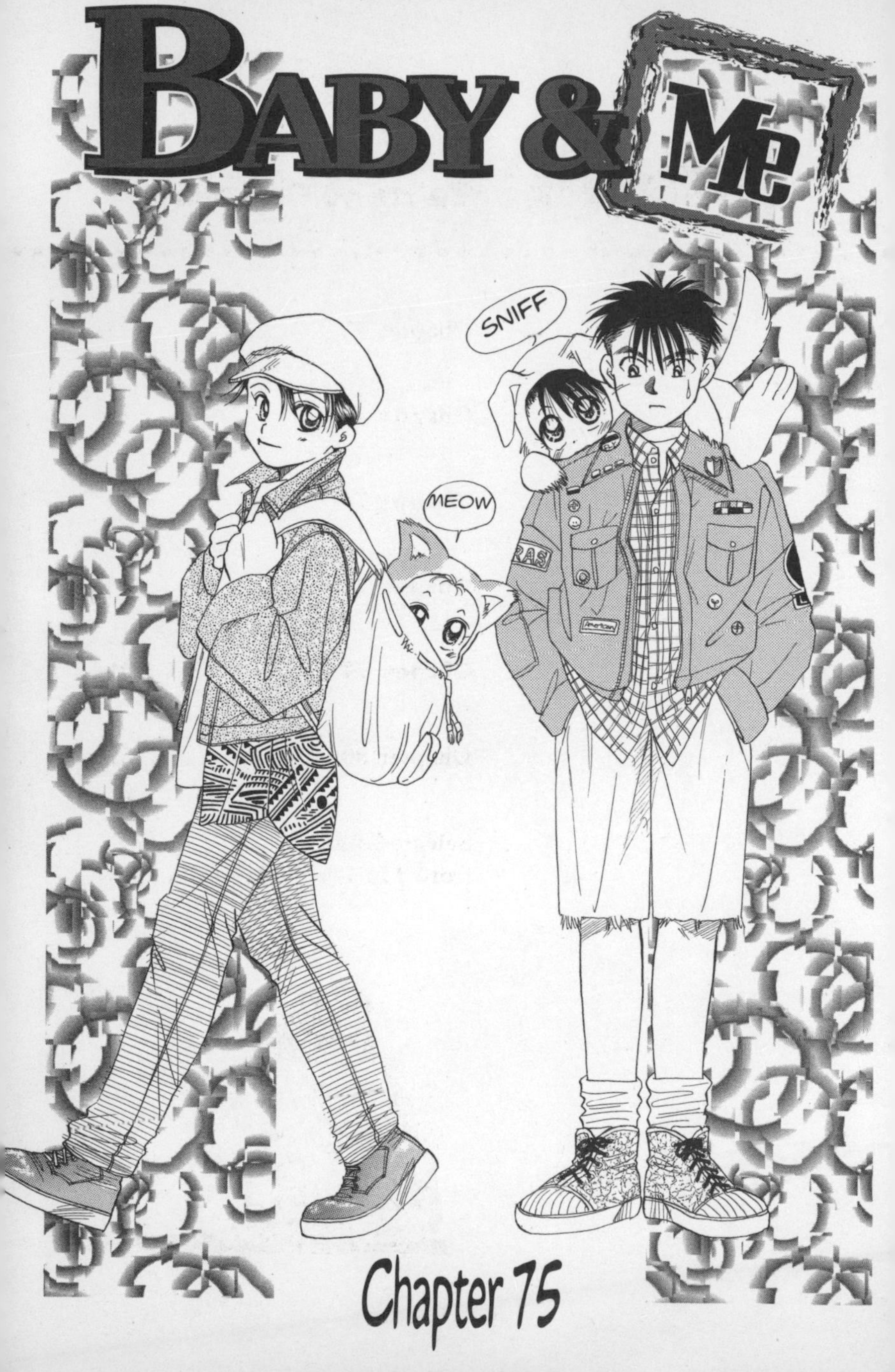
BABY & ME
SNIFF
MEOW
Chapter 75

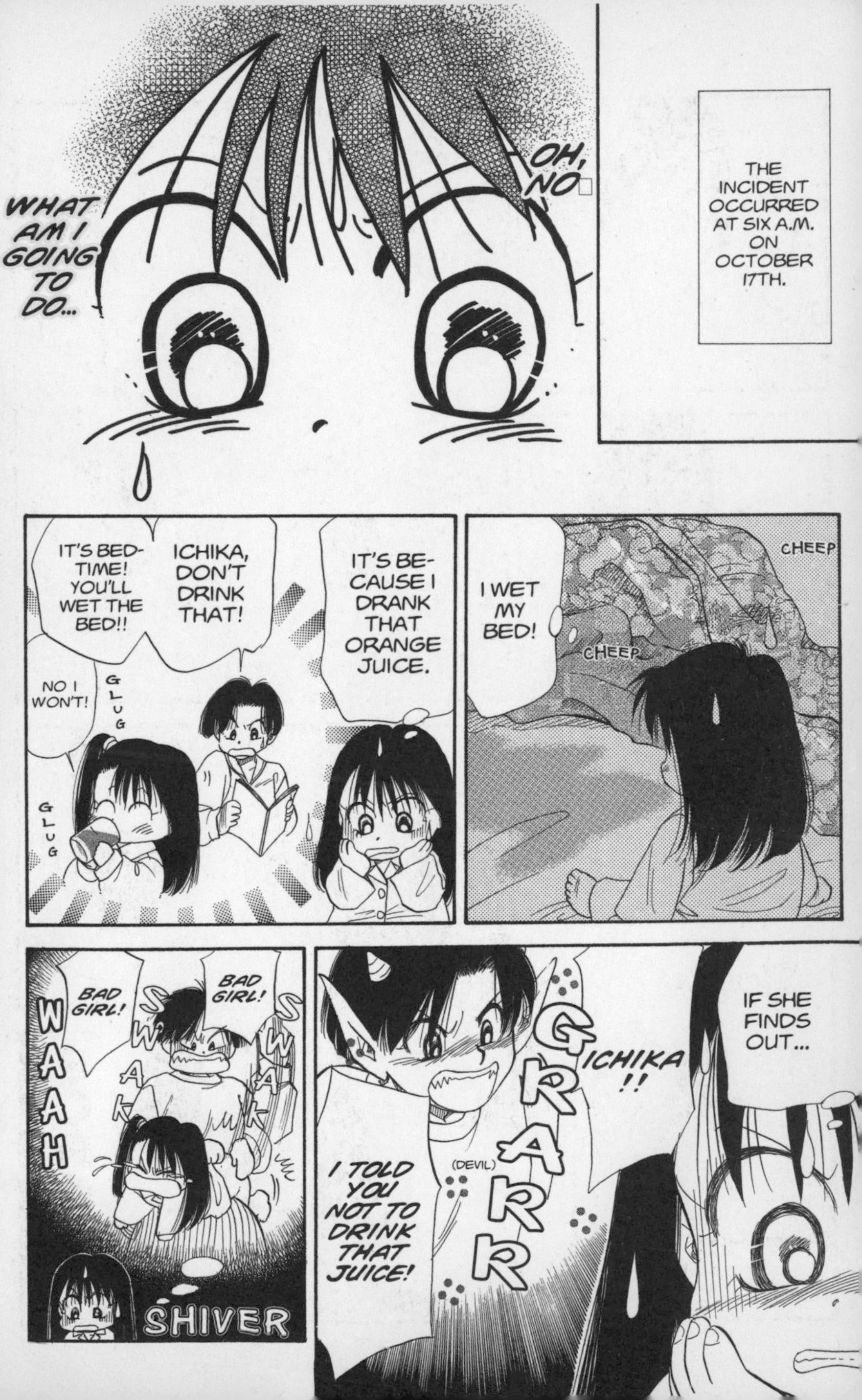
THE INCIDENT OCCURRED AT SIX A.M. ON OCTOBER 17TH.
OH, NO
WHAT AM I GOING TO DO...
CHEEP
I WET MY BED!
CHEEP
IT'S BE-CAUSE I DRANK THAT ORANGE JUICE.
ICHIKA, DON'T DRINK THAT!
IT'S BED-TIME! YOU'LL WET THE BED!!
NO I WON'T!
GLUG
GLUG
IF SHE FINDS OUT...
ICHIKA!!
GRARR
(DEVIL)
I TOLD YOU NOT TO DRINK THAT JUICE!
BAD GIRL!
SWAK
BAD GIRL!
SWAK
WAAAH
SHIVER

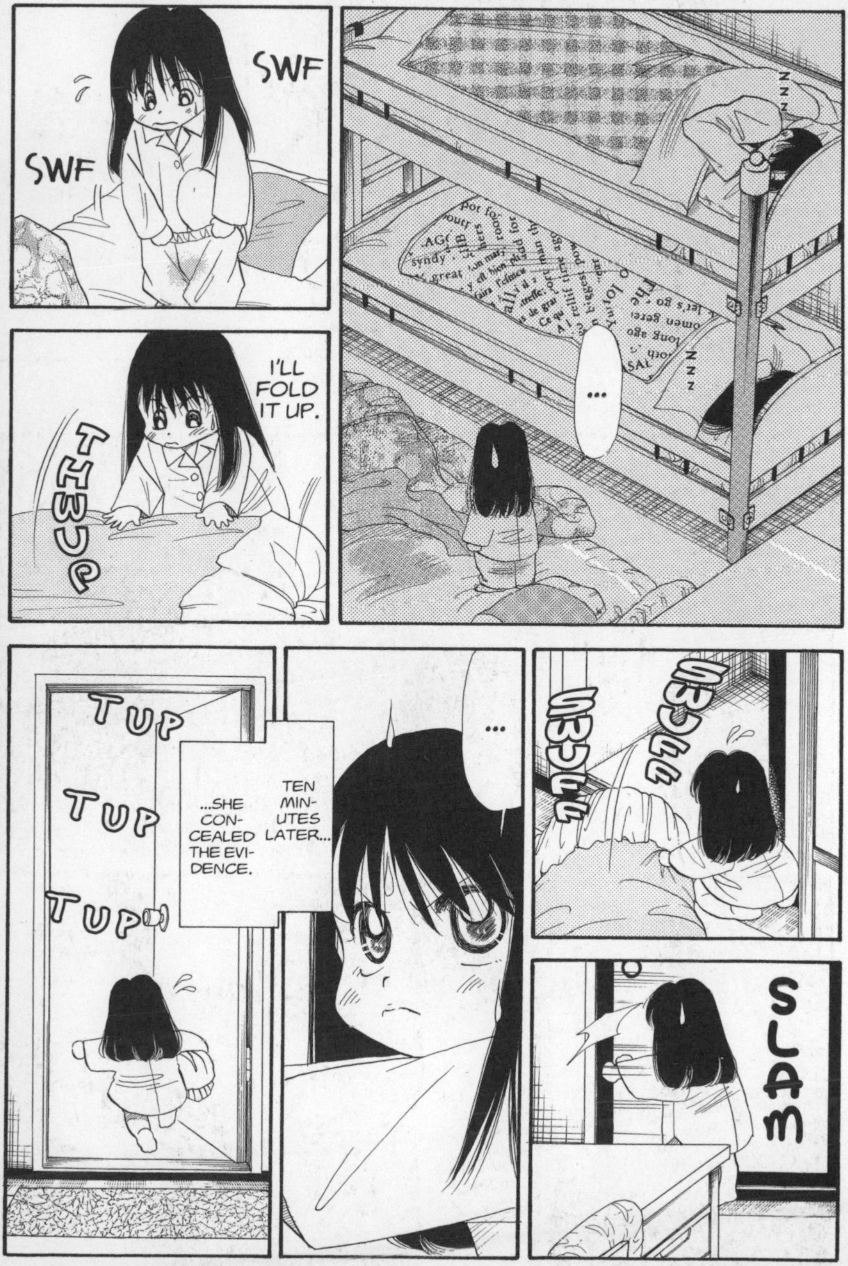
Z Z Z
...
Z Z Z
SWF
SWF
I'LL FOLD IT UP.
THWUP
SWUFF
SWUFF
SLAM
...
TEN MIN-UTES LATER...
...SHE CON-CEALED THE EVI-DENCE.
TUP
TUP
TUP

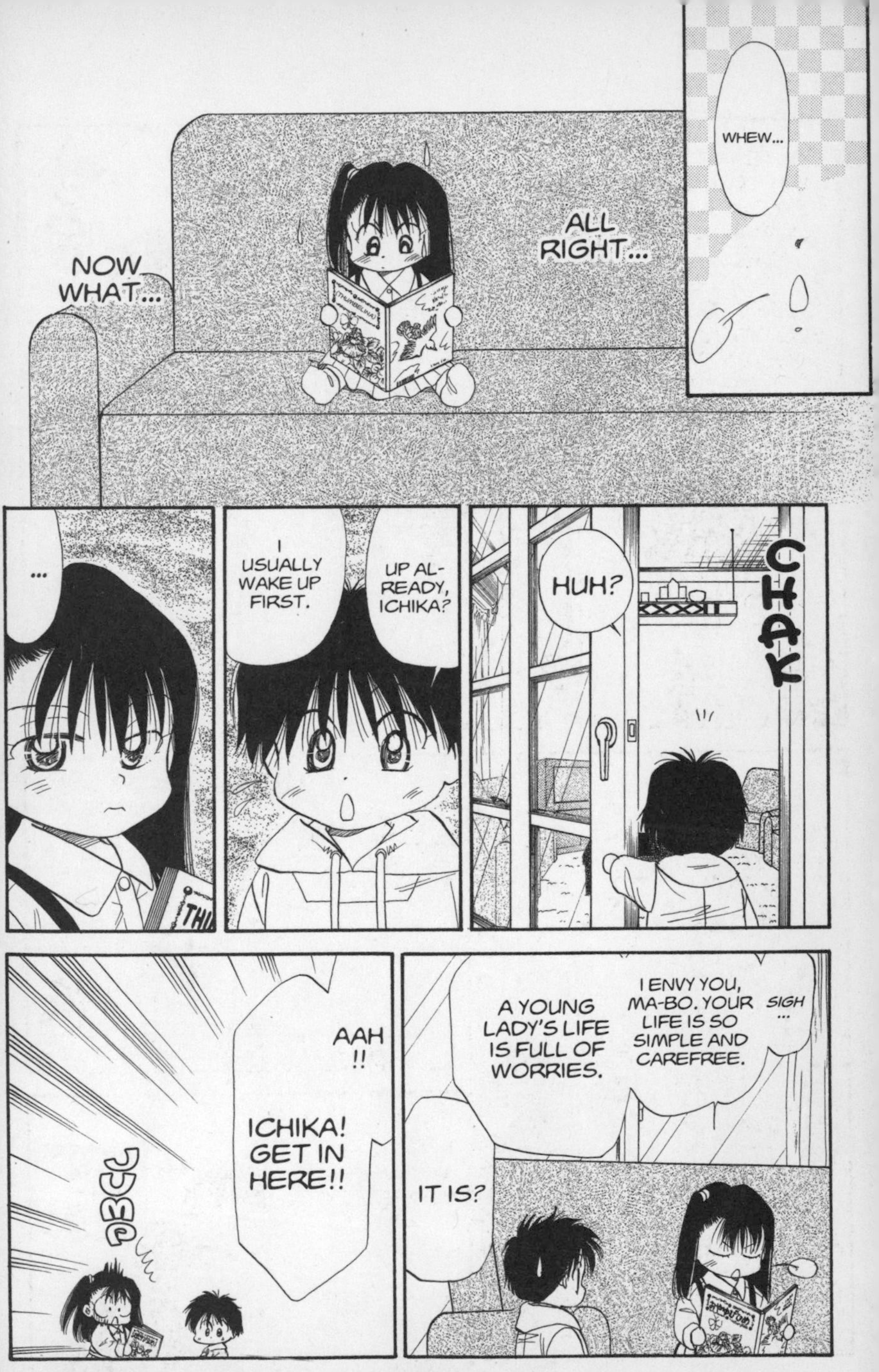
WHEW...
ALL RIGHT...
NOW WHAT...
HUH?
CHAK
UP AL-READY, ICHIKA?
I USUALLY WAKE UP FIRST.
...
SIGH ...
I ENVY YOU, MA-BO. YOUR LIFE IS SO SIMPLE AND CAREFREE.
A YOUNG LADY'S LIFE IS FULL OF WORRIES.
IT IS?
AAH !!
ICHIKA! GET IN HERE!!
JUMP

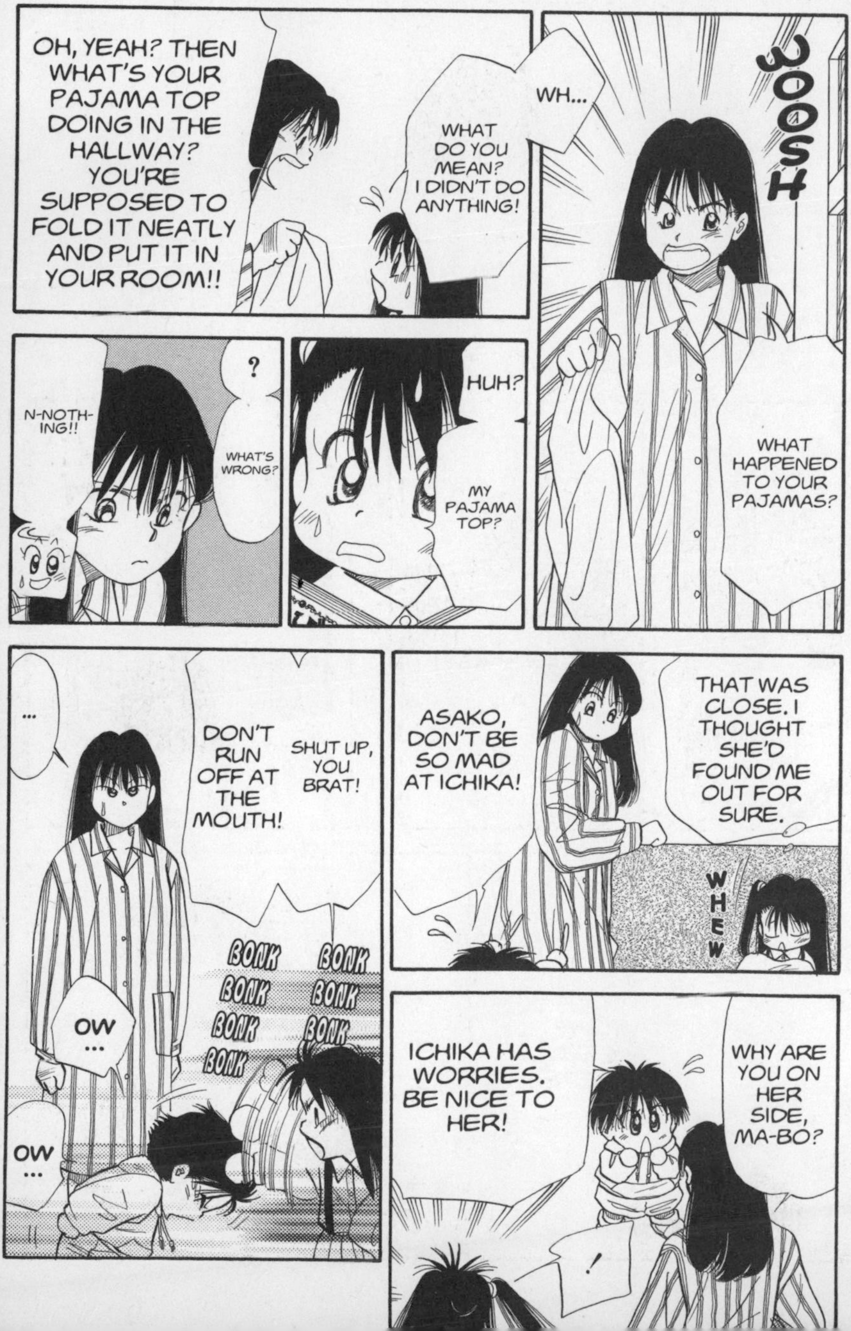
WOOSH
WH...
WHAT HAPPENED TO YOUR PAJAMAS?
WHAT DO YOU MEAN? I DIDN'T DO ANYTHING!
OH, YEAH? THEN WHAT'S YOUR PAJAMA TOP DOING IN THE HALLWAY? YOU'RE SUPPOSED TO FOLD IT NEATLY AND PUT IT IN YOUR ROOM!!
HUH?
MY PAJAMA TOP?
?
WHAT'S WRONG?
N-NOTHING!!
THAT WAS CLOSE. I THOUGHT SHE'D FOUND ME OUT FOR SURE.
WHEW
ASAKO, DON'T BE SO MAD AT ICHIKA!
WHY ARE YOU ON HER SIDE, MA-BO?
ICHIKA HAS WORRIES. BE NICE TO HER!
!
SHUT UP, YOU BRAT!
DON'T RUN OFF AT THE MOUTH!
...
BONK BONK BONK
BONK BONK BONK BONK
OW...
OW...

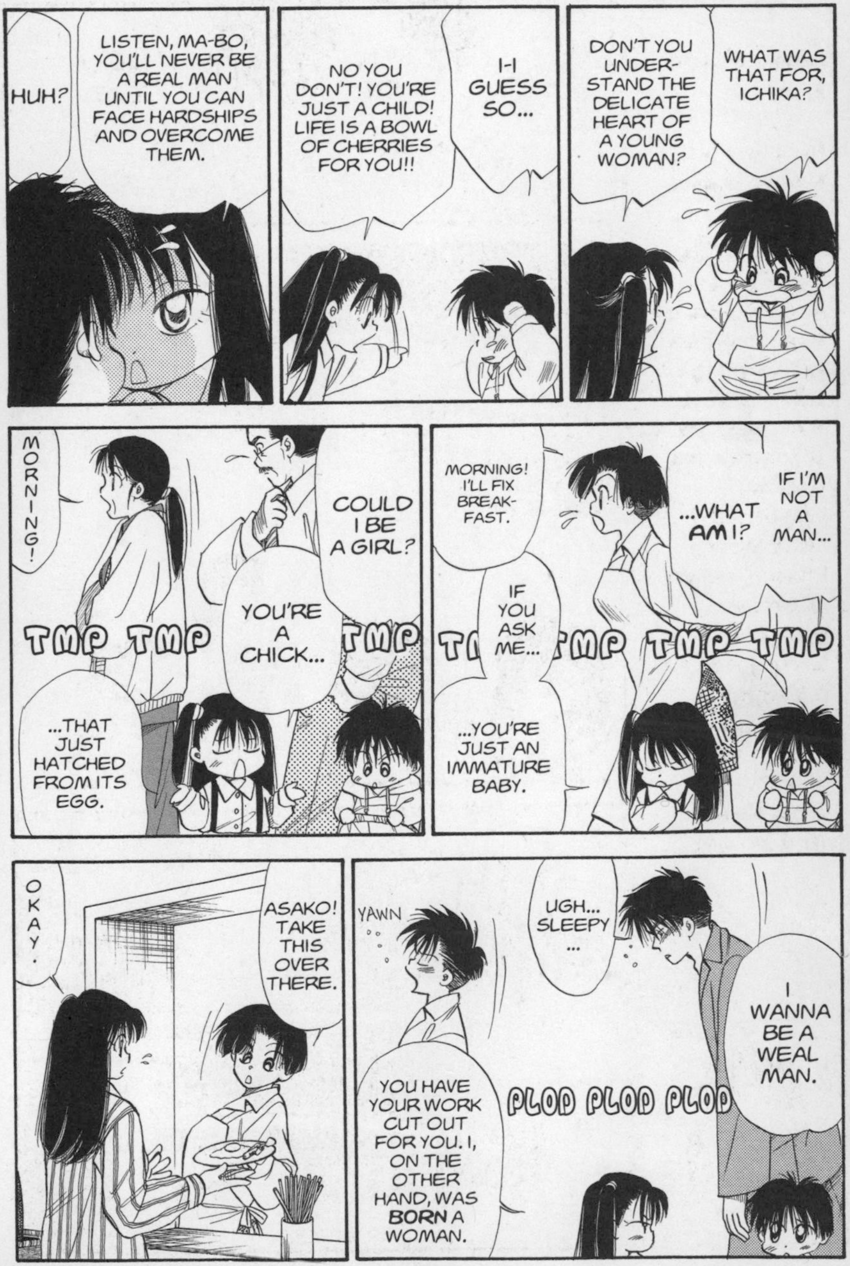
WHAT WAS THAT FOR, ICHIKA?
DON'T YOU UNDERSTAND THE DELICATE HEART OF A YOUNG WOMAN?
I-I GUESS SO...
NO YOU DON'T! YOU'RE JUST A CHILD! LIFE IS A BOWL OF CHERRIES FOR YOU!!
LISTEN, MA-BO, YOU'LL NEVER BE A REAL MAN UNTIL YOU CAN FACE HARDSHIPS AND OVERCOME THEM.
HUH?
IF I'M NOT A MAN...
...WHAT **AM** I?
MORNING! I'LL FIX BREAK-FAST.
IF YOU ASK ME...
TMP TMP TMP
...YOU'RE JUST AN IMMATURE BABY.
COULD I BE A GIRL?
MORNING!
YOU'RE A CHICK...
TMP TMP TMP
...THAT JUST HATCHED FROM ITS EGG.
I WANNA BE A WEAL MAN.
UGH... SLEEPY...
YAWN
PLOD PLOD PLOD
YOU HAVE YOUR WORK CUT OUT FOR YOU. I, ON THE OTHER HAND, WAS **BORN** A WOMAN.
ASAKO! TAKE THIS OVER THERE.
OKAY.

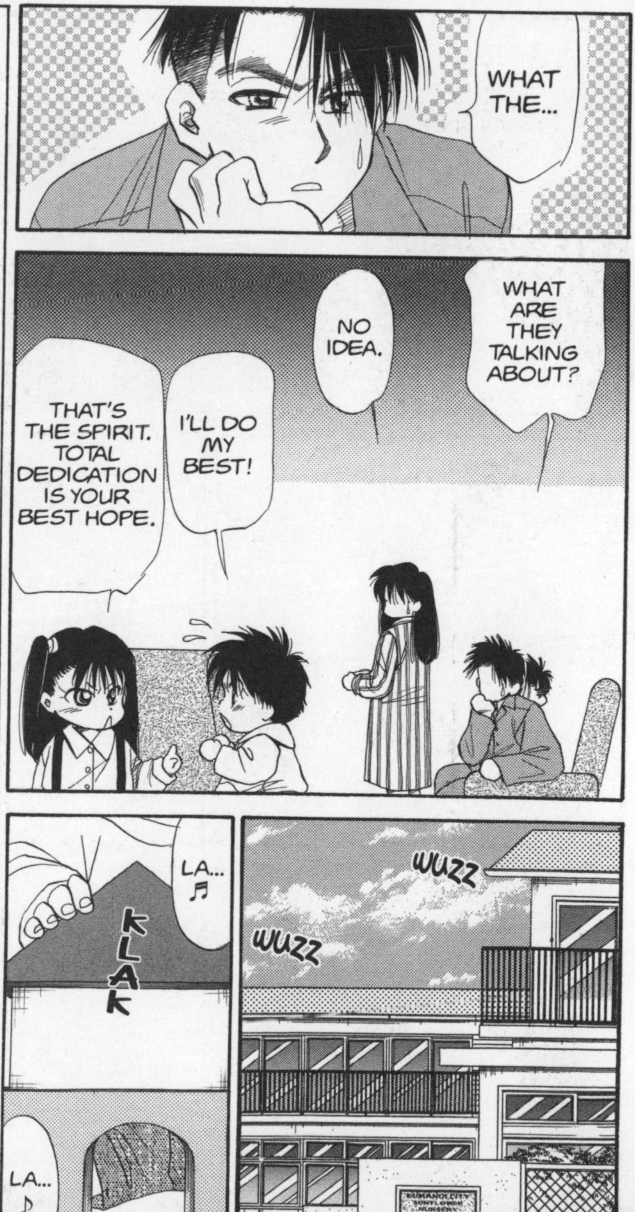
WHAT THE...
WHAT ARE THEY TALKING ABOUT?
NO IDEA.
I'LL DO MY BEST!
THAT'S THE SPIRIT. TOTAL DEDICATION IS YOUR BEST HOPE.
WUZZ
WUZZ
LA... ♬
KLAK
LA... ♪

Author's Note Part 1

Hello, this is Marimo Ragawa.

As I write this, I have a huge swollen cheek from having my lower left wisdom tooth pulled. It's been three days, but it's still painful and bleeding.
I'm worried about the trip I have planned for tomorrow.
(I hope I'll be able to enjoy food.)
It takes me a whole hour to eat a meal right now. Well, they say eating slowly is good for you.

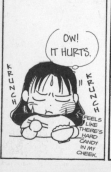

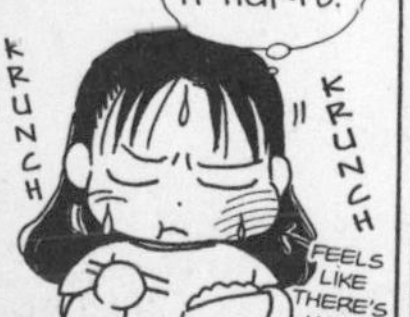
OW! IT HURTS.
KRUNCH
KRUNCH
FEELS LIKE THERE'S HARD CANDY IN MY CHEEK.

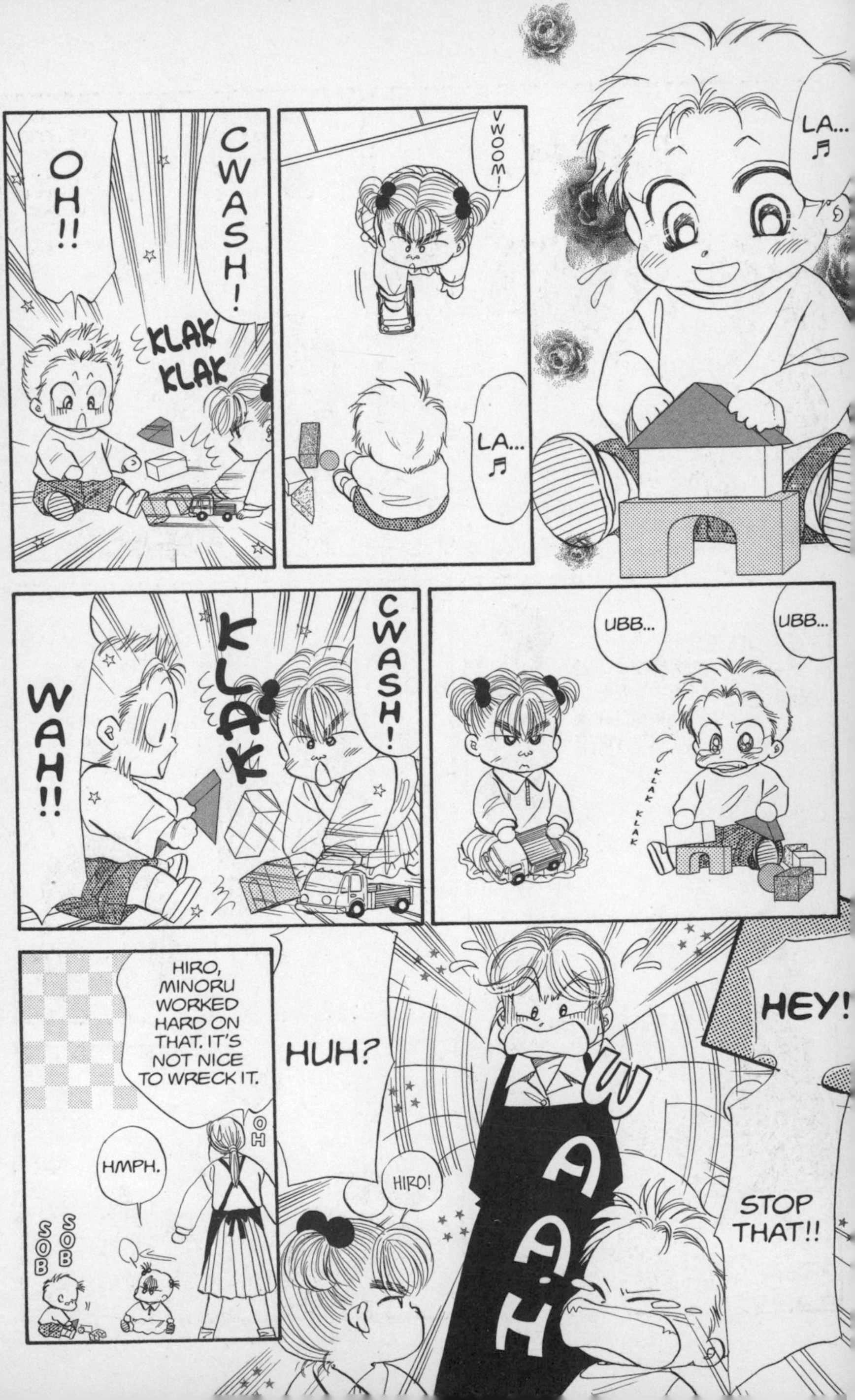

LA... ♬
VWOOM!
LA... ♬
CWASH!
OH!!
KLAK KLAK
UBB...
UBB...
KLAK KLAK
CWASH!
KLAK
WAH!!
HEY!
STOP THAT!!
WAAH
HIRO!
HUH?
HIRO, MINORU WORKED HARD ON THAT. IT'S NOT NICE TO WRECK IT.
OH
HMPH.
SOB SOB

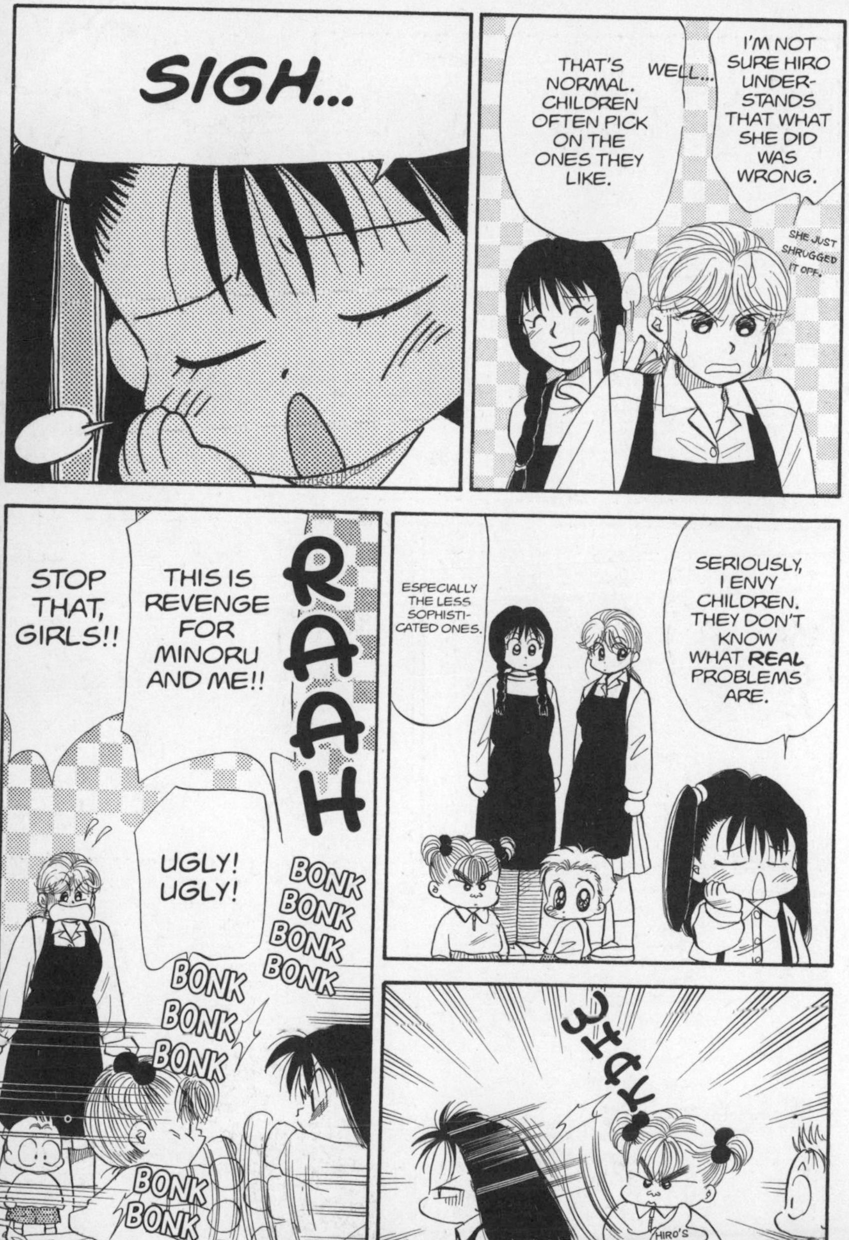
I'M NOT SURE HIRO UNDERSTANDS THAT WHAT SHE DID WAS WRONG.
WELL...
THAT'S NORMAL. CHILDREN OFTEN PICK ON THE ONES THEY LIKE.
SHE JUST SHRUGGED IT OFF.
SIGH...
SERIOUSLY, I ENVY CHILDREN. THEY DON'T KNOW WHAT **REAL** PROBLEMS ARE.
ESPECIALLY THE LESS SOPHISTICATED ONES.
HIRO'S HAND
RAAH
THIS IS REVENGE FOR MINORU AND ME!!
STOP THAT, GIRLS!!
UGLY! UGLY!
BONK BONK BONK BONK
BONK BONK BONK
BONK BONK

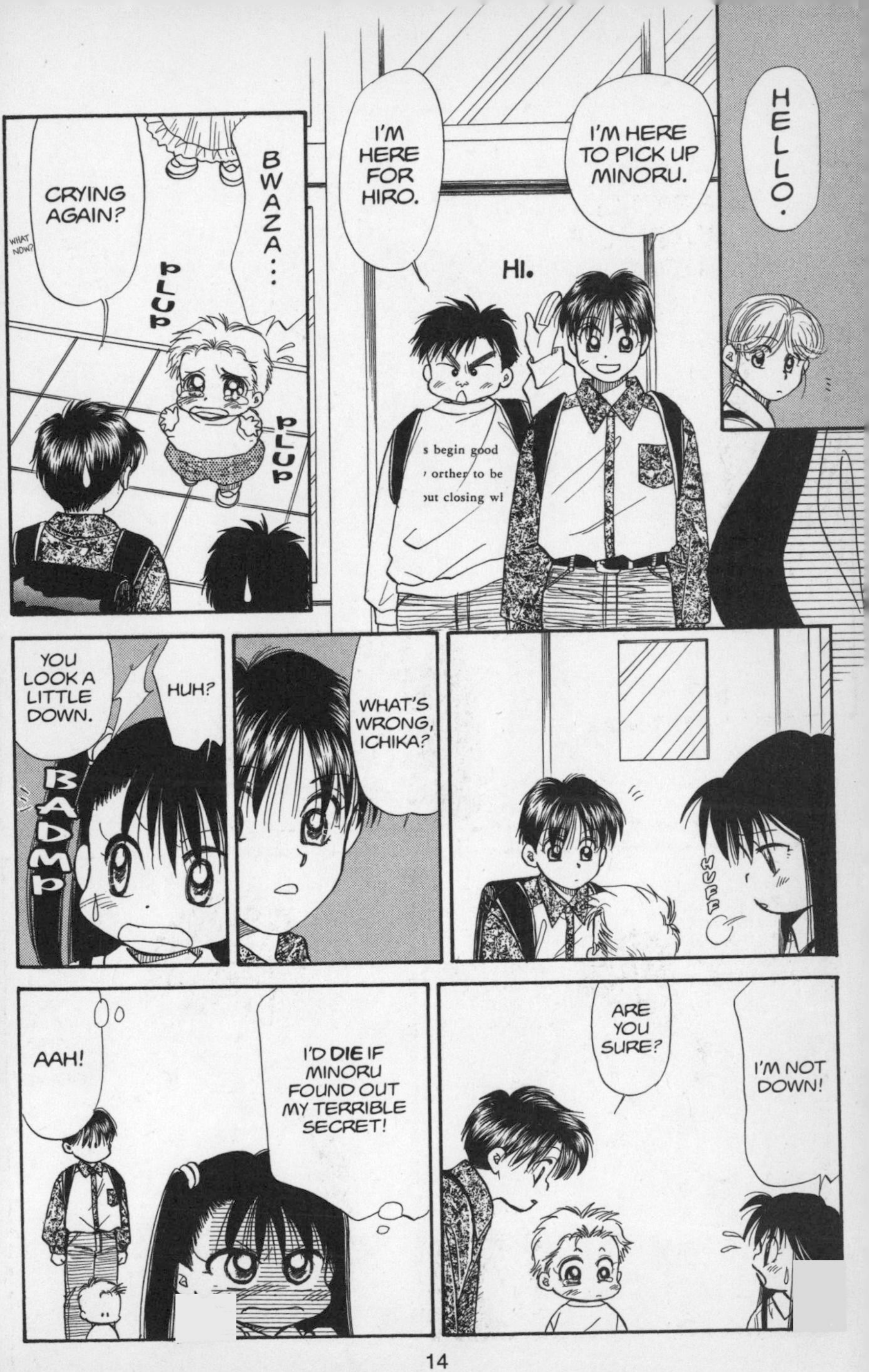
HELLO.
I'M HERE TO PICK UP MINORU.
HI.
I'M HERE FOR HIRO.
BWAZA...
CRYING AGAIN?
WHAT NOW?
PLUP
PLUP
HUFF
WHAT'S WRONG, ICHIKA?
HUH?
YOU LOOK A LITTLE DOWN.
BADMP
I'M NOT DOWN!
ARE YOU SURE?
I'D **DIE** IF MINORU FOUND OUT MY TERRIBLE SECRET!
AAH!

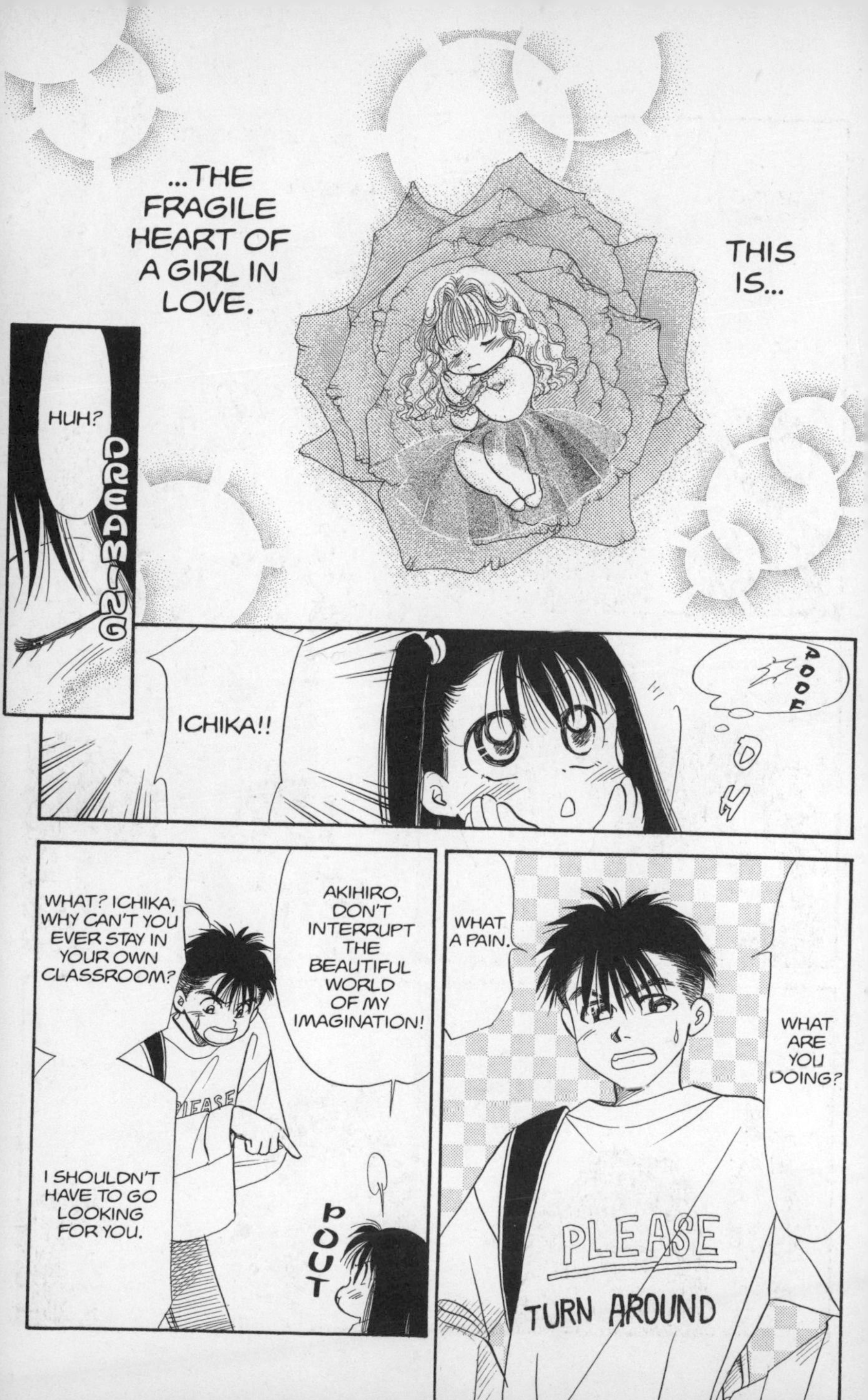
THIS IS...
...THE FRAGILE HEART OF A GIRL IN LOVE.
HUH?
DREAMING
POOF
OH
ICHIKA!!
WHAT ARE YOU DOING?
WHAT A PAIN.
AKIHIRO, DON'T INTERRUPT THE BEAUTIFUL WORLD OF MY IMAGINATION!
POUT
WHAT? ICHIKA, WHY CAN'T YOU EVER STAY IN YOUR OWN CLASSROOM?
I SHOULDN'T HAVE TO GO LOOKING FOR YOU.
PLEASE
TURN AROUND

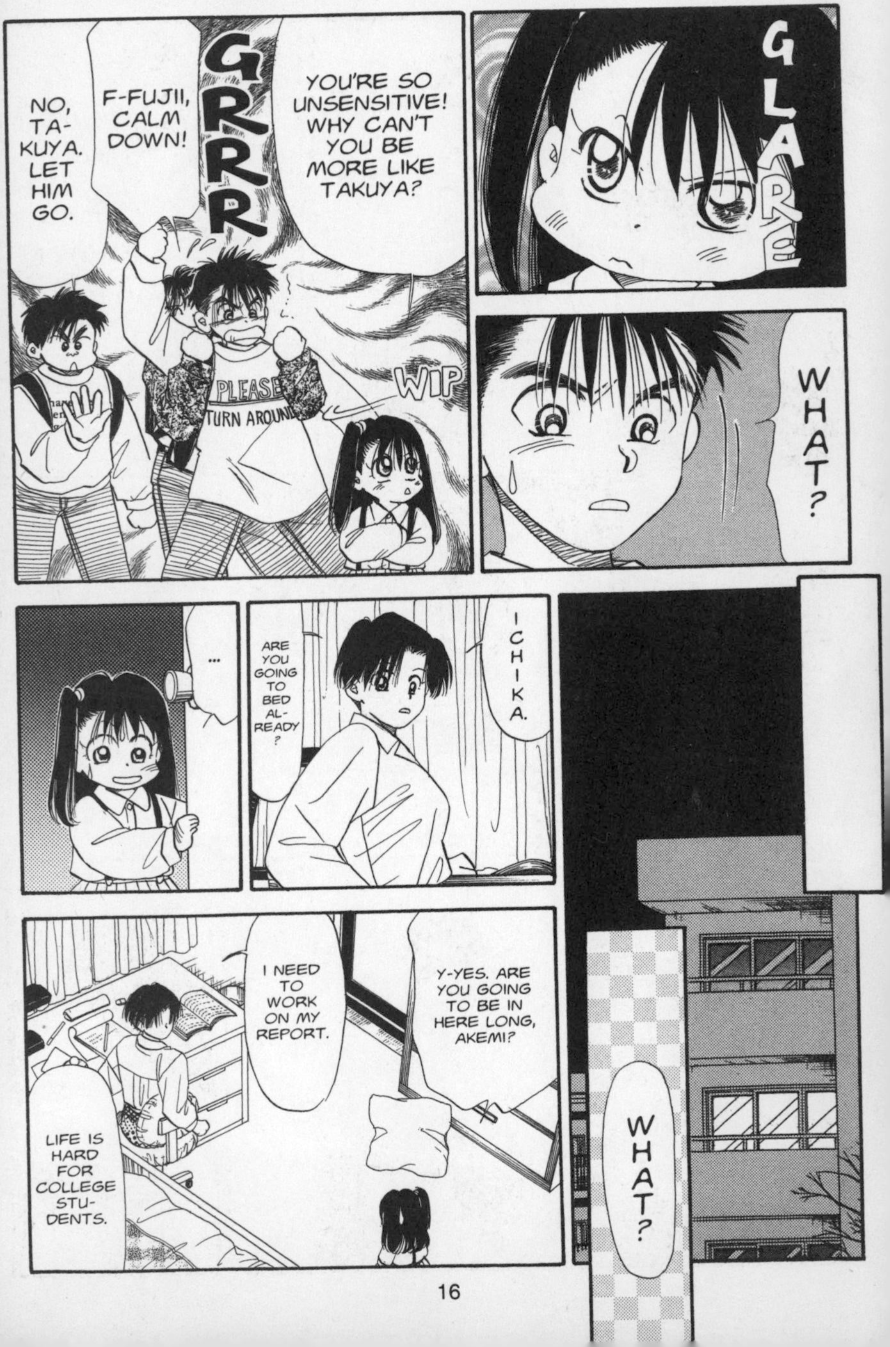
GLARE
WHAT?
YOU'RE SO UNSENSITIVE! WHY CAN'T YOU BE MORE LIKE TAKUYA?
GRRR
F-FUJII, CALM DOWN!
NO, TA-KUYA. LET HIM GO.
PLEASE TURN AROUND
WIP
WHAT?
ICHIKA.
ARE YOU GOING TO BED AL-READY?
...
Y-YES. ARE YOU GOING TO BE IN HERE LONG, AKEMI?
I NEED TO WORK ON MY REPORT.
LIFE IS HARD FOR COLLEGE STU-DENTS.

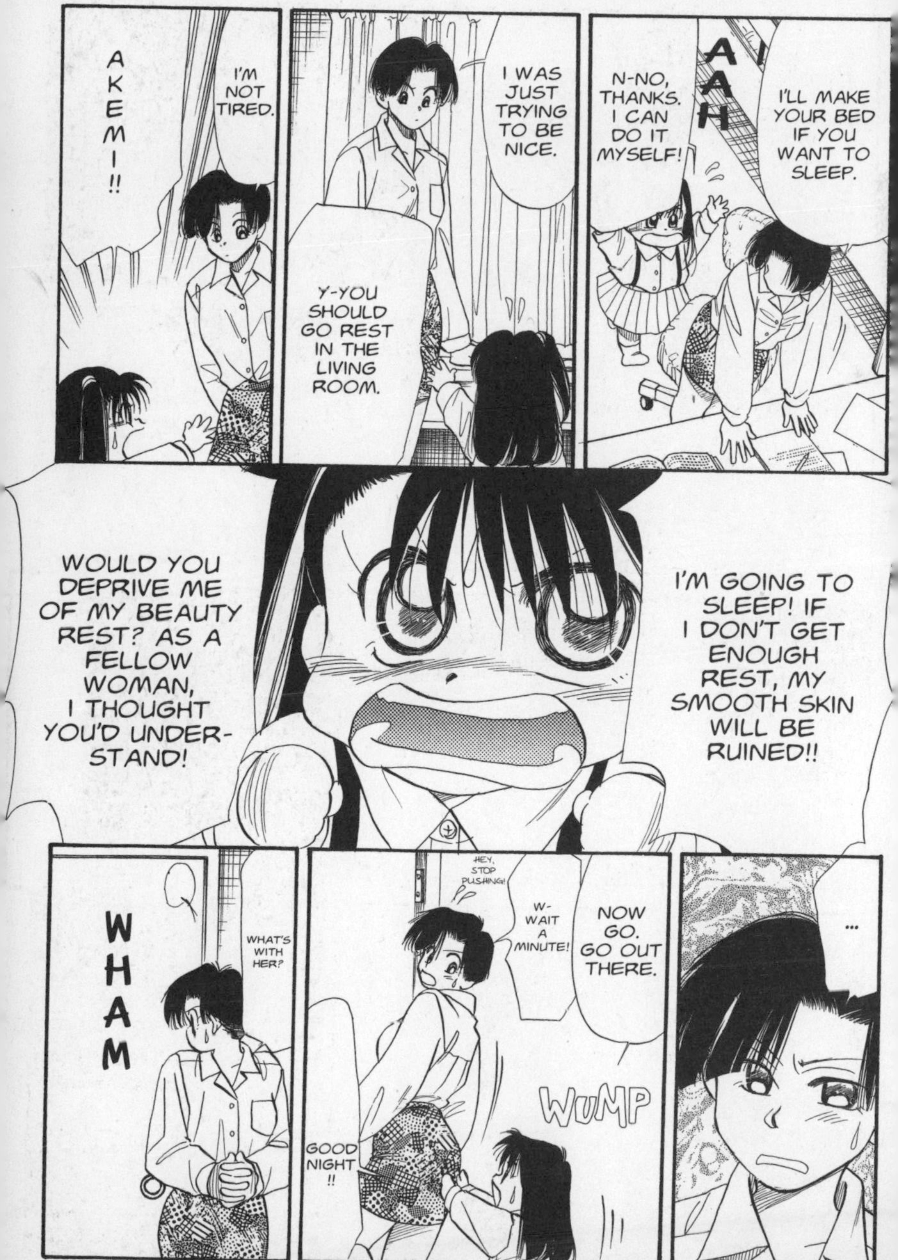
I'LL MAKE YOUR BED IF YOU WANT TO SLEEP.
AAH
N-NO, THANKS. I CAN DO IT MYSELF!
I WAS JUST TRYING TO BE NICE.
Y-YOU SHOULD GO REST IN THE LIVING ROOM.
I'M NOT TIRED.
AKEMI!!
I'M GOING TO SLEEP! IF I DON'T GET ENOUGH REST, MY SMOOTH SKIN WILL BE RUINED!!
WOULD YOU DEPRIVE ME OF MY BEAUTY REST? AS A FELLOW WOMAN, I THOUGHT YOU'D UNDER-STAND!
...
NOW GO. GO OUT THERE.
W-WAIT A MINUTE!
HEY, STOP PUSHING!
WUMP
GOOD NIGHT!!
WHAM
WHAT'S WITH HER?

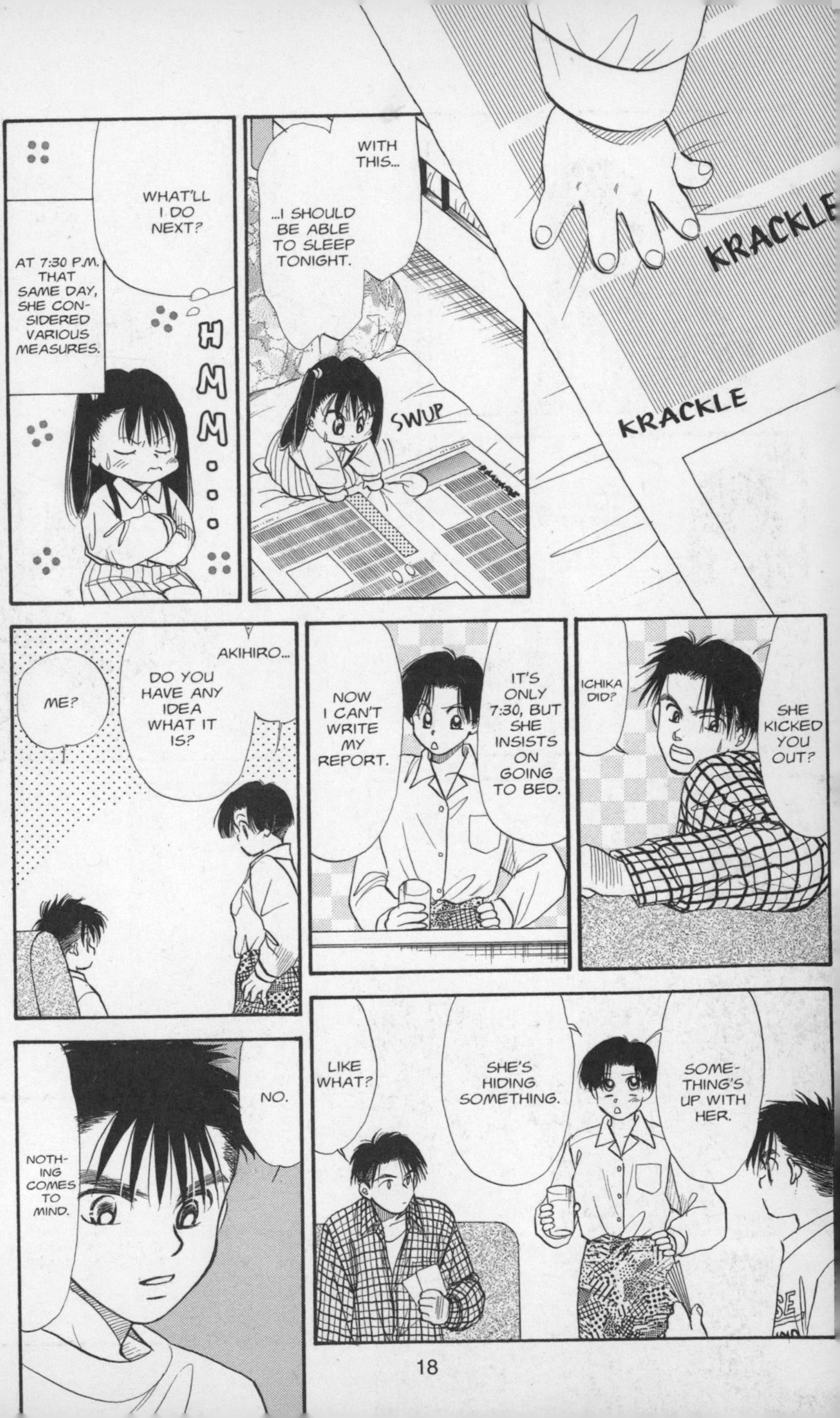
KRACKLE
KRACKLE
WITH THIS...
...I SHOULD BE ABLE TO SLEEP TONIGHT.
SWUP
WHAT'LL I DO NEXT?
AT 7:30 P.M. THAT SAME DAY, SHE CONSIDERED VARIOUS MEASURES.
HMM...
SHE KICKED YOU OUT?
ICHIKA DID?
IT'S ONLY 7:30, BUT SHE INSISTS ON GOING TO BED.
NOW I CAN'T WRITE MY REPORT.
AKIHIRO...
DO YOU HAVE ANY IDEA WHAT IT IS?
ME?
SOMETHING'S UP WITH HER.
SHE'S HIDING SOMETHING.
LIKE WHAT?
NO.
NOTHING COMES TO MIND.

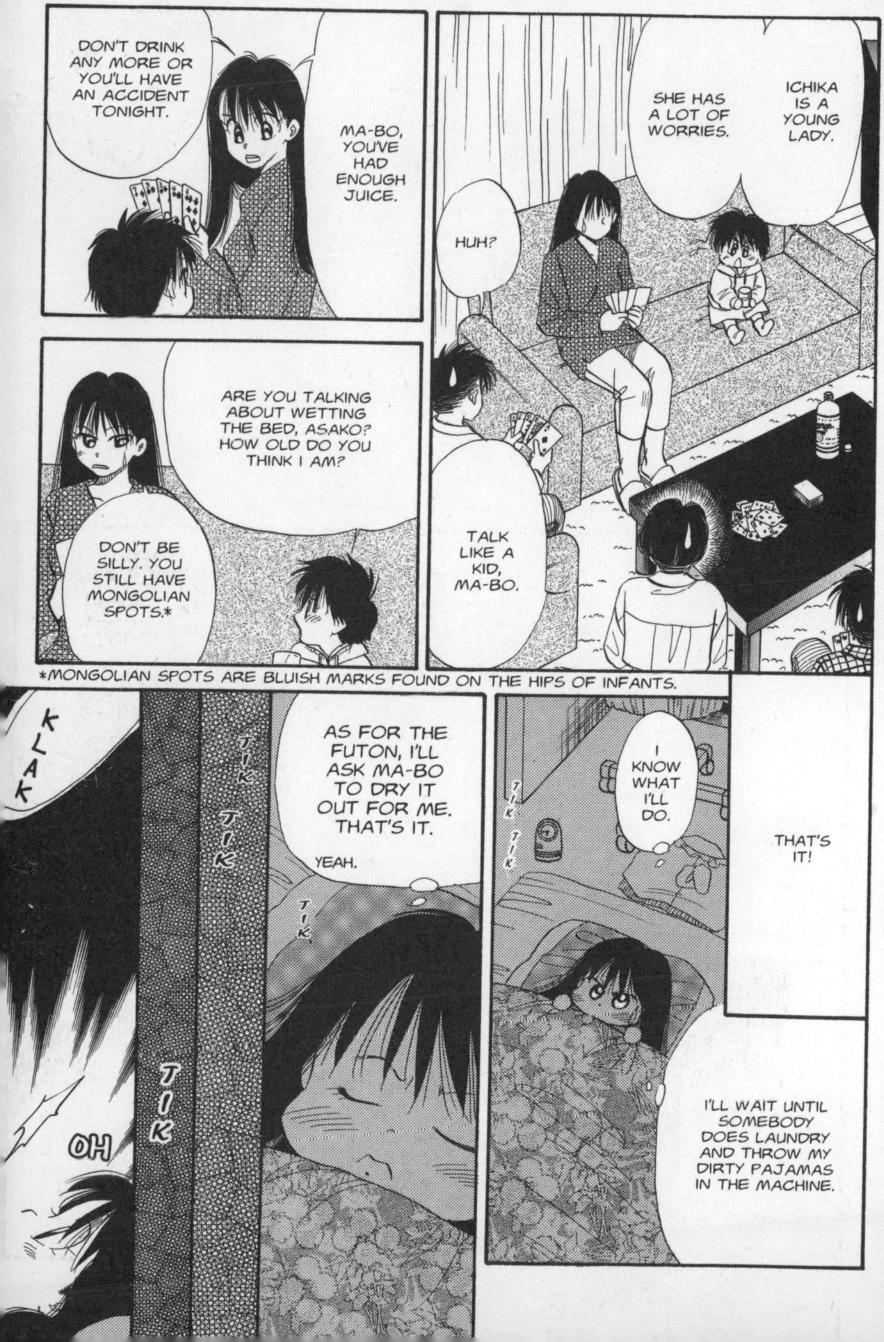
ICHIKA IS A YOUNG LADY.
SHE HAS A LOT OF WORRIES.
HUH?
TALK LIKE A KID, MA-BO.
MA-BO, YOU'VE HAD ENOUGH JUICE.
DON'T DRINK ANY MORE OR YOU'LL HAVE AN ACCIDENT TONIGHT.
ARE YOU TALKING ABOUT WETTING THE BED, ASAKO? HOW OLD DO YOU THINK I AM?
DON'T BE SILLY. YOU STILL HAVE MONGOLIAN SPOTS.*
THAT'S IT!
I KNOW WHAT I'LL DO.
I'LL WAIT UNTIL SOMEBODY DOES LAUNDRY AND THROW MY DIRTY PAJAMAS IN THE MACHINE.
TIK TIK
AS FOR THE FUTON, I'LL ASK MA-BO TO DRY IT OUT FOR ME. THAT'S IT.
YEAH.
TIK
TIK TIK
TIK
KLAK
OH

*MONGOLIAN SPOTS ARE BLUISH MARKS FOUND ON THE HIPS OF INFANTS.

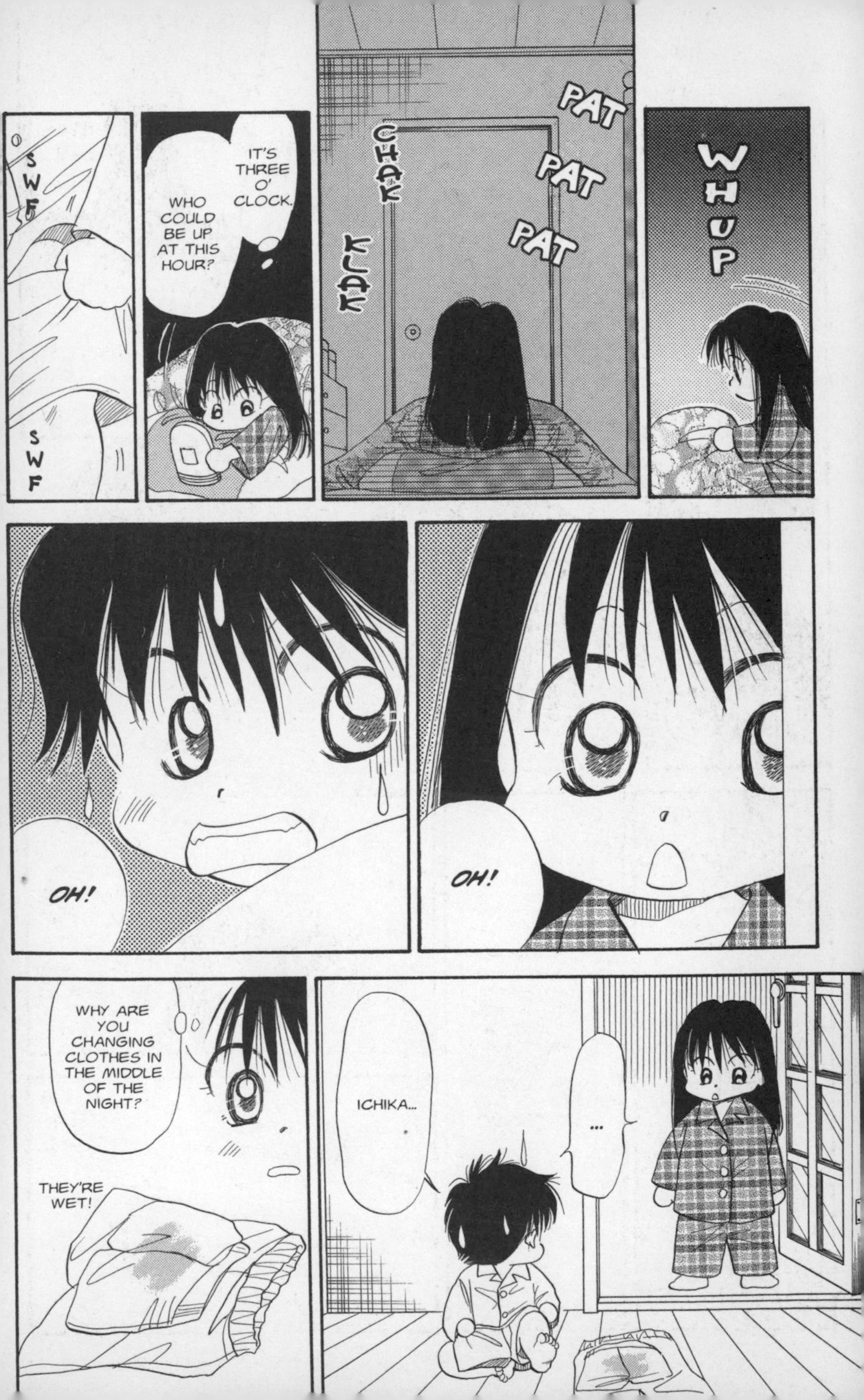
WHUP
PAT PAT PAT
CHAK KLAK
IT'S THREE O' CLOCK.
WHO COULD BE UP AT THIS HOUR?
SWF
SWF
OH!
OH!
...
ICHIKA...
WHY ARE YOU CHANGING CLOTHES IN THE MIDDLE OF THE NIGHT?
THEY'RE WET!

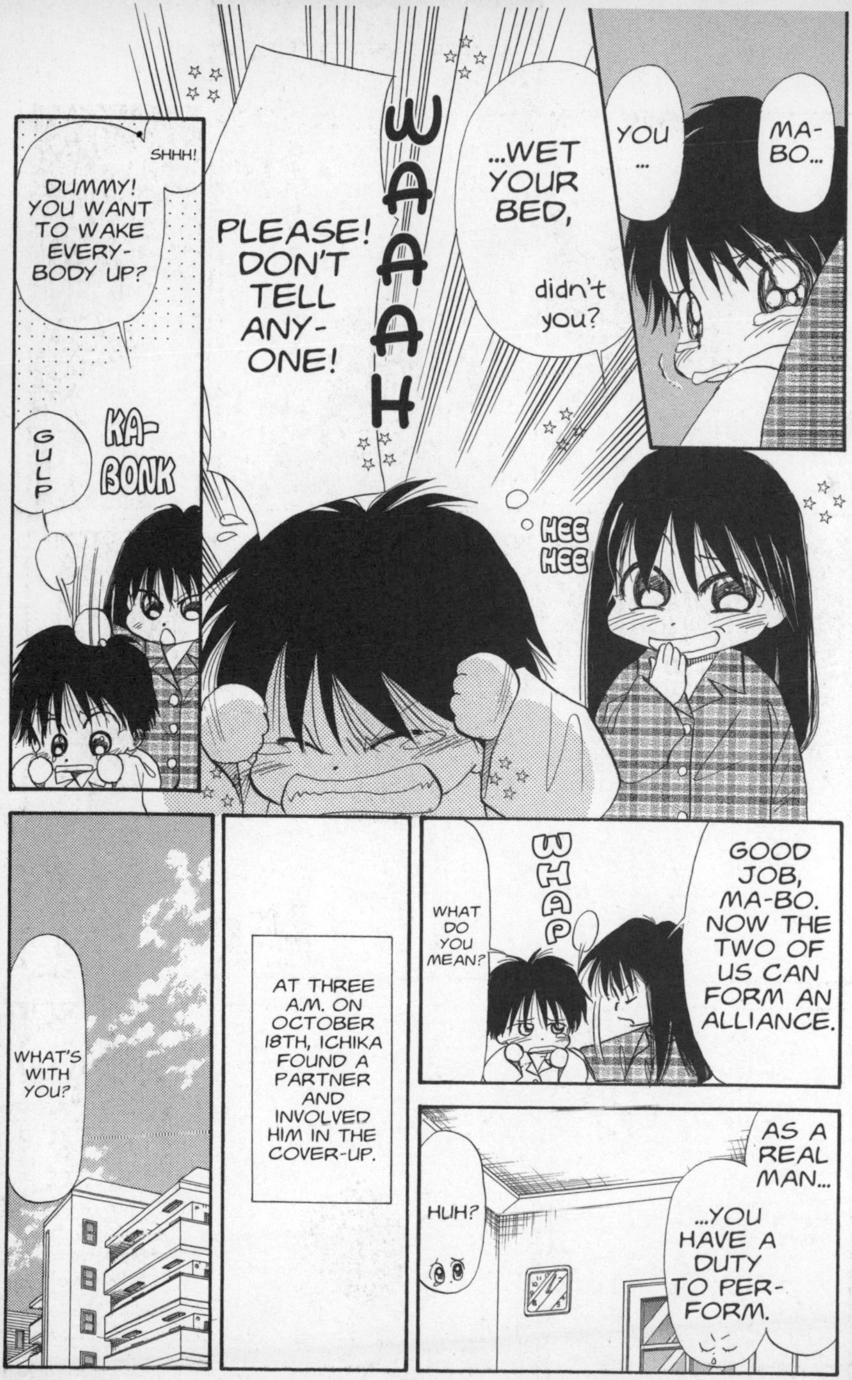
MA-BO...
YOU ...
...WET YOUR BED,
didn't you?
WAAAAH
PLEASE! DON'T TELL ANY-ONE!
HEE HEE
SHHH!
DUMMY! YOU WANT TO WAKE EVERY-BODY UP?
KA-BONK
GULP
GOOD JOB, MA-BO. NOW THE TWO OF US CAN FORM AN ALLIANCE.
WHAP
WHAT DO YOU MEAN?
AS A REAL MAN...
...YOU HAVE A DUTY TO PER-FORM.
HUH?
AT THREE A.M. ON OCTOBER 18TH, ICHIKA FOUND A PARTNER AND INVOLVED HIM IN THE COVER-UP.
WHAT'S WITH YOU?

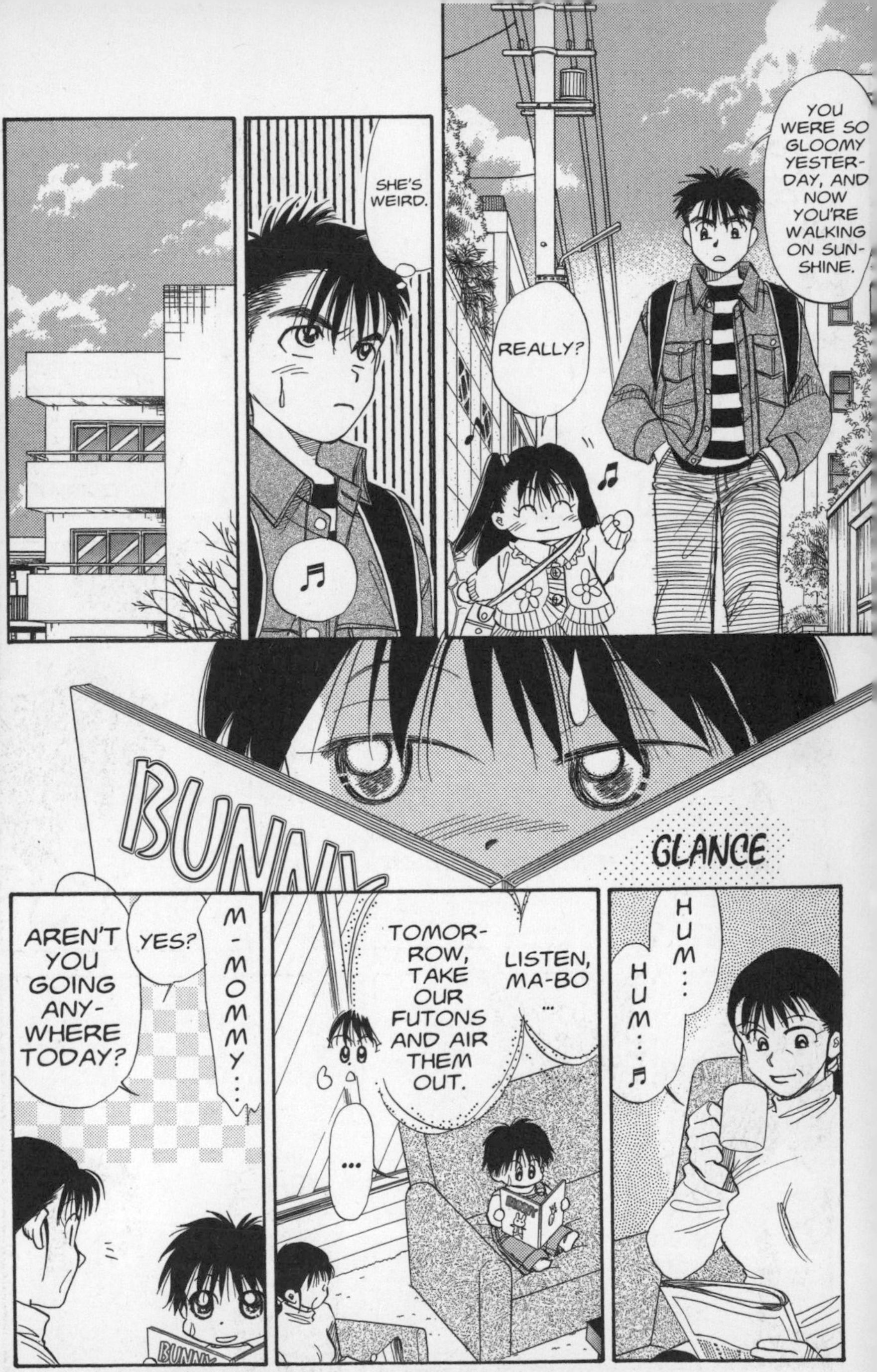
YOU WERE SO GLOOMY YESTERDAY, AND NOW YOU'RE WALKING ON SUNSHINE.
REALLY?
SHE'S WEIRD.
BUNNY
GLANCE
HUM... HUM...
LISTEN, MA-BO ...
TOMORROW, TAKE OUR FUTONS AND AIR THEM OUT.
...
M-MOMMY...
YES?
AREN'T YOU GOING ANYWHERE TODAY?
BUNNY

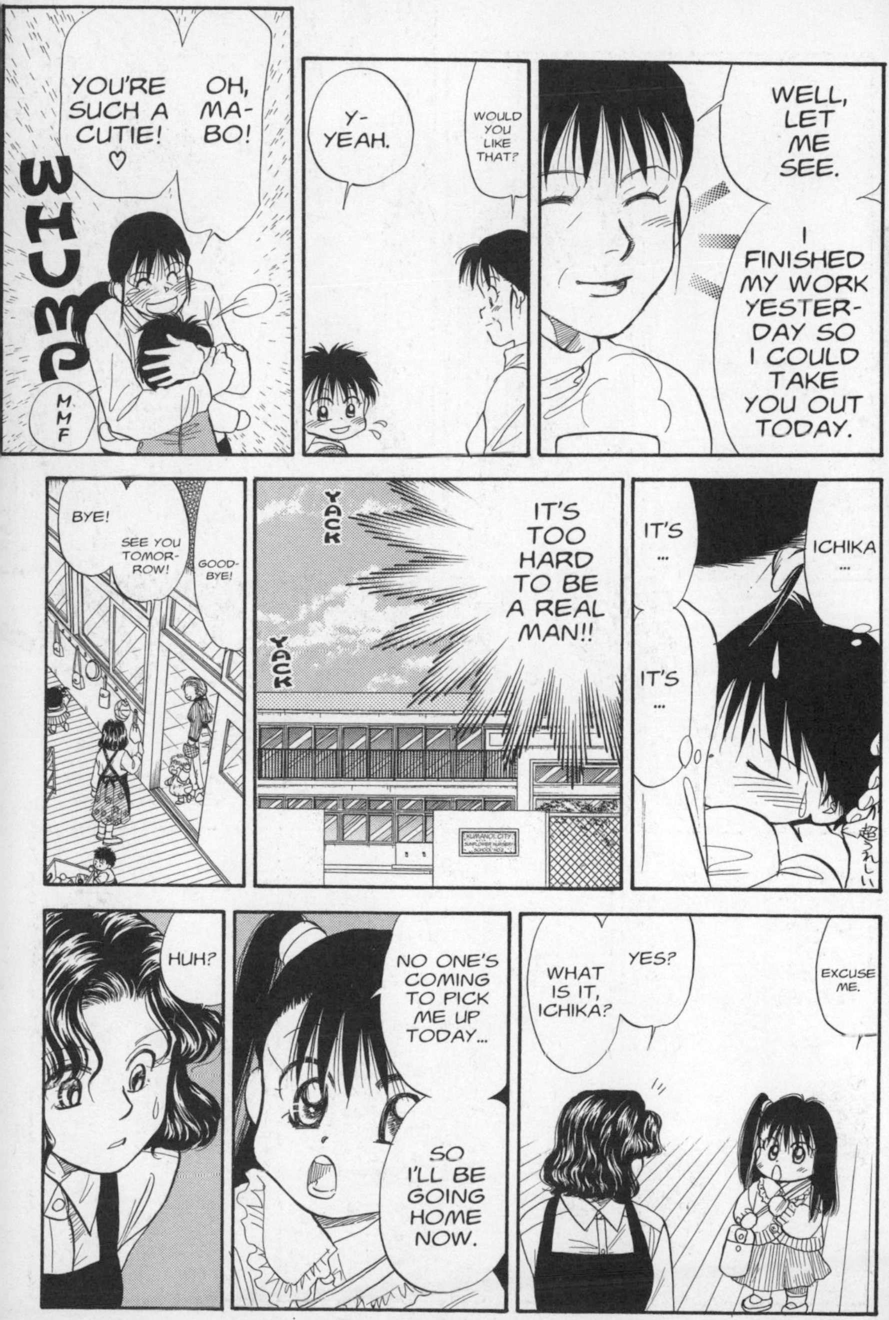

WELL, LET ME SEE.
I FINISHED MY WORK YESTER-DAY SO I COULD TAKE YOU OUT TODAY.
WOULD YOU LIKE THAT?
Y-YEAH.
OH, MA-BO!
YOU'RE SUCH A CUTIE! ♡
WHUMP
MMF
ICHIKA...
IT'S...
IT'S...
IT'S TOO HARD TO BE A REAL MAN!!
YACK
YACK
BYE!
SEE YOU TOMOR-ROW!
GOOD-BYE!
EXCUSE ME.
YES?
WHAT IS IT, ICHIKA?
NO ONE'S COMING TO PICK ME UP TODAY...
SO I'LL BE GOING HOME NOW.
HUH?

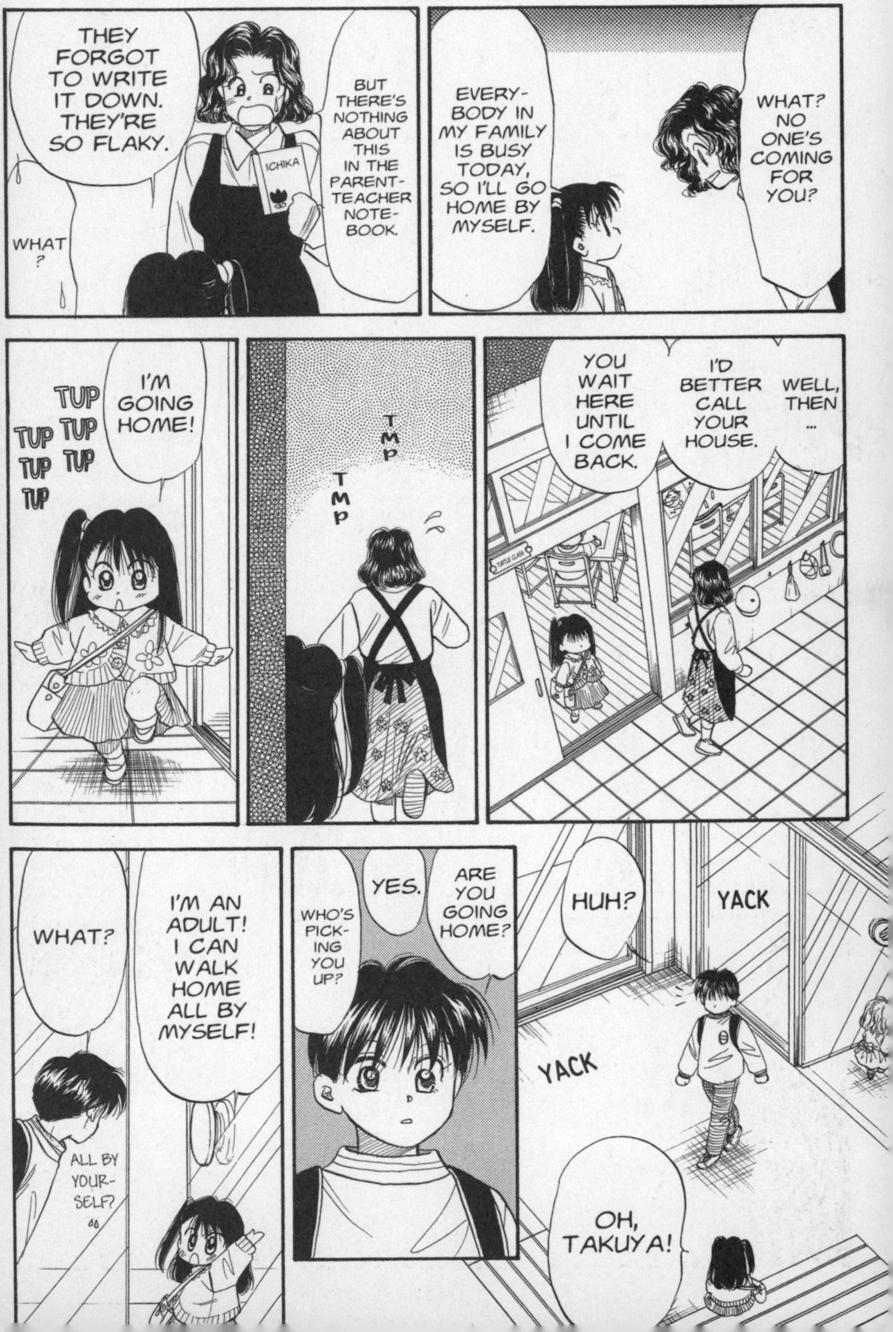
WHAT? NO ONE'S COMING FOR YOU?
EVERY-BODY IN MY FAMILY IS BUSY TODAY, SO I'LL GO HOME BY MYSELF.
BUT THERE'S NOTHING ABOUT THIS IN THE PARENT-TEACHER NOTE-BOOK.
ICHIKA
THEY FORGOT TO WRITE IT DOWN. THEY'RE SO FLAKY.
WHAT?
WELL, THEN ...
I'D BETTER CALL YOUR HOUSE.
YOU WAIT HERE UNTIL I COME BACK.
TMP
TMP
I'M GOING HOME!
TUP TUP TUP
TUP TUP TUP
TUP
YACK
HUH?
YACK
OH, TAKUYA!
ARE YOU GOING HOME?
YES.
WHO'S PICK-ING YOU UP?
I'M AN ADULT! I CAN WALK HOME ALL BY MYSELF!
WHAT?
ALL BY YOUR-SELF?

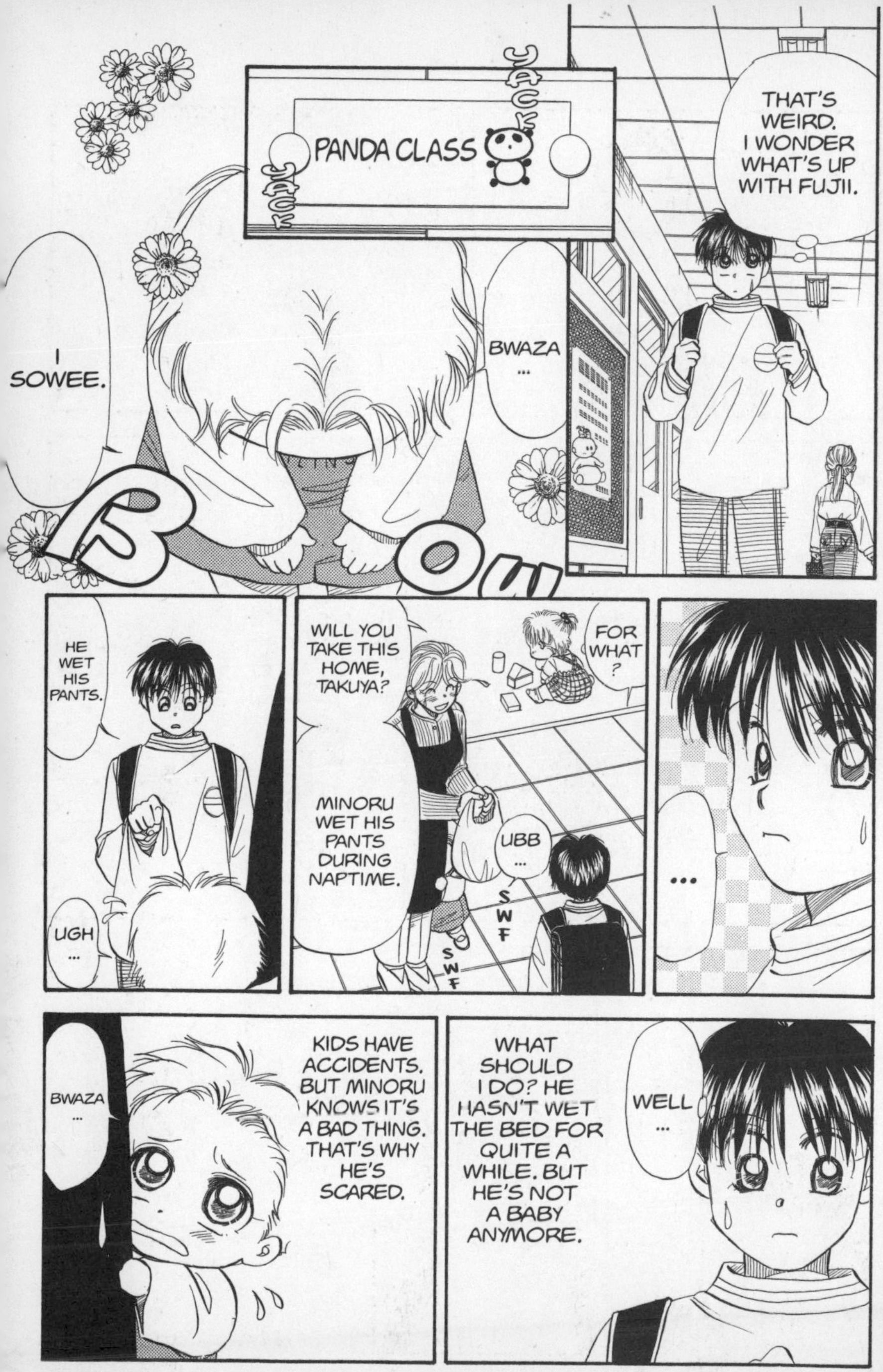
THAT'S WEIRD. I WONDER WHAT'S UP WITH FUJII.
JACK
PANDA CLASS
JACK
BWAZA ...
I SOWEE.
BOU
...
FOR WHAT ?
WILL YOU TAKE THIS HOME, TAKUYA?
MINORU WET HIS PANTS DURING NAPTIME.
UBB ...
SWF
SWF
HE WET HIS PANTS.
UGH ...
WELL ...
WHAT SHOULD I DO? HE HASN'T WET THE BED FOR QUITE A WHILE. BUT HE'S NOT A BABY ANYMORE.
KIDS HAVE ACCIDENTS. BUT MINORU KNOWS IT'S A BAD THING. THAT'S WHY HE'S SCARED.
BWAZA ...

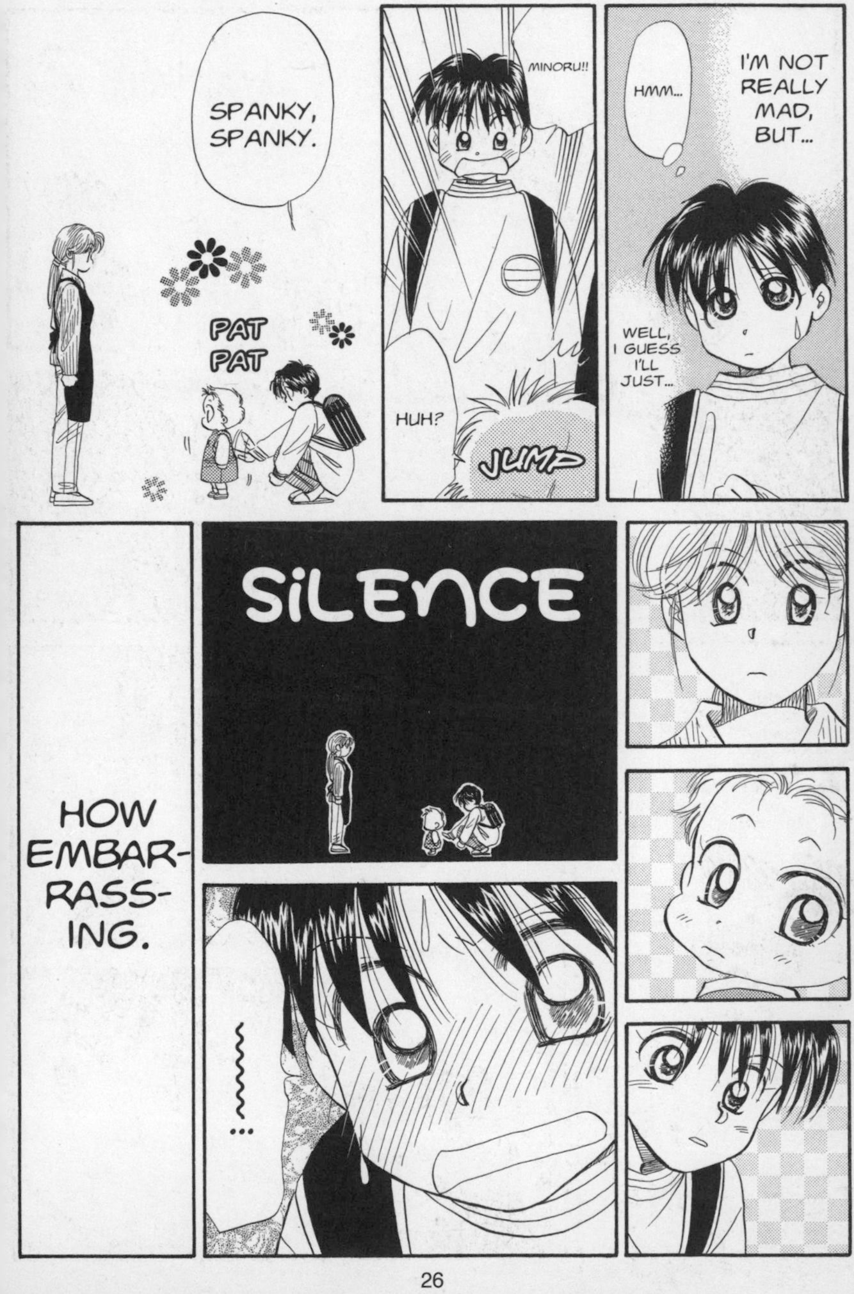
I'M NOT REALLY MAD, BUT...
HMM...
WELL, I GUESS I'LL JUST...
MINORU!!
HUH?
JUMP
SPANKY, SPANKY.
PAT PAT
SILENCE
...
HOW EMBARRASSING.

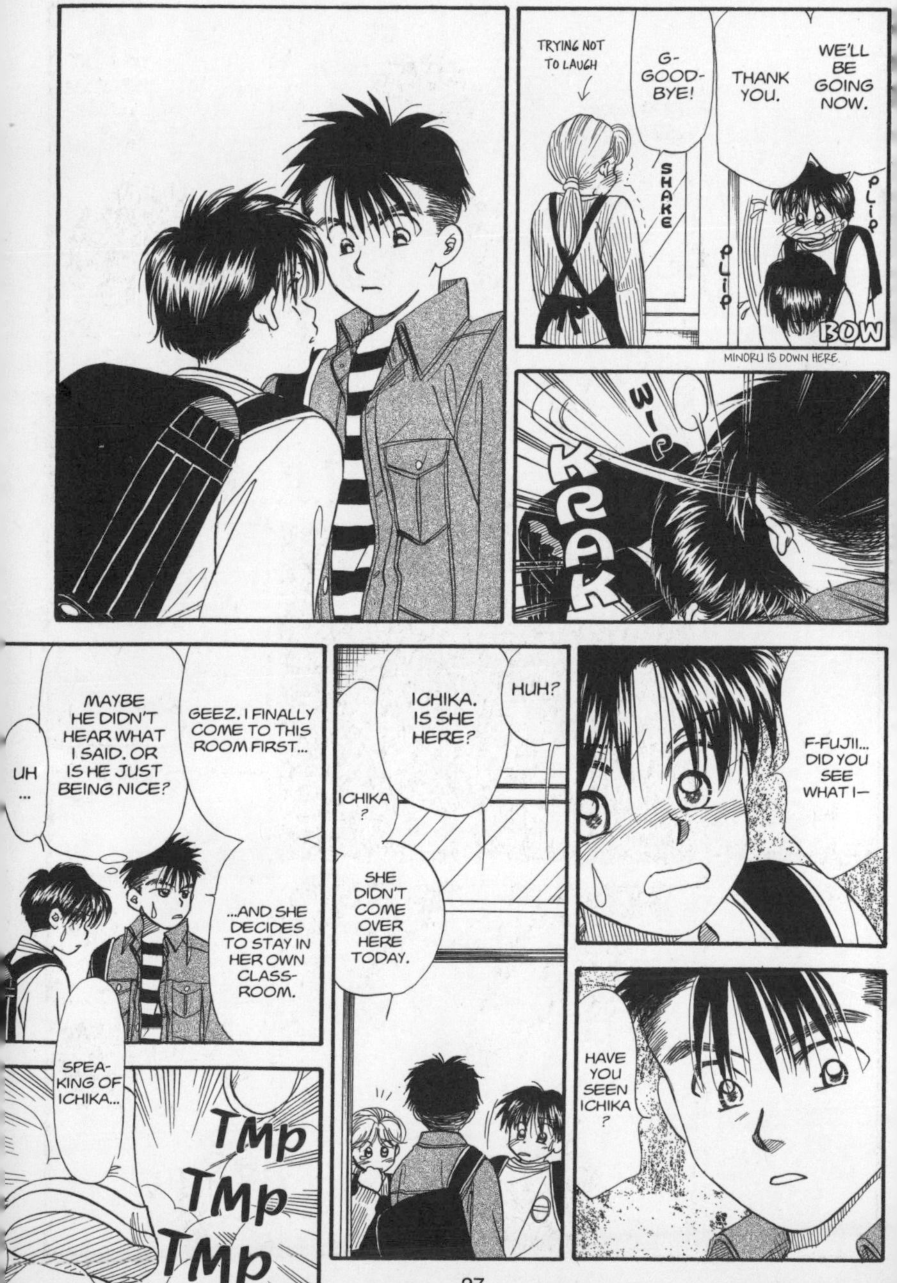
WE'LL BE GOING NOW.
THANK YOU.
G-GOODBYE!
TRYING NOT TO LAUGH
SHAKE
PLIP PLIP
BOW
MINORU IS DOWN HERE.
WIP
KRAK
F-FUJII... DID YOU SEE WHAT I—
HAVE YOU SEEN ICHIKA?
HUH?
ICHIKA. IS SHE HERE?
ICHIKA?
SHE DIDN'T COME OVER HERE TODAY.
GEEZ. I FINALLY COME TO THIS ROOM FIRST...
MAYBE HE DIDN'T HEAR WHAT I SAID. OR IS HE JUST BEING NICE?
UH...
...AND SHE DECIDES TO STAY IN HER OWN CLASS-ROOM.
SPEA-KING OF ICHIKA...
TMP TMP TMP

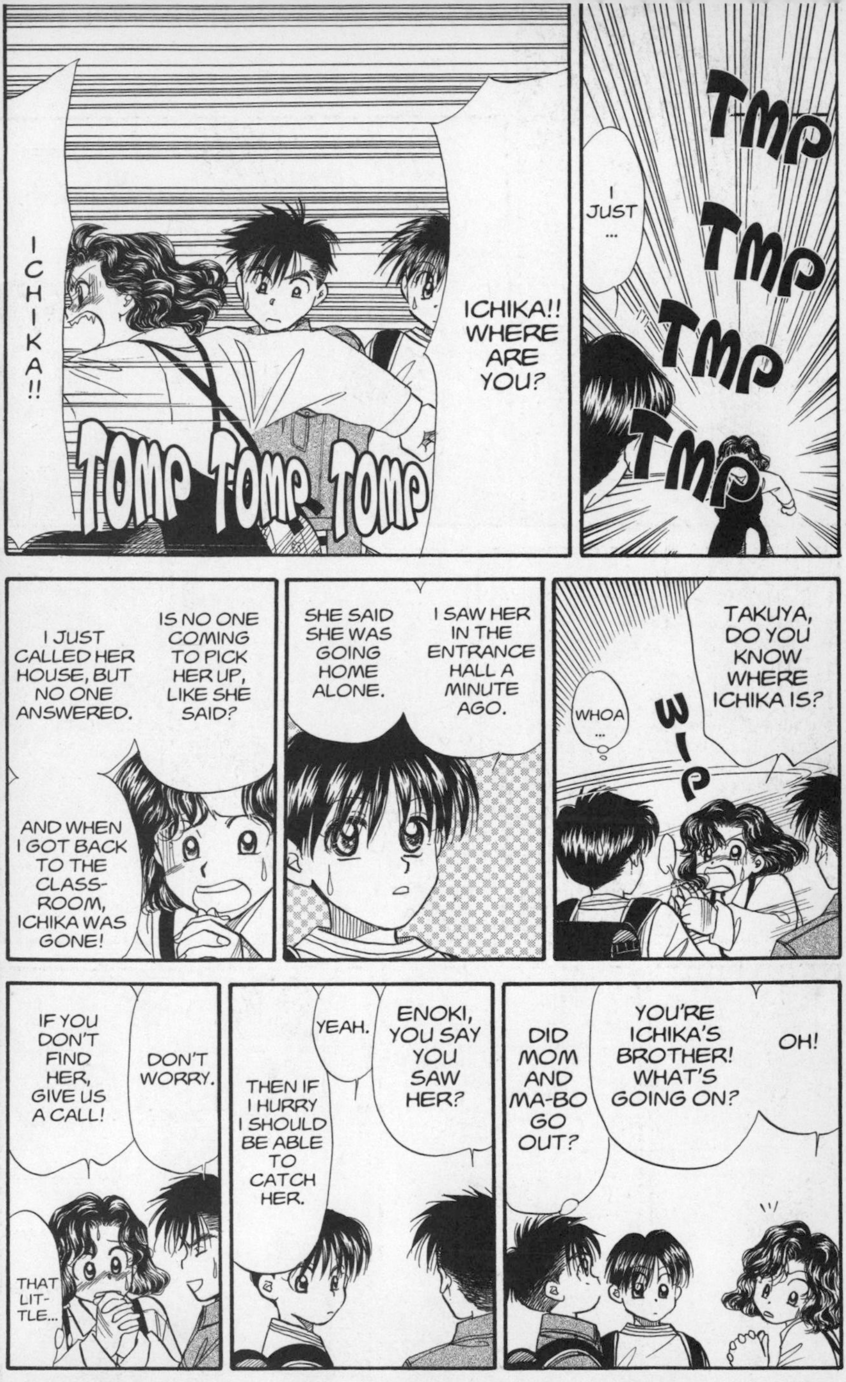
TMP TMP TMP TMP TMP
I JUST ...
ICHIKA!! WHERE ARE YOU?
ICHIKA!!
TOMP TOMP TOMP
TAKUYA, DO YOU KNOW WHERE ICHIKA IS?
WIP
WHOA ...
I SAW HER IN THE ENTRANCE HALL A MINUTE AGO.
SHE SAID SHE WAS GOING HOME ALONE.
IS NO ONE COMING TO PICK HER UP, LIKE SHE SAID?
I JUST CALLED HER HOUSE, BUT NO ONE ANSWERED.
AND WHEN I GOT BACK TO THE CLASS-ROOM, ICHIKA WAS GONE!
OH!
YOU'RE ICHIKA'S BROTHER! WHAT'S GOING ON?
DID MOM AND MA-BO GO OUT?
ENOKI, YOU SAY YOU SAW HER?
YEAH.
THEN IF I HURRY I SHOULD BE ABLE TO CATCH HER.
DON'T WORRY.
IF YOU DON'T FIND HER, GIVE US A CALL!
THAT LIT-TLE...

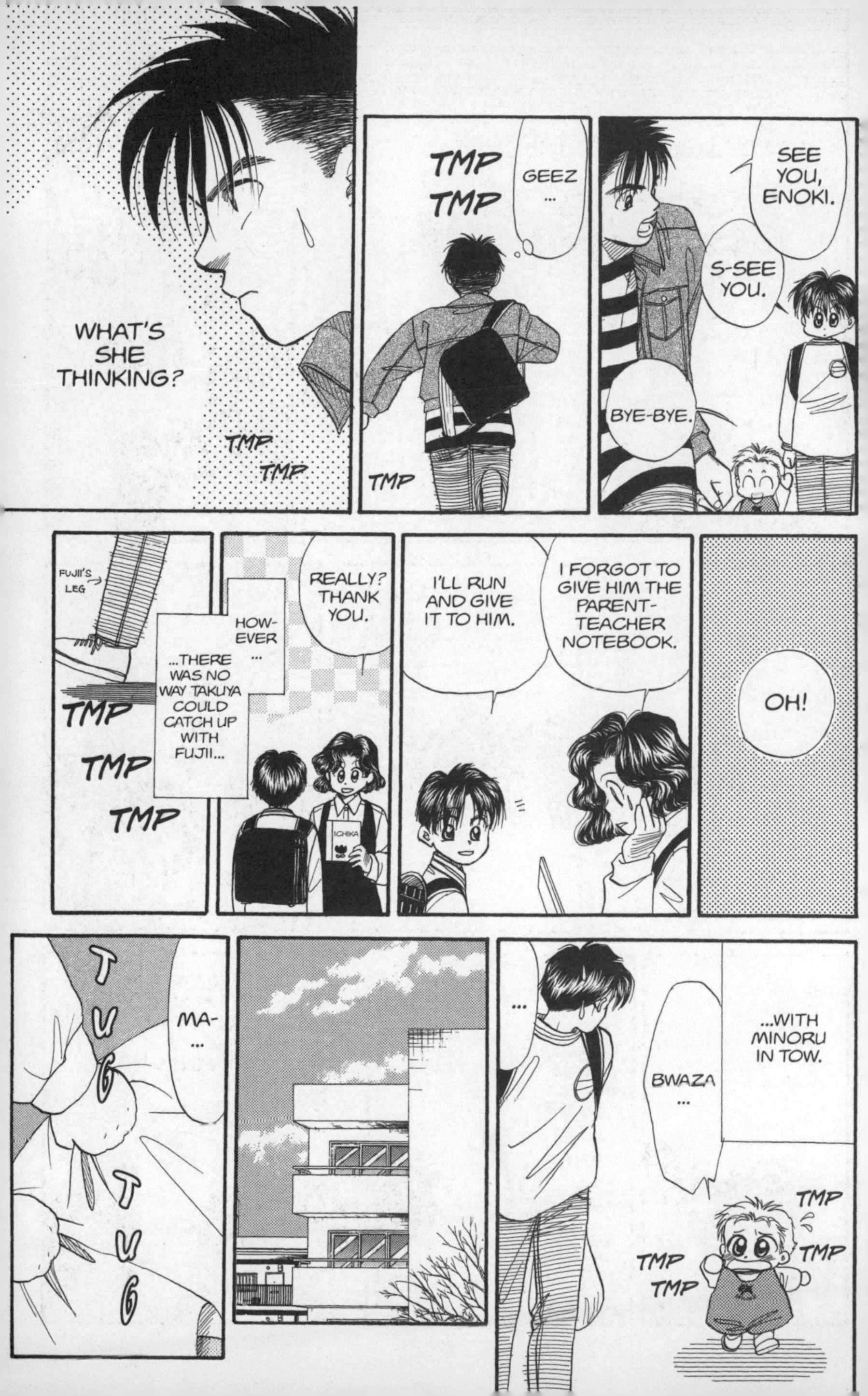
SEE YOU, ENOKI.
S-SEE YOU.
BYE-BYE.
TMP TMP
GEEZ ...
TMP
WHAT'S SHE THINKING?
TMP TMP
OH!
I FORGOT TO GIVE HIM THE PARENT-TEACHER NOTEBOOK.
I'LL RUN AND GIVE IT TO HIM.
REALLY? THANK YOU.
HOW-EVER ...
...THERE WAS NO WAY TAKUYA COULD CATCH UP WITH FUJII...
ICHIKA
FUJII'S LEG
TMP TMP TMP
...WITH MINORU IN TOW.
BWAZA ...
...
TMP TMP TMP TMP
MA- ...
TUG TUG

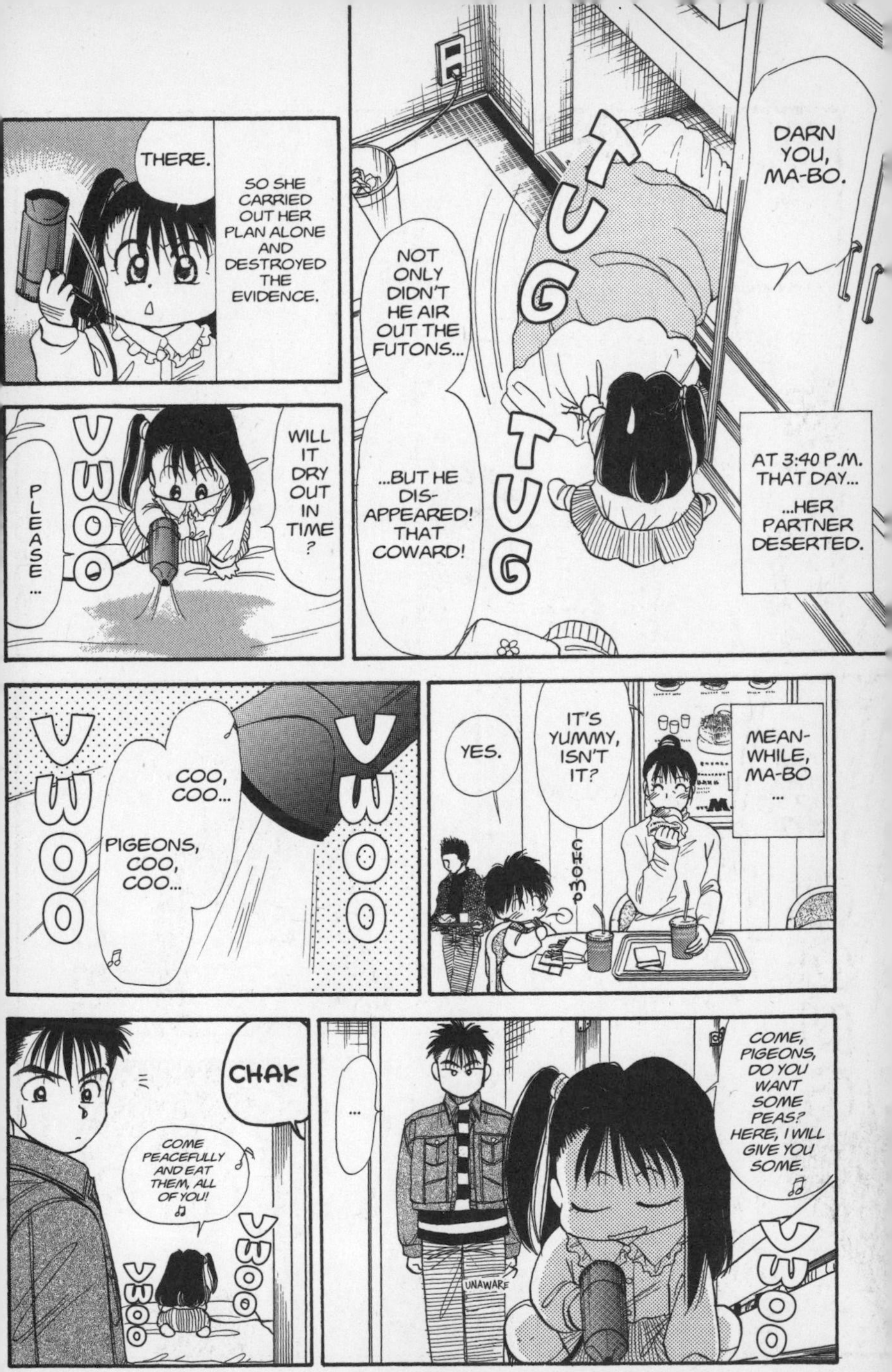
DARN YOU, MA-BO.
AT 3:40 P.M. THAT DAY... ...HER PARTNER DESERTED.
TUG
TUG
NOT ONLY DIDN'T HE AIR OUT THE FUTONS...
...BUT HE DIS-APPEARED! THAT COWARD!
THERE.
SO SHE CARRIED OUT HER PLAN ALONE AND DESTROYED THE EVIDENCE.
WILL IT DRY OUT IN TIME?
PLEASE...
VWOO
MEAN-WHILE, MA-BO...
IT'S YUMMY, ISN'T IT?
YES.
CHOMP
VWOO
COO, COO...
PIGEONS, COO, COO...
VWOO
COME, PIGEONS, DO YOU WANT SOME PEAS? HERE, I WILL GIVE YOU SOME.
VWOO
...
UNAWARE
CHAK
COME PEACEFULLY AND EAT THEM, ALL OF YOU!
VWOO
VWOO

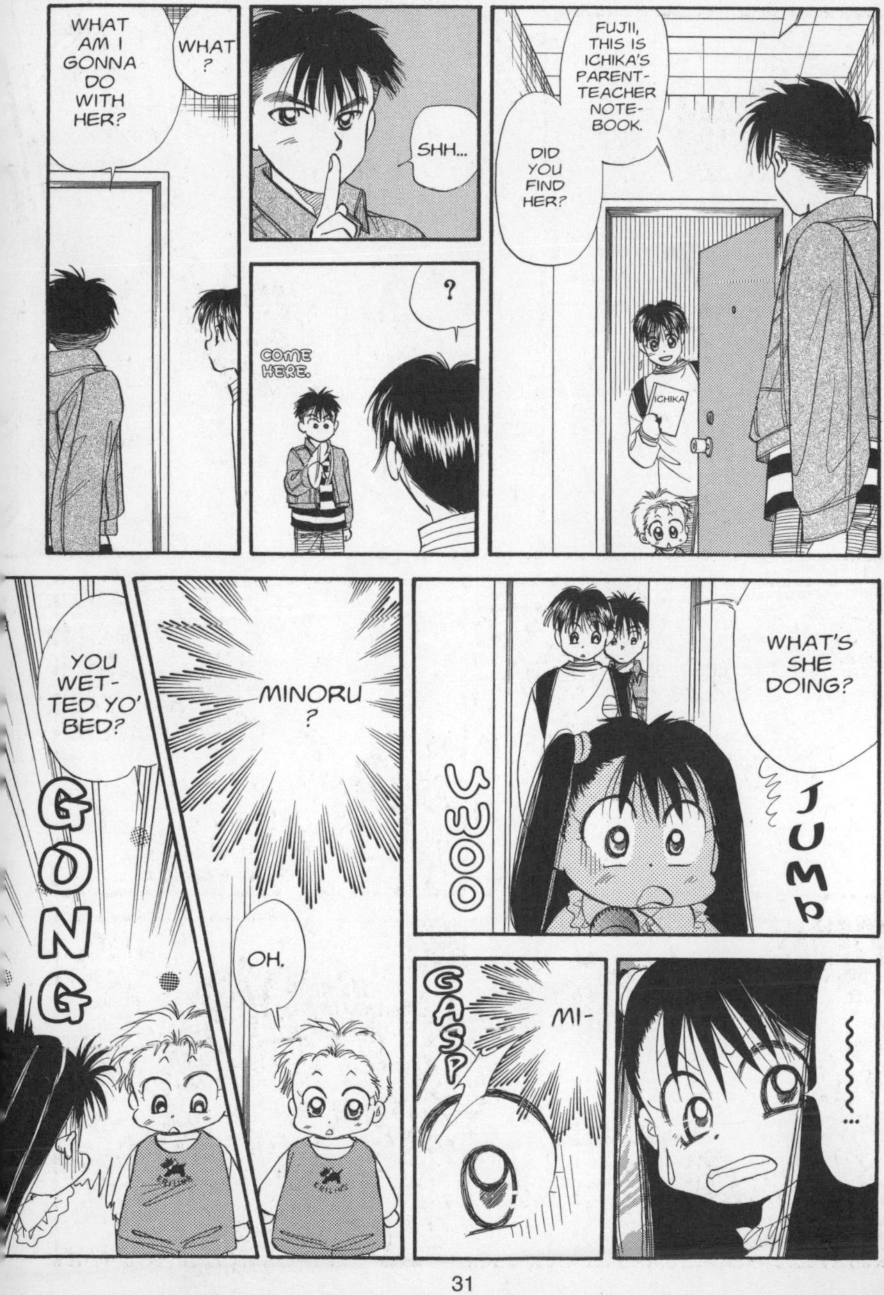
FUJII, THIS IS ICHIKA'S PARENT-TEACHER NOTE-BOOK.
DID YOU FIND HER?
ICHIKA
SHH...
?
COME HERE.
WHAT?
WHAT AM I GONNA DO WITH HER?
WHAT'S SHE DOING?
JUMP
UWOO
......
MI-
GASP
MINORU?
OH.
YOU WETTED YO' BED?
GONG

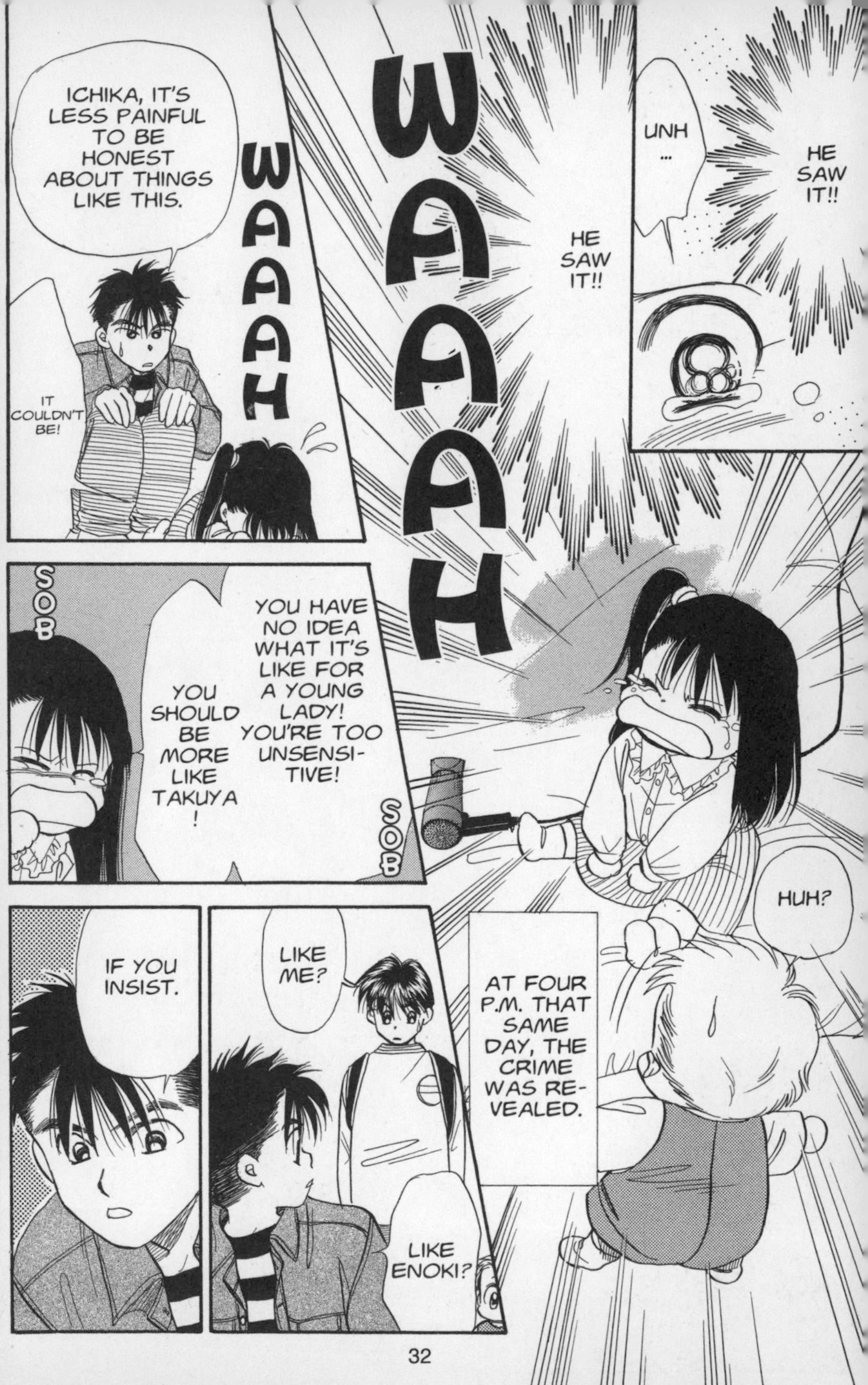
UNH ...
HE SAW IT!!
HE SAW IT!!
WAAAAH
WAAAH
ICHIKA, IT'S LESS PAINFUL TO BE HONEST ABOUT THINGS LIKE THIS.
IT COULDN'T BE!
SOB
YOU HAVE NO IDEA WHAT IT'S LIKE FOR A YOUNG LADY! YOU'RE TOO UNSENSI-TIVE!
YOU SHOULD BE MORE LIKE TAKUYA!
SOB
HUH?
AT FOUR P.M. THAT SAME DAY, THE CRIME WAS RE-VEALED.
LIKE ME?
LIKE ENOKI?
IF YOU INSIST.

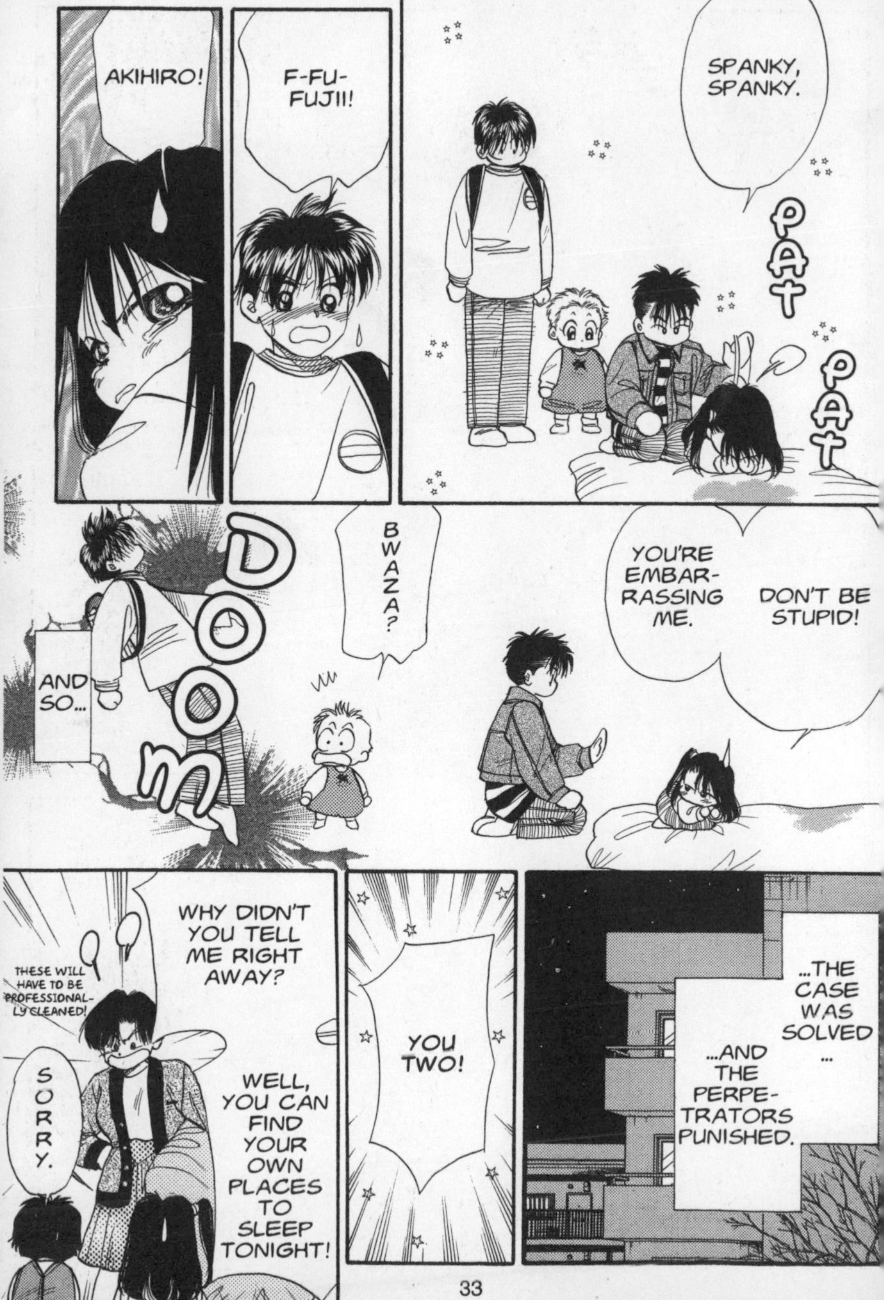

SPANKY, SPANKY.
PAT
PAT
F-FU-FUJII!
AKIHIRO!
DON'T BE STUPID!
YOU'RE EMBAR-RASSING ME.
BWAZA?
DOOM
AND SO...
...THE CASE WAS SOLVED...
...AND THE PERPE-TRATORS PUNISHED.
YOU TWO!
WHY DIDN'T YOU TELL ME RIGHT AWAY?
WELL, YOU CAN FIND YOUR OWN PLACES TO SLEEP TONIGHT!
THESE WILL HAVE TO BE PROFESSIONAL-LY CLEANED!
SORRY.

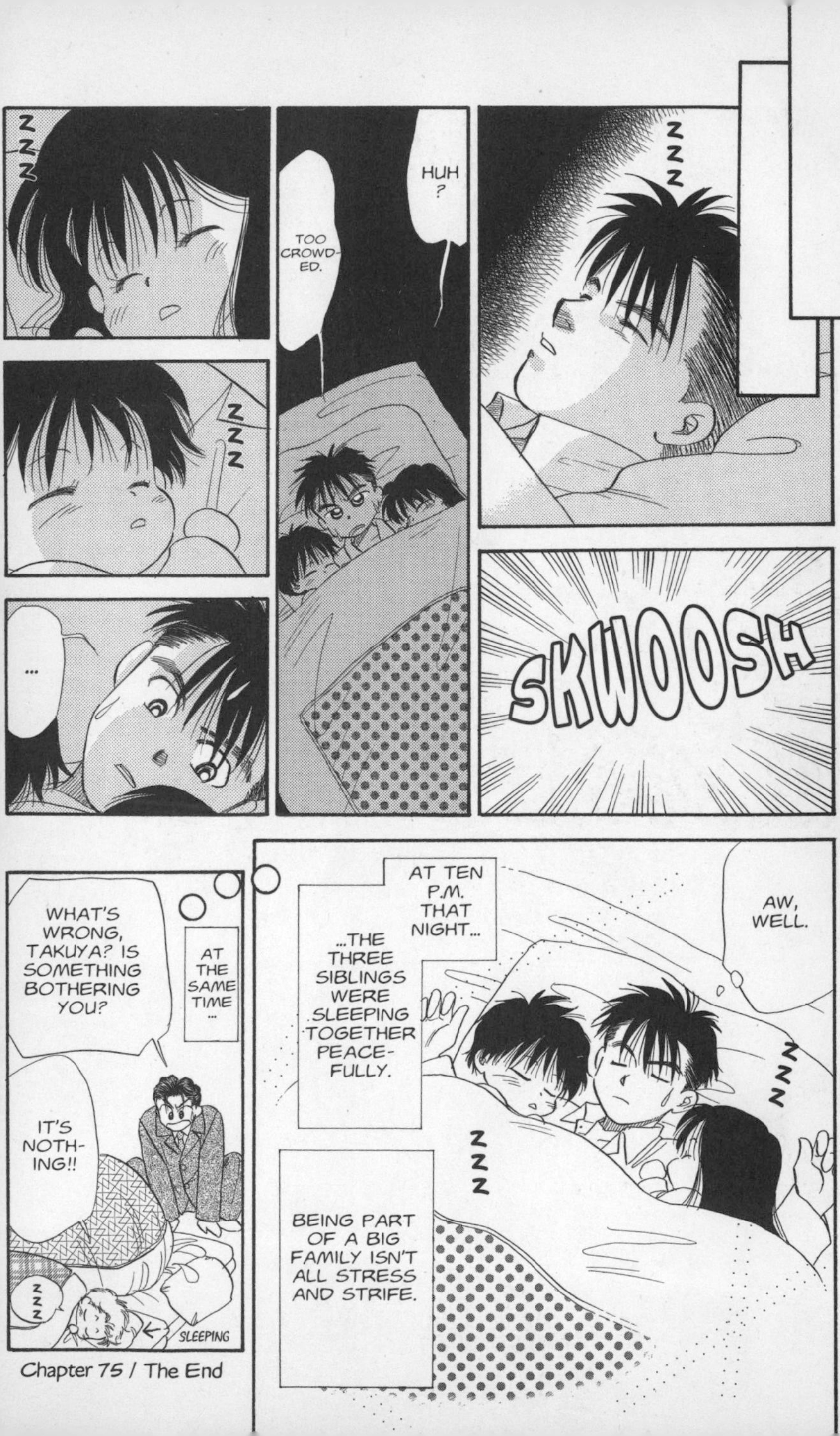
Z Z Z
SKWOOSH
HUH?
TOO CROWDED.
Z Z Z
Z Z Z
...
AW, WELL.
AT TEN P.M. THAT NIGHT...
...THE THREE SIBLINGS WERE SLEEPING TOGETHER PEACEFULLY.
Z Z Z
Z Z Z
BEING PART OF A BIG FAMILY ISN'T ALL STRESS AND STRIFE.
AT THE SAME TIME...
WHAT'S WRONG, TAKUYA? IS SOMETHING BOTHERING YOU?
IT'S NOTHING!!
Z Z Z
SLEEPING

Chapter 75 / The End

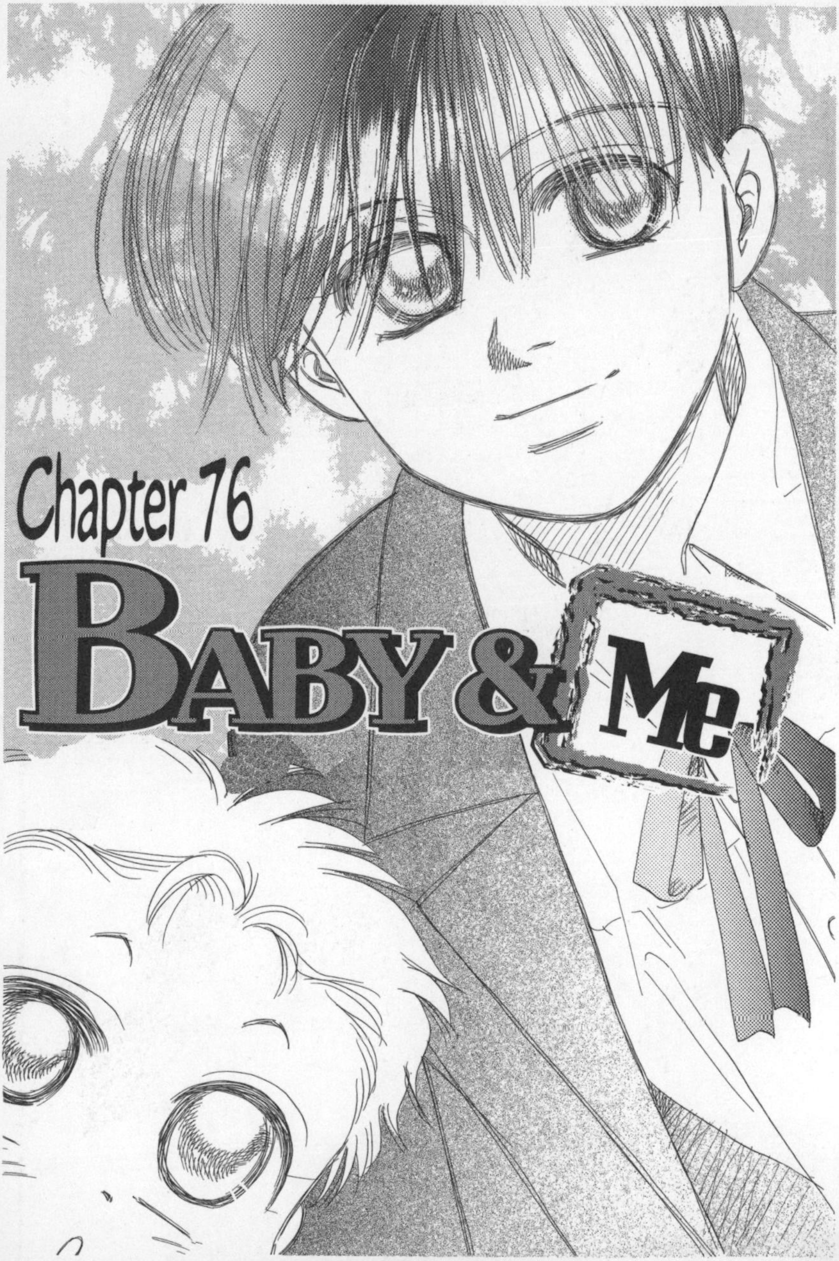
Chapter 76
BABY & Me

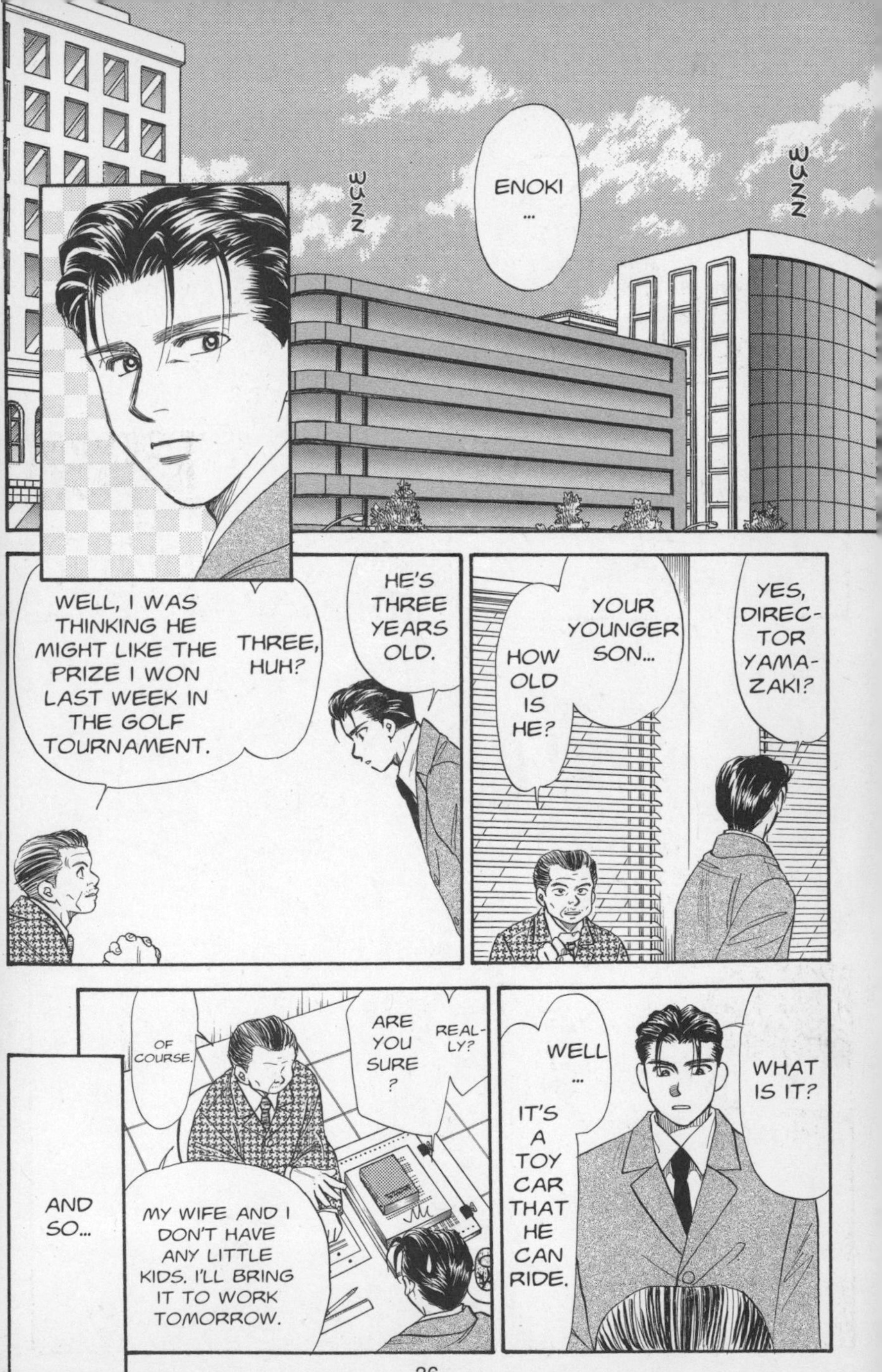
BUZZ
ENOKI ...
BUZZ
YES, DIRECTOR YAMAZAKI?
YOUR YOUNGER SON...
HOW OLD IS HE?
HE'S THREE YEARS OLD.
THREE, HUH?
WELL, I WAS THINKING HE MIGHT LIKE THE PRIZE I WON LAST WEEK IN THE GOLF TOURNAMENT.
WHAT IS IT?
WELL ...
IT'S A TOY CAR THAT HE CAN RIDE.
REAL-LY?
ARE YOU SURE?
OF COURSE.
MY WIFE AND I DON'T HAVE ANY LITTLE KIDS. I'LL BRING IT TO WORK TOMORROW.
AND SO...

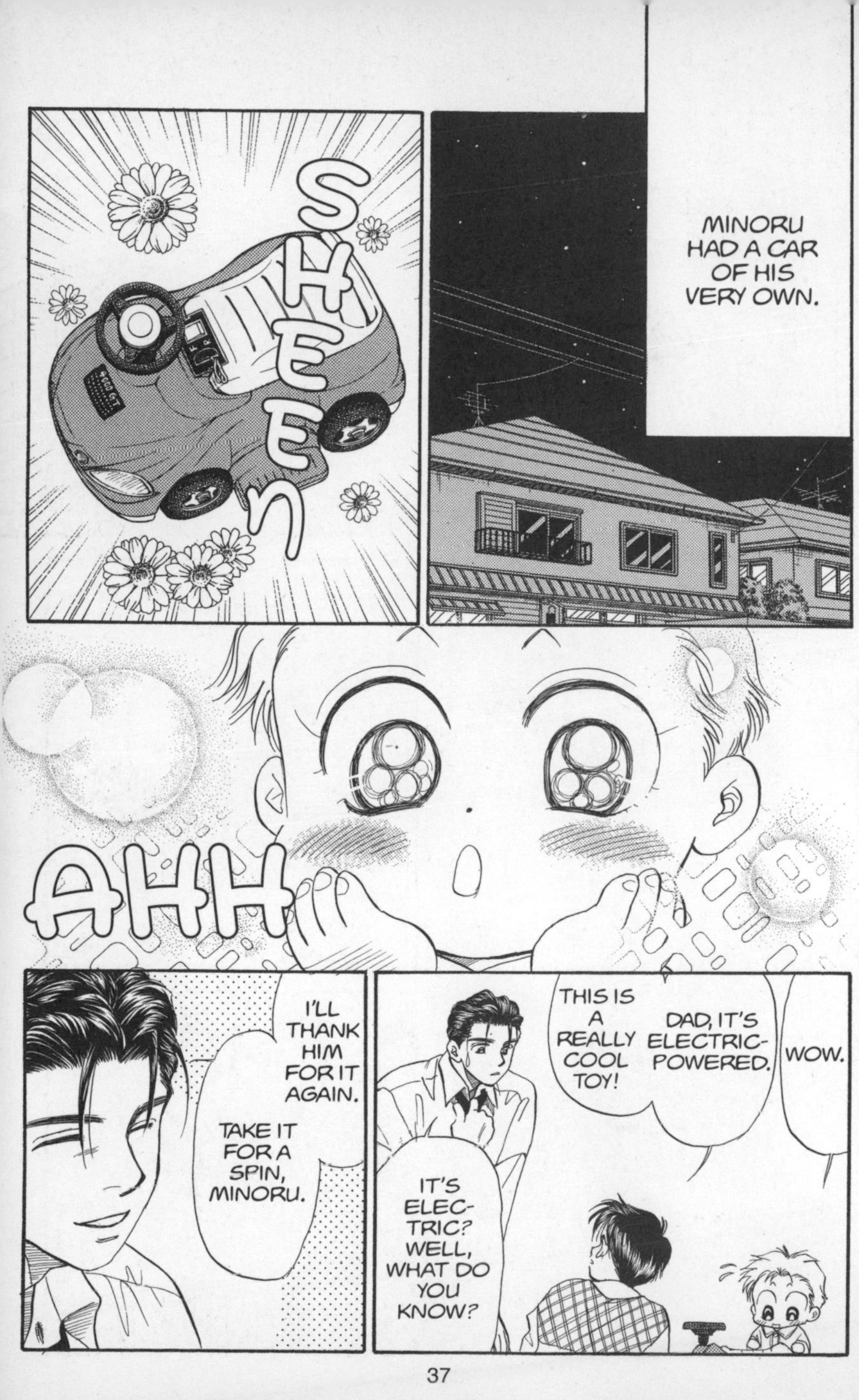
MINORU HAD A CAR OF HIS VERY OWN.
SHEEN
AHH
WOW.
DAD, IT'S ELECTRIC-POWERED.
THIS IS A REALLY COOL TOY!
IT'S ELECTRIC? WELL, WHAT DO YOU KNOW?
I'LL THANK HIM FOR IT AGAIN.
TAKE IT FOR A SPIN, MINORU.

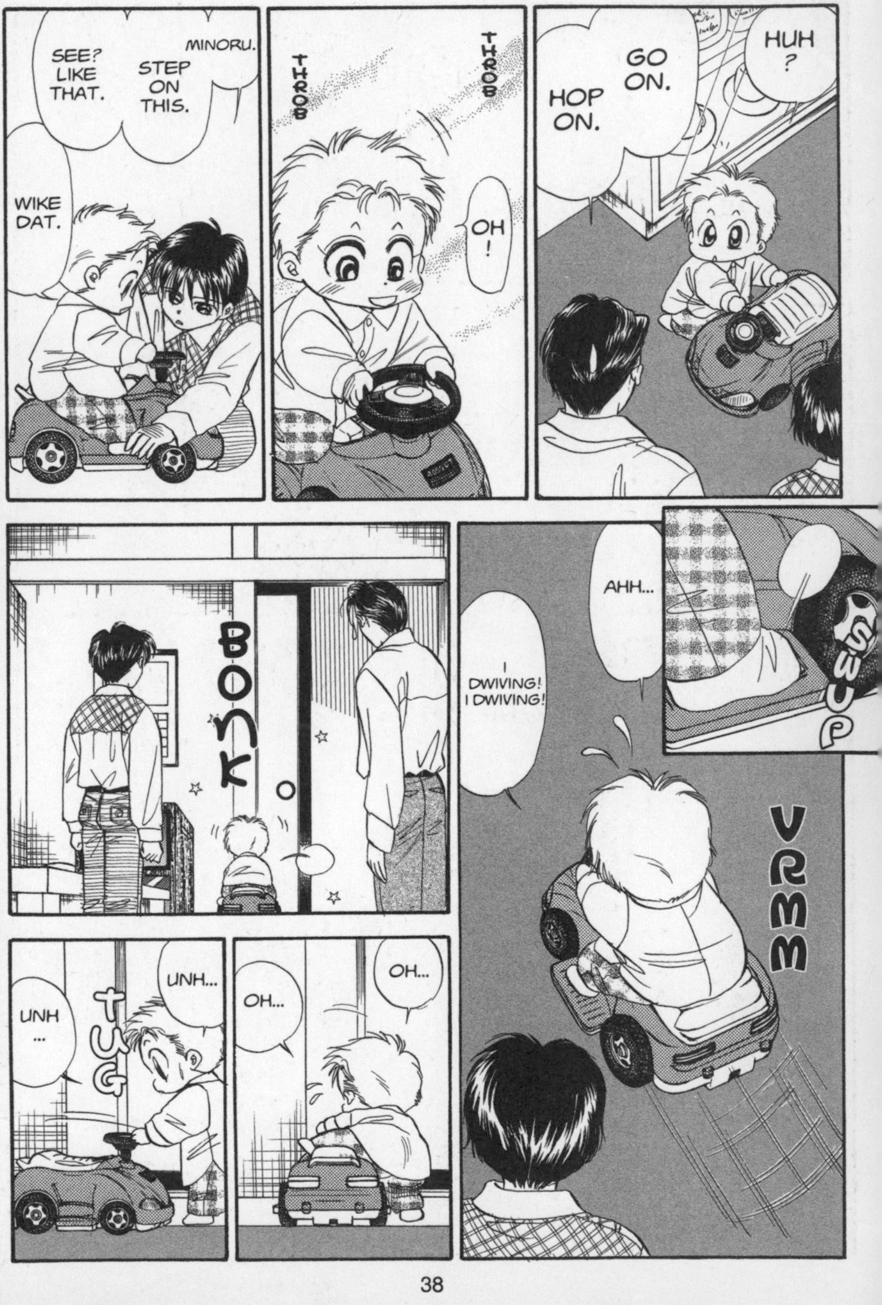
HUH?
GO ON.
HOP ON.
THROB
THROB
OH!
MINORU.
STEP ON THIS.
SEE? LIKE THAT.
WIKE DAT.
SWUP
AHH...
I DWIVING! I DWIVING!
VRMM
BONK
OH...
OH...
UNH...
UNH ...
TUG

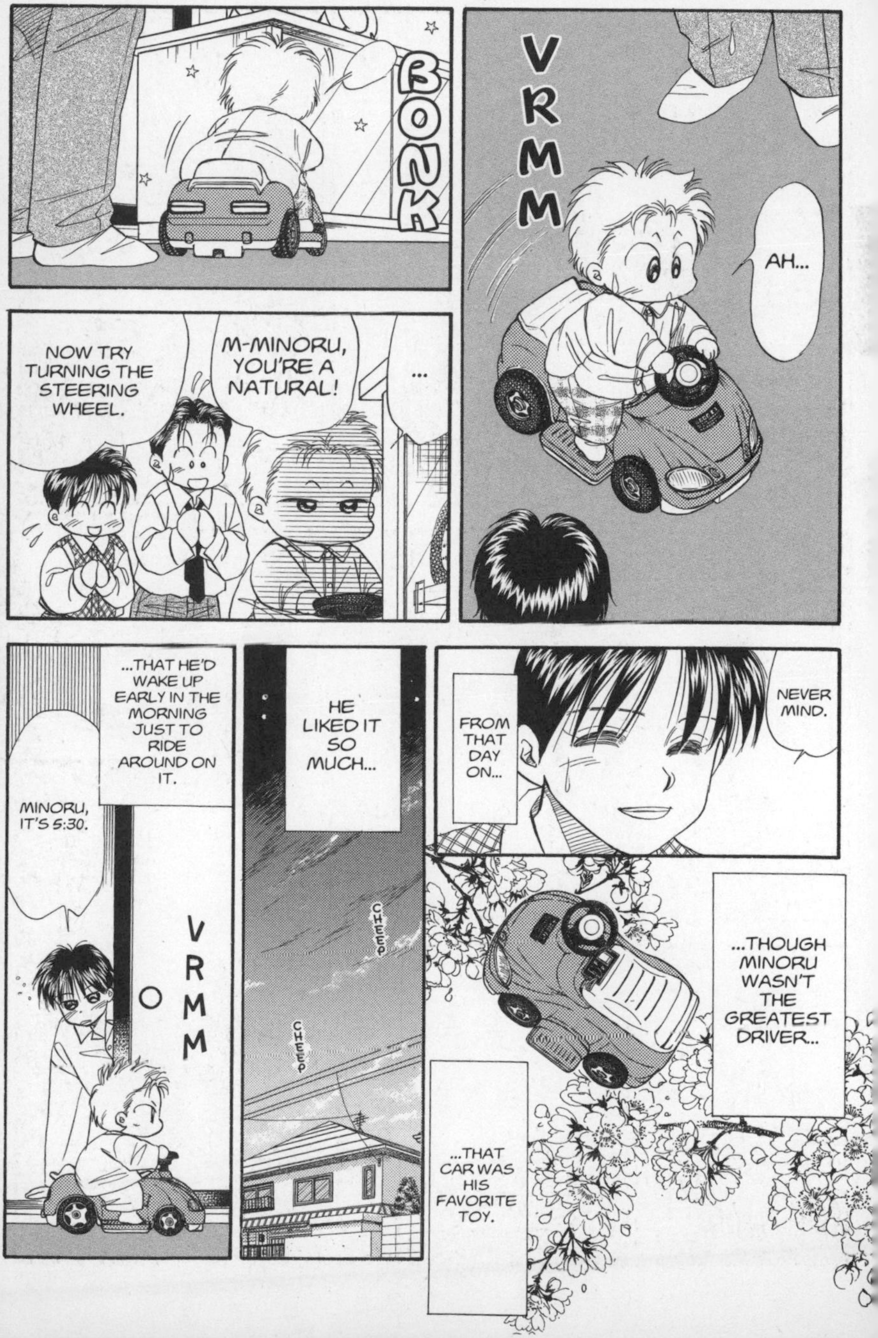
VRMM
AH...
BONK
...
M-MINORU, YOU'RE A NATURAL!
NOW TRY TURNING THE STEERING WHEEL.
NEVER MIND.
FROM THAT DAY ON...
HE LIKED IT SO MUCH...
CHEEP
CHEEP
...THAT HE'D WAKE UP EARLY IN THE MORNING JUST TO RIDE AROUND ON IT.
MINORU, IT'S 5:30.
VRMM
O
...THOUGH MINORU WASN'T THE GREATEST DRIVER...
...THAT CAR WAS HIS FAVORITE TOY.

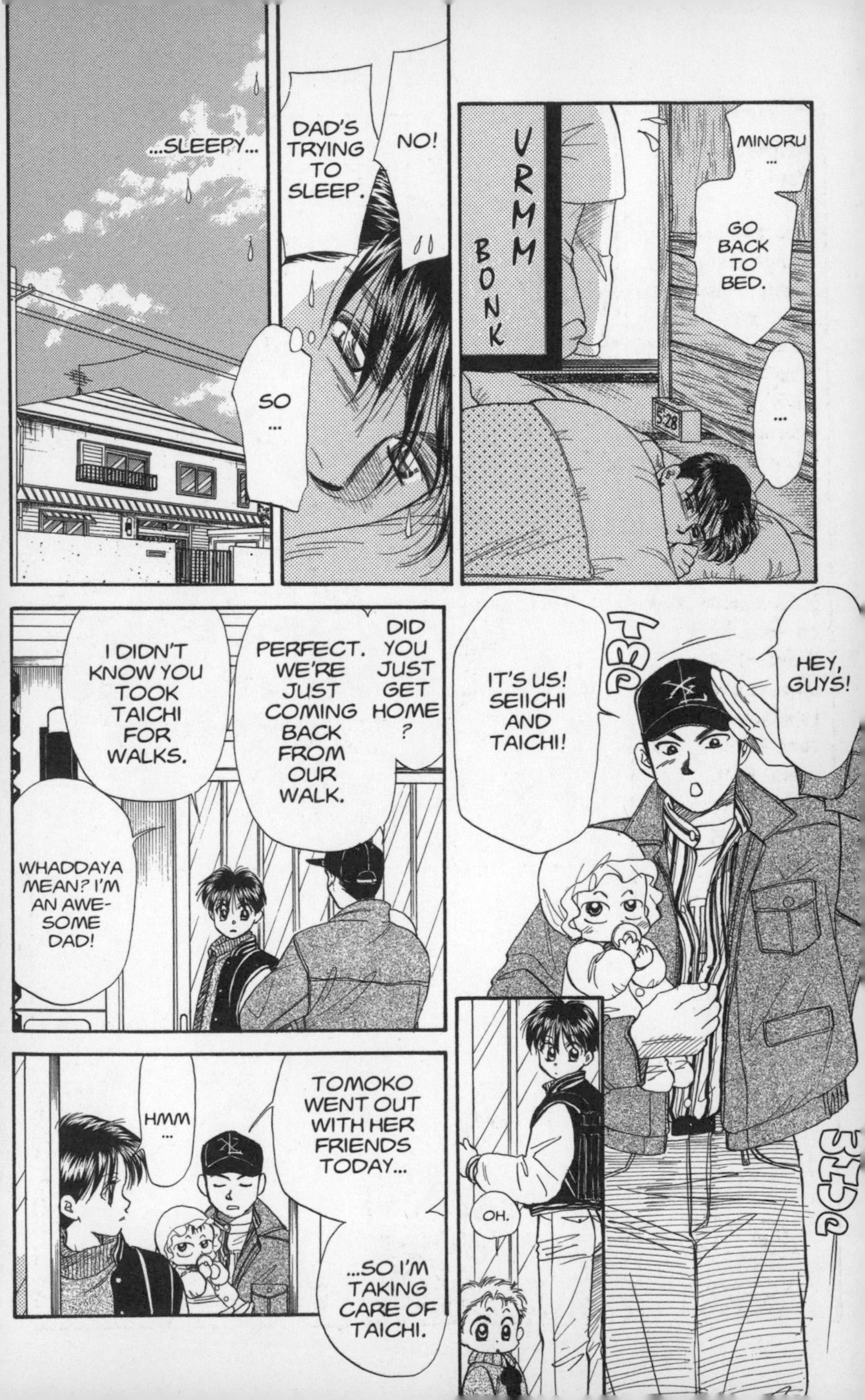
MINORU ...
GO BACK TO BED.
URMM
BONK
... ...
NO!
DAD'S TRYING TO SLEEP.
SO ...
...SLEEPY...
HEY, GUYS!
TMP
IT'S US! SEIICHI AND TAICHI!
SLIDE
OH.
DID YOU JUST GET HOME?
PERFECT. WE'RE JUST COMING BACK FROM OUR WALK.
I DIDN'T KNOW YOU TOOK TAICHI FOR WALKS.
WHADDAYA MEAN? I'M AN AWESOME DAD!
TOMOKO WENT OUT WITH HER FRIENDS TODAY...
HMM ...
...SO I'M TAKING CARE OF TAICHI.

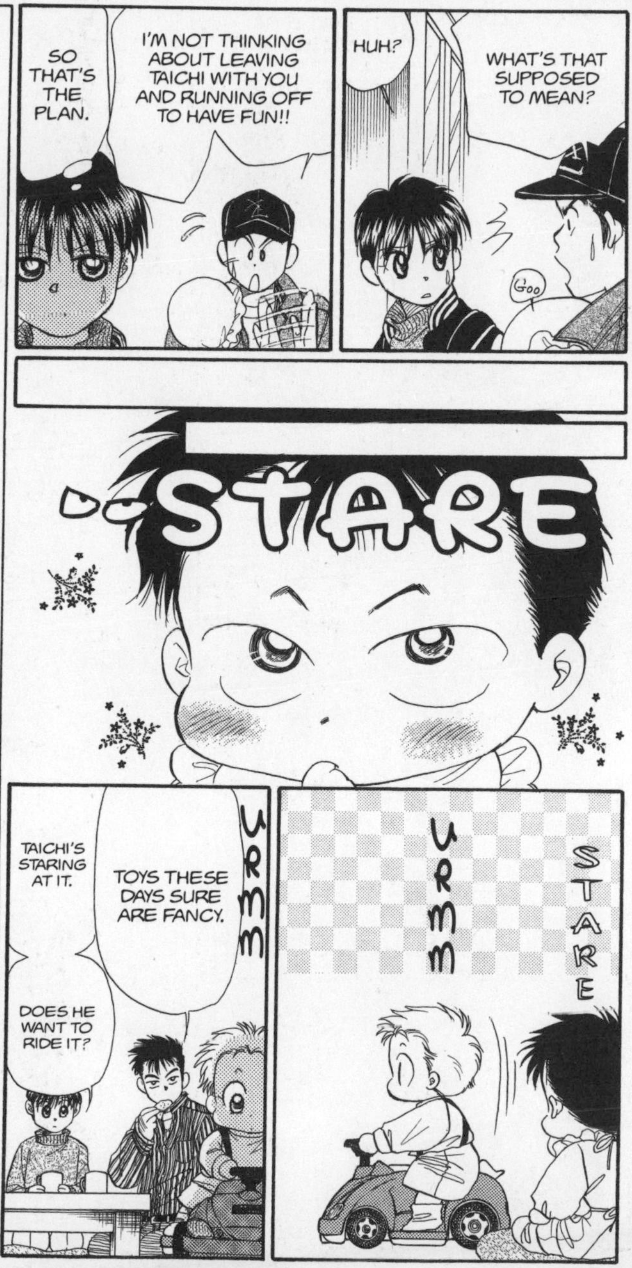
HUH?
WHAT'S THAT SUPPOSED TO MEAN?
Goo
I'M NOT THINKING ABOUT LEAVING TAICHI WITH YOU AND RUNNING OFF TO HAVE FUN!!
SO THAT'S THE PLAN.
STARE
STARE
URMM
URMM
TOYS THESE DAYS SURE ARE FANCY.
TAICHI'S STARING AT IT.
DOES HE WANT TO RIDE IT?

Author's Note Part 2

I worked on a manga story for adults called "New York, New York" right before I did Chapter 75. As a result, my characters in Chapter 75 lack some of their chubbiness and seem kind of plain. After a manga artist works on something different, it takes a day of rehabilitation to be back in the groove again. Blah blah...So I tried to "shrink" my young characters in Chapter 76. Let me tell you, it's not easy to break a habit once you have it.

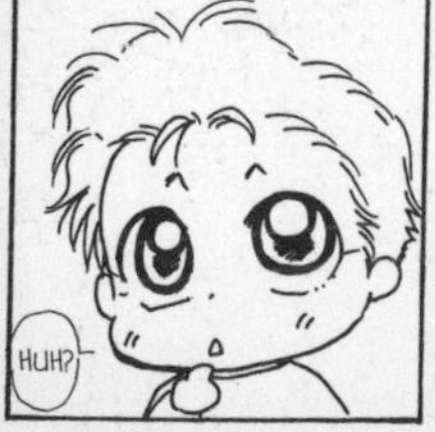
HUH?

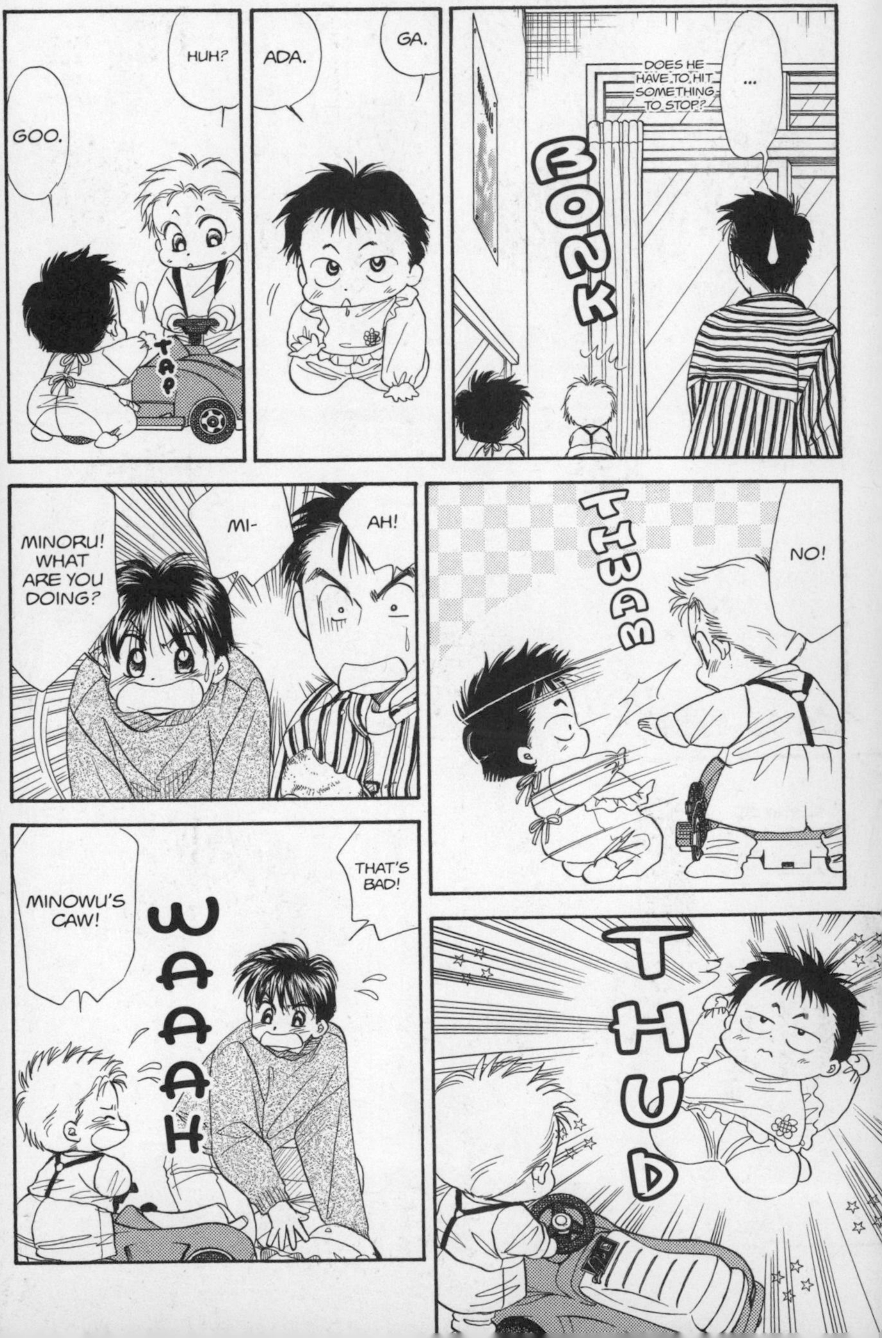
...
DOES HE HAVE TO HIT SOMETHING TO STOP?
BONK
GA.
ADA.
HUH?
GOO.
TAP
NO!
THWAM
AH!
MI-
MINORU! WHAT ARE YOU DOING?
THUD
THAT'S BAD!
WAAAAH
MINOWU'S CAW!

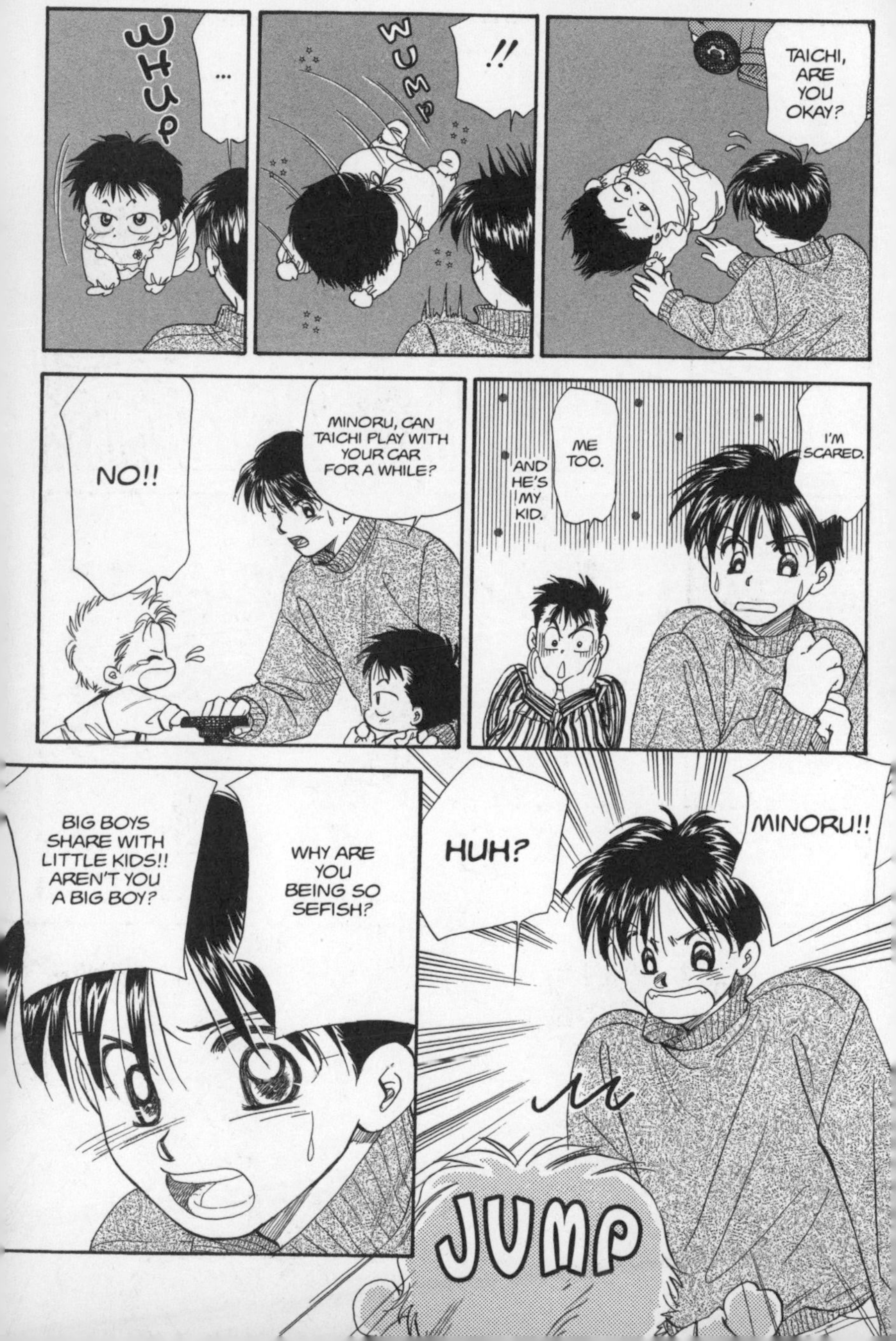

TAICHI, ARE YOU OKAY?
!!
WUMP
...
WHUP
I'M SCARED.
ME TOO.
AND HE'S MY KID.
MINORU, CAN TAICHI PLAY WITH YOUR CAR FOR A WHILE?
NO!!
MINORU!!
HUH?
JUMP
WHY ARE YOU BEING SO SEFISH?
BIG BOYS SHARE WITH LITTLE KIDS!! AREN'T YOU A BIG BOY?

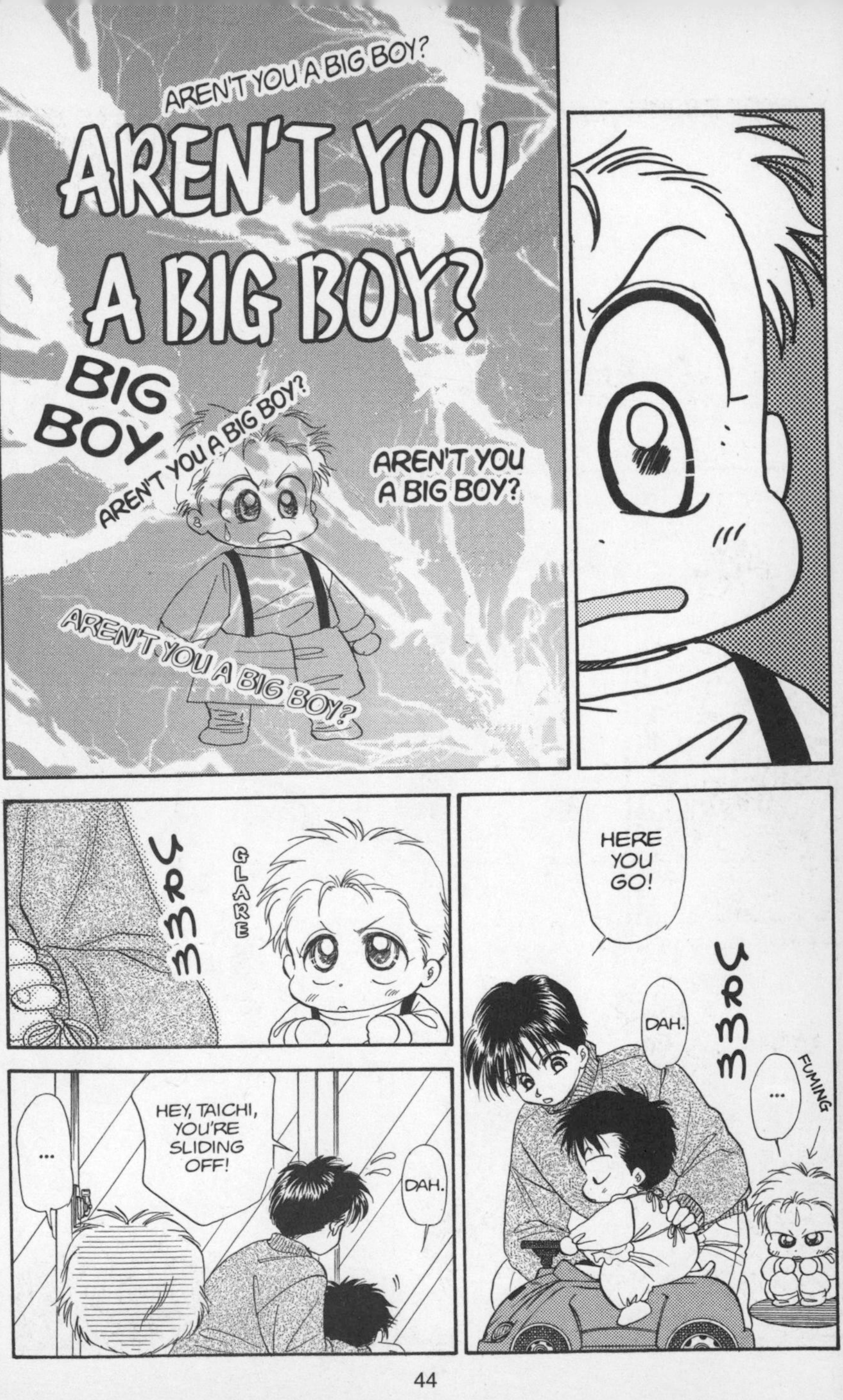

AREN'T YOU A BIG BOY?
AREN'T YOU A BIG BOY?
BIG BOY
AREN'T YOU A BIG BOY?
AREN'T YOU A BIG BOY?
AREN'T YOU A BIG BOY?
HERE YOU GO!
URMM
DAH.
...
FUMING
URMM
GLARE
DAH.
HEY, TAICHI, YOU'RE SLIDING OFF!
...

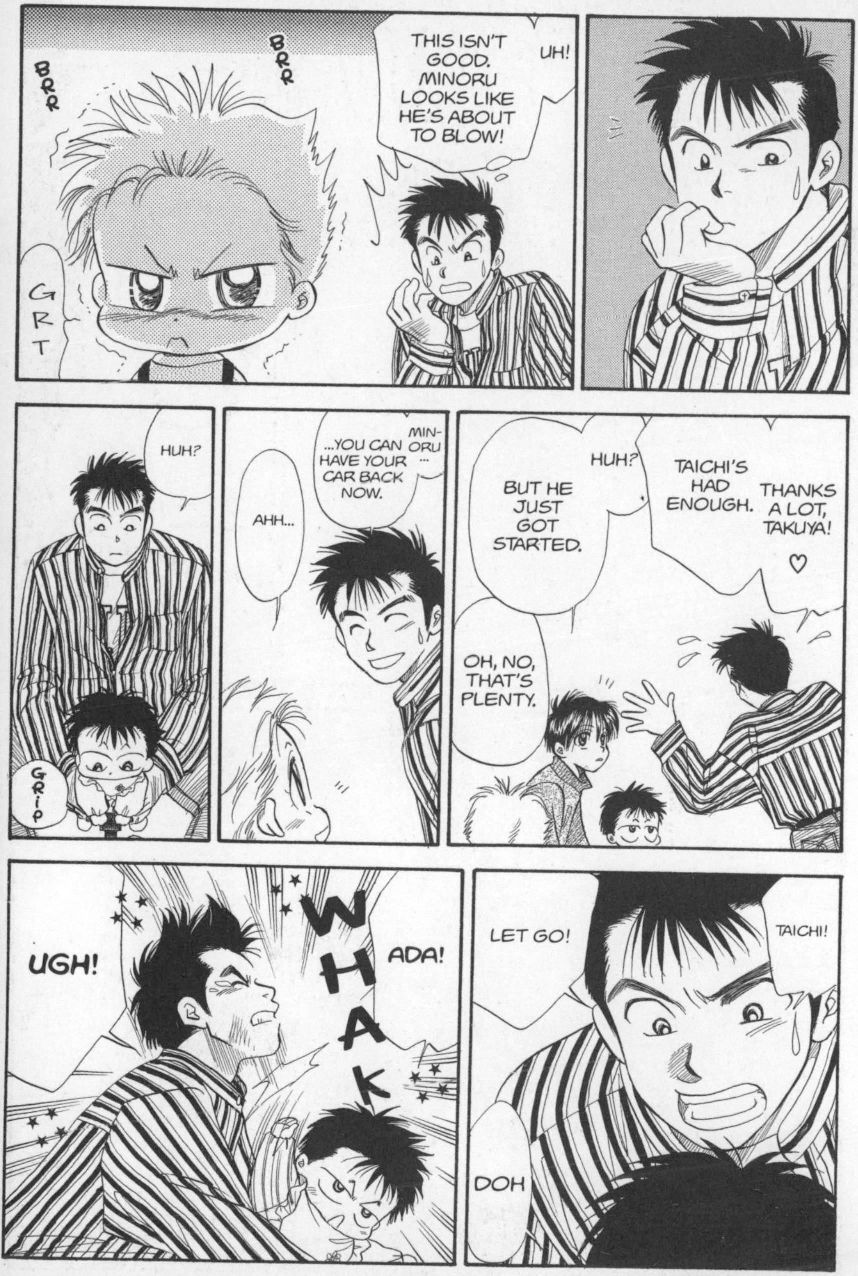
UH!
THIS ISN'T GOOD. MINORU LOOKS LIKE HE'S ABOUT TO BLOW!
BRR
BRR
GRT
THANKS A LOT, TAKUYA! ♡
TAICHI'S HAD ENOUGH.
HUH?
BUT HE JUST GOT STARTED.
OH, NO, THAT'S PLENTY.
MIN-ORU ...
...YOU CAN HAVE YOUR CAR BACK NOW.
AHH...
HUH?
GRIP
TAICHI!
LET GO!
DOH
ADA!
WHAK
UGH!

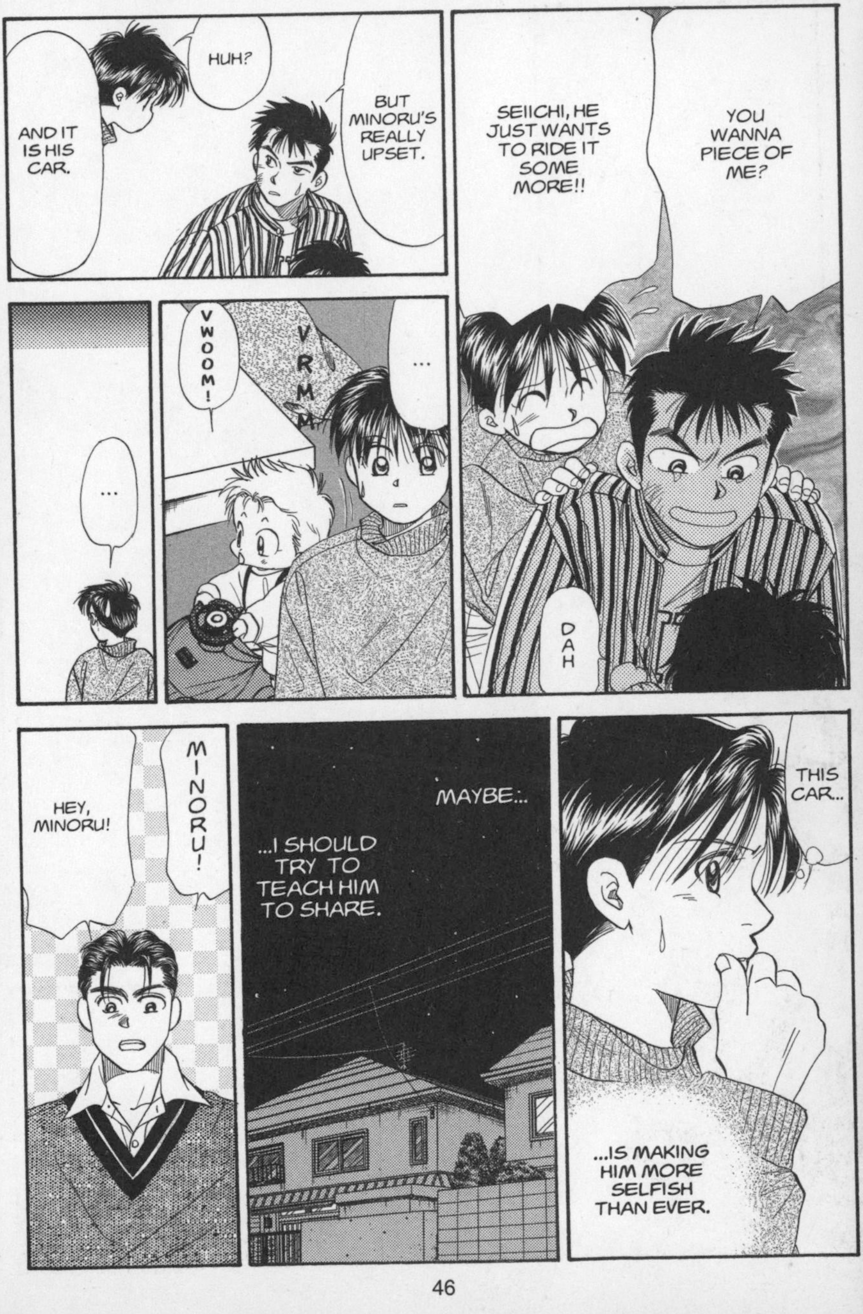
YOU WANNA PIECE OF ME?
SEIICHI, HE JUST WANTS TO RIDE IT SOME MORE!!
DAH
BUT MINORU'S REALLY UPSET.
HUH?
AND IT IS HIS CAR.
...
VRMM
VWOOM!
...
THIS CAR...
...IS MAKING HIM MORE SELFISH THAN EVER.
MAYBE...
...I SHOULD TRY TO TEACH HIM TO SHARE.
MINORU!
HEY, MINORU!

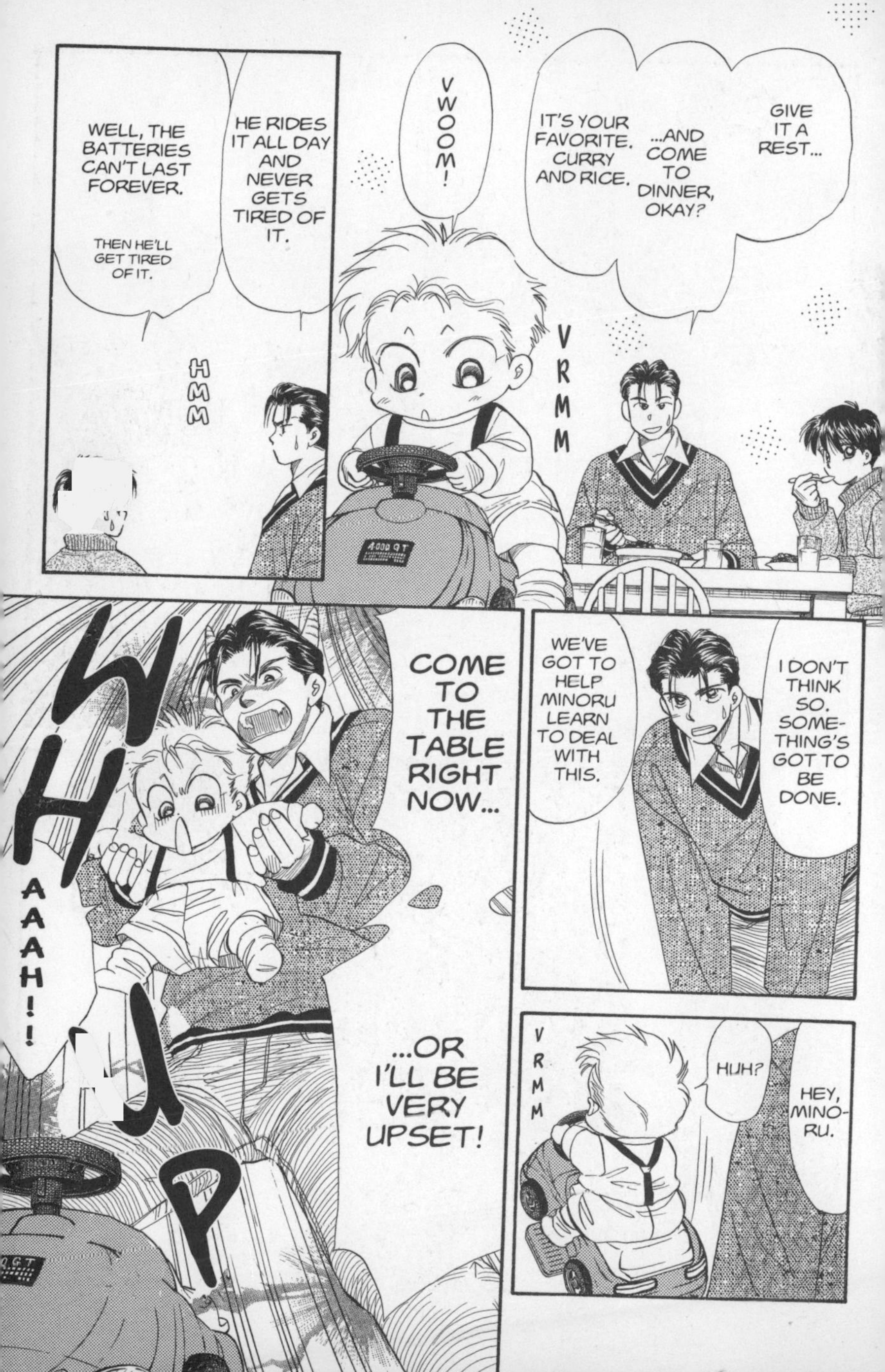
GIVE IT A REST...
...AND COME TO DINNER, OKAY?
IT'S YOUR FAVORITE. CURRY AND RICE.
VWOOM!
VRMM
HE RIDES IT ALL DAY AND NEVER GETS TIRED OF IT.
WELL, THE BATTERIES CAN'T LAST FOREVER.
THEN HE'LL GET TIRED OF IT.
HMM
I DON'T THINK SO. SOME-THING'S GOT TO BE DONE.
WE'VE GOT TO HELP MINORU LEARN TO DEAL WITH THIS.
HEY, MINO-RU.
HUH?
VRMM
COME TO THE TABLE RIGHT NOW...
...OR I'LL BE VERY UPSET!
WHUP
AAAAH!!

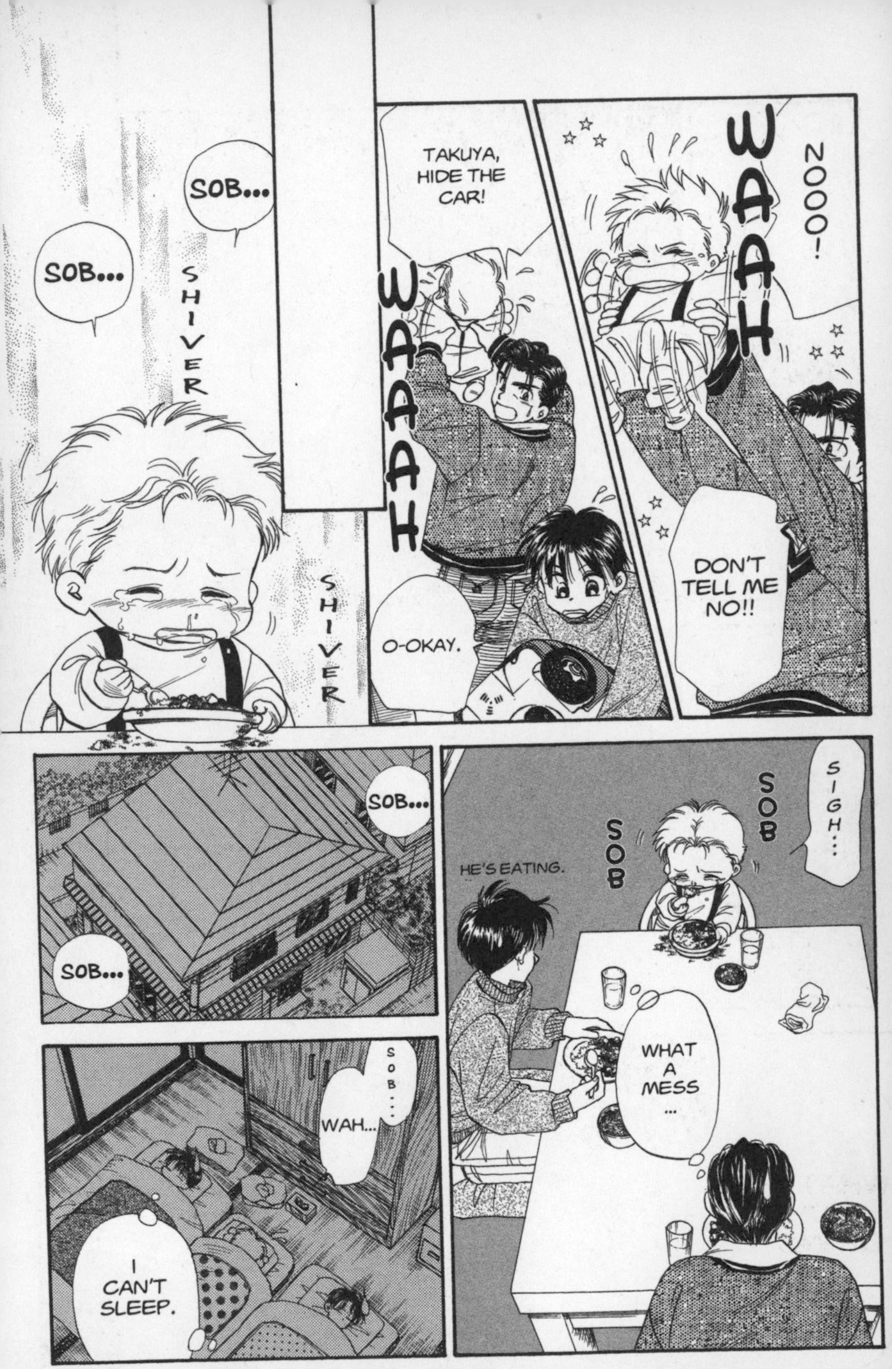
WAAH
NOOO!
DON'T TELL ME NO!!
TAKUYA, HIDE THE CAR!
WAAAH
O-OKAY.
SOB...
SOB...
SHIVER
SHIVER
SIGH...
SOB
SOB
HE'S EATING.
WHAT A MESS...
SOB...
SOB...
SOB...
WAH...
I CAN'T SLEEP.

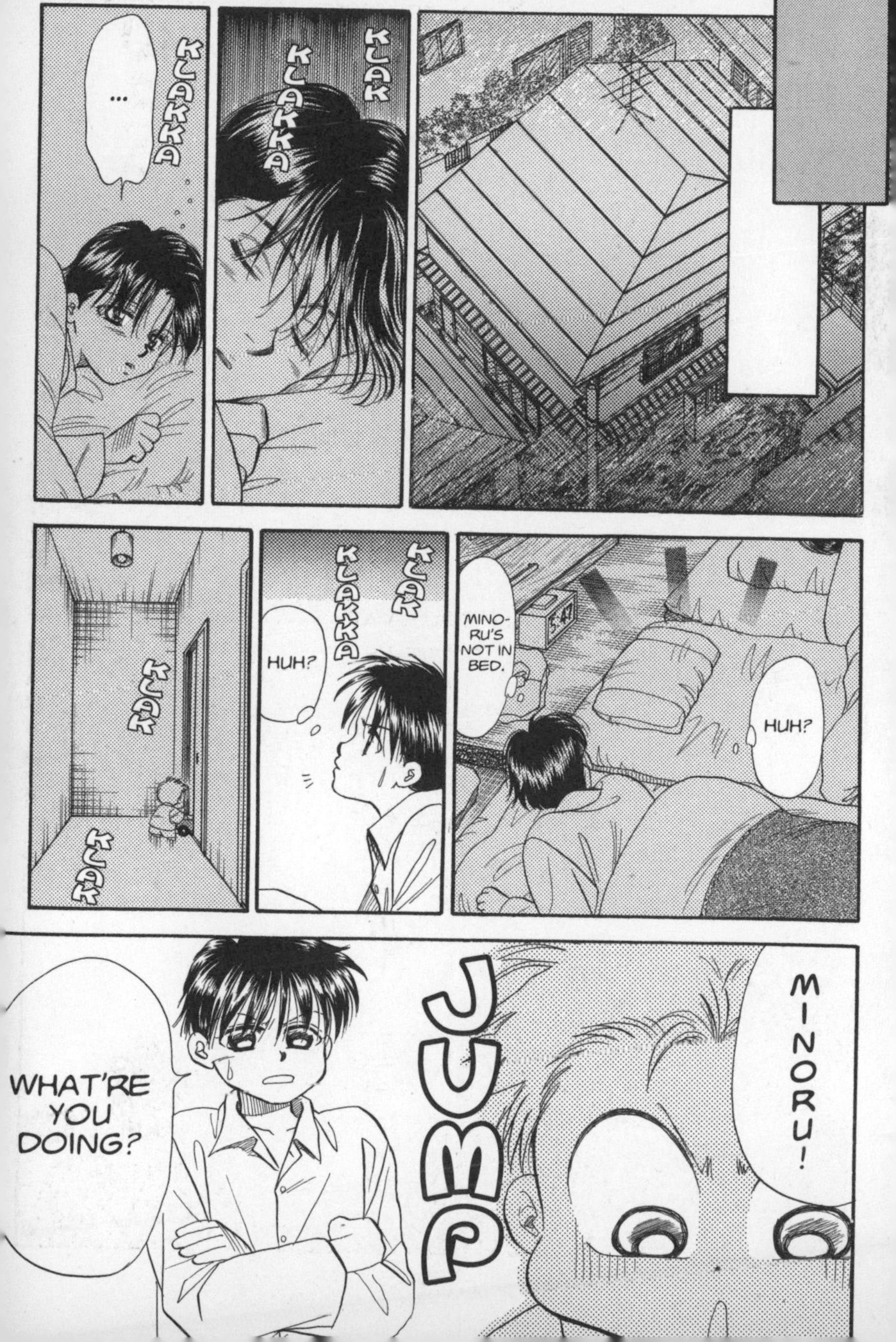
KLAK
KLAKKA
...
KLAKKA
HUH?
MINORU'S NOT IN BED.
KLAK
KLAKKA
HUH?
KLAK
KLAK
MINORU!
JUMP
WHAT'RE YOU DOING?

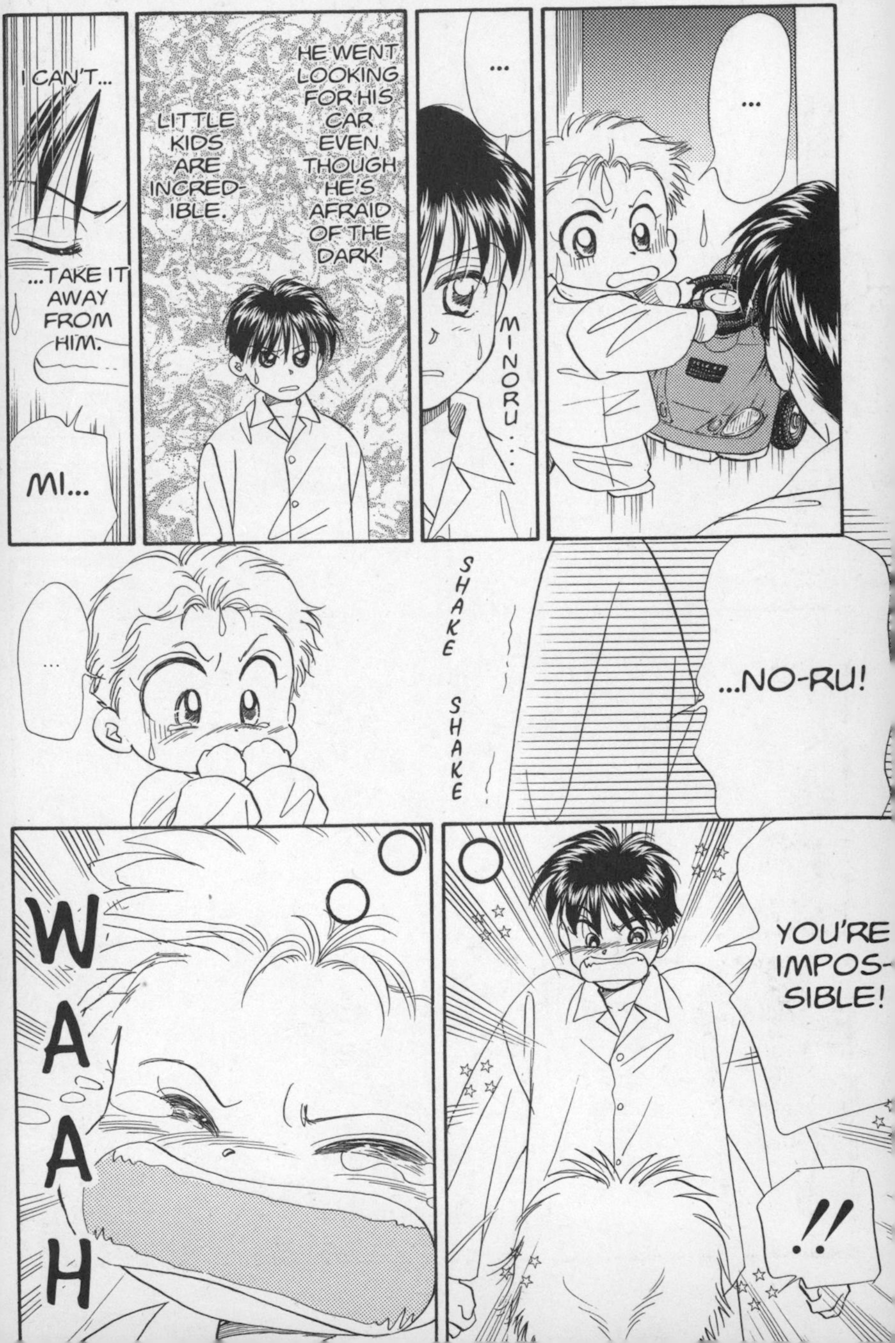
…
…
MINORU…
HE WENT LOOKING FOR HIS CAR EVEN THOUGH HE'S AFRAID OF THE DARK!
LITTLE KIDS ARE INCREDIBLE.
I CAN'T…
…TAKE IT AWAY FROM HIM.
MI…
…NO-RU!
SHAKE SHAKE
…
YOU'RE IMPOSSIBLE!
!!
WAAAH

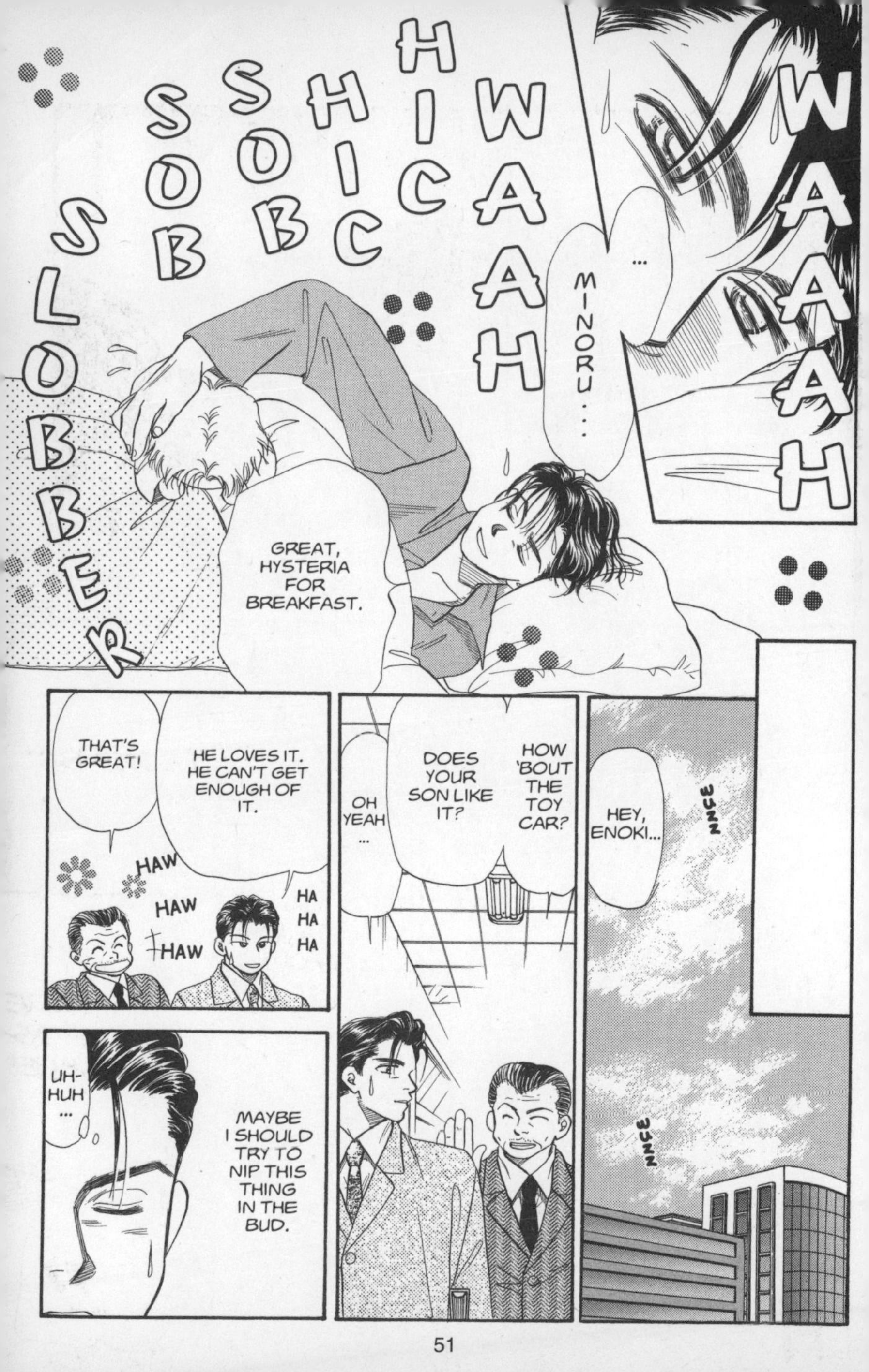
WAAAH
...
MINORU...
WAAH
HIC
HIC
SOB
SOB
SLOBBER
GREAT, HYSTERIA FOR BREAKFAST.
HEY, ENOKI...
WUNN
WUNN
HOW 'BOUT THE TOY CAR?
DOES YOUR SON LIKE IT?
OH YEAH...
HE LOVES IT. HE CAN'T GET ENOUGH OF IT.
THAT'S GREAT!
HA HA HA
HAW HAW HAW
UH-HUH...
MAYBE I SHOULD TRY TO NIP THIS THING IN THE BUD.

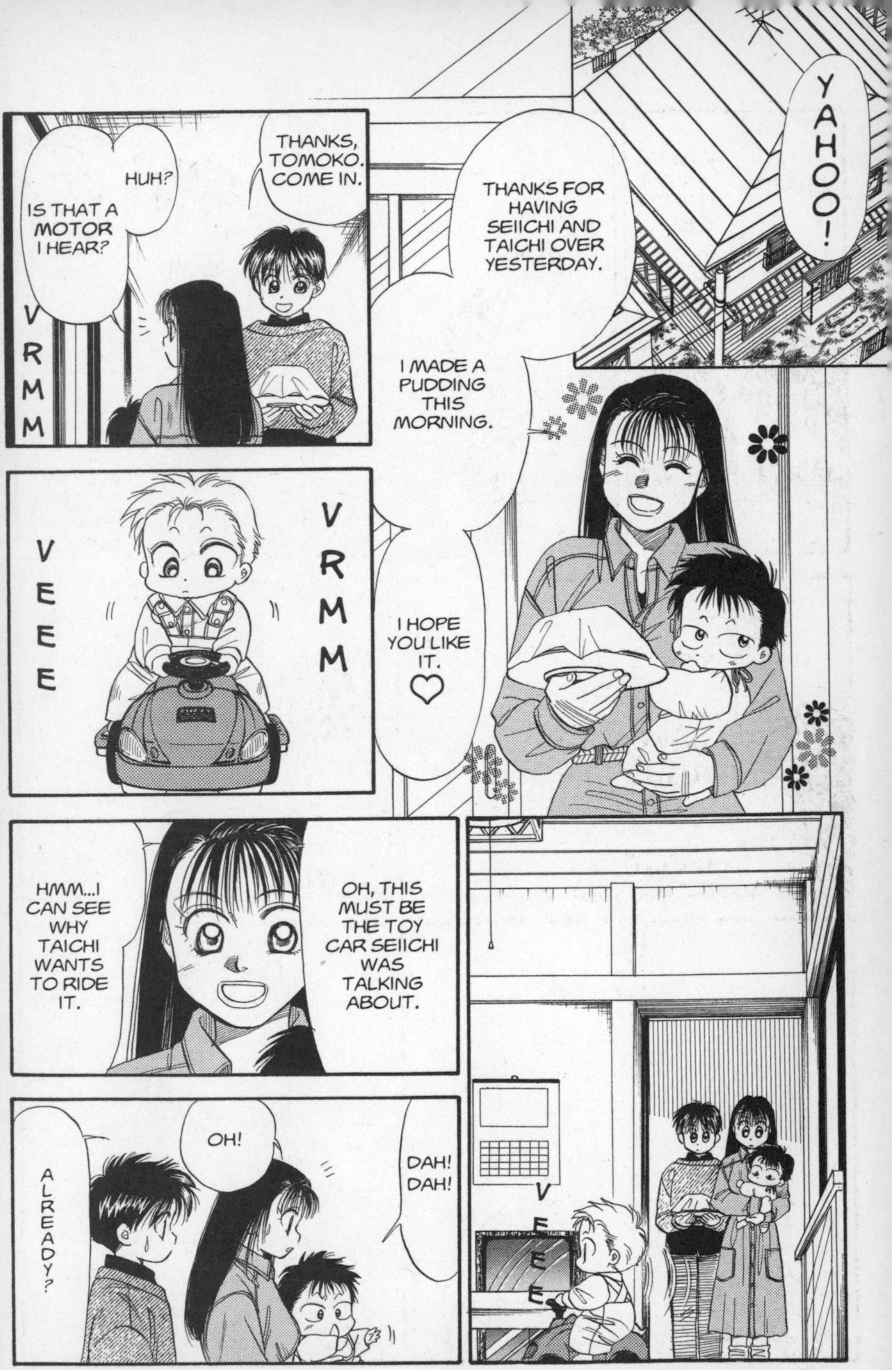
YAHOO!
THANKS FOR HAVING SEIICHI AND TAICHI OVER YESTERDAY.
I MADE A PUDDING THIS MORNING.
I HOPE YOU LIKE IT. ♡
THANKS, TOMOKO. COME IN.
HUH? IS THAT A MOTOR I HEAR?
VRMM
VRMM
VEEE
VEEE
OH, THIS MUST BE THE TOY CAR SEIICHI WAS TALKING ABOUT.
HMM...I CAN SEE WHY TAICHI WANTS TO RIDE IT.
DAH! DAH!
OH!
ALREADY?

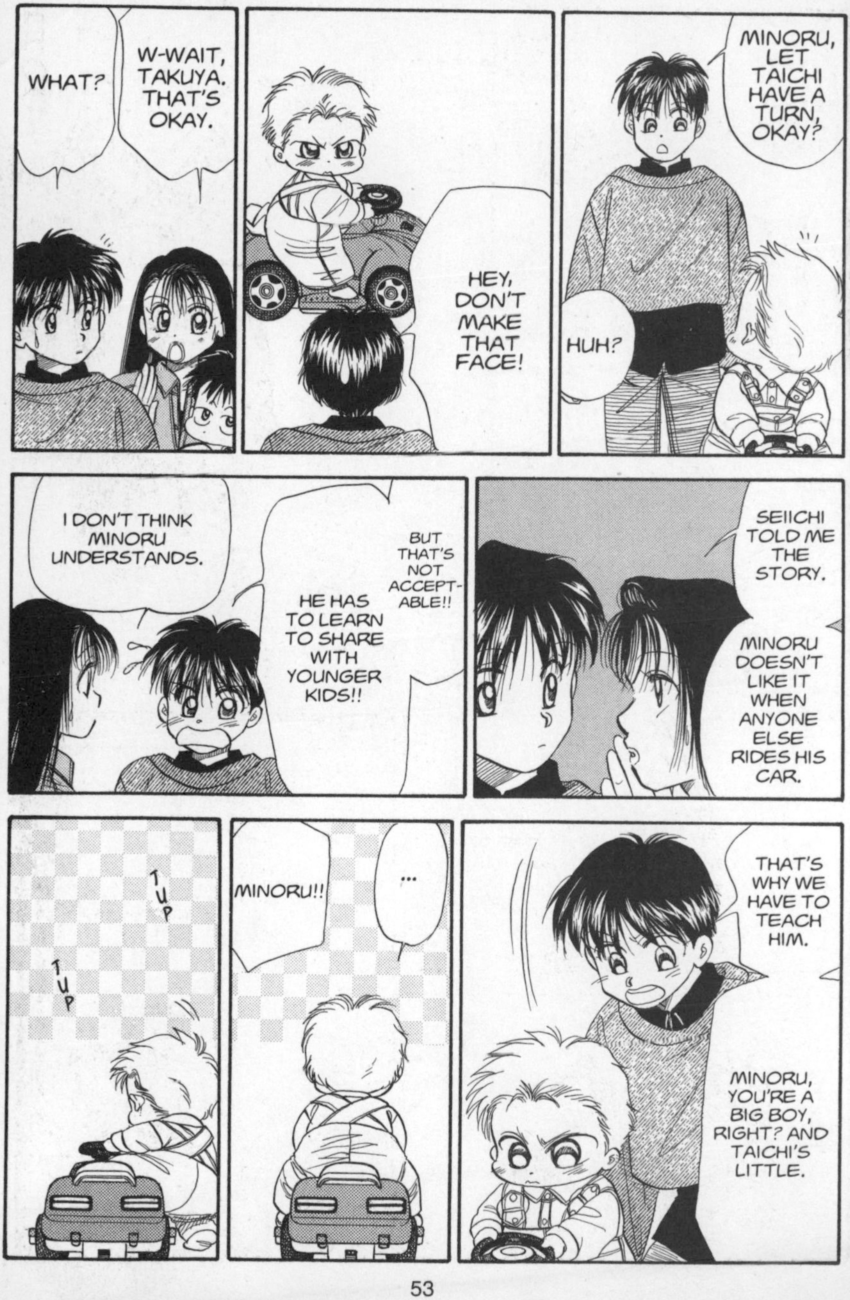
MINORU, LET TAICHI HAVE A TURN, OKAY?
HUH?
HEY, DON'T MAKE THAT FACE!
W-WAIT, TAKUYA. THAT'S OKAY.
WHAT?
SEIICHI TOLD ME THE STORY.
MINORU DOESN'T LIKE IT WHEN ANYONE ELSE RIDES HIS CAR.
BUT THAT'S NOT ACCEPT-ABLE!!
HE HAS TO LEARN TO SHARE WITH YOUNGER KIDS!!
I DON'T THINK MINORU UNDERSTANDS.
THAT'S WHY WE HAVE TO TEACH HIM.
MINORU, YOU'RE A BIG BOY, RIGHT? AND TAICHI'S LITTLE.
...
MINORU!!
TUP
TUP

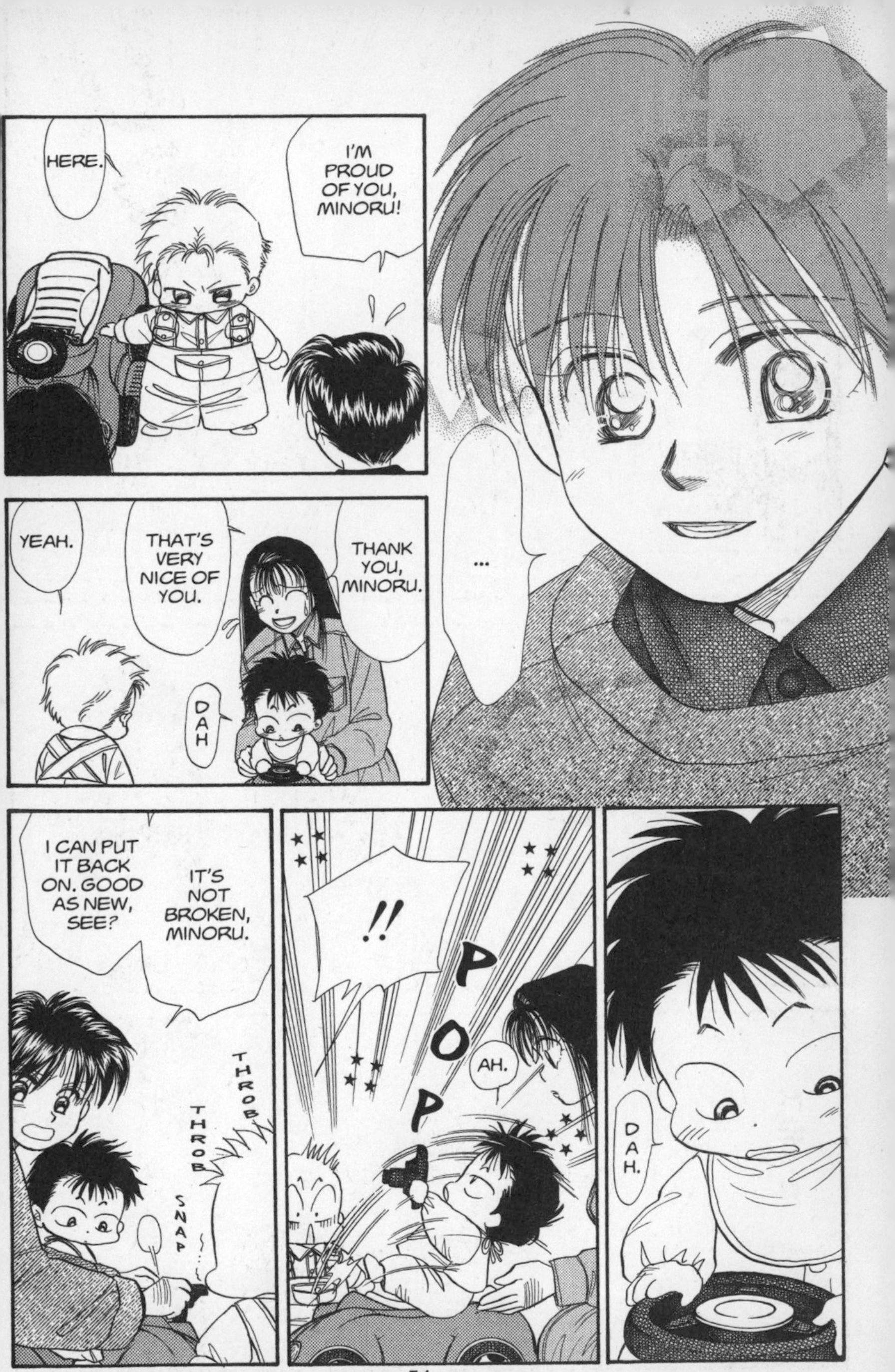
...
I'M PROUD OF YOU, MINORU!
HERE.
THANK YOU, MINORU.
THAT'S VERY NICE OF YOU.
YEAH.
DAH
DAH.
!!
POP
AH.
IT'S NOT BROKEN, MINORU.
I CAN PUT IT BACK ON. GOOD AS NEW, SEE?
THROB
THROB
SNAP

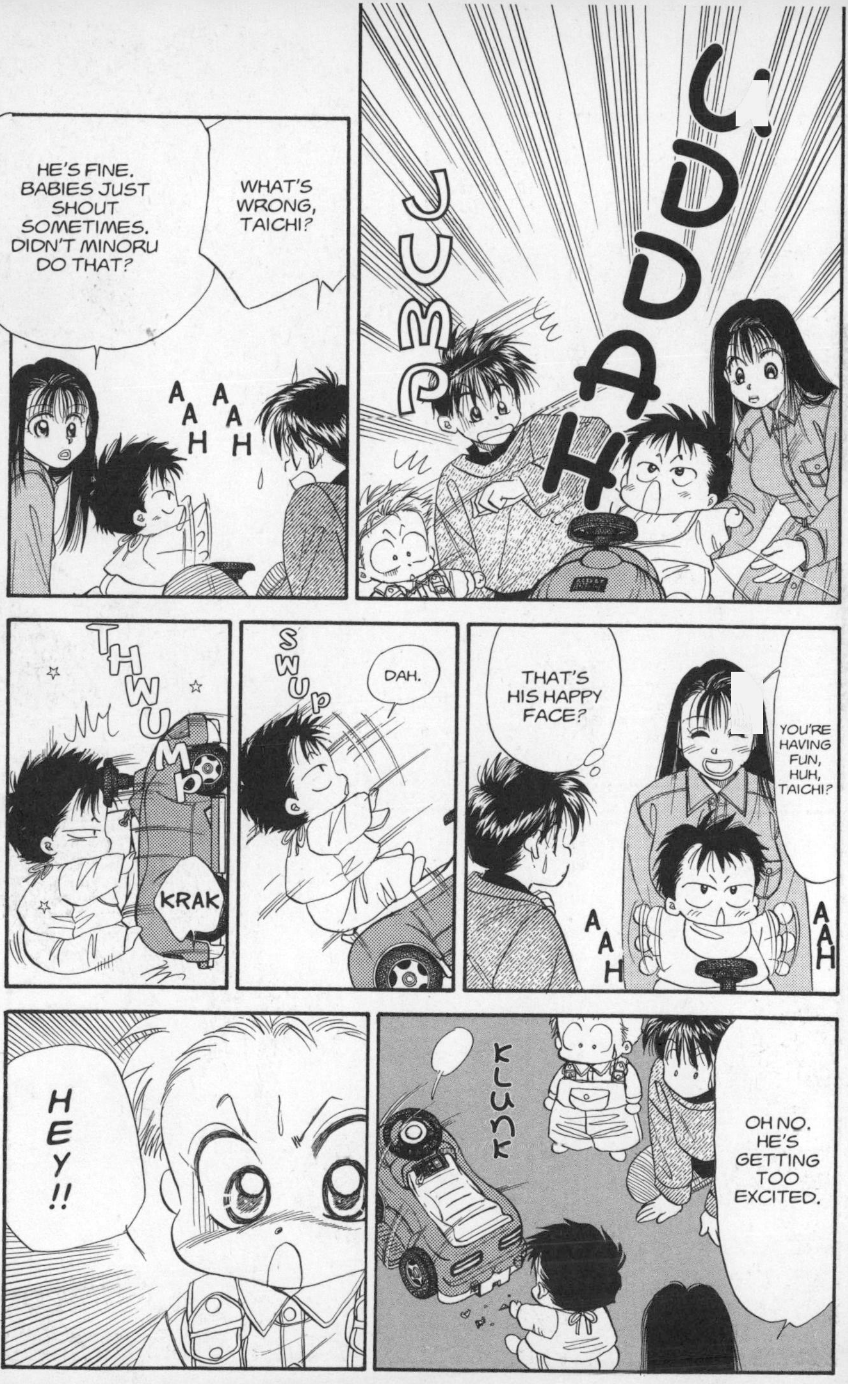
WHAT'S WRONG, TAICHI?
HE'S FINE. BABIES JUST SHOUT SOMETIMES. DIDN'T MINORU DO THAT?
AAH
AAH
YOU'RE HAVING FUN, HUH, TAICHI?
AAH
THAT'S HIS HAPPY FACE?
AAH
SWUp
DAH.
THWUMp
KRAK
OH NO. HE'S GETTING TOO EXCITED.
KLUNK
HEY!!

OH!

T-TAKE IT EASY, MINORU.

IT'S OKAY...

I'M SO SORRY!

SHAKE
SHAKE
SHAKE

DAMAGED

WHAT?

?!

SOB
...

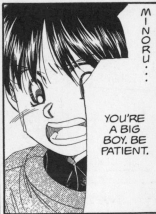

MINORU...

YOU'RE A BIG BOY. BE PATIENT.

I FELT WEIRD...

...FOR A SECOND THERE...

WHAT WAS THAT?

SOB...

...

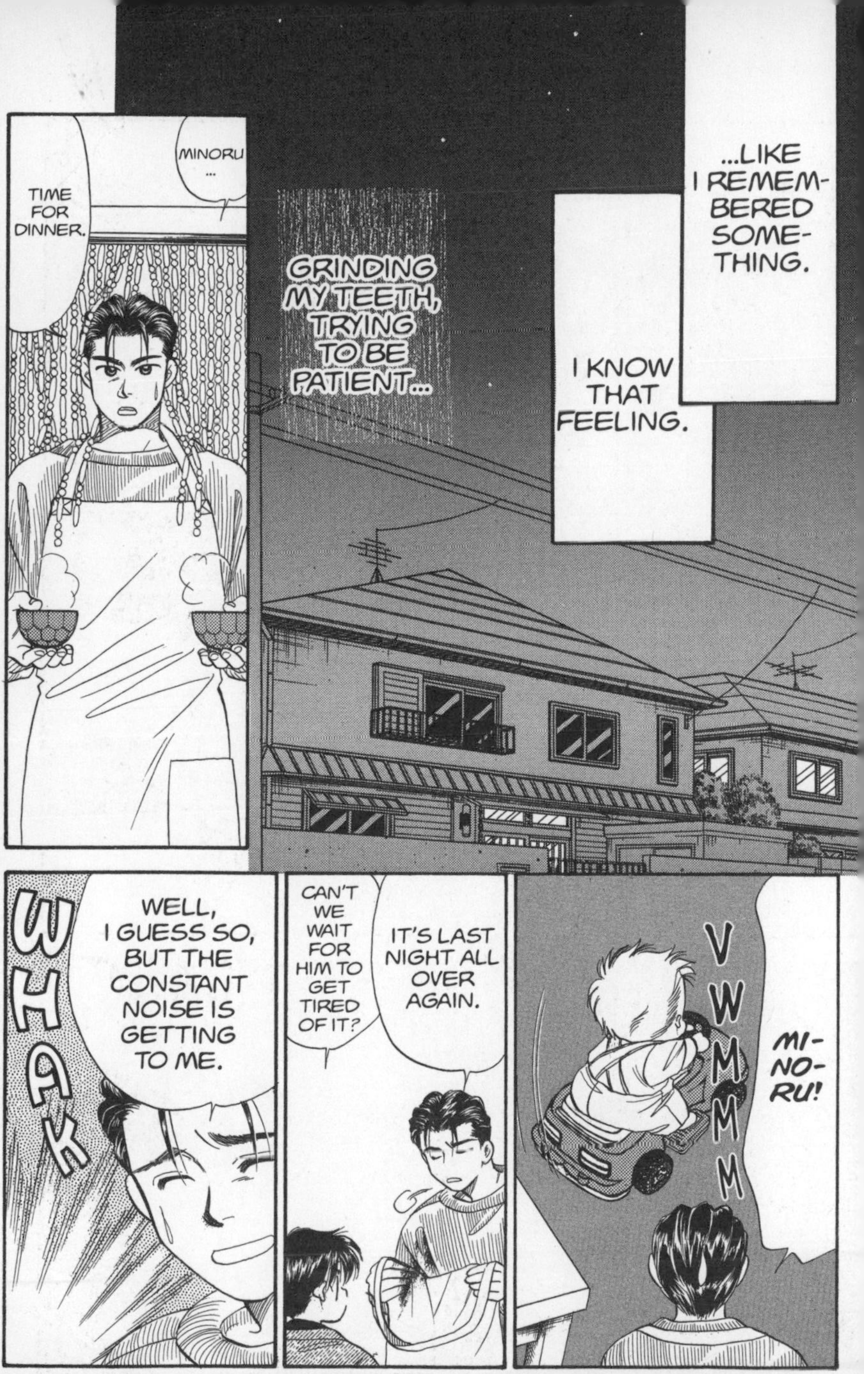
...LIKE I REMEMBERED SOMETHING.
I KNOW THAT FEELING.
GRINDING MY TEETH, TRYING TO BE PATIENT...
MINORU ...
TIME FOR DINNER.
VWMMM
MI-NO-RU!
IT'S LAST NIGHT ALL OVER AGAIN.
CAN'T WE WAIT FOR HIM TO GET TIRED OF IT?
WELL, I GUESS SO, BUT THE CONSTANT NOISE IS GETTING TO ME.
WHAK

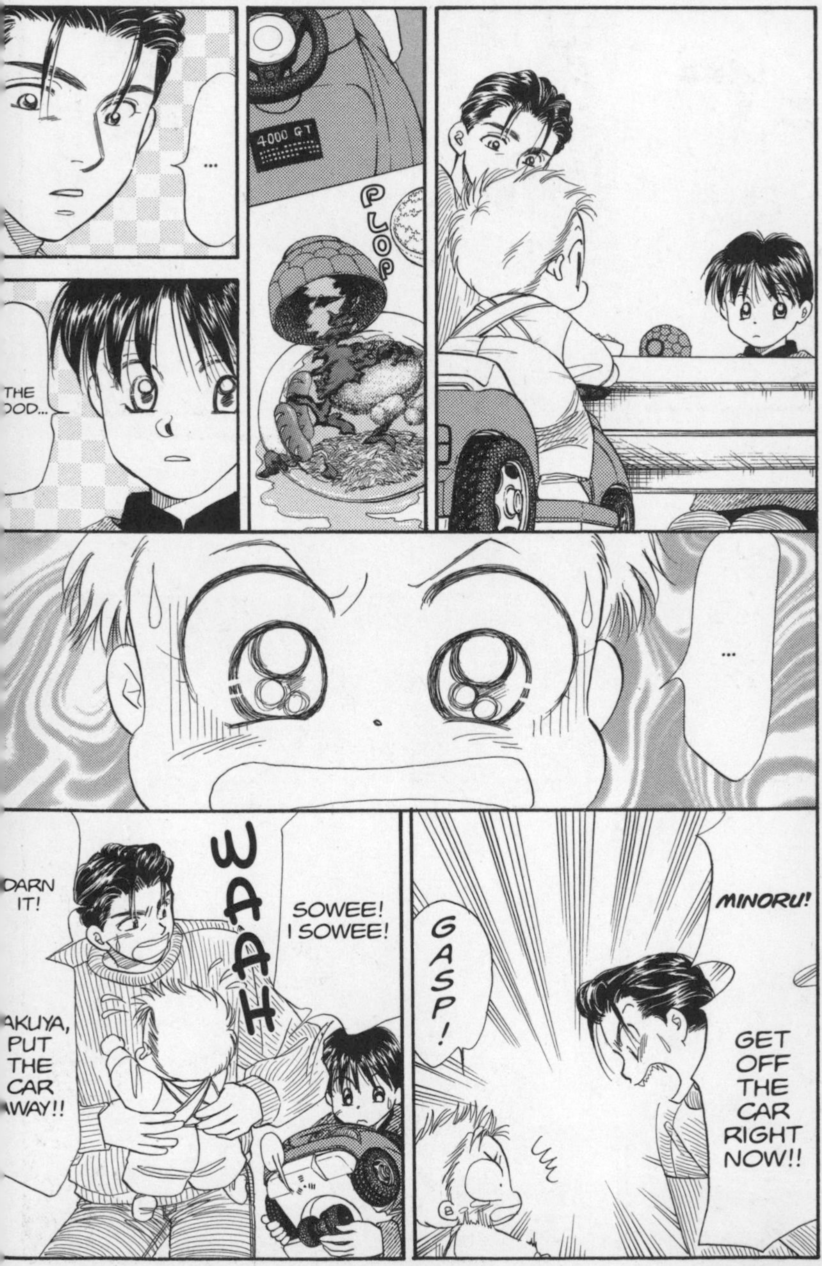
PLOP
4000 GT
...
THE OOD...
...
MINORU!
GASP!
GET OFF THE CAR RIGHT NOW!!
SOWEE! I SOWEE!
WAAH
DARN IT!
AKUYA, PUT THE CAR WAY!!

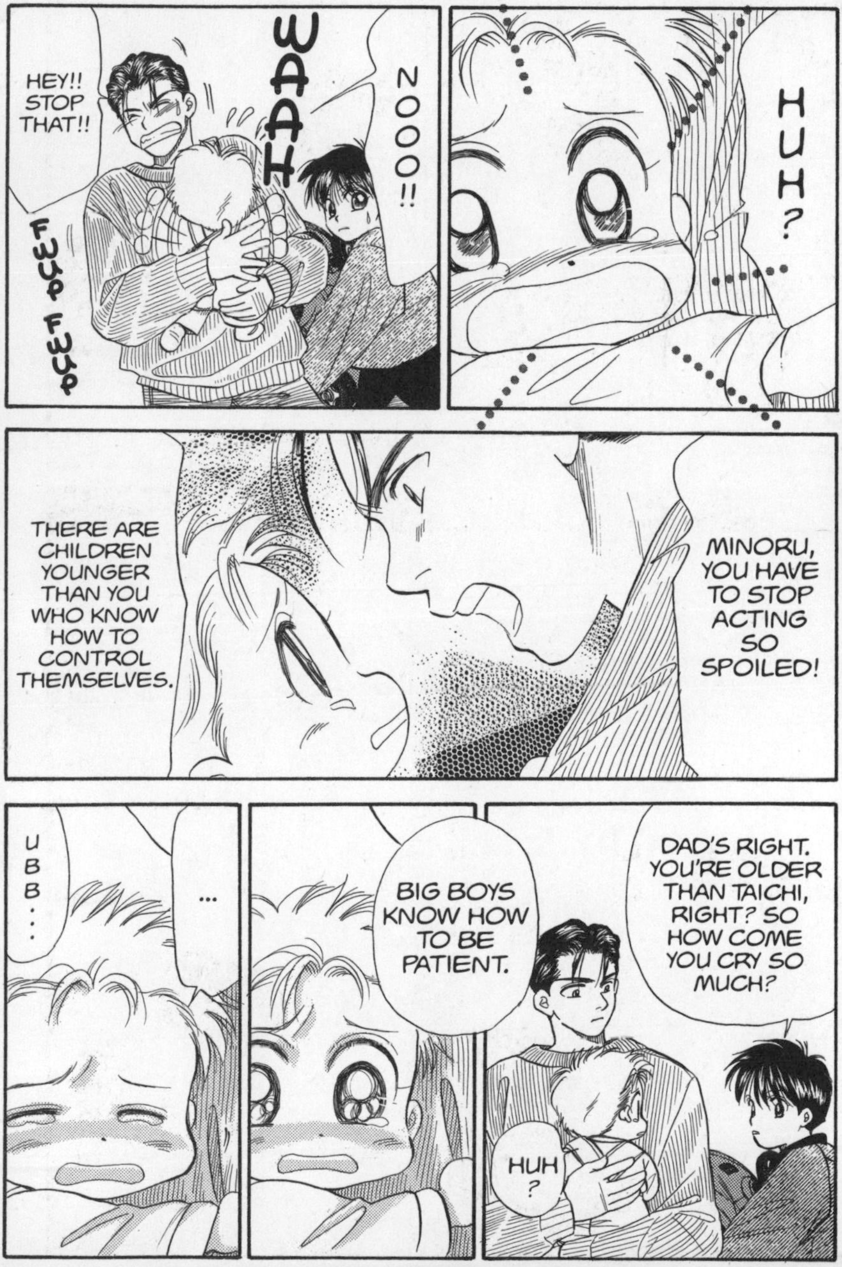
HUH?
NOOOO!!
WAAH
HEY!! STOP THAT!!
FWUP FWUP
MINORU, YOU HAVE TO STOP ACTING SO SPOILED!
THERE ARE CHILDREN YOUNGER THAN YOU WHO KNOW HOW TO CONTROL THEMSELVES.
DAD'S RIGHT. YOU'RE OLDER THAN TAICHI, RIGHT? SO HOW COME YOU CRY SO MUCH?
HUH?
BIG BOYS KNOW HOW TO BE PATIENT.
...
UBB...

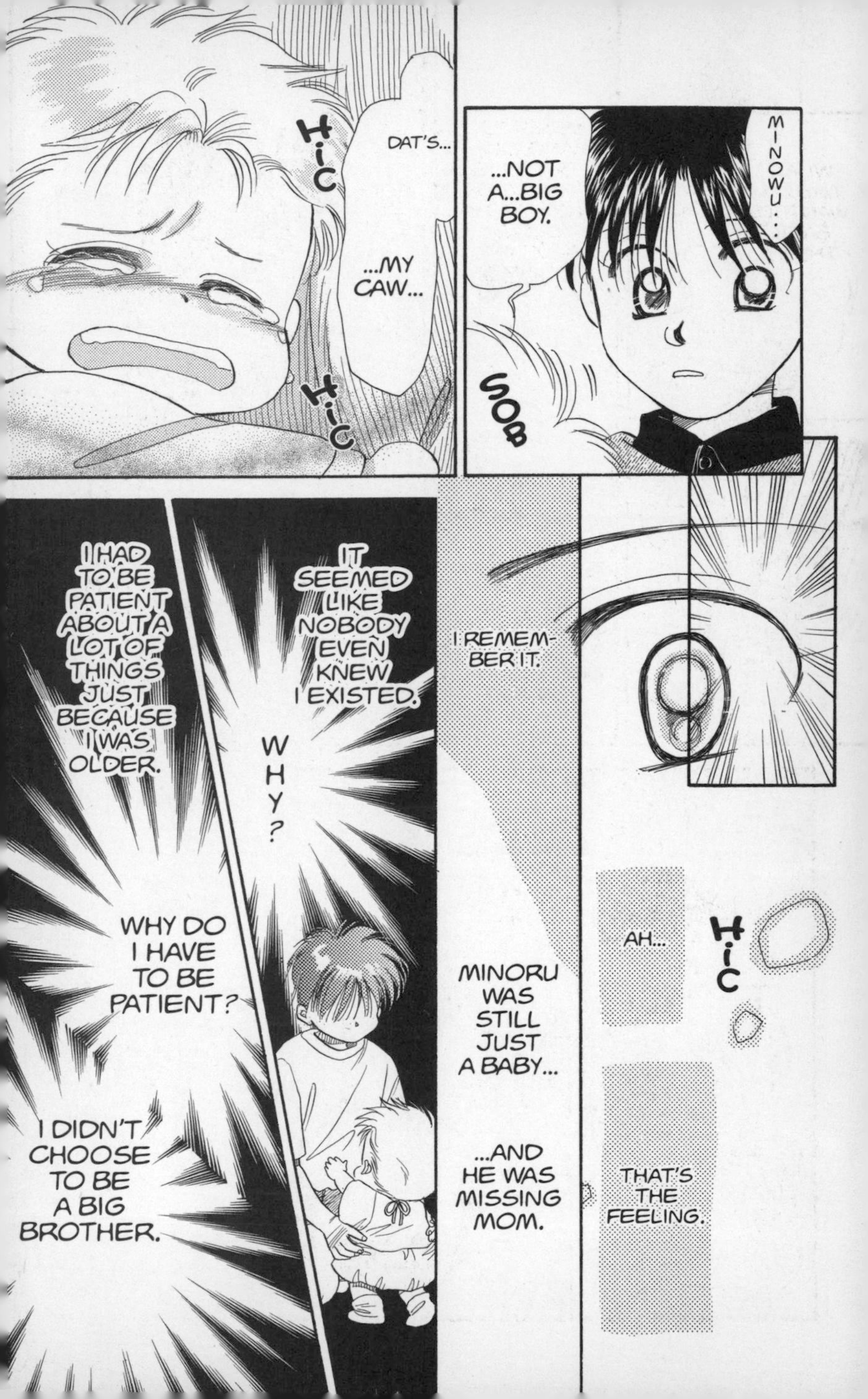

MINOWU...
...NOT A...BIG BOY.
SOB
HIC
DAT'S...
...MY CAW...
HIC
HIC
AH...
THAT'S THE FEELING.
I REMEMBER IT.
MINORU WAS STILL JUST A BABY...
...AND HE WAS MISSING MOM.
IT SEEMED LIKE NOBODY EVEN KNEW I EXISTED.
I HAD TO BE PATIENT ABOUT A LOT OF THINGS JUST BECAUSE I WAS OLDER.
WHY?
WHY DO I HAVE TO BE PATIENT?
I DIDN'T CHOOSE TO BE A BIG BROTHER.

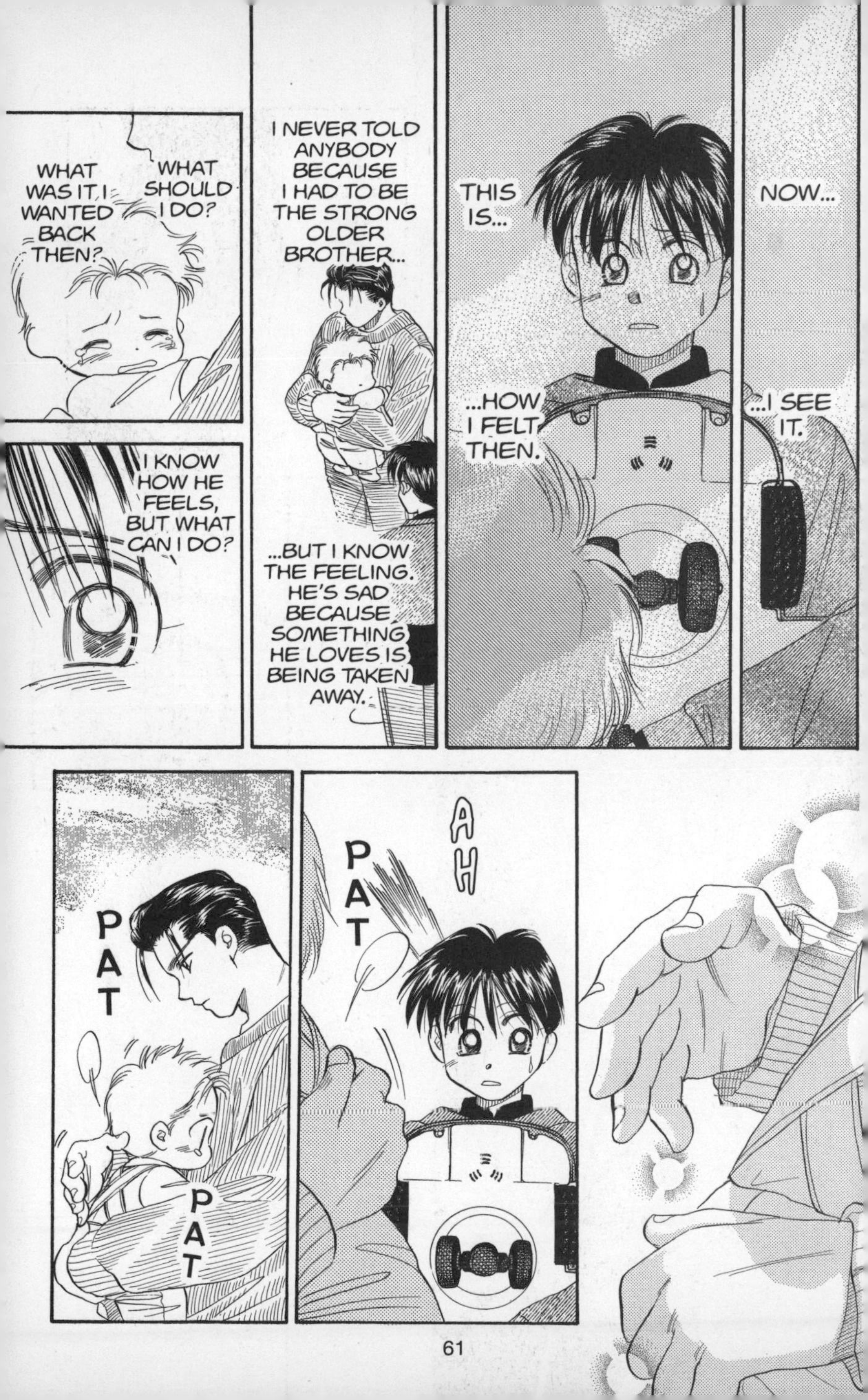
NOW...
...I SEE IT.
THIS IS...
...HOW I FELT THEN.
I NEVER TOLD ANYBODY BECAUSE I HAD TO BE THE STRONG OLDER BROTHER...
...BUT I KNOW THE FEELING. HE'S SAD BECAUSE SOMETHING HE LOVES IS BEING TAKEN AWAY.
WHAT SHOULD I DO?
WHAT WAS IT I WANTED BACK THEN?
I KNOW HOW HE FEELS, BUT WHAT CAN I DO?
AH
PAT
PAT
PAT
PAT
PAT
PAT

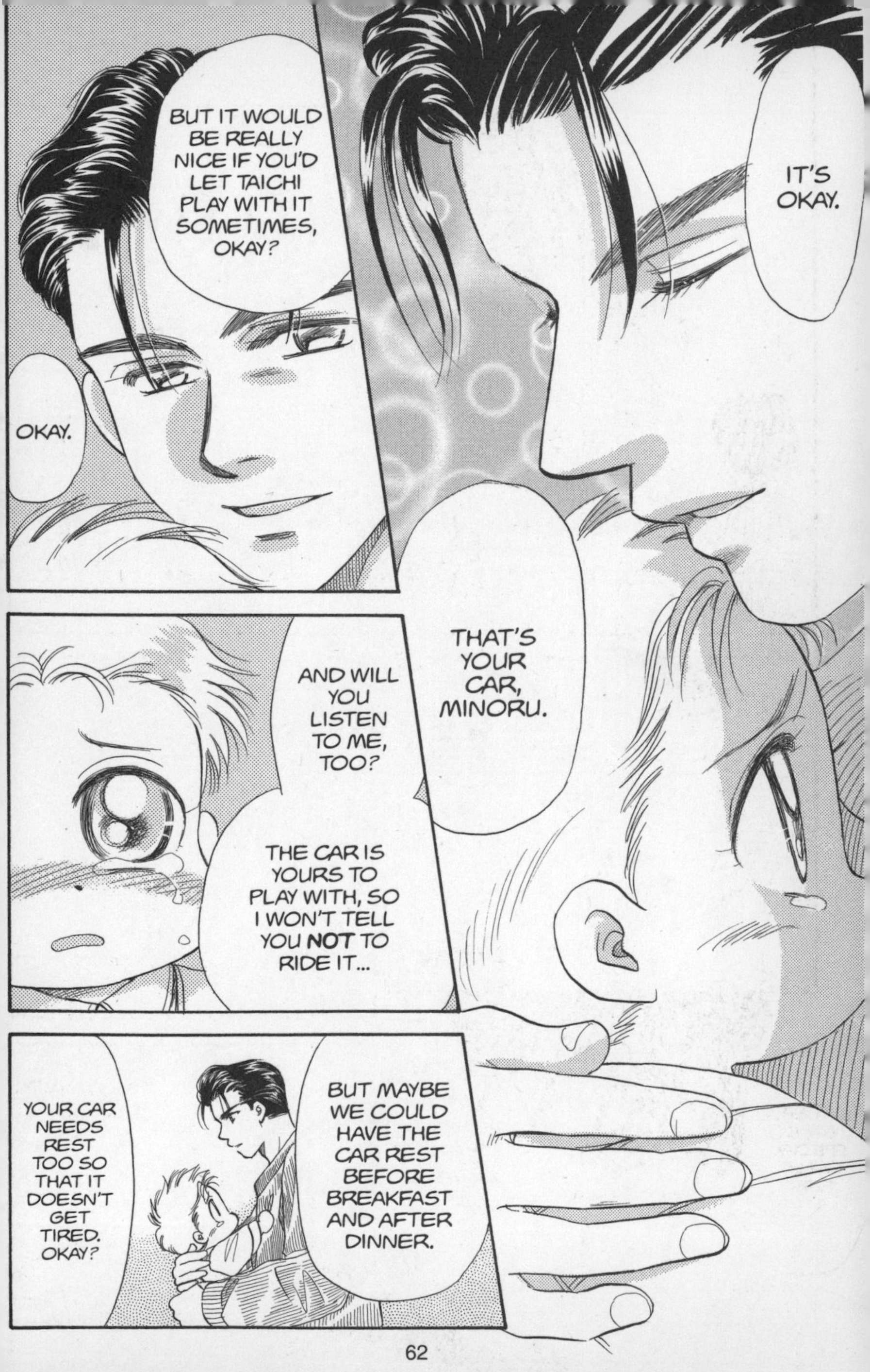
IT'S OKAY.
THAT'S YOUR CAR, MINORU.
BUT IT WOULD BE REALLY NICE IF YOU'D LET TAICHI PLAY WITH IT SOMETIMES, OKAY?
OKAY.
AND WILL YOU LISTEN TO ME, TOO?
THE CAR IS YOURS TO PLAY WITH, SO I WON'T TELL YOU **NOT** TO RIDE IT...
BUT MAYBE WE COULD HAVE THE CAR REST BEFORE BREAKFAST AND AFTER DINNER.
YOUR CAR NEEDS REST TOO SO THAT IT DOESN'T GET TIRED. OKAY?

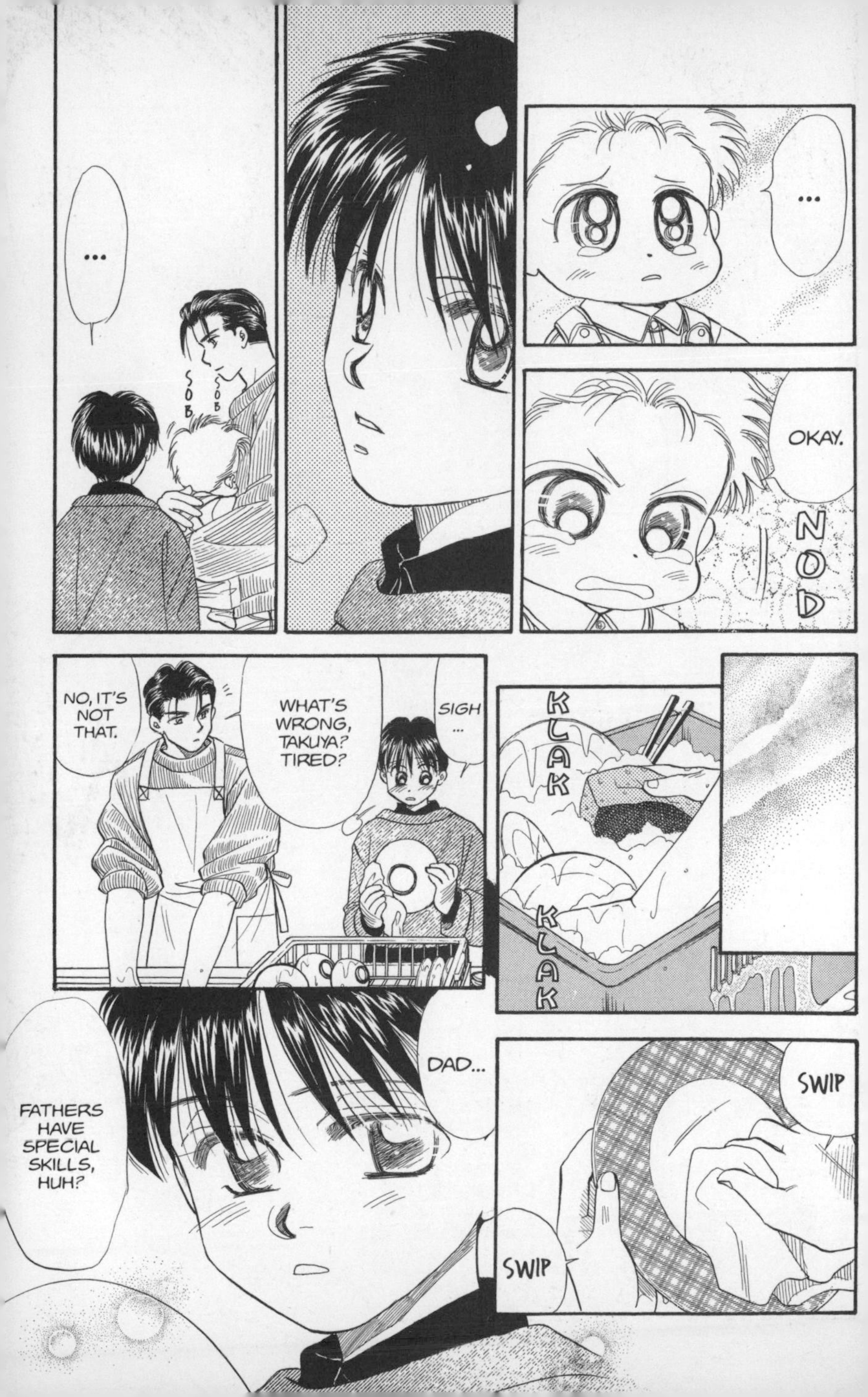
...
OKAY.
NOD
...
SOB SOB
KLAK KLAK
SIGH ...
WHAT'S WRONG, TAKUYA? TIRED?
NO, IT'S NOT THAT.
SWIP
SWIP
DAD...
FATHERS HAVE SPECIAL SKILLS, HUH?

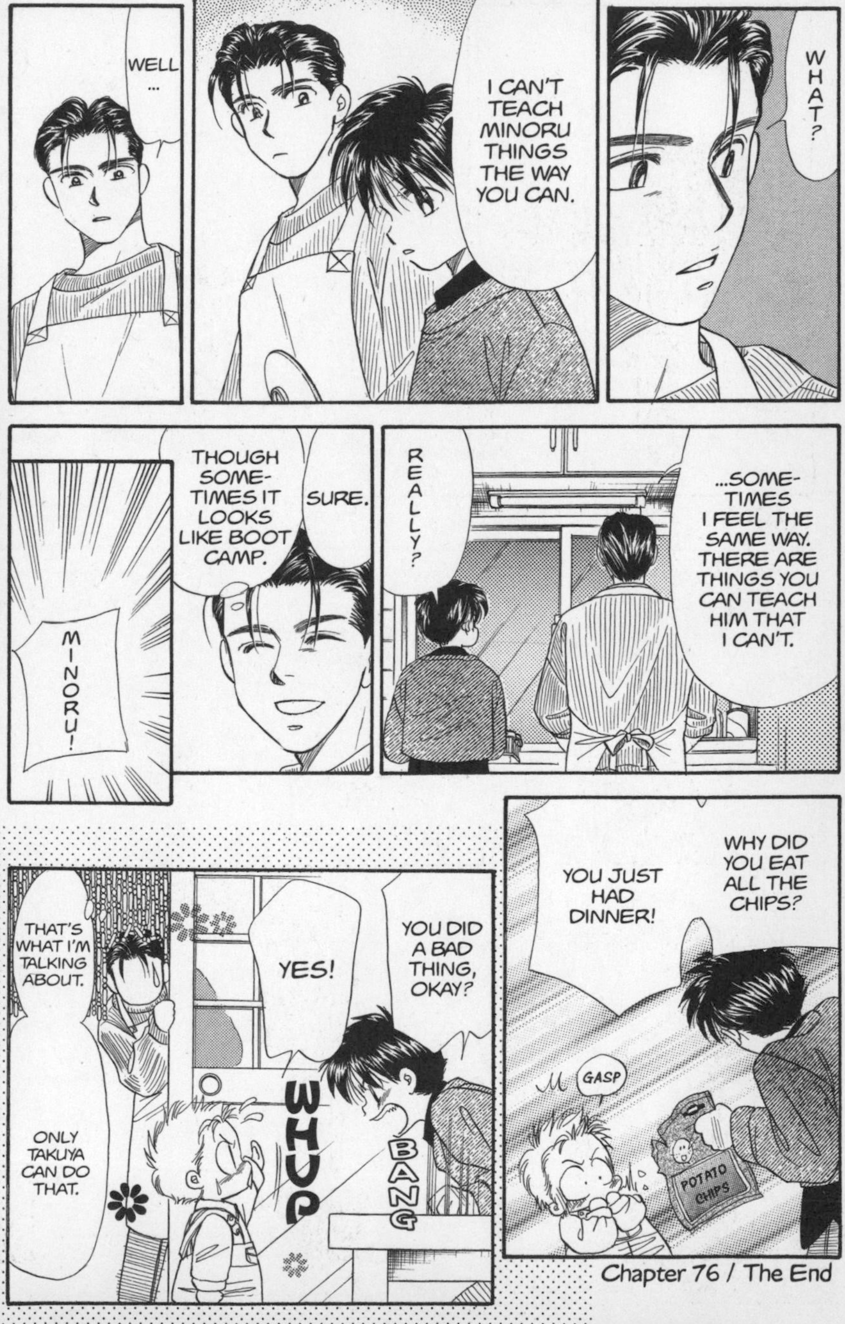
WHAT?
I CAN'T TEACH MINORU THINGS THE WAY YOU CAN.
WELL ...
...SOME-TIMES I FEEL THE SAME WAY. THERE ARE THINGS YOU CAN TEACH HIM THAT I CAN'T.
REALLY?
SURE.
THOUGH SOME-TIMES IT LOOKS LIKE BOOT CAMP.
MINORU!
WHY DID YOU EAT ALL THE CHIPS?
YOU JUST HAD DINNER!
GASP
POTATO CHIPS
YOU DID A BAD THING, OKAY?
YES!
WHUP
BANG
THAT'S WHAT I'M TALKING ABOUT.
ONLY TAKUYA CAN DO THAT.

Chapter 76 / The End

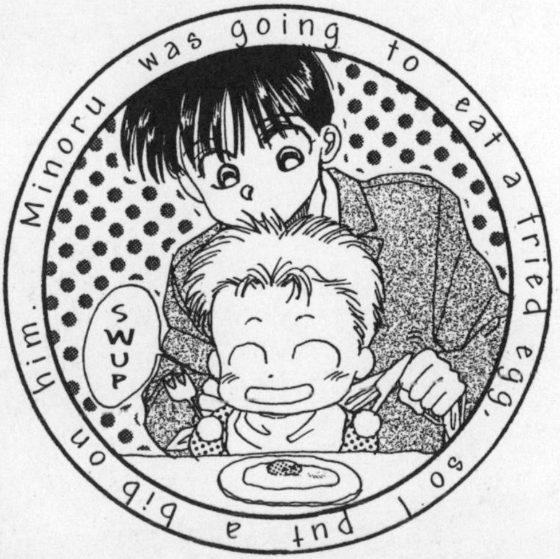
Minoru was going to eat a fried egg, so I put a bib on him.
SWUP

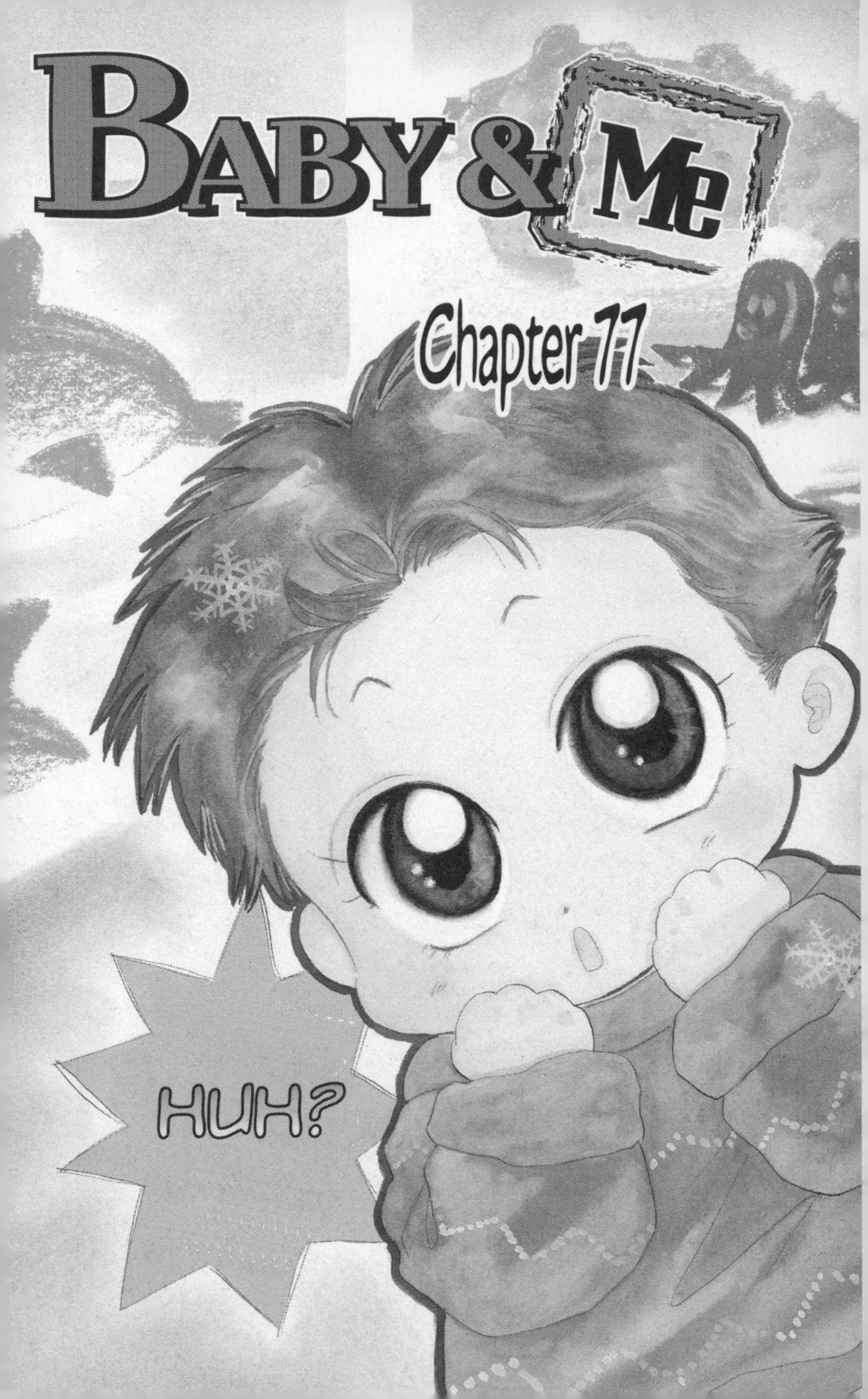
BABY & ME
Chapter 77
HUH?

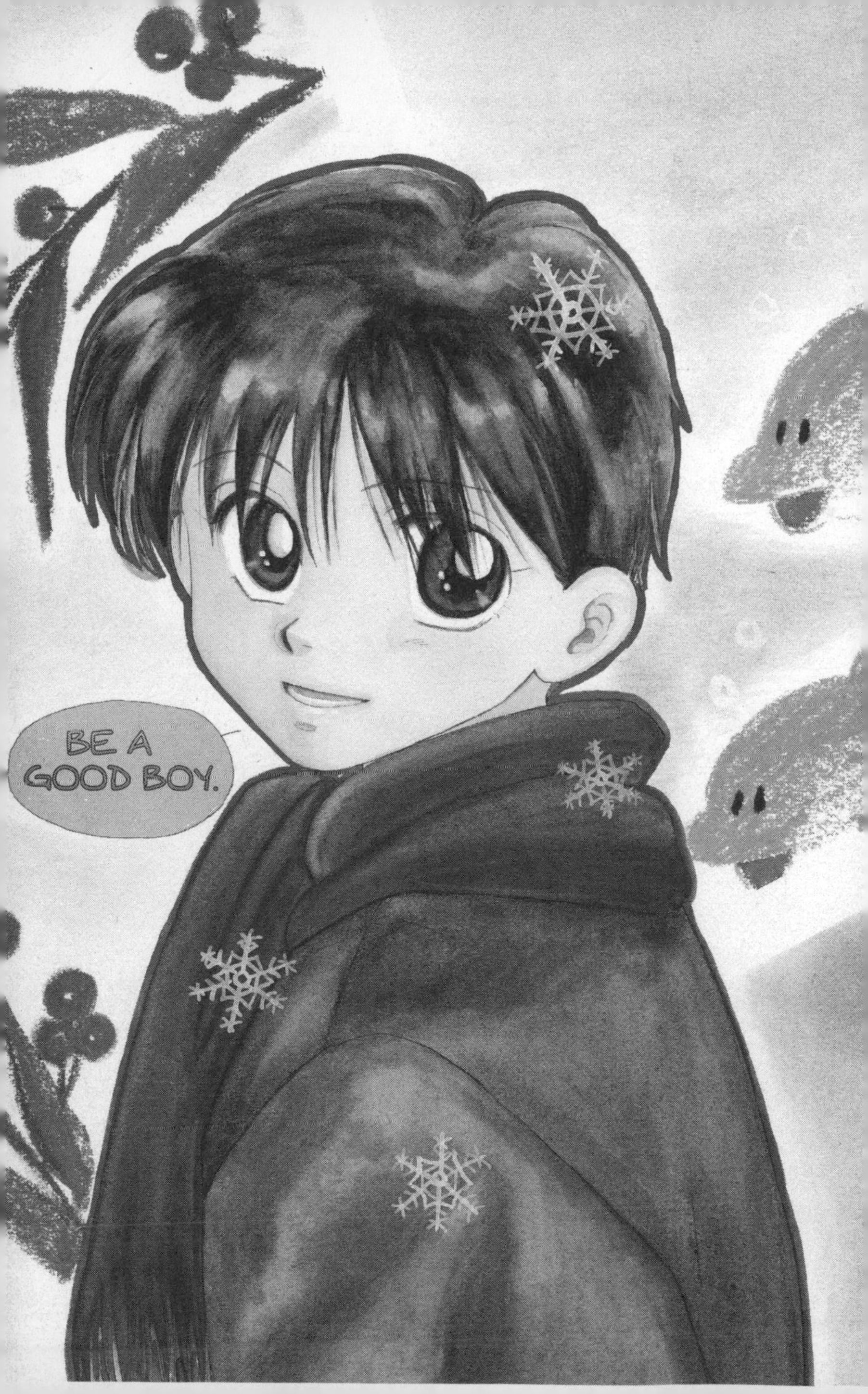
BE A GOOD BOY.

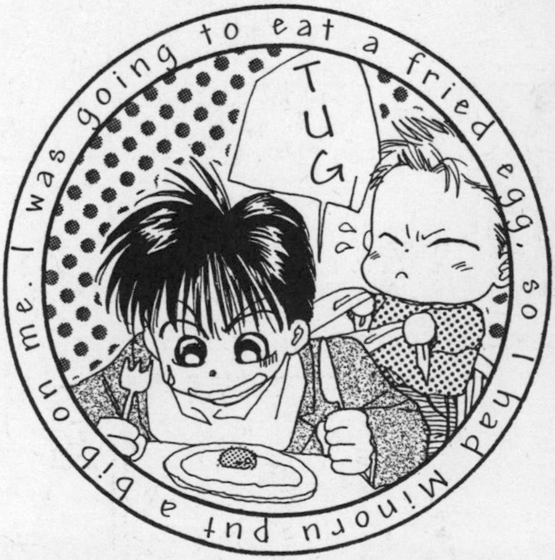
I was going to eat a fried egg, so I had Minoru put a bib on me.
TUG

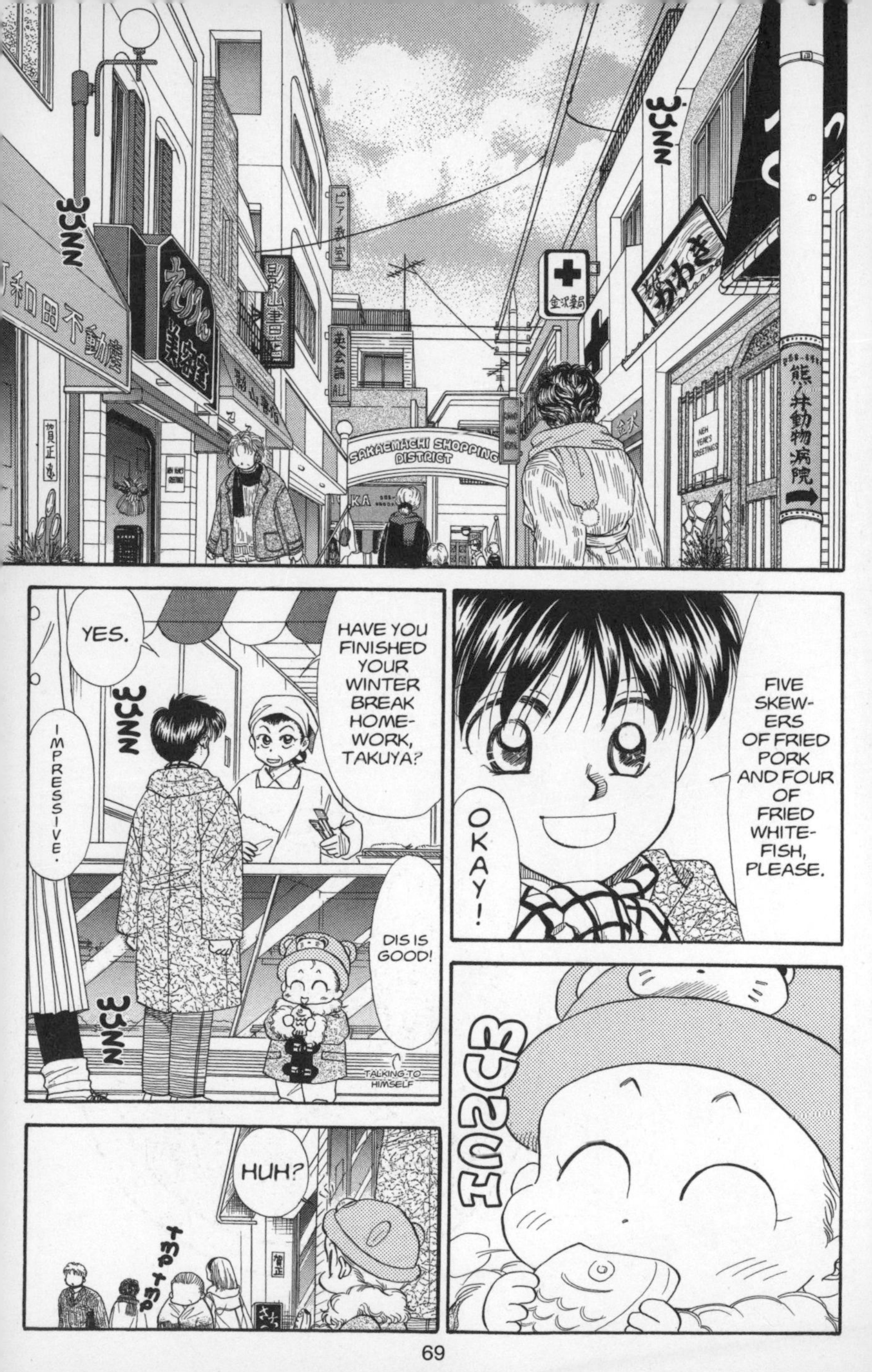
SAKAEMACHI SHOPPING DISTRICT
NEW YEAR'S GREETINGS
FIVE SKEWERS OF FRIED PORK AND FOUR OF FRIED WHITEFISH, PLEASE.
OKAY!
HAVE YOU FINISHED YOUR WINTER BREAK HOMEWORK, TAKUYA?
YES.
IMPRESSIVE.
DIS IS GOOD!
TALKING TO HIMSELF
MUNCH
HUH?

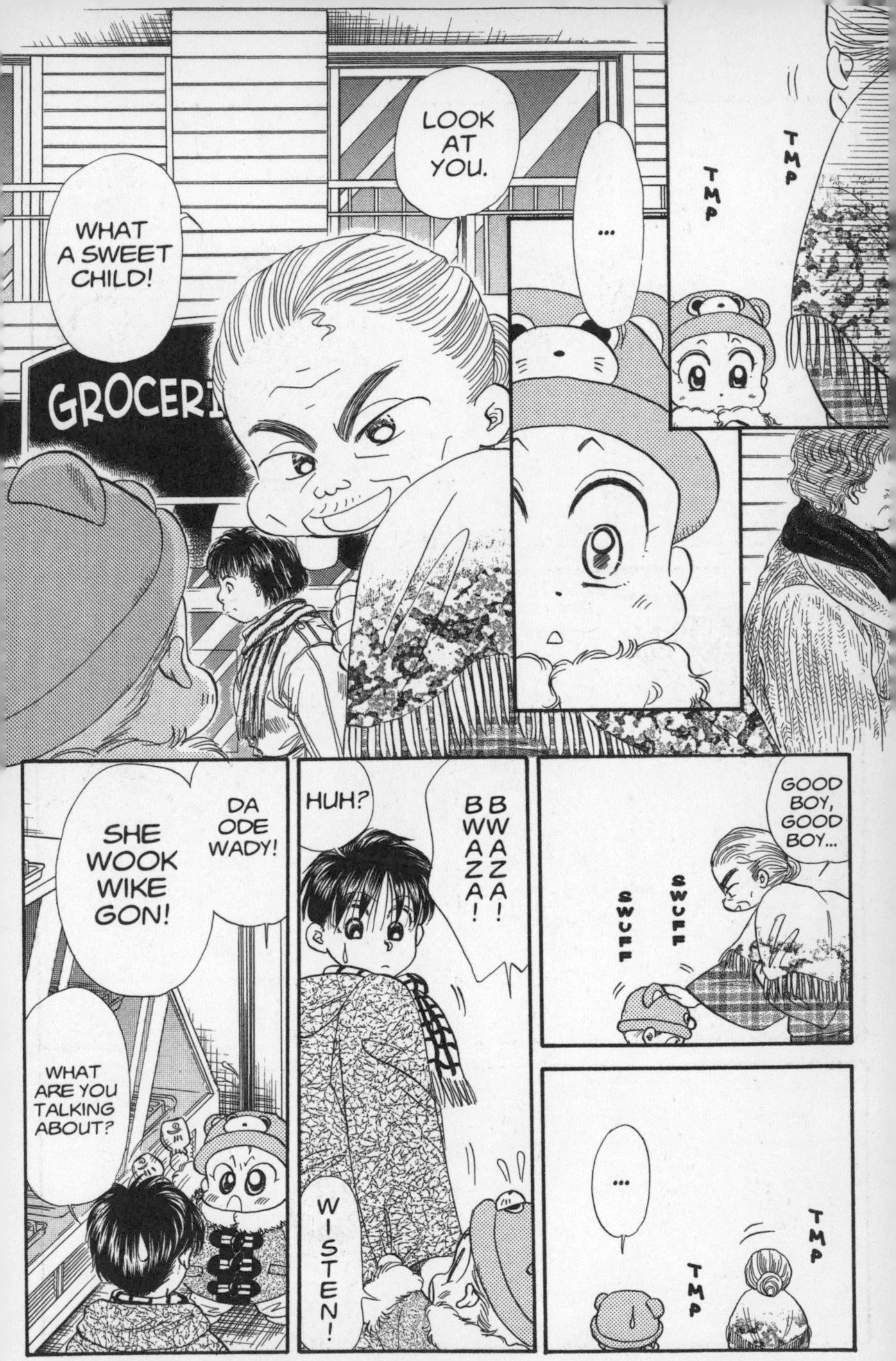

TMP
TMP
...
LOOK AT YOU.
WHAT A SWEET CHILD!
GROCERI
GOOD BOY, GOOD BOY...
SWUFF
SWUFF
...
TMP
TMP
BWAZA!
BWAZA!
HUH?
WISTEN!
DA ODE WADY!
SHE WOOK WIKE GON!
WHAT ARE YOU TALKING ABOUT?

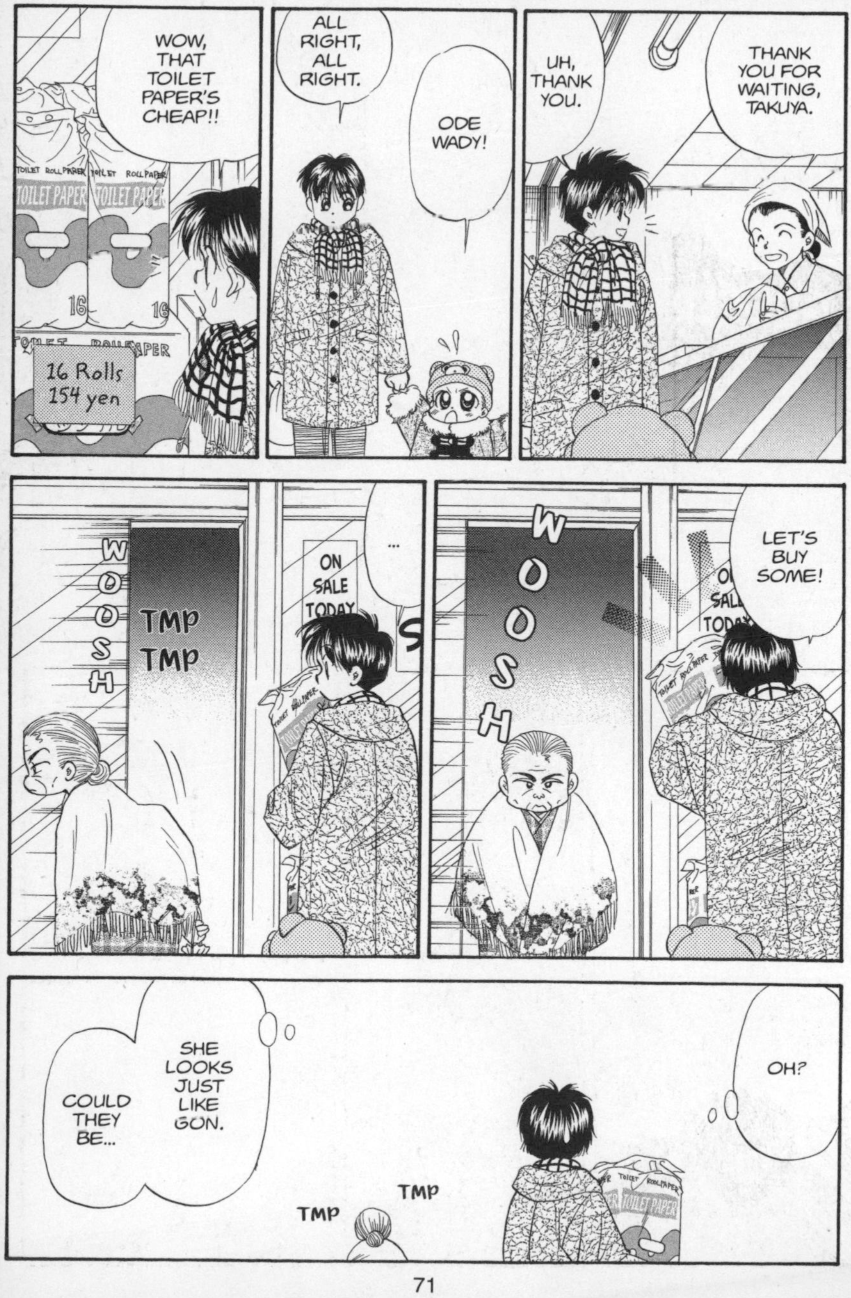
THANK YOU FOR WAITING, TAKUYA.
UH, THANK YOU.
ODE WADY!
ALL RIGHT, ALL RIGHT.
WOW, THAT TOILET PAPER'S CHEAP!!
TOILET ROLLPAPER TOILET ROLLPAPER
TOILET PAPER TOILET PAPER
16 Rolls 154 yen
LET'S BUY SOME!
WOOSH
...
ON SALE TODAY
WOOSH
TMP TMP
OH?
SHE LOOKS JUST LIKE GON.
COULD THEY BE...
TMP
TMP

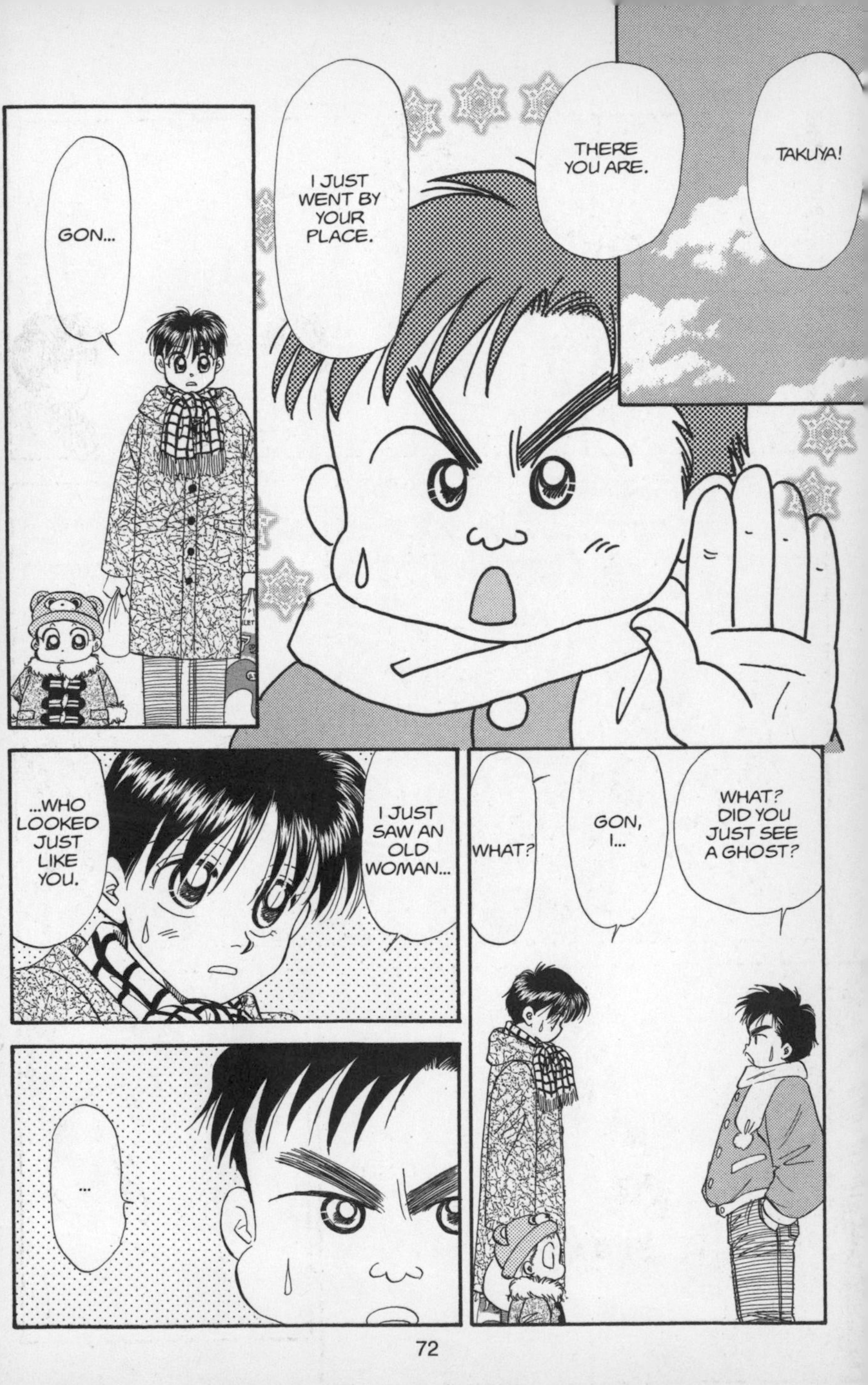
TAKUYA!
THERE YOU ARE.
I JUST WENT BY YOUR PLACE.
GON...
WHAT? DID YOU JUST SEE A GHOST?
GON, I...
WHAT?
I JUST SAW AN OLD WOMAN...
...WHO LOOKED JUST LIKE YOU.
...

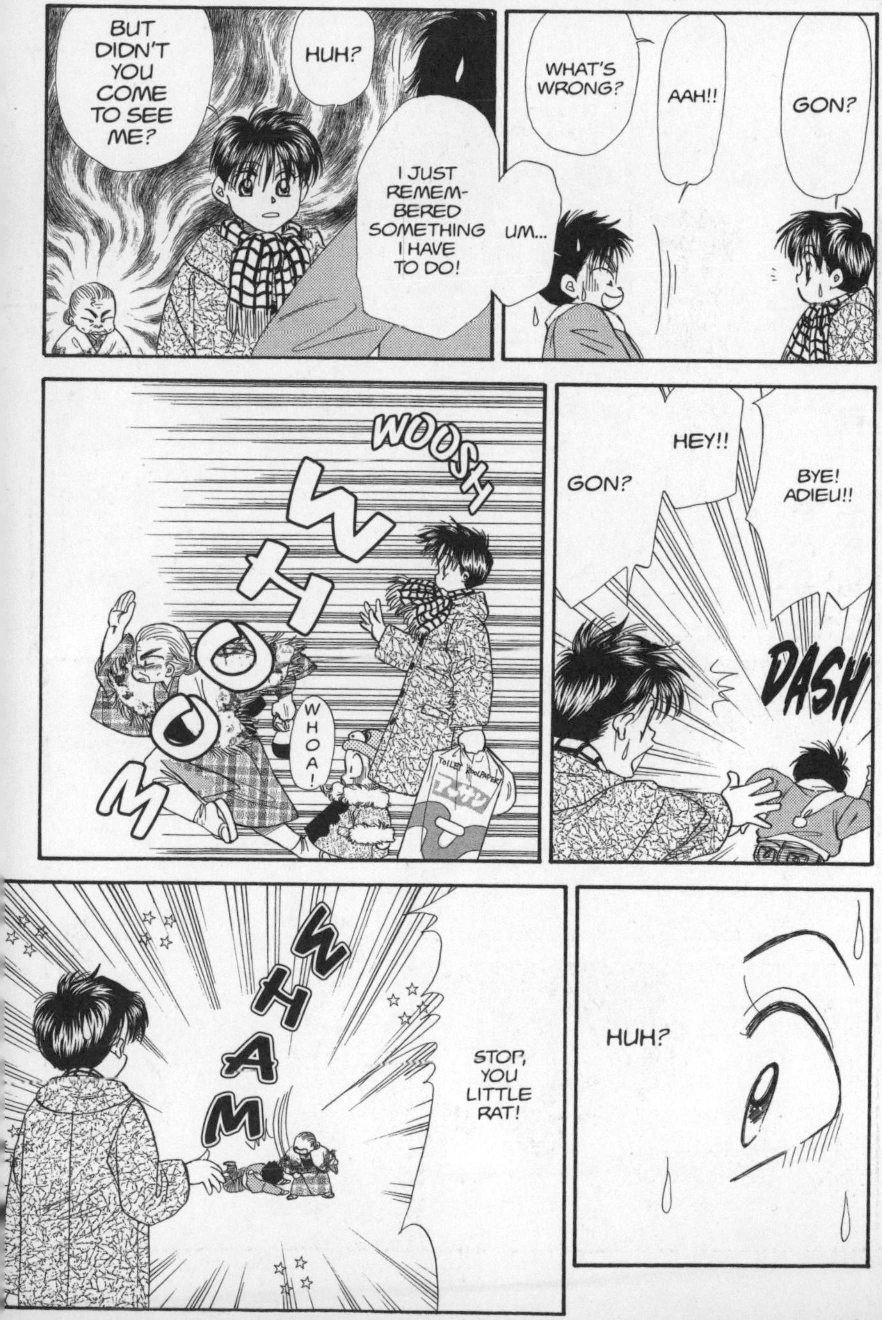
GON?
AAH!!
WHAT'S WRONG?
UM...
I JUST REMEMBERED SOMETHING I HAVE TO DO!
HUH?
BUT DIDN'T YOU COME TO SEE ME?
BYE! ADIEU!!
HEY!!
GON?
DASH
WOOSH
WHOOM
WHOA!
HUH?
STOP, YOU LITTLE RAT!
WHAM

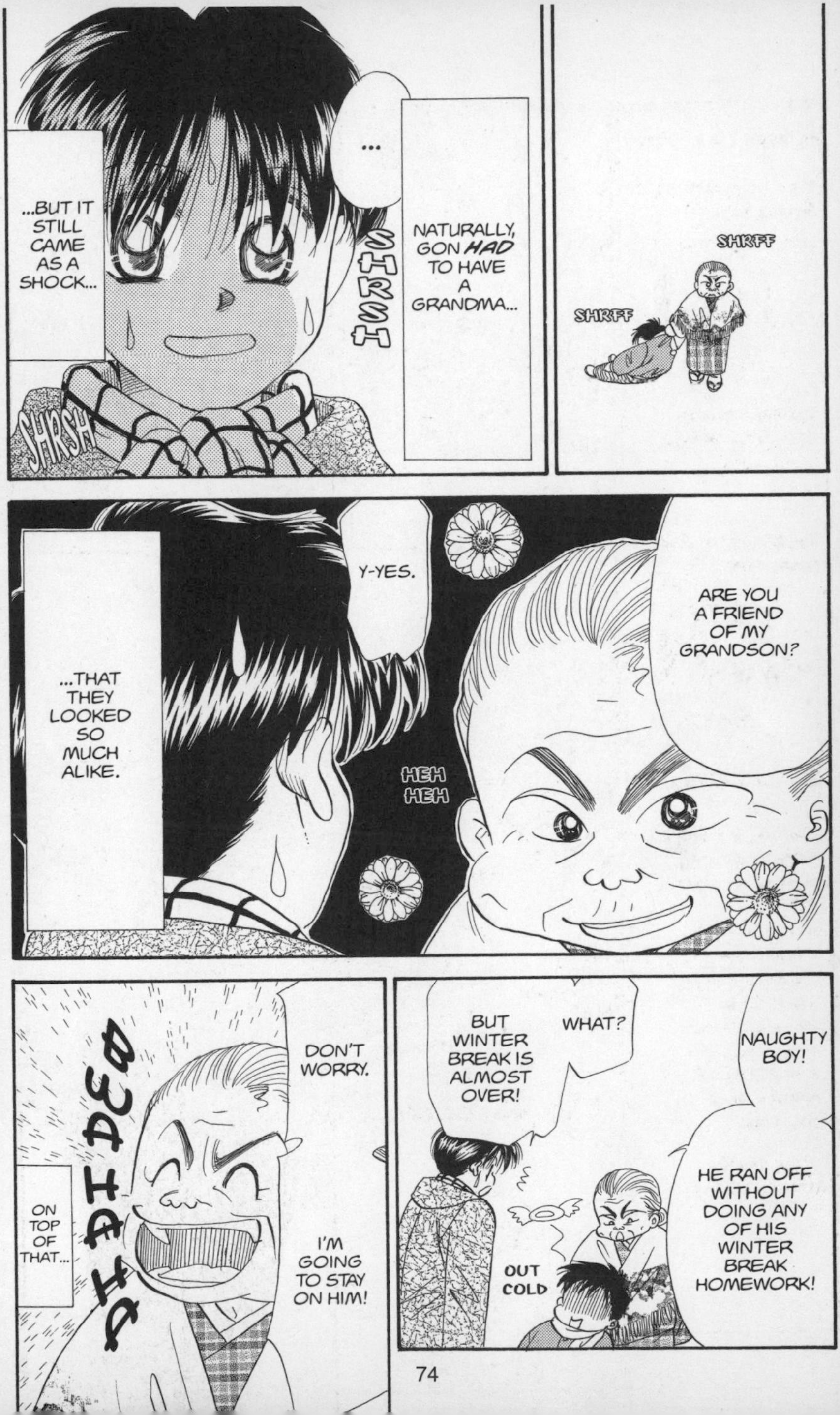
SHRFF
SHRFF
...
NATURALLY, GON *HAD* TO HAVE A GRANDMA...
SHRSH
...BUT IT STILL CAME AS A SHOCK...
SHRSH
ARE YOU A FRIEND OF MY GRANDSON?
Y-YES.
HEH HEH
...THAT THEY LOOKED SO MUCH ALIKE.
NAUGHTY BOY!
HE RAN OFF WITHOUT DOING ANY OF HIS WINTER BREAK HOMEWORK!
WHAT?
BUT WINTER BREAK IS ALMOST OVER!
OUT COLD
DON'T WORRY.
I'M GOING TO STAY ON HIM!
ON TOP OF THAT...

Author's Note : Part 3

The History of Tadakichi Gotoh's Hair

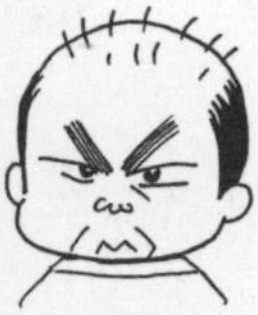

Tadakichi through Volume Six Before

↓

Tadakichi after Volume Seven After

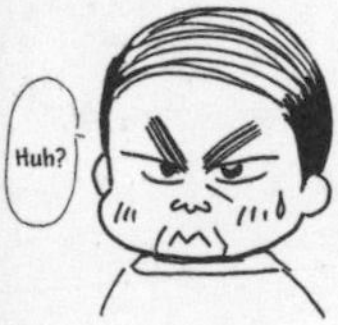

Huh?

Hair restoration treatment?

Can you guess what I liked most about working on chapter 77?
I really enjoyed drawing Shotaro Gotoh as a young man! But it was a lot of work researching uniforms of military schools for those few panels.

I found out the uniforms differed a lot.

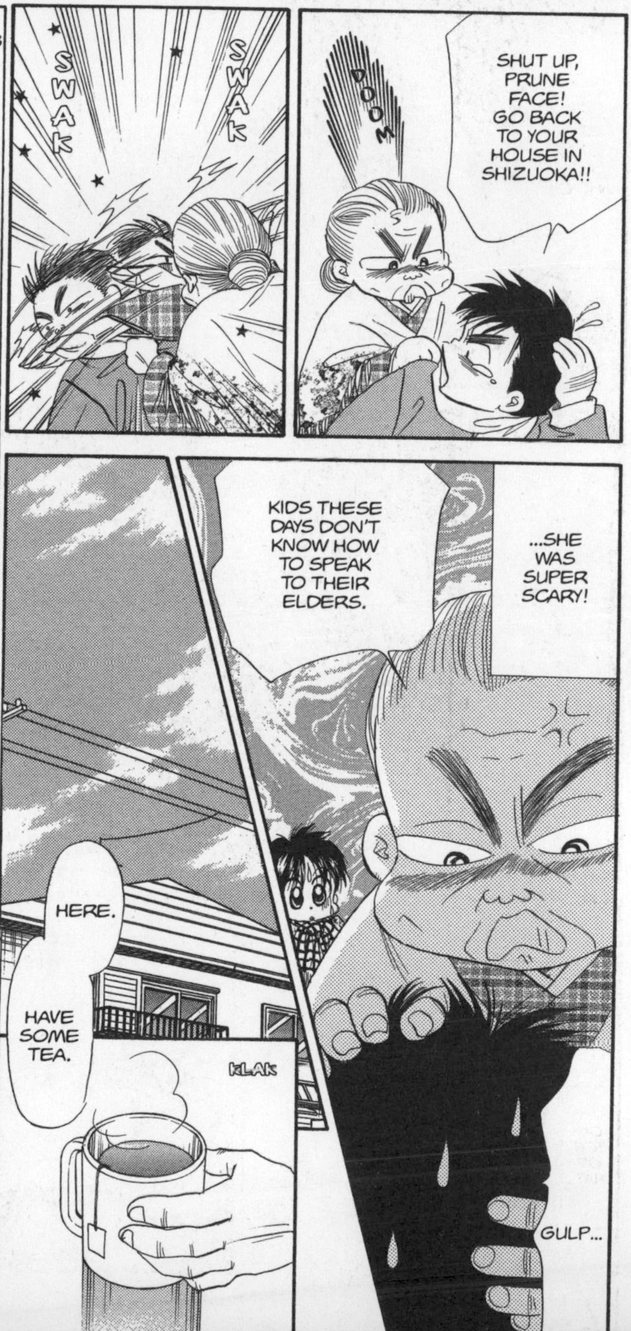

DOOM
SHUT UP, PRUNE FACE! GO BACK TO YOUR HOUSE IN SHIZUOKA!!
SWAK
SWAK
KIDS THESE DAYS DON'T KNOW HOW TO SPEAK TO THEIR ELDERS.
...SHE WAS SUPER SCARY!
GULP...
HERE.
HAVE SOME TEA.
KLAK

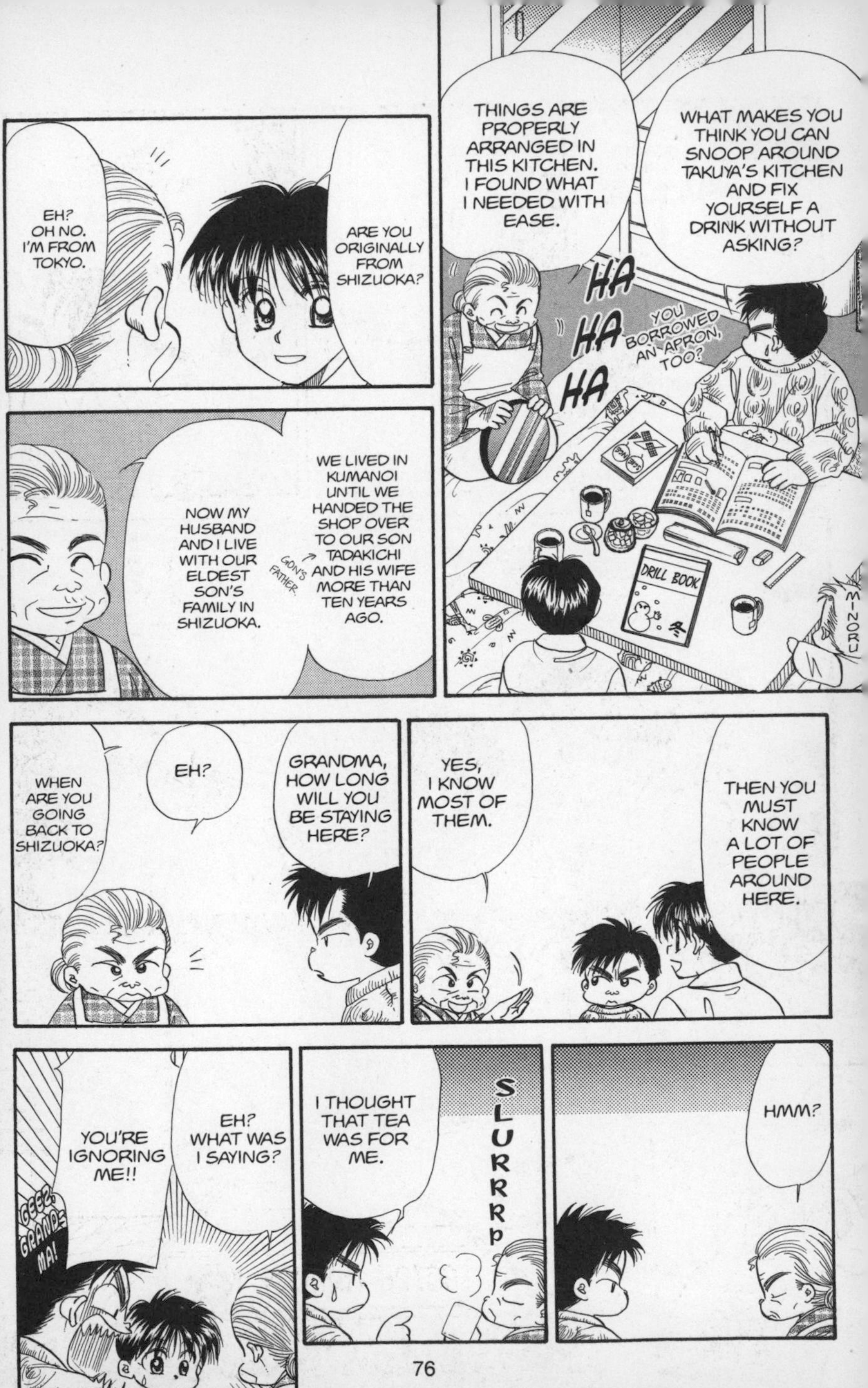

WHAT MAKES YOU THINK YOU CAN SNOOP AROUND TAKUYA'S KITCHEN AND FIX YOURSELF A DRINK WITHOUT ASKING?
THINGS ARE PROPERLY ARRANGED IN THIS KITCHEN. I FOUND WHAT I NEEDED WITH EASE.
HA HA HA
YOU BORROWED AN APRON, TOO?
DRILL BOOK
MINORU
ARE YOU ORIGINALLY FROM SHIZUOKA?
EH? OH NO. I'M FROM TOKYO.
WE LIVED IN KUMANOI UNTIL WE HANDED THE SHOP OVER TO OUR SON TADAKICHI AND HIS WIFE MORE THAN TEN YEARS AGO.
GON'S FATHER
NOW MY HUSBAND AND I LIVE WITH OUR ELDEST SON'S FAMILY IN SHIZUOKA.
THEN YOU MUST KNOW A LOT OF PEOPLE AROUND HERE.
YES, I KNOW MOST OF THEM.
GRANDMA, HOW LONG WILL YOU BE STAYING HERE?
EH?
WHEN ARE YOU GOING BACK TO SHIZUOKA?
HMM?
SLURRRP
I THOUGHT THAT TEA WAS FOR ME.
EH? WHAT WAS I SAYING?
YOU'RE IGNORING ME!!
GEEZ, GRANDMA!

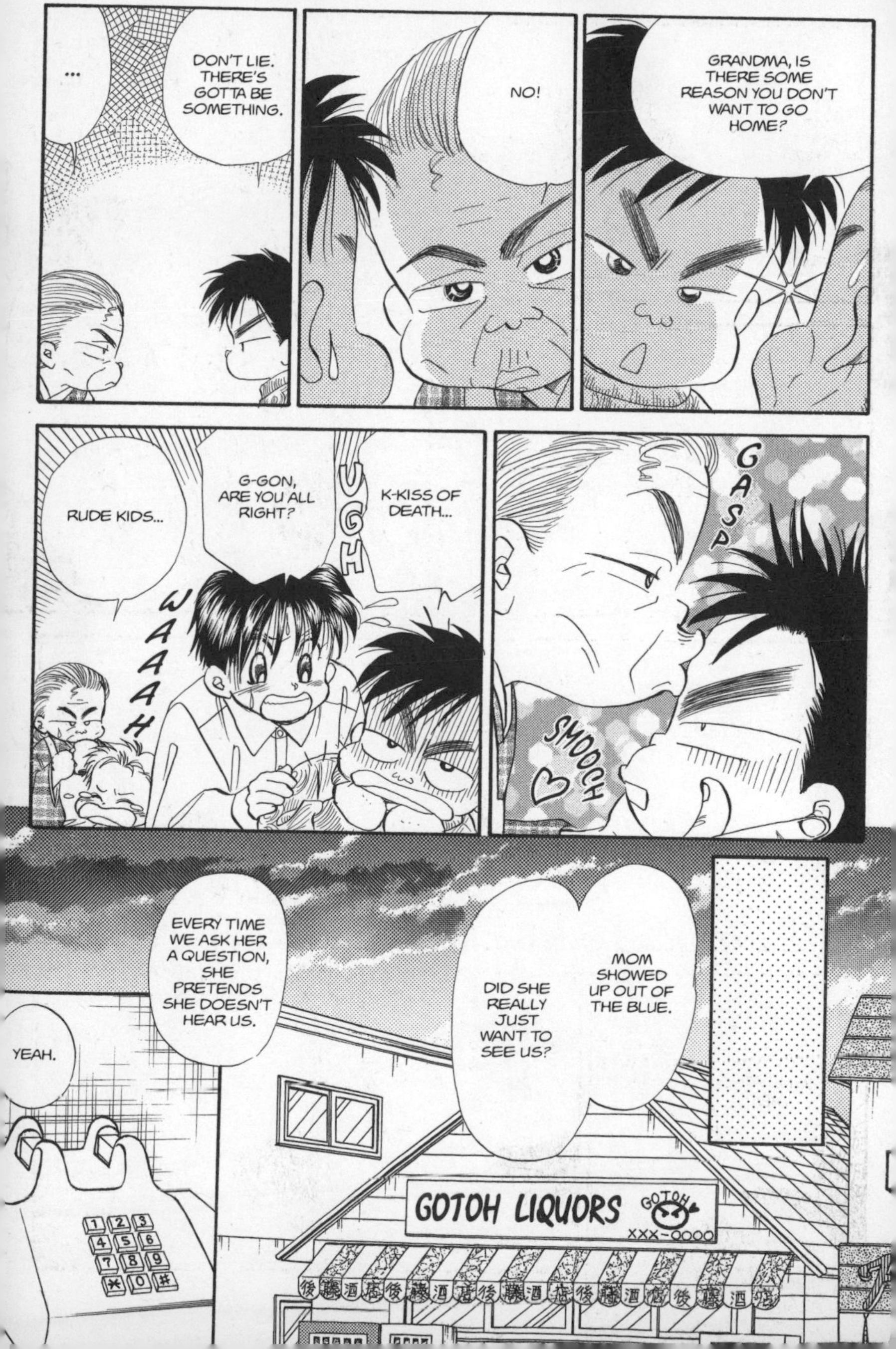
GRANDMA, IS THERE SOME REASON YOU DON'T WANT TO GO HOME?
NO!
DON'T LIE. THERE'S GOTTA BE SOMETHING.
...
GASP
SMOOCH
K-KISS OF DEATH...
UGH
G-GON, ARE YOU ALL RIGHT?
WAAAAH
RUDE KIDS...
MOM SHOWED UP OUT OF THE BLUE.
DID SHE REALLY JUST WANT TO SEE US?
EVERY TIME WE ASK HER A QUESTION, SHE PRETENDS SHE DOESN'T HEAR US.
YEAH.
GOTOH LIQUORS
GOTOH
XXX-0000
後藤酒店後藤酒店後藤酒店後藤酒店後藤酒店

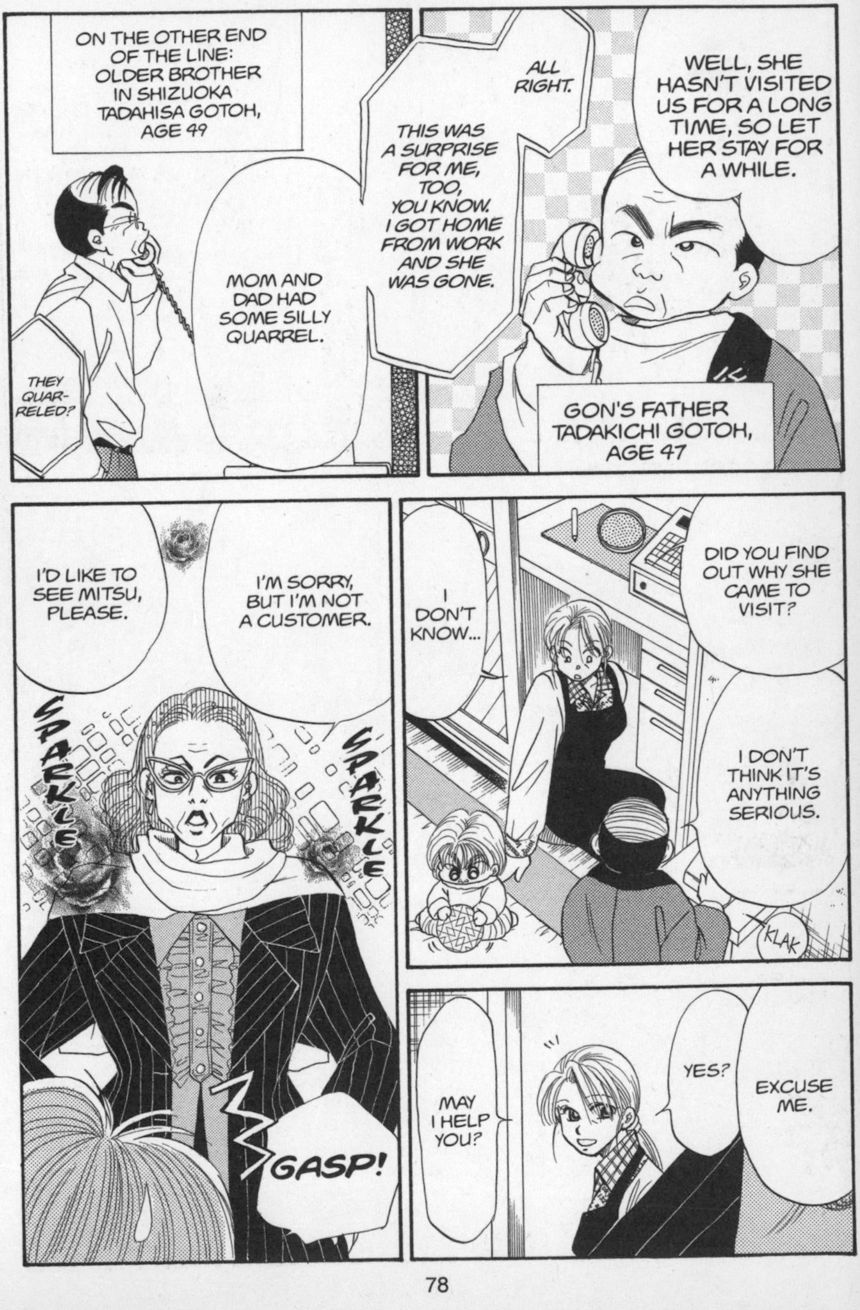
WELL, SHE HASN'T VISITED US FOR A LONG TIME, SO LET HER STAY FOR A WHILE.
ALL RIGHT.
GON'S FATHER TADAKICHI GOTOH, AGE 47
ON THE OTHER END OF THE LINE: OLDER BROTHER IN SHIZUOKA TADAHISA GOTOH, AGE 49
THIS WAS A SURPRISE FOR ME, TOO, YOU KNOW. I GOT HOME FROM WORK AND SHE WAS GONE.
MOM AND DAD HAD SOME SILLY QUARREL.
THEY QUARRELED?
DID YOU FIND OUT WHY SHE CAME TO VISIT?
I DON'T KNOW...
I DON'T THINK IT'S ANYTHING SERIOUS.
KLAK
EXCUSE ME.
YES?
MAY I HELP YOU?
I'M SORRY, BUT I'M NOT A CUSTOMER.
I'D LIKE TO SEE MITSU, PLEASE.
SPARKLE
SPARKLE
GASP!

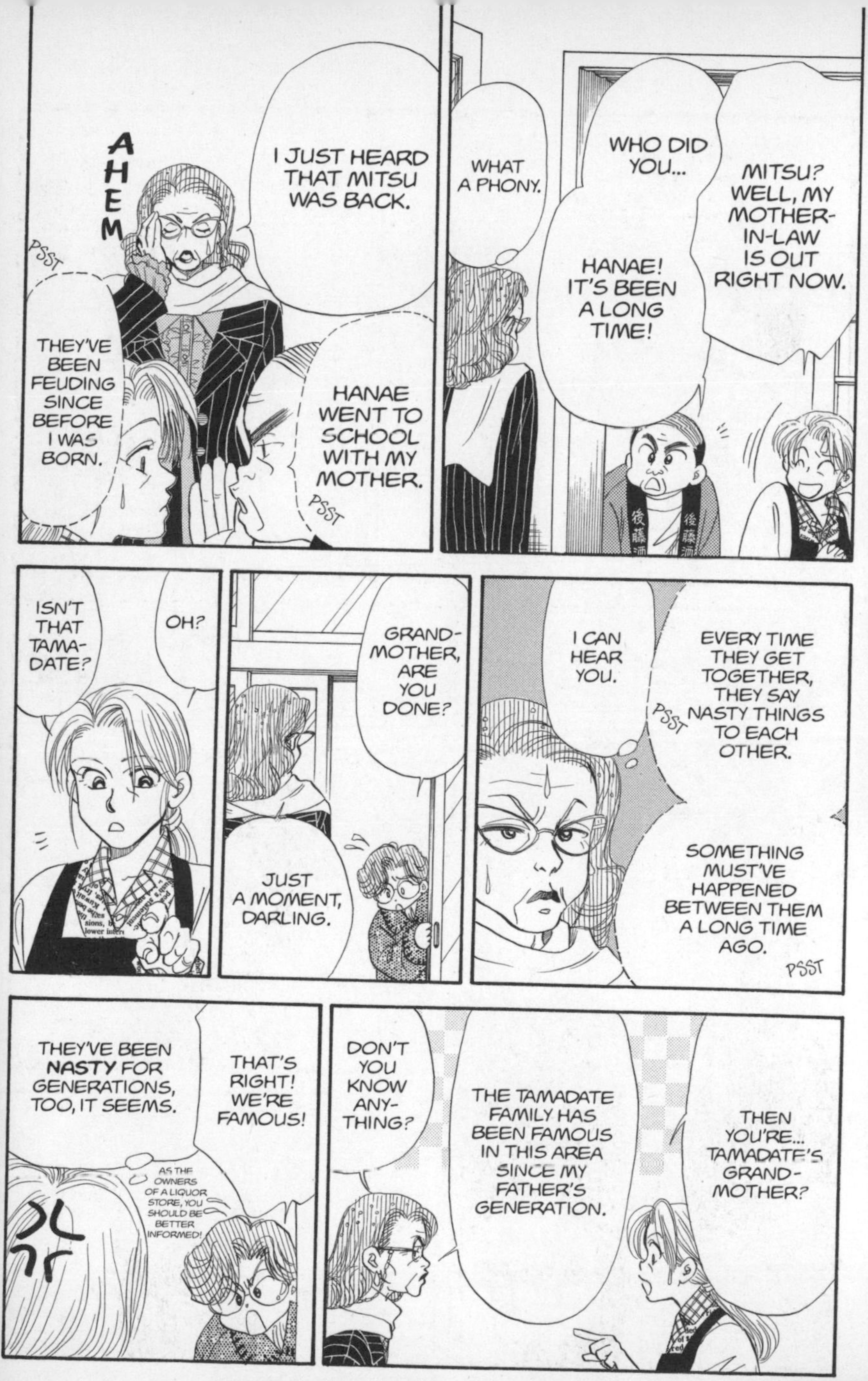
MITSU? WELL, MY MOTHER-IN-LAW IS OUT RIGHT NOW.
WHO DID YOU...
WHAT A PHONY.
HANAE! IT'S BEEN A LONG TIME!
I JUST HEARD THAT MITSU WAS BACK.
AHEM
HANAE WENT TO SCHOOL WITH MY MOTHER.
PSST
THEY'VE BEEN FEUDING SINCE BEFORE I WAS BORN.
PSST
EVERY TIME THEY GET TOGETHER, THEY SAY NASTY THINGS TO EACH OTHER.
PSST
I CAN HEAR YOU.
SOMETHING MUST'VE HAPPENED BETWEEN THEM A LONG TIME AGO.
PSST
GRAND-MOTHER, ARE YOU DONE?
JUST A MOMENT, DARLING.
OH?
ISN'T THAT TAMA-DATE?
THEN YOU'RE... TAMADATE'S GRAND-MOTHER?
THE TAMADATE FAMILY HAS BEEN FAMOUS IN THIS AREA SINCE MY FATHER'S GENERATION.
DON'T YOU KNOW ANY-THING?
THAT'S RIGHT! WE'RE FAMOUS!
AS THE OWNERS OF A LIQUOR STORE, YOU SHOULD BE BETTER INFORMED!
THEY'VE BEEN **NASTY** FOR GENERATIONS, TOO, IT SEEMS.

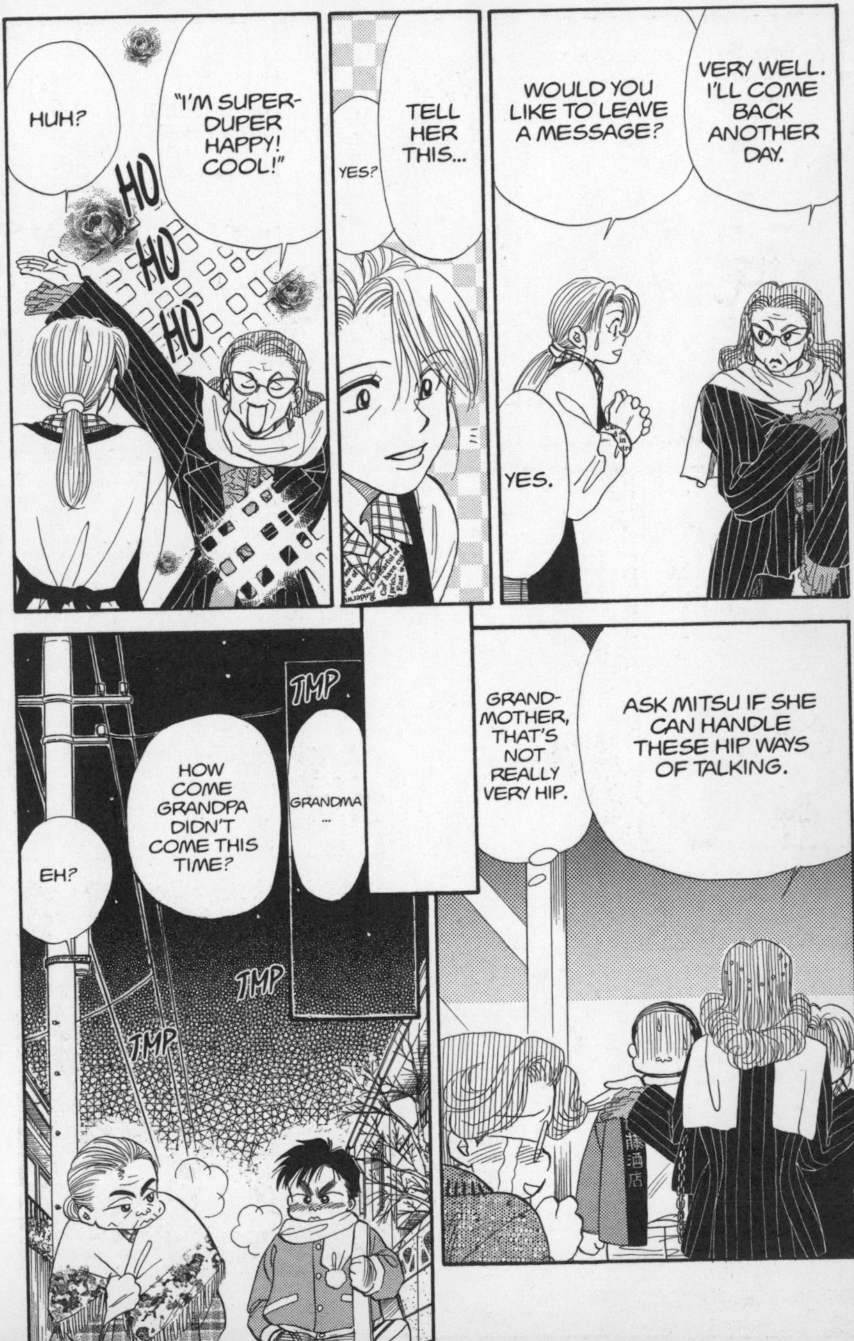
VERY WELL. I'LL COME BACK ANOTHER DAY.
WOULD YOU LIKE TO LEAVE A MESSAGE?
YES.
TELL HER THIS...
YES?
"I'M SUPER-DUPER HAPPY! COOL!"
HO HO HO
HUH?
ASK MITSU IF SHE CAN HANDLE THESE HIP WAYS OF TALKING.
GRAND-MOTHER, THAT'S NOT REALLY VERY HIP.
藤酒店
TMP
GRANDMA...
HOW COME GRANDPA DIDN'T COME THIS TIME?
EH?
TMP
TMP

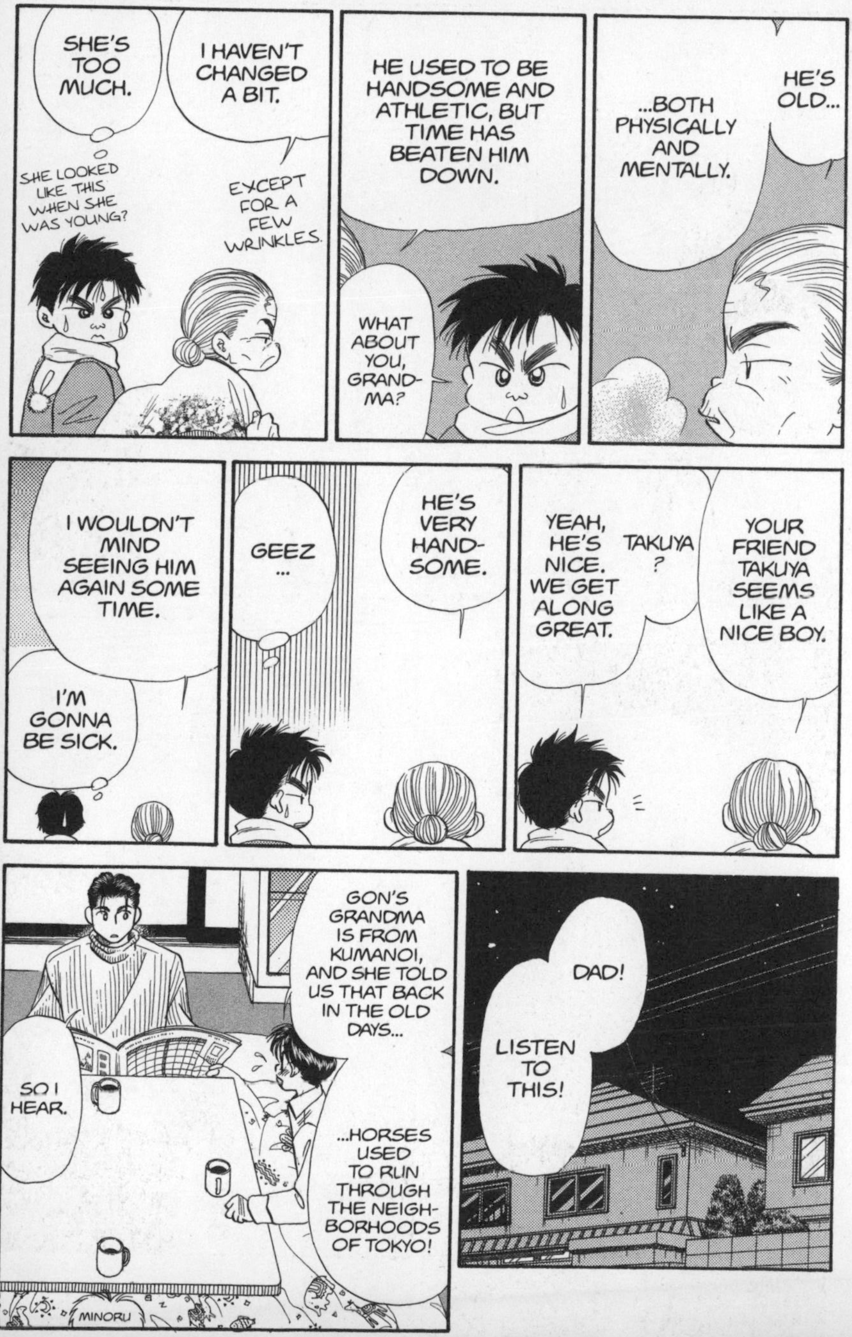
HE'S OLD...
...BOTH PHYSICALLY AND MENTALLY.
HE USED TO BE HANDSOME AND ATHLETIC, BUT TIME HAS BEATEN HIM DOWN.
WHAT ABOUT YOU, GRAND-MA?
I HAVEN'T CHANGED A BIT.
SHE'S TOO MUCH.
EXCEPT FOR A FEW WRINKLES.
SHE LOOKED LIKE THIS WHEN SHE WAS YOUNG?
YOUR FRIEND TAKUYA SEEMS LIKE A NICE BOY.
TAKUYA ?
YEAH, HE'S NICE. WE GET ALONG GREAT.
HE'S VERY HAND-SOME.
GEEZ ...
I WOULDN'T MIND SEEING HIM AGAIN SOME TIME.
I'M GONNA BE SICK.
DAD!
LISTEN TO THIS!
GON'S GRANDMA IS FROM KUMANOI, AND SHE TOLD US THAT BACK IN THE OLD DAYS...
...HORSES USED TO RUN THROUGH THE NEIGH-BORHOODS OF TOKYO!
SO I HEAR.
MINORU

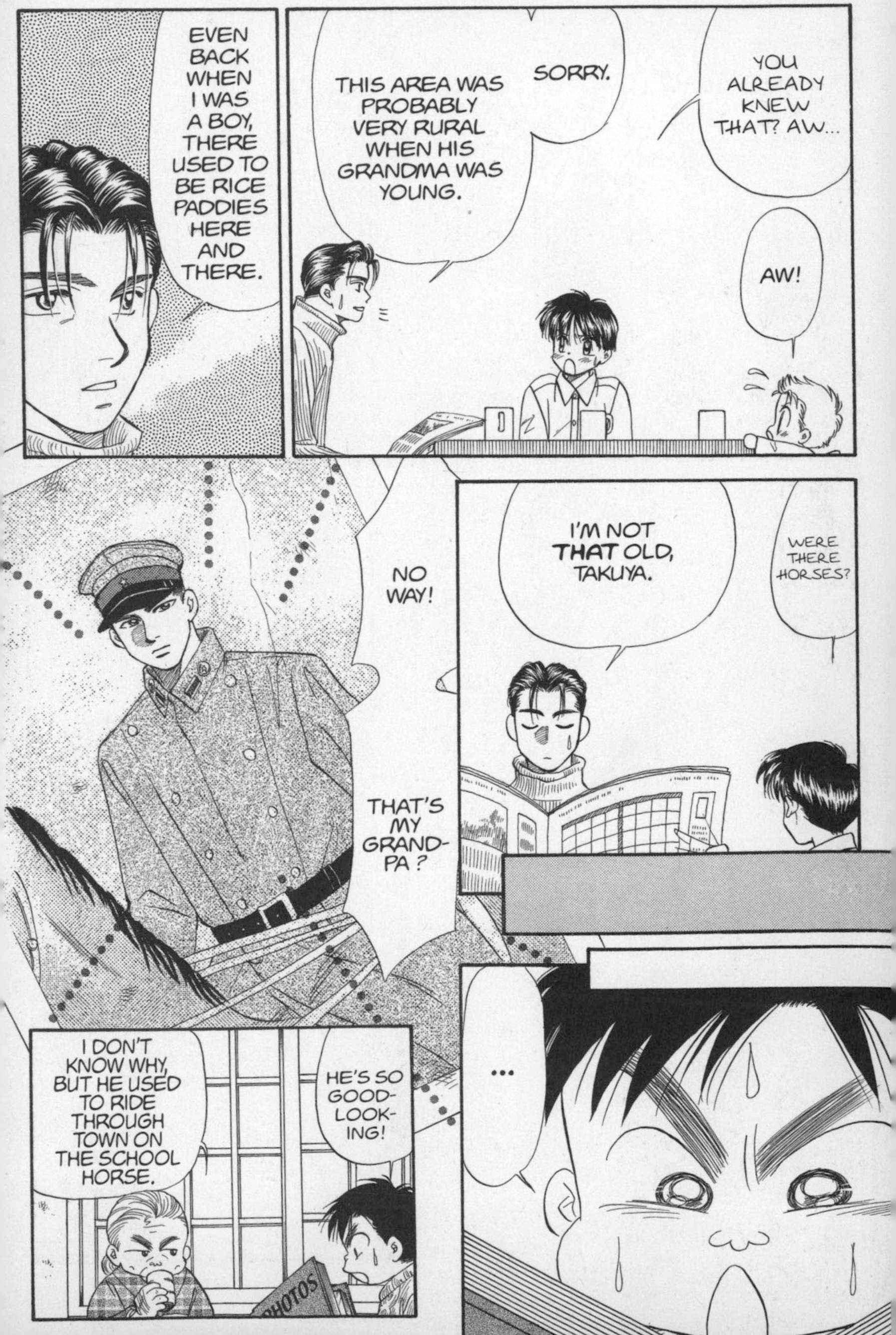
YOU ALREADY KNEW THAT? AW...
AW!
SORRY.
THIS AREA WAS PROBABLY VERY RURAL WHEN HIS GRANDMA WAS YOUNG.
EVEN BACK WHEN I WAS A BOY, THERE USED TO BE RICE PADDIES HERE AND THERE.
WERE THERE HORSES?
I'M NOT **THAT** OLD, TAKUYA.
...
NO WAY!
THAT'S MY GRAND-PA ?
HE'S SO GOOD-LOOK-ING!
I DON'T KNOW WHY, BUT HE USED TO RIDE THROUGH TOWN ON THE SCHOOL HORSE.
PHOTOS

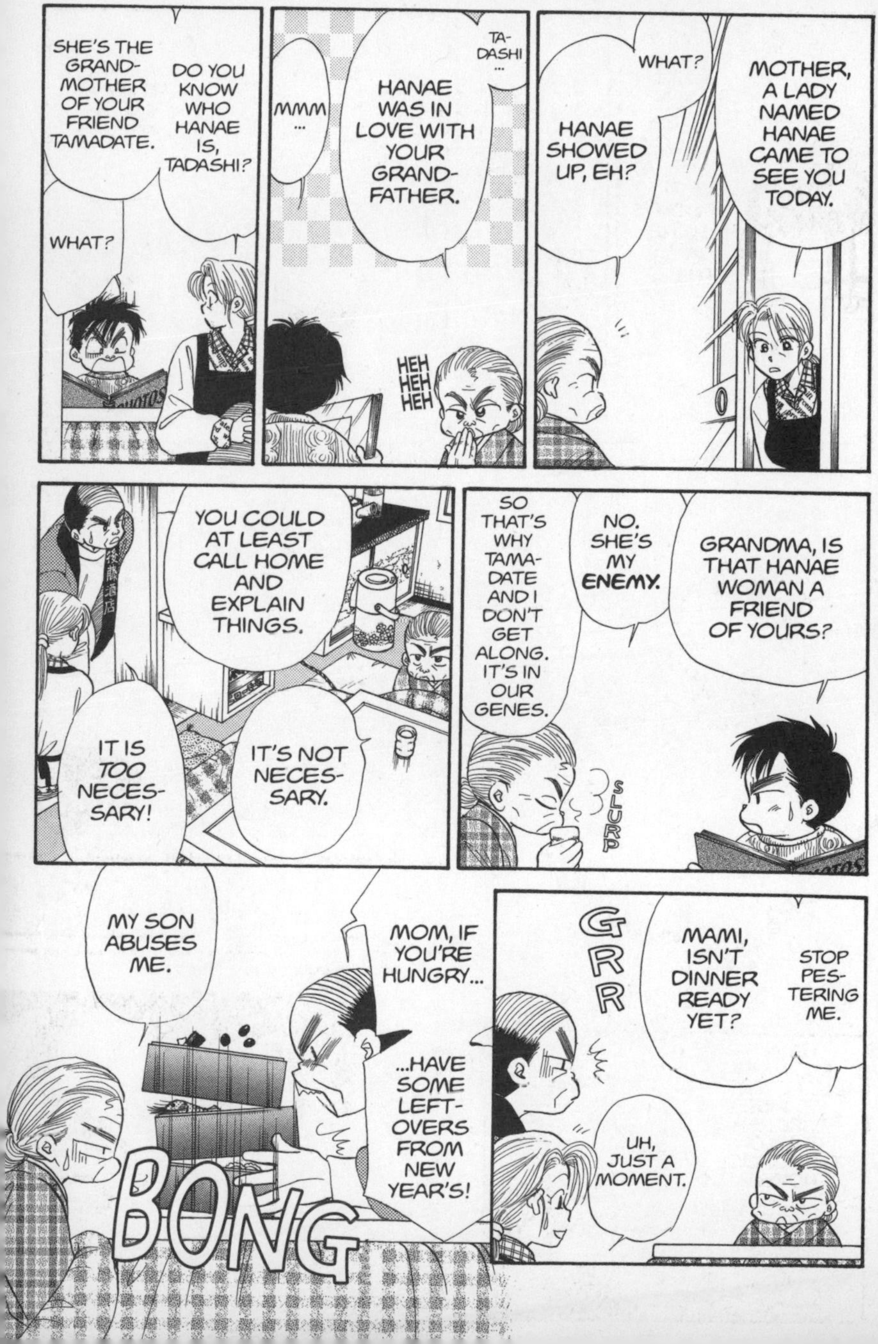
MOTHER, A LADY NAMED HANAE CAME TO SEE YOU TODAY.
WHAT?
HANAE SHOWED UP, EH?
TADASHI ...
HANAE WAS IN LOVE WITH YOUR GRANDFATHER.
MMM ...
HEH HEH HEH
DO YOU KNOW WHO HANAE IS, TADASHI?
SHE'S THE GRANDMOTHER OF YOUR FRIEND TAMADATE.
WHAT?
GRANDMA, IS THAT HANAE WOMAN A FRIEND OF YOURS?
NO. SHE'S MY **ENEMY.**
SO THAT'S WHY TAMADATE AND I DON'T GET ALONG. IT'S IN OUR GENES.
SLURP
YOU COULD AT LEAST CALL HOME AND EXPLAIN THINGS.
IT'S NOT NECESSARY.
IT IS *TOO* NECESSARY!
MAMI, ISN'T DINNER READY YET?
GRR
STOP PESTERING ME.
UH, JUST A MOMENT.
MOM, IF YOU'RE HUNGRY...
...HAVE SOME LEFTOVERS FROM NEW YEAR'S!
MY SON ABUSES ME.
BONG

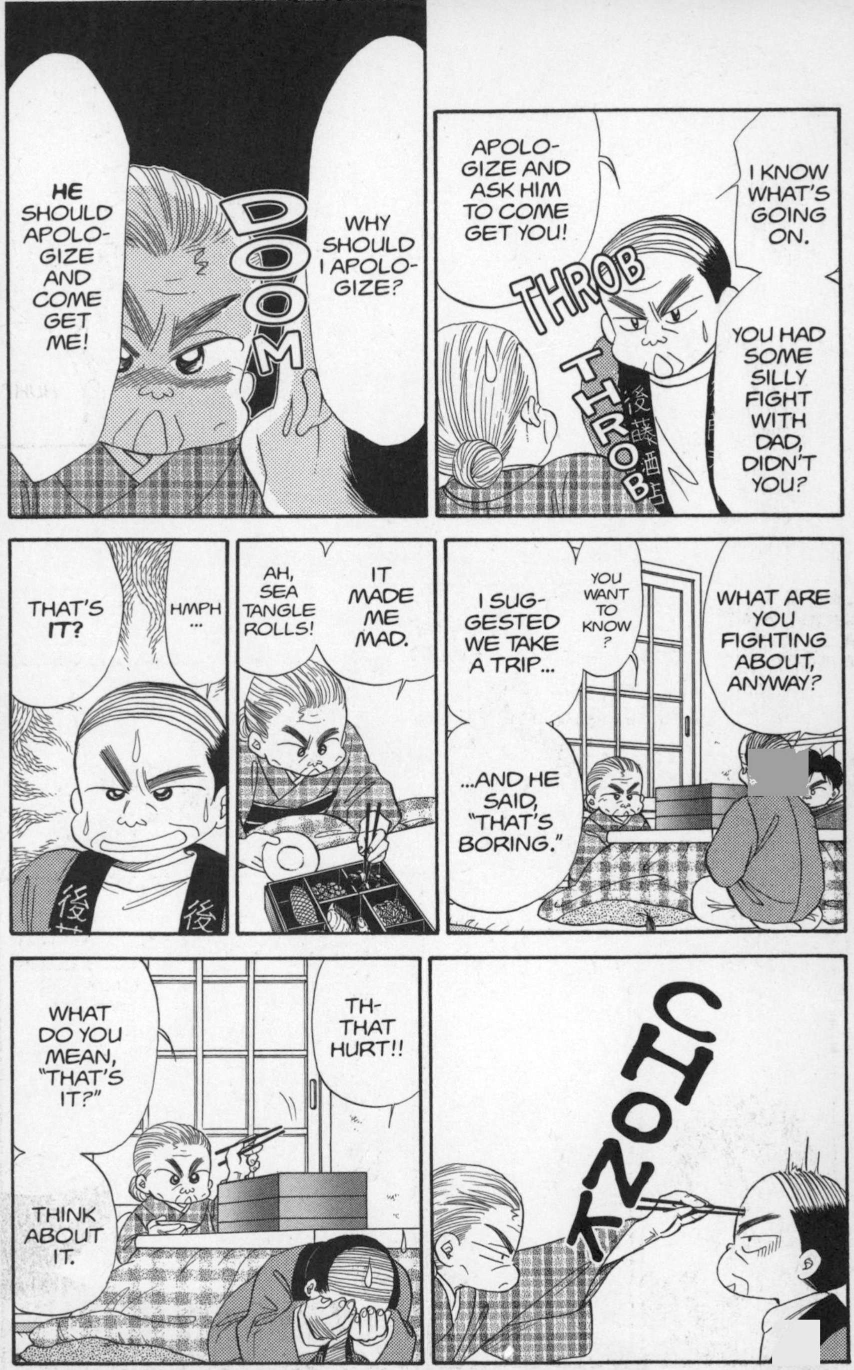
I KNOW WHAT'S GOING ON.
YOU HAD SOME SILLY FIGHT WITH DAD, DIDN'T YOU?
APOLO-GIZE AND ASK HIM TO COME GET YOU!
THROB THROB
後藤酒店
WHY SHOULD I APOLO-GIZE?
DOOM
HE SHOULD APOLO-GIZE AND COME GET ME!
WHAT ARE YOU FIGHTING ABOUT, ANYWAY?
YOU WANT TO KNOW?
I SUG-GESTED WE TAKE A TRIP...
...AND HE SAID, "THAT'S BORING."
IT MADE ME MAD.
AH, SEA TANGLE ROLLS!
HMPH...
THAT'S IT?
CHONK
TH-THAT HURT!!
WHAT DO YOU MEAN, "THAT'S IT?"
THINK ABOUT IT.

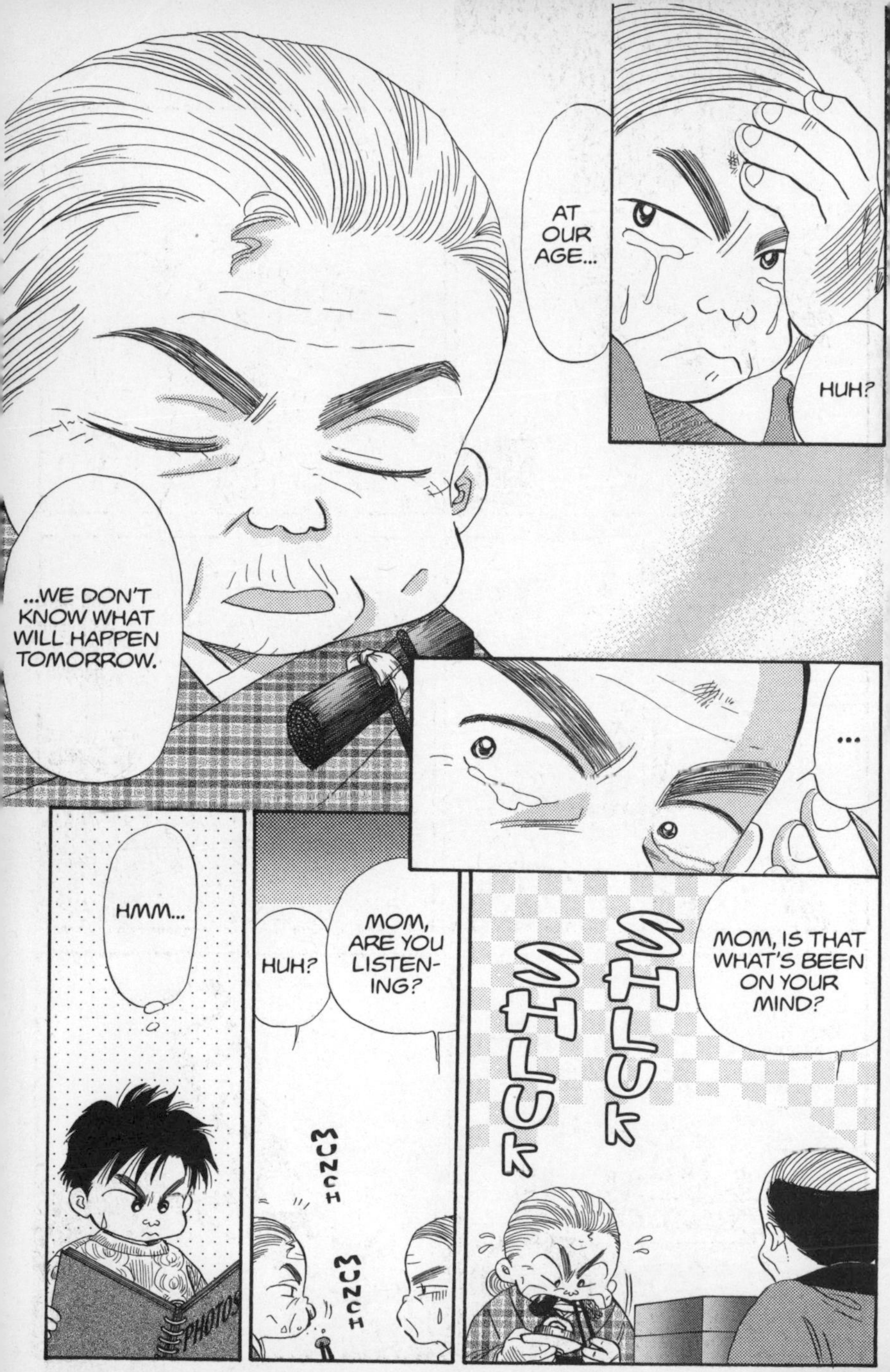
AT OUR AGE...
HUH?
...WE DON'T KNOW WHAT WILL HAPPEN TOMORROW.
...
MOM, IS THAT WHAT'S BEEN ON YOUR MIND?
SHLUK
SHLUK
MOM, ARE YOU LISTEN-ING?
HUH?
MUNCH
MUNCH
HMM...
PHOTOS

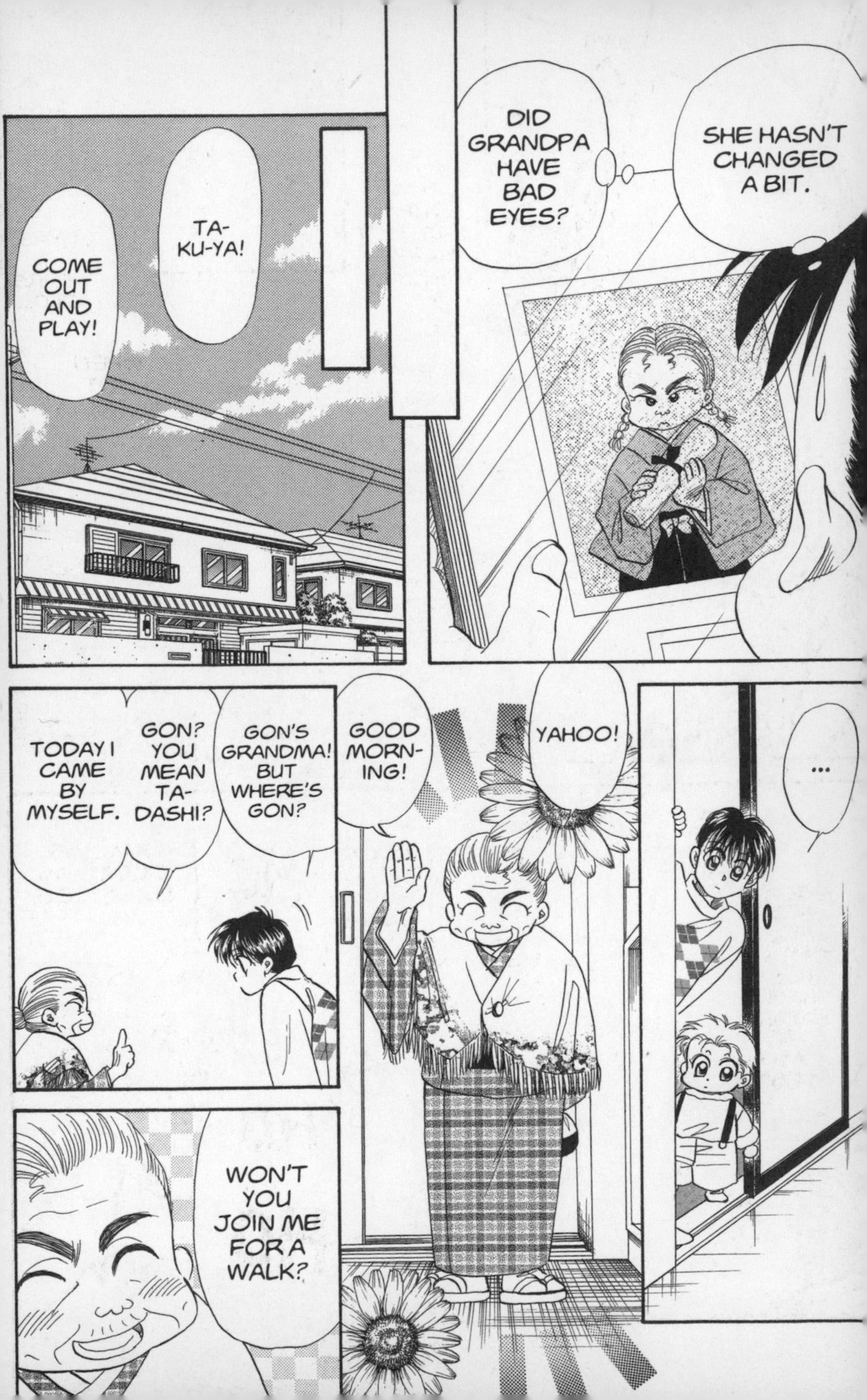
SHE HASN'T CHANGED A BIT.
DID GRANDPA HAVE BAD EYES?
TA-KU-YA!
COME OUT AND PLAY!
...
YAHOO!
GOOD MORN-ING!
GON'S GRANDMA! BUT WHERE'S GON?
GON? YOU MEAN TA-DASHI?
TODAY I CAME BY MYSELF.
WON'T YOU JOIN ME FOR A WALK?

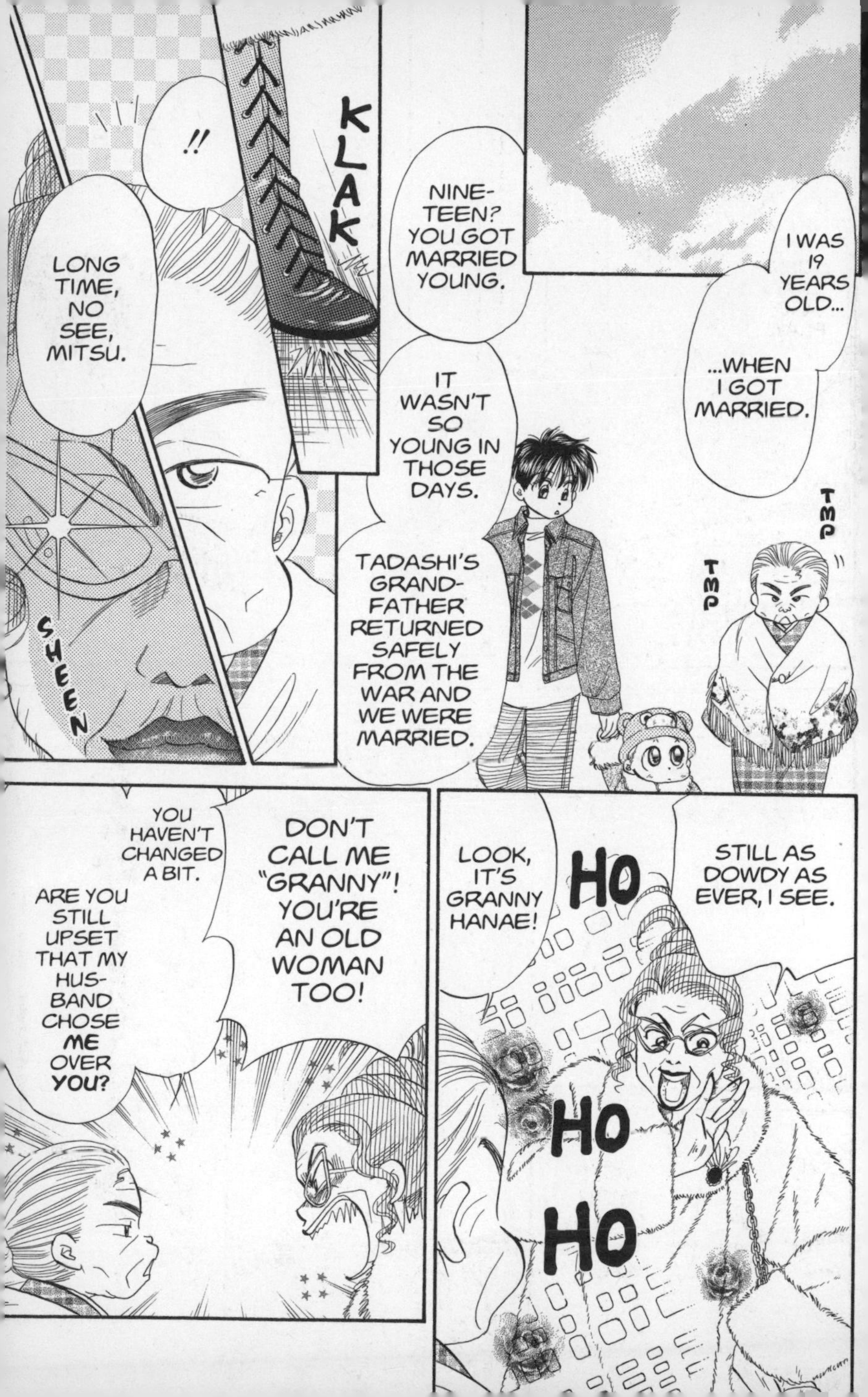
I WAS 19 YEARS OLD...
...WHEN I GOT MARRIED.
NINE-TEEN? YOU GOT MARRIED YOUNG.
IT WASN'T SO YOUNG IN THOSE DAYS.
TADASHI'S GRAND-FATHER RETURNED SAFELY FROM THE WAR AND WE WERE MARRIED.
TMP
TMP
KLAK
!!
LONG TIME, NO SEE, MITSU.
SHEEN
STILL AS DOWDY AS EVER, I SEE.
HO HO HO
LOOK, IT'S GRANNY HANAE!
DON'T CALL ME "GRANNY"! YOU'RE AN OLD WOMAN TOO!
YOU HAVEN'T CHANGED A BIT.
ARE YOU STILL UPSET THAT MY HUS-BAND CHOSE ME OVER YOU?

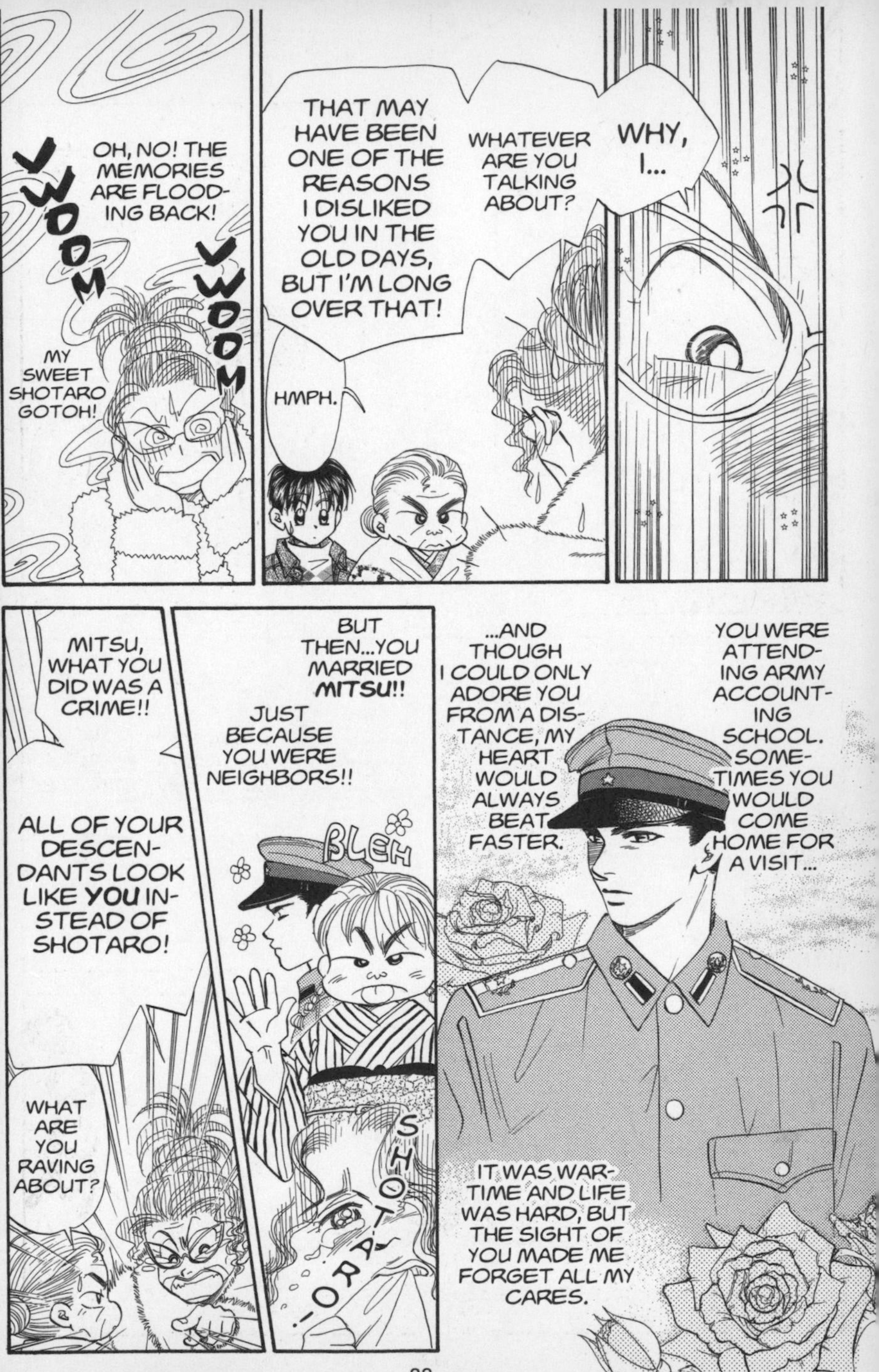
WHY, I...
WHATEVER ARE YOU TALKING ABOUT?
THAT MAY HAVE BEEN ONE OF THE REASONS I DISLIKED YOU IN THE OLD DAYS, BUT I'M LONG OVER THAT!
HMPH.
OH, NO! THE MEMORIES ARE FLOODING BACK!
VWOOM VWOOM
VWOOM
MY SWEET SHOTARO GOTOH!
YOU WERE ATTENDING ARMY ACCOUNTING SCHOOL. SOMETIMES YOU WOULD COME HOME FOR A VISIT...
...AND THOUGH I COULD ONLY ADORE YOU FROM A DISTANCE, MY HEART WOULD ALWAYS BEAT FASTER.
IT WAS WARTIME AND LIFE WAS HARD, BUT THE SIGHT OF YOU MADE ME FORGET ALL MY CARES.
BUT THEN...YOU MARRIED **MITSU**!!
JUST BECAUSE YOU WERE NEIGHBORS!!
BLEH
SHOTARO-O!
MITSU, WHAT YOU DID WAS A CRIME!!
ALL OF YOUR DESCENDANTS LOOK LIKE **YOU** INSTEAD OF SHOTARO!
WHAT ARE YOU RAVING ABOUT?

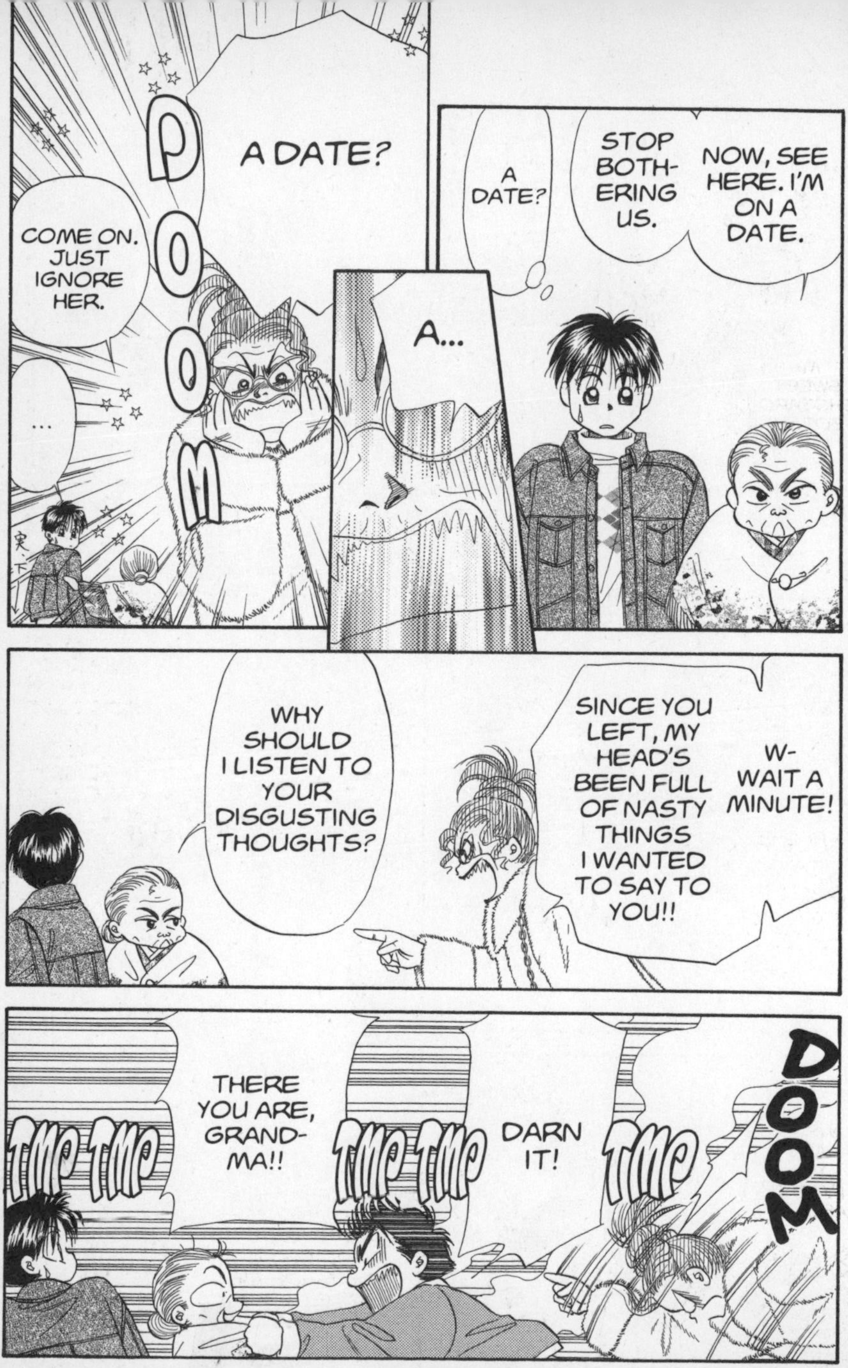
NOW, SEE HERE. I'M ON A DATE.
STOP BOTH-ERING US.
A DATE?
A...
A DATE?
DOOM
COME ON. JUST IGNORE HER.
...
W-WAIT A MINUTE!
SINCE YOU LEFT, MY HEAD'S BEEN FULL OF NASTY THINGS I WANTED TO SAY TO YOU!!
WHY SHOULD I LISTEN TO YOUR DISGUSTING THOUGHTS?
DOOM
TMP
DARN IT!
TMP TMP
THERE YOU ARE, GRAND-MA!!
TMP TMP

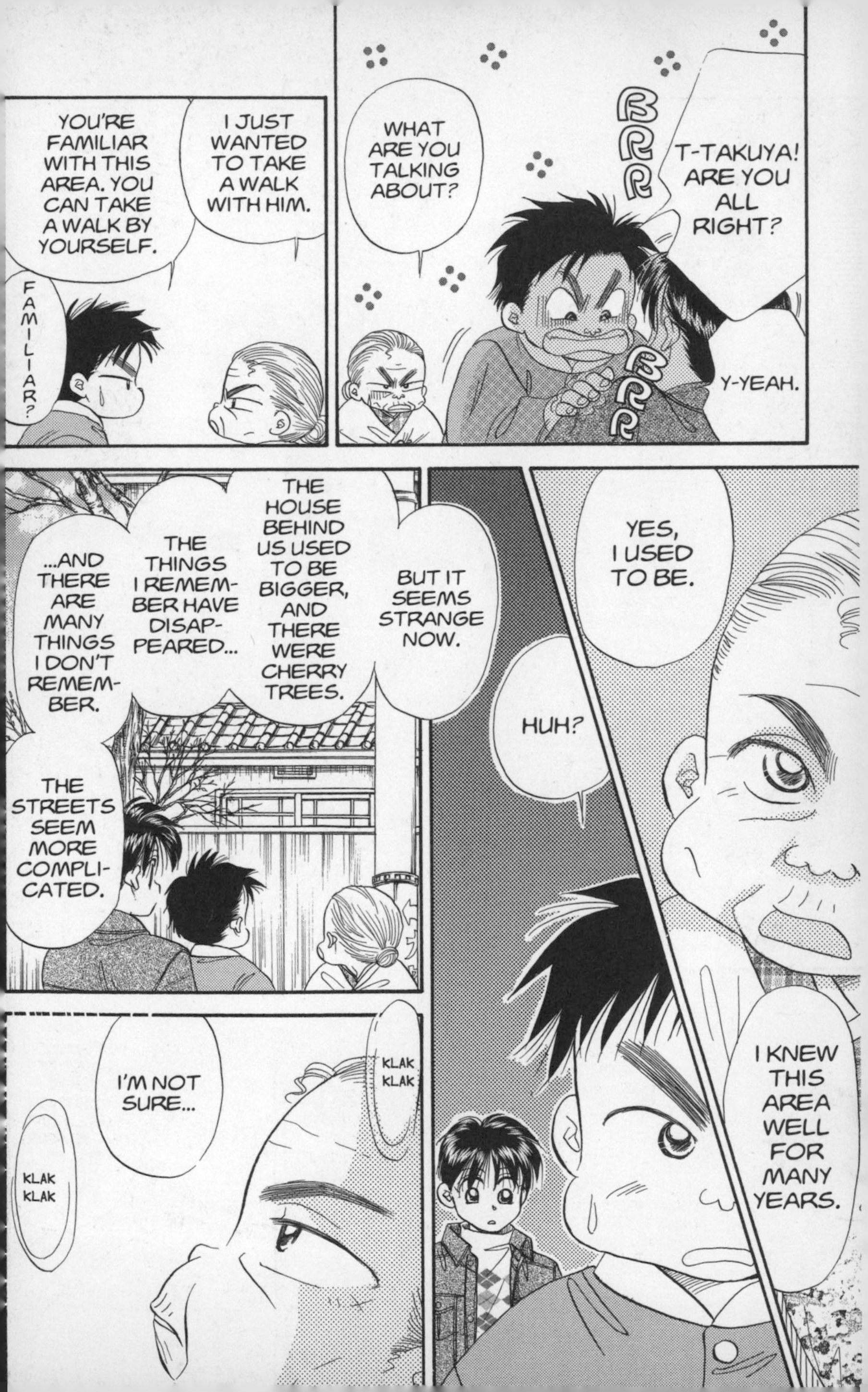

T-TAKUYA! ARE YOU ALL RIGHT?
BRR
WHAT ARE YOU TALKING ABOUT?
BRR
Y-YEAH.
I JUST WANTED TO TAKE A WALK WITH HIM.
YOU'RE FAMILIAR WITH THIS AREA. YOU CAN TAKE A WALK BY YOURSELF.
FAMILIAR?
YES, I USED TO BE.
HUH?
I KNEW THIS AREA WELL FOR MANY YEARS.
BUT IT SEEMS STRANGE NOW.
THE HOUSE BEHIND US USED TO BE BIGGER, AND THERE WERE CHERRY TREES.
THE THINGS I REMEMBER HAVE DISAPPEARED...
...AND THERE ARE MANY THINGS I DON'T REMEMBER.
THE STREETS SEEM MORE COMPLICATED.
KLAK KLAK
I'M NOT SURE...
KLAK KLAK

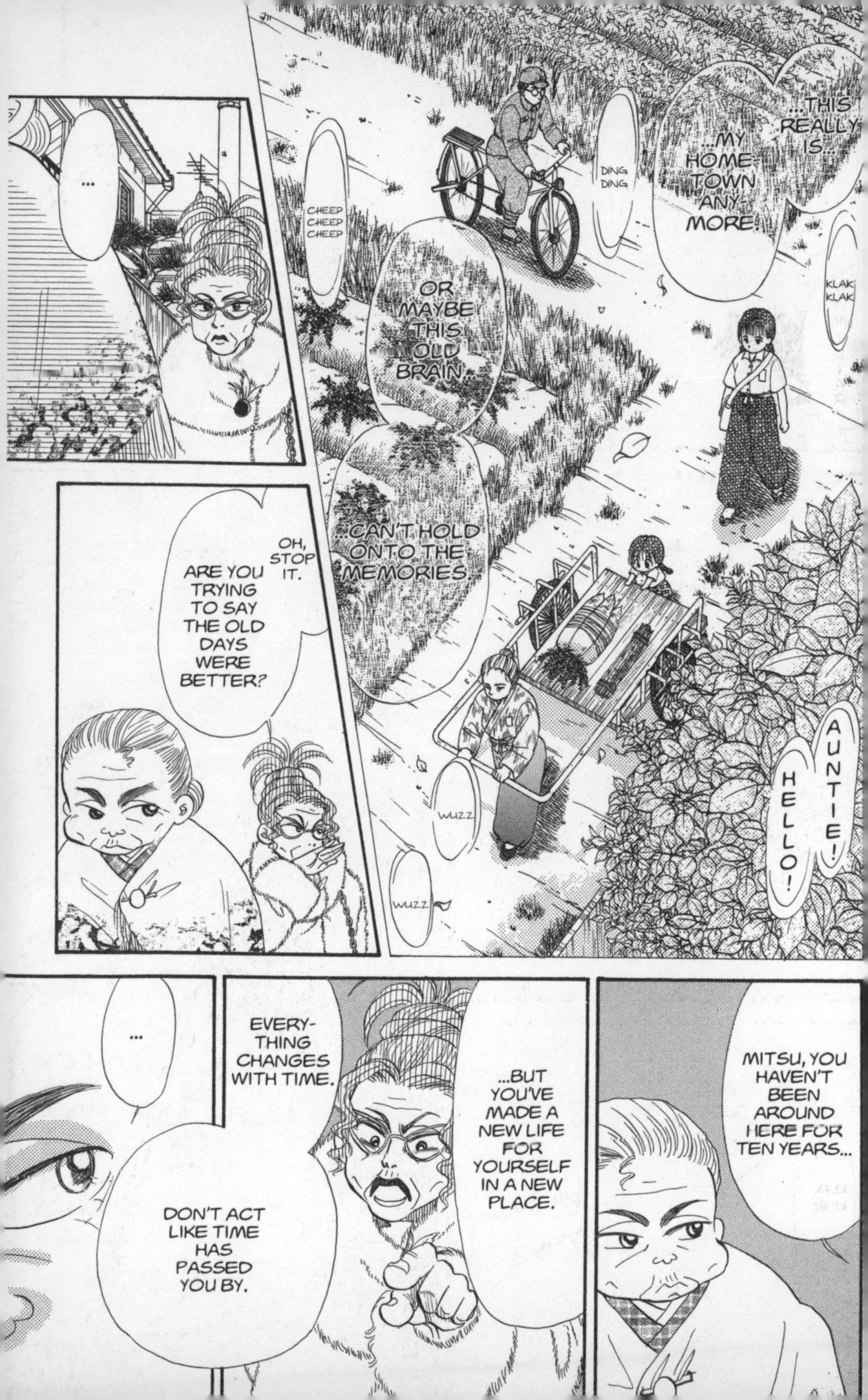
...THIS REALLY IS...
...MY HOME-TOWN ANY-MORE.
KLAK KLAK
DING DING
OR MAYBE THIS OLD BRAIN...
CHEEP CHEEP CHEEP
...CAN'T HOLD ONTO THE MEMORIES.
AUNTIE!
HELLO!
WUZZ
WUZZ
...
OH, STOP IT.
ARE YOU TRYING TO SAY THE OLD DAYS WERE BETTER?
MITSU, YOU HAVEN'T BEEN AROUND HERE FOR TEN YEARS...
EVERY-THING CHANGES WITH TIME.
...BUT YOU'VE MADE A NEW LIFE FOR YOURSELF IN A NEW PLACE.
...
DON'T ACT LIKE TIME HAS PASSED YOU BY.

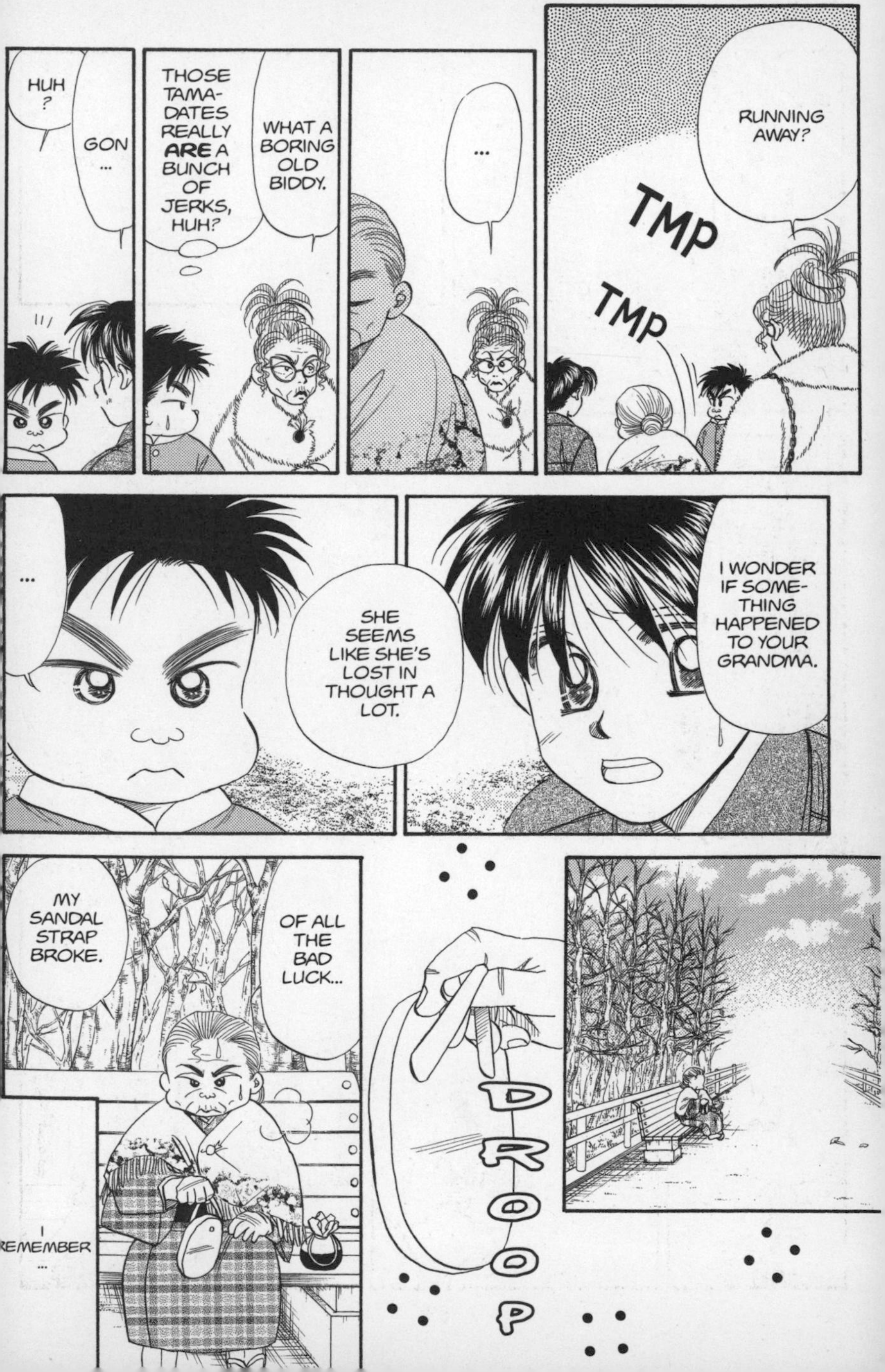
RUNNING AWAY?
TMP
TMP
...
WHAT A BORING OLD BIDDY.
THOSE TAMADATES REALLY **ARE** A BUNCH OF JERKS, HUH?
GON ...
HUH ?
I WONDER IF SOMETHING HAPPENED TO YOUR GRANDMA.
SHE SEEMS LIKE SHE'S LOST IN THOUGHT A LOT.
...
DROOP
OF ALL THE BAD LUCK...
MY SANDAL STRAP BROKE.
I REMEMBER ...

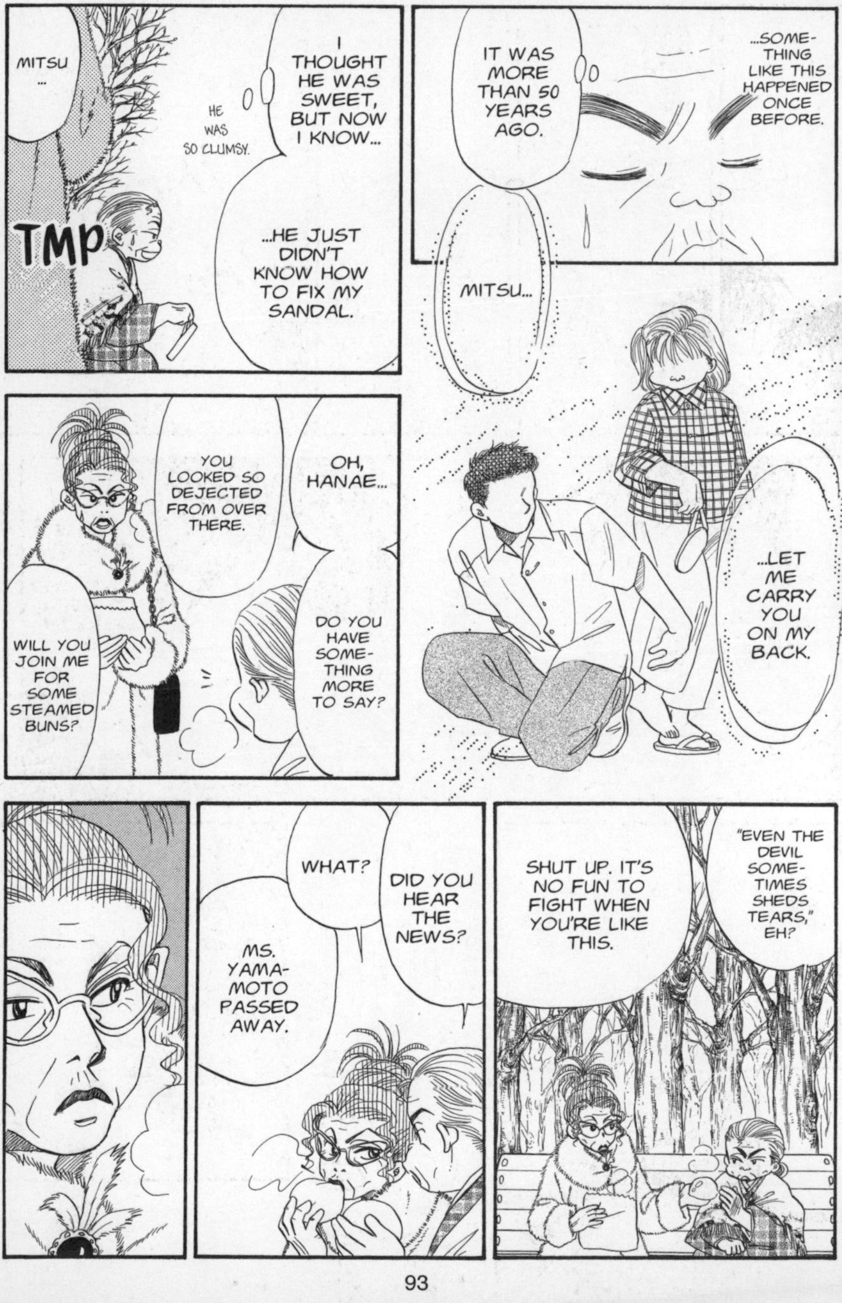
...SOME-THING LIKE THIS HAPPENED ONCE BEFORE.
IT WAS MORE THAN 50 YEARS AGO.
I THOUGHT HE WAS SWEET, BUT NOW I KNOW...
...HE JUST DIDN'T KNOW HOW TO FIX MY SANDAL.
HE WAS SO CLUMSY.
MITSU ...
TMP
MITSU...
...LET ME CARRY YOU ON MY BACK.
OH, HANAE...
YOU LOOKED SO DEJECTED FROM OVER THERE.
DO YOU HAVE SOME-THING MORE TO SAY?
WILL YOU JOIN ME FOR SOME STEAMED BUNS?
"EVEN THE DEVIL SOME-TIMES SHEDS TEARS," EH?
SHUT UP. IT'S NO FUN TO FIGHT WHEN YOU'RE LIKE THIS.
DID YOU HEAR THE NEWS?
WHAT?
MS. YAMA-MOTO PASSED AWAY.

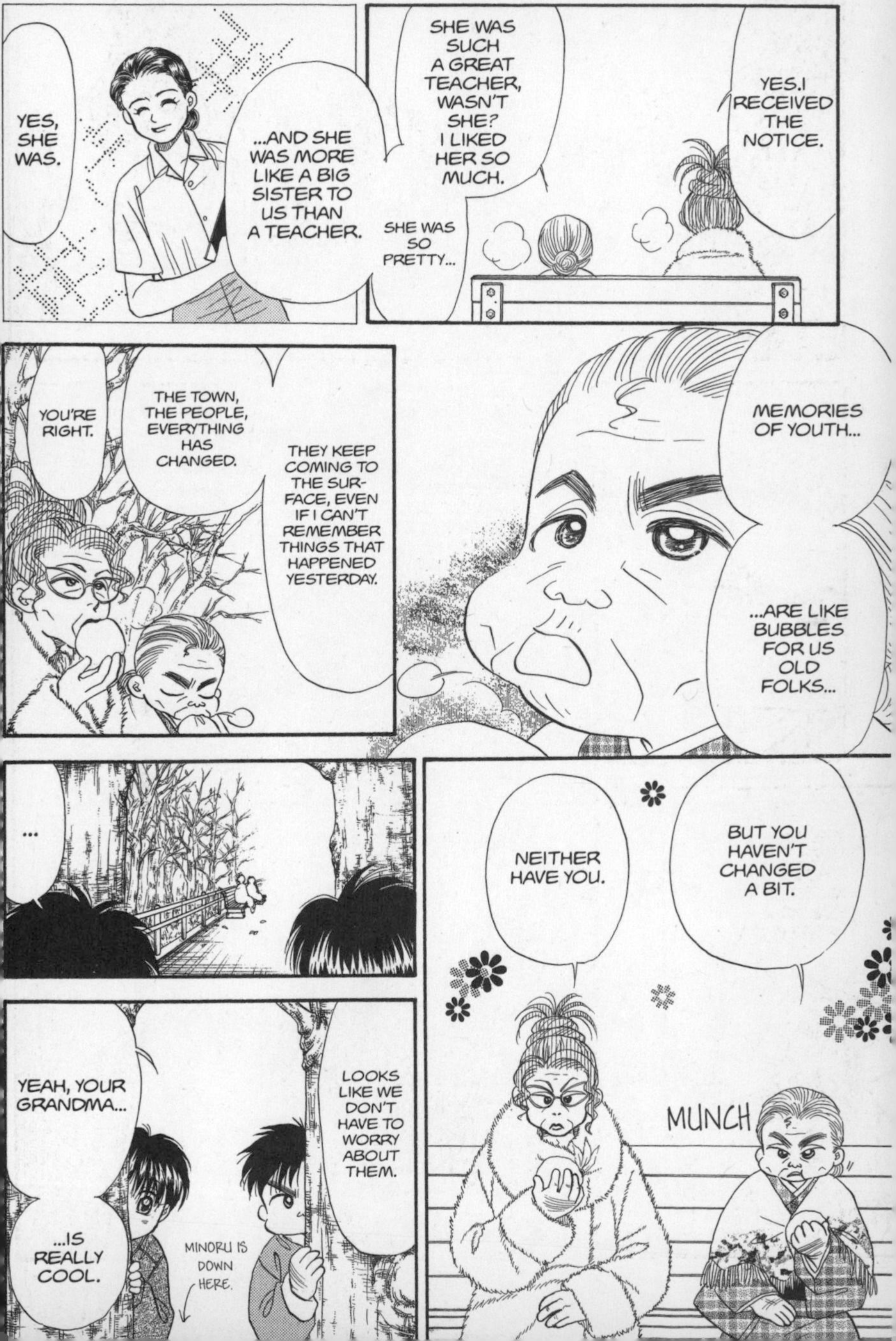
YES. I RECEIVED THE NOTICE.
SHE WAS SUCH A GREAT TEACHER, WASN'T SHE? I LIKED HER SO MUCH.
SHE WAS SO PRETTY...
...AND SHE WAS MORE LIKE A BIG SISTER TO US THAN A TEACHER.
YES, SHE WAS.
MEMORIES OF YOUTH...
...ARE LIKE BUBBLES FOR US OLD FOLKS...
THEY KEEP COMING TO THE SUR-FACE, EVEN IF I CAN'T REMEMBER THINGS THAT HAPPENED YESTERDAY.
THE TOWN, THE PEOPLE, EVERYTHING HAS CHANGED.
YOU'RE RIGHT.
BUT YOU HAVEN'T CHANGED A BIT.
NEITHER HAVE YOU.
MUNCH
...
LOOKS LIKE WE DON'T HAVE TO WORRY ABOUT THEM.
YEAH, YOUR GRANDMA...
...IS REALLY COOL.
MINORU IS DOWN HERE.

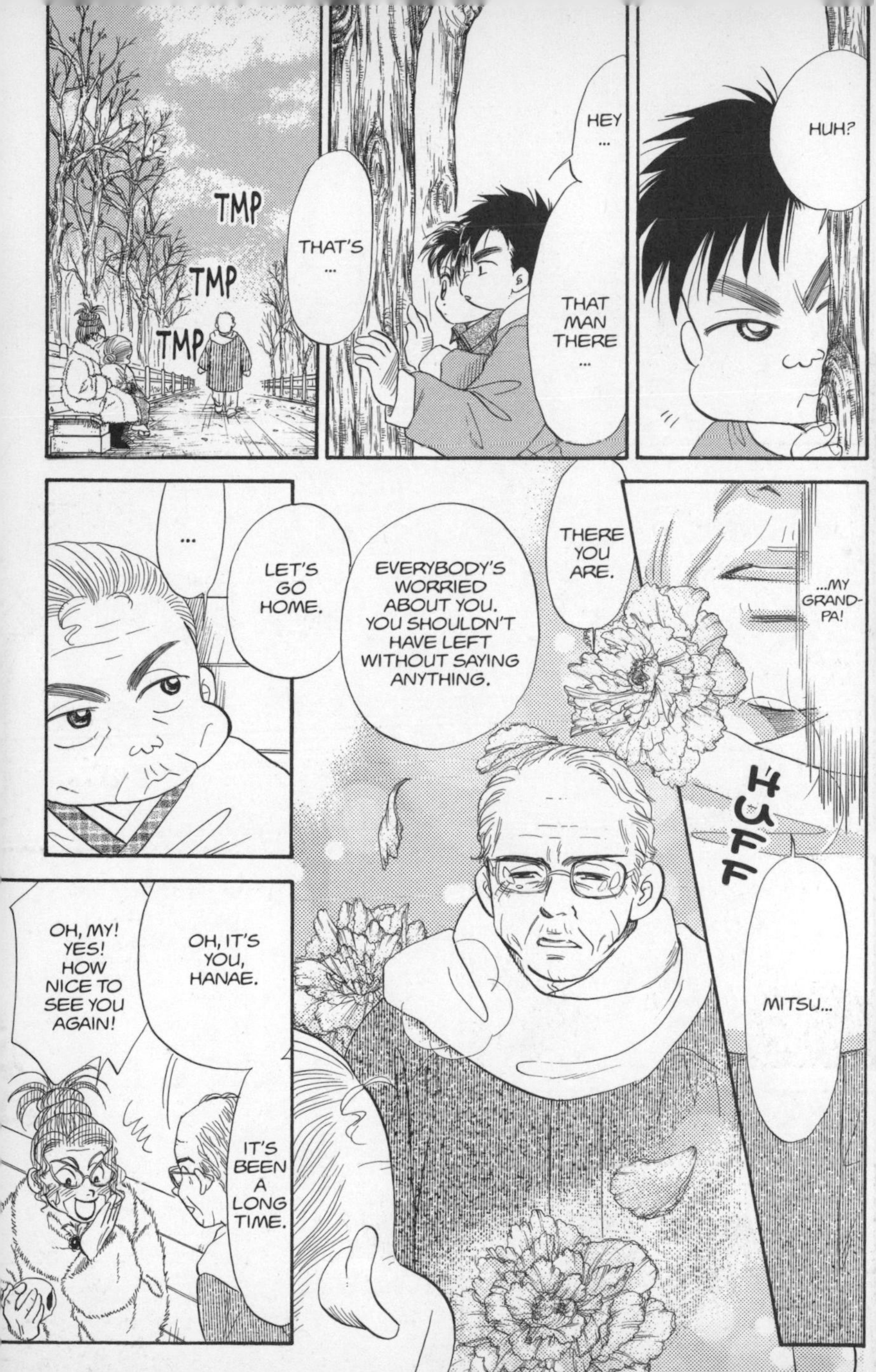
HUH?
HEY ...
THAT MAN THERE ...
THAT'S ...
TMP
TMP
TMP
...MY GRANDPA!
THERE YOU ARE.
HUFF
MITSU...
EVERYBODY'S WORRIED ABOUT YOU. YOU SHOULDN'T HAVE LEFT WITHOUT SAYING ANYTHING.
LET'S GO HOME.
...
OH, IT'S YOU, HANAE.
IT'S BEEN A LONG TIME.
OH, MY! YES! HOW NICE TO SEE YOU AGAIN!

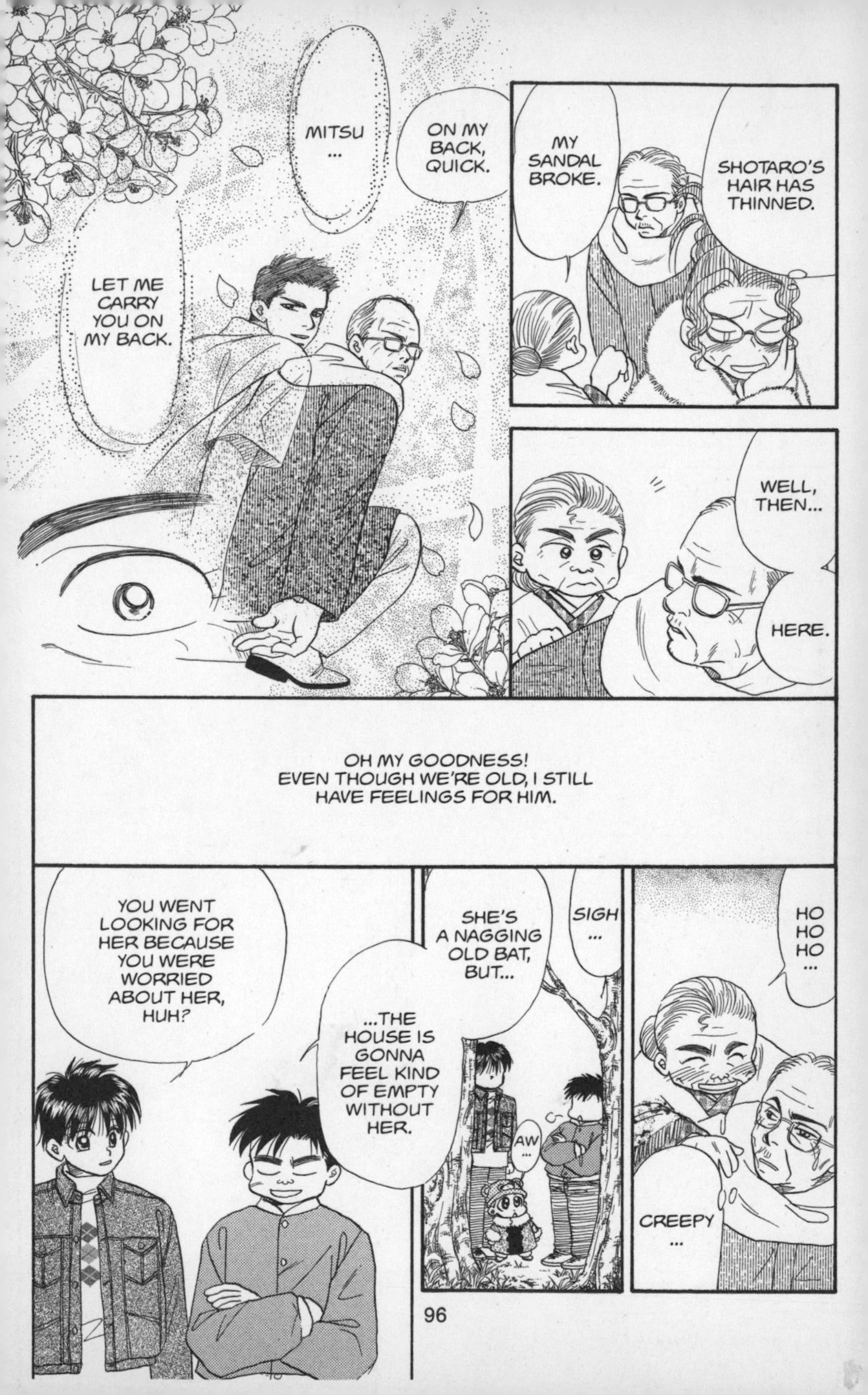
SHOTARO'S HAIR HAS THINNED.
MY SANDAL BROKE.
WELL, THEN...
HERE.
ON MY BACK, QUICK.
MITSU ...
LET ME CARRY YOU ON MY BACK.
OH MY GOODNESS! EVEN THOUGH WE'RE OLD, I STILL HAVE FEELINGS FOR HIM.
HO HO HO ...
CREEPY ...
SIGH ...
SHE'S A NAGGING OLD BAT, BUT...
...THE HOUSE IS GONNA FEEL KIND OF EMPTY WITHOUT HER.
AW ...
YOU WENT LOOKING FOR HER BECAUSE YOU WERE WORRIED ABOUT HER, HUH?

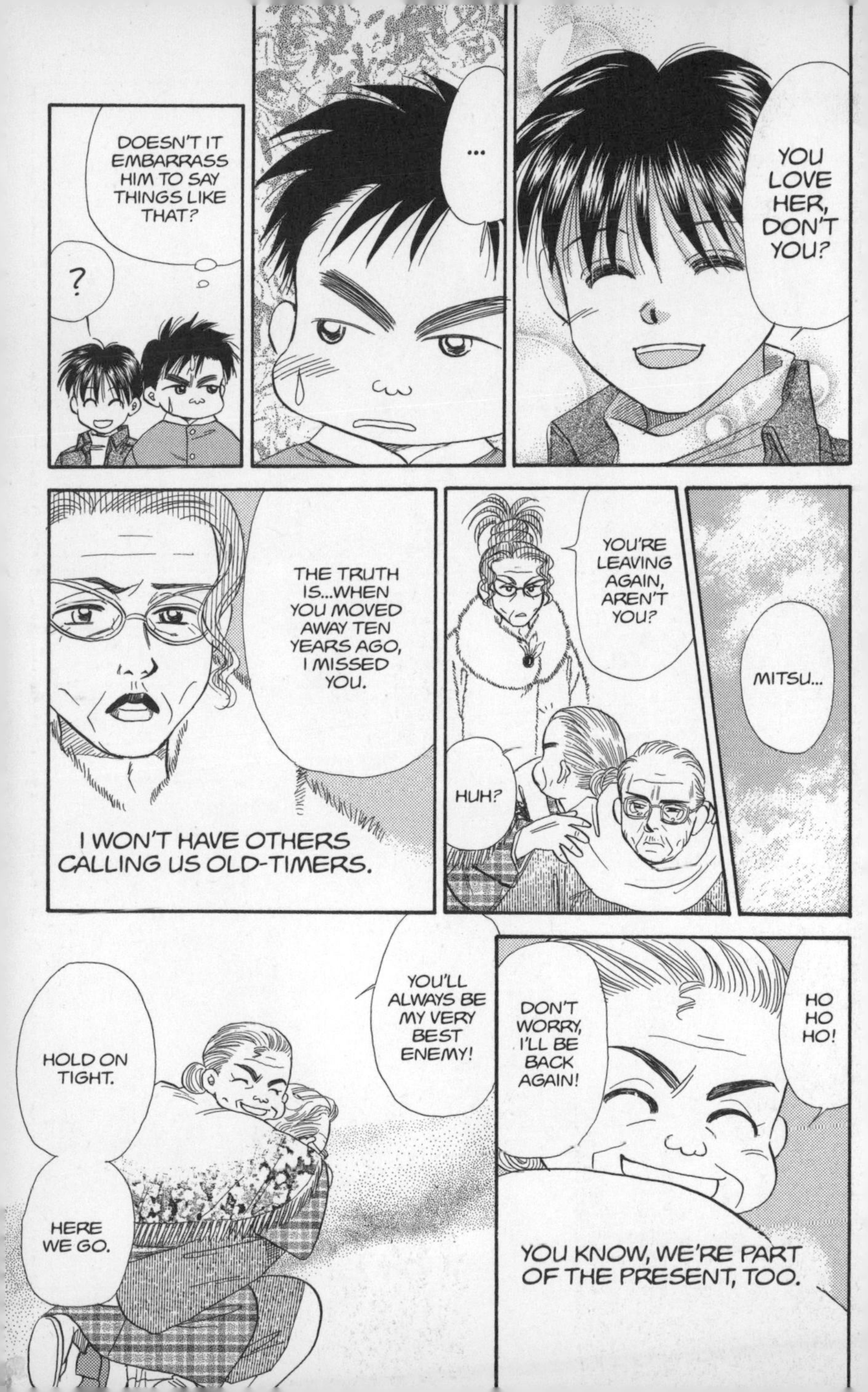
YOU LOVE HER, DON'T YOU?
...
DOESN'T IT EMBARRASS HIM TO SAY THINGS LIKE THAT?
?
MITSU...
YOU'RE LEAVING AGAIN, AREN'T YOU?
HUH?
THE TRUTH IS...WHEN YOU MOVED AWAY TEN YEARS AGO, I MISSED YOU.
I WON'T HAVE OTHERS CALLING US OLD-TIMERS.
HO HO HO!
DON'T WORRY, I'LL BE BACK AGAIN!
YOU KNOW, WE'RE PART OF THE PRESENT, TOO.
YOU'LL ALWAYS BE MY VERY BEST ENEMY!
HOLD ON TIGHT.
HERE WE GO.

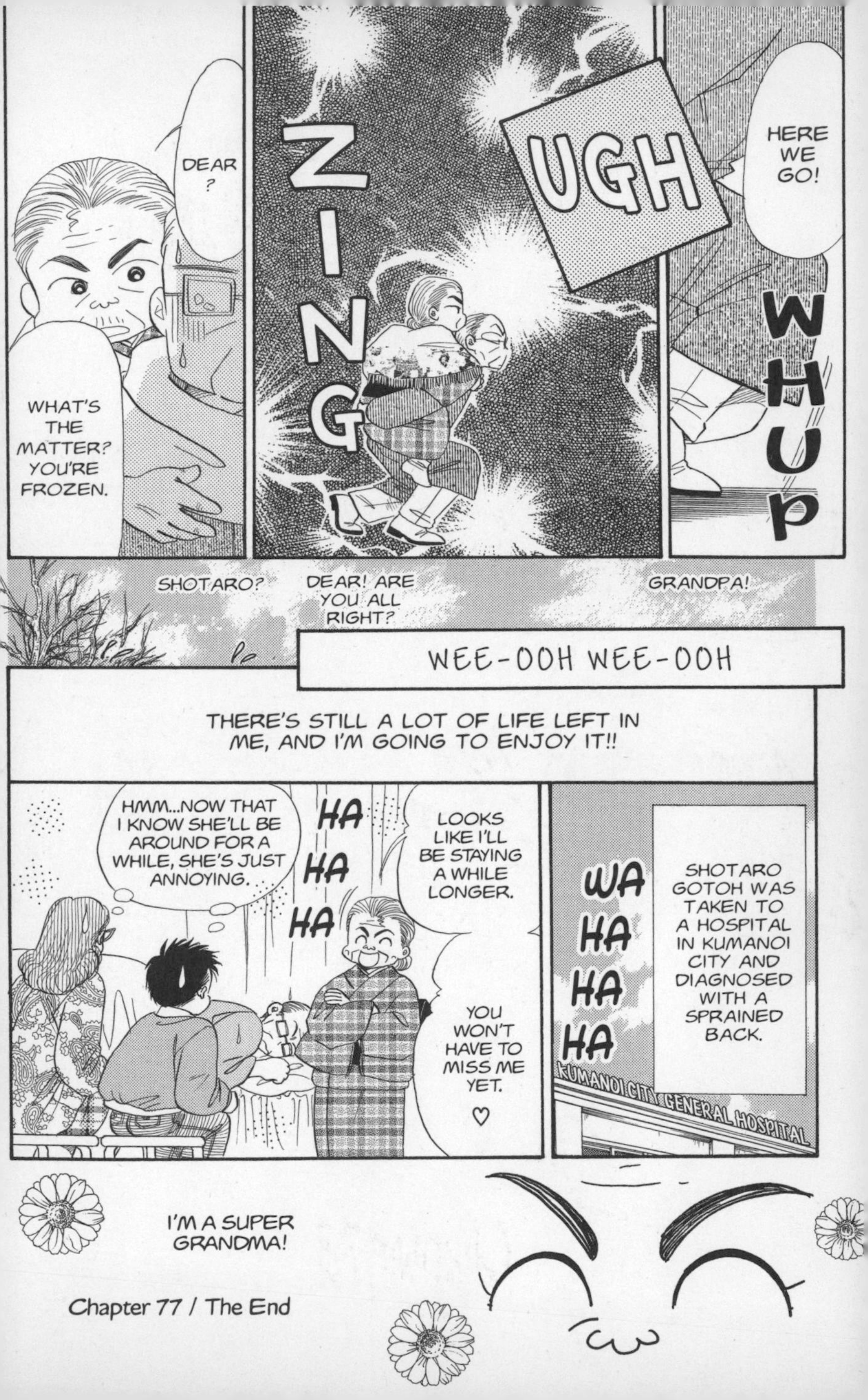
HERE WE GO!
WHUP
UGH
ZING
DEAR?
WHAT'S THE MATTER? YOU'RE FROZEN.
GRANDPA!
DEAR! ARE YOU ALL RIGHT?
SHOTARO?
WEE-OOH WEE-OOH
THERE'S STILL A LOT OF LIFE LEFT IN ME, AND I'M GOING TO ENJOY IT!!
SHOTARO GOTOH WAS TAKEN TO A HOSPITAL IN KUMANOI CITY AND DIAGNOSED WITH A SPRAINED BACK.
WA HA HA HA HA
KUMANOI CITY GENERAL HOSPITAL
LOOKS LIKE I'LL BE STAYING A WHILE LONGER.
YOU WON'T HAVE TO MISS ME YET. ♡
HA HA HA
HMM...NOW THAT I KNOW SHE'LL BE AROUND FOR A WHILE, SHE'S JUST ANNOYING.
I'M A SUPER GRANDMA!

Chapter 77 / The End

BABY & Me

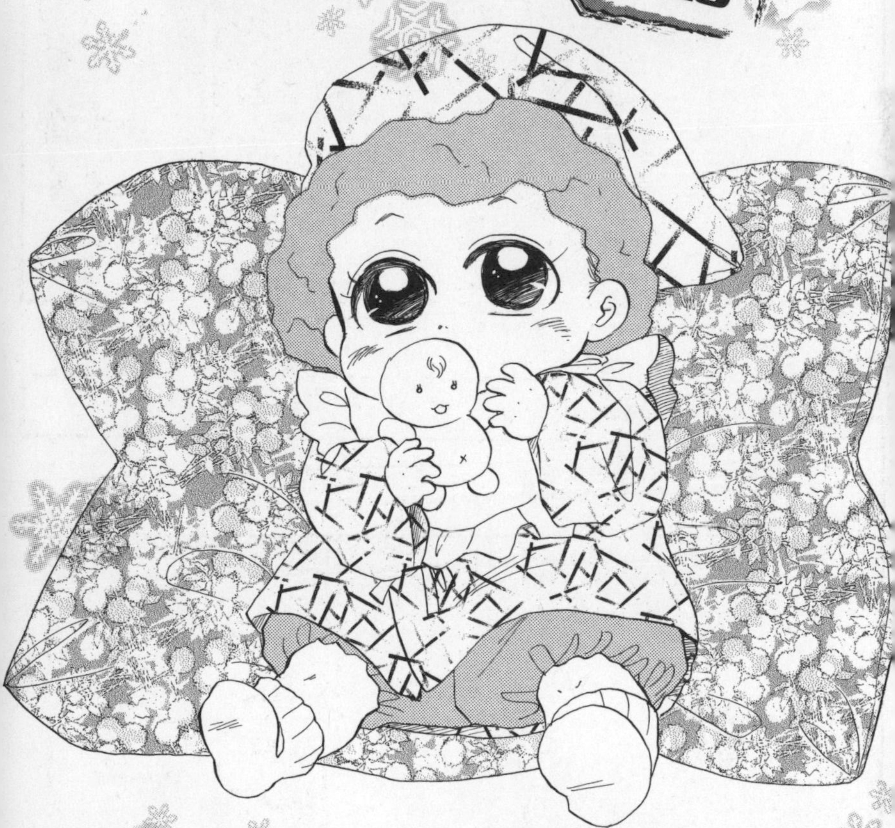

minoru.

Chapter 78

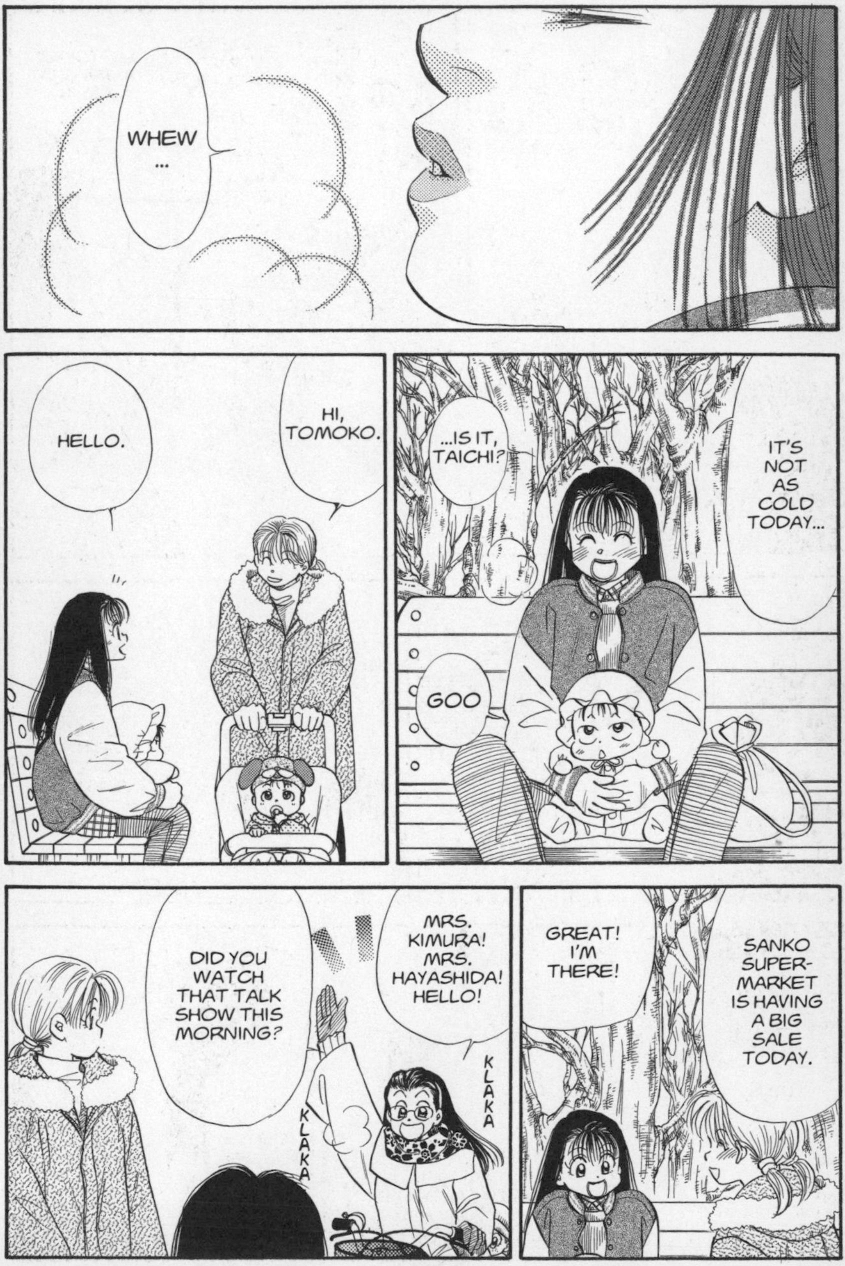
WHEW ...
IT'S NOT AS COLD TODAY...
...IS IT, TAICHI?
GOO
HI, TOMOKO.
HELLO.
SANKO SUPER-MARKET IS HAVING A BIG SALE TODAY.
GREAT! I'M THERE!
MRS. KIMURA! MRS. HAYASHIDA! HELLO!
KLAKA
KLAKA
DID YOU WATCH THAT TALK SHOW THIS MORNING?

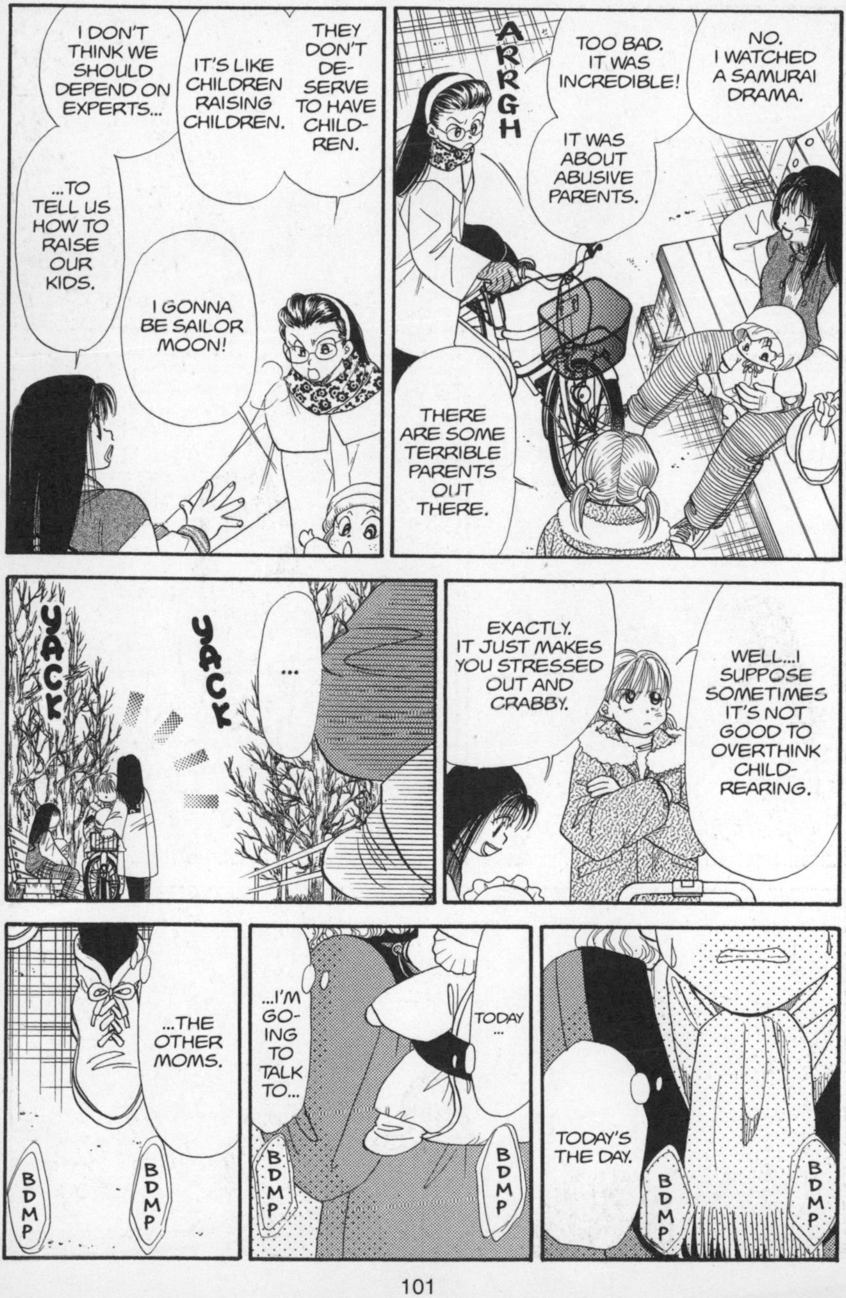
NO. I WATCHED A SAMURAI DRAMA.
TOO BAD. IT WAS INCREDIBLE!
IT WAS ABOUT ABUSIVE PARENTS.
ARRGH
THERE ARE SOME TERRIBLE PARENTS OUT THERE.
THEY DON'T DE- SERVE TO HAVE CHILD- REN.
IT'S LIKE CHILDREN RAISING CHILDREN.
I DON'T THINK WE SHOULD DEPEND ON EXPERTS...
...TO TELL US HOW TO RAISE OUR KIDS.
I GONNA BE SAILOR MOON!
WELL...I SUPPOSE SOMETIMES IT'S NOT GOOD TO OVERTHINK CHILD- REARING.
EXACTLY. IT JUST MAKES YOU STRESSED OUT AND CRABBY.
...
YACK
YACK
BDMP
TODAY'S THE DAY.
BDMP
TODAY ...
BDMP
...I'M GO- ING TO TALK TO...
BDMP
...THE OTHER MOMS.
BDMP
BDMP

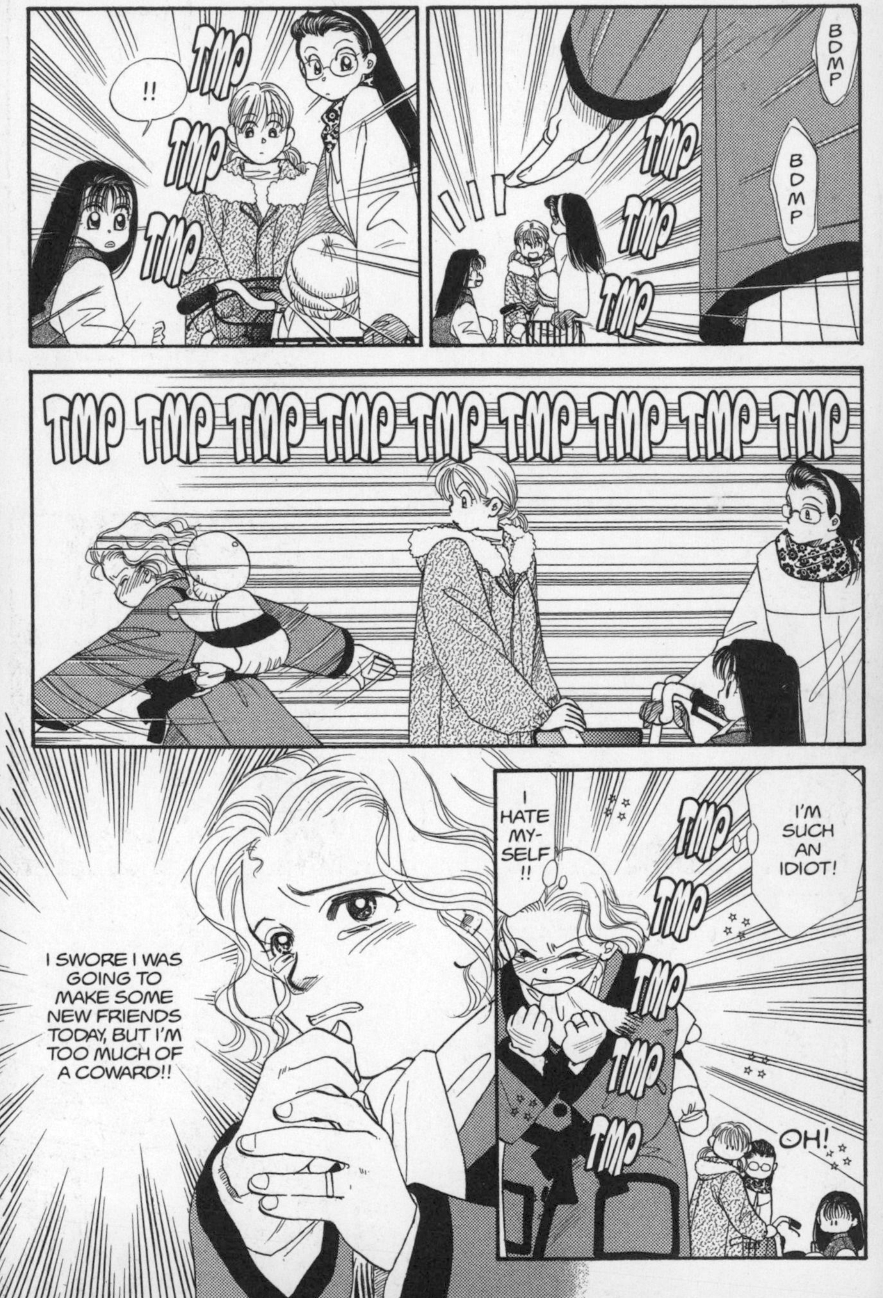
BDMP
BDMP
TMP
TMP
TMP
TMP
TMP
TMP
!!
TMP TMP TMP TMP TMP TMP TMP TMP TMP
I'M SUCH AN IDIOT!
I HATE MY-SELF!!
TMP
TMP
TMP
TMP
TMP
OH!
I SWORE I WAS GOING TO MAKE SOME NEW FRIENDS TODAY, BUT I'M TOO MUCH OF A COWARD!!

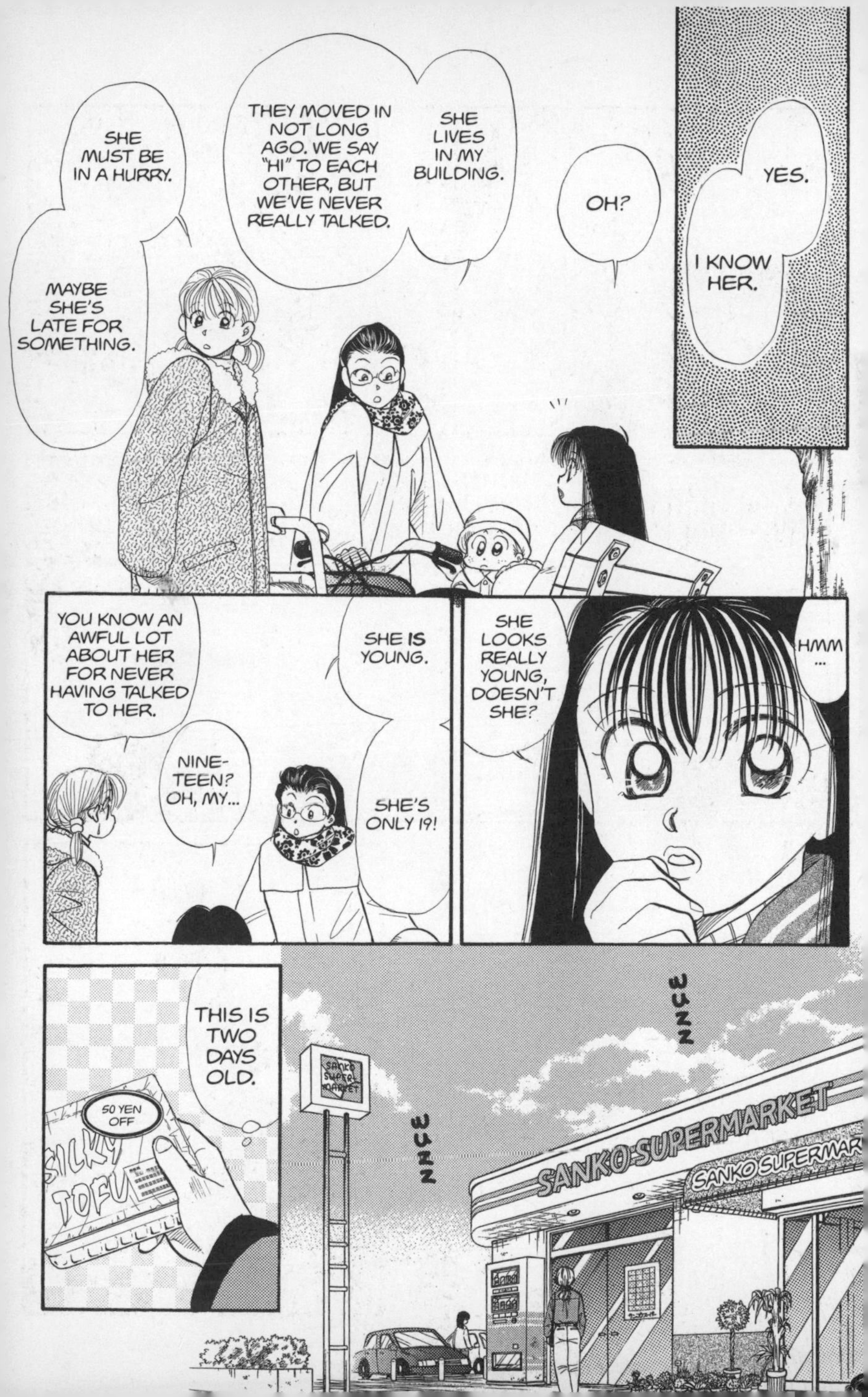
YES.
I KNOW HER.
OH?
SHE LIVES IN MY BUILDING.
THEY MOVED IN NOT LONG AGO. WE SAY "HI" TO EACH OTHER, BUT WE'VE NEVER REALLY TALKED.
SHE MUST BE IN A HURRY.
MAYBE SHE'S LATE FOR SOMETHING.
HMM...
SHE LOOKS REALLY YOUNG, DOESN'T SHE?
SHE **IS** YOUNG.
SHE'S ONLY 19!
NINE-TEEN? OH, MY...
YOU KNOW AN AWFUL LOT ABOUT HER FOR NEVER HAVING TALKED TO HER.
SANKO SUPERMARKET
SANKO SUPERMARKET
SANKO SUPERMAR
THIS IS TWO DAYS OLD.
50 YEN OFF
SILKY TOFU

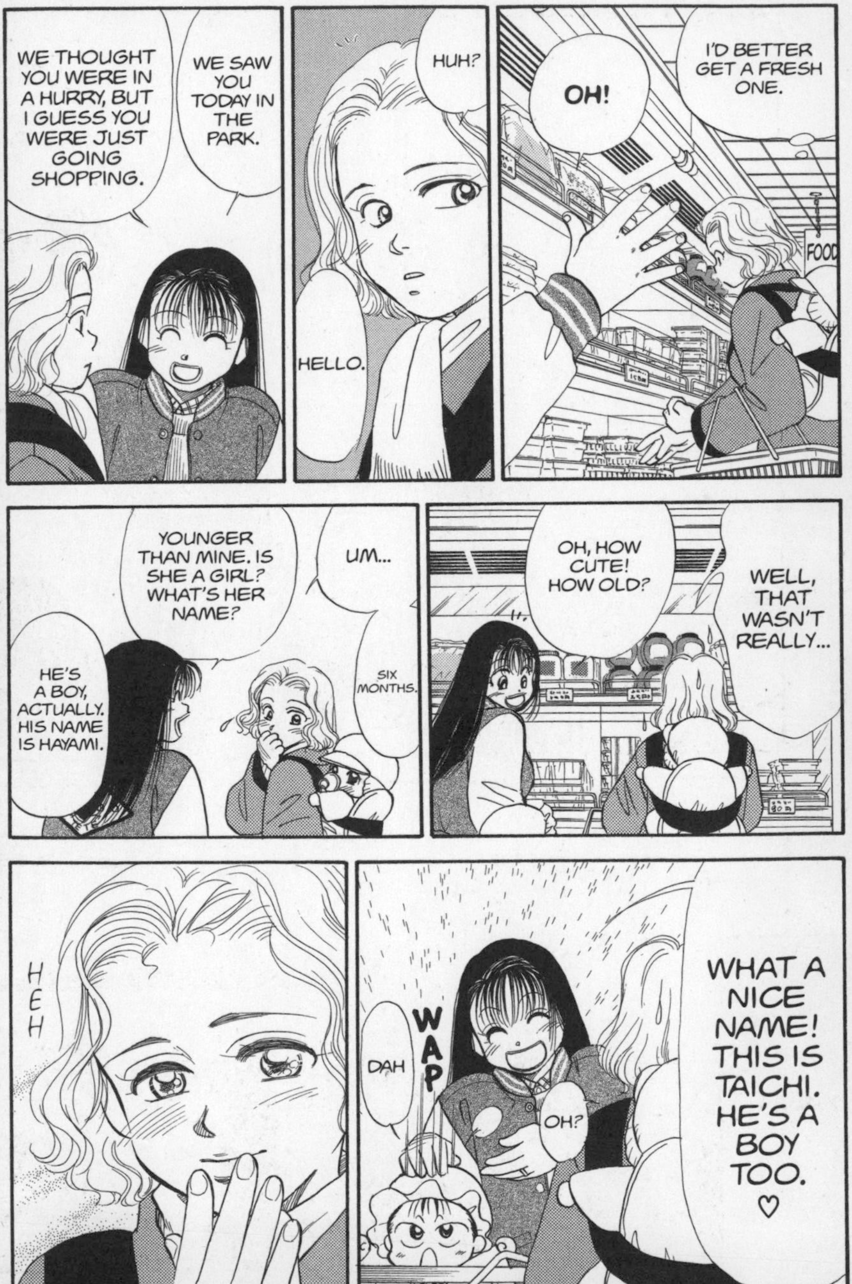
I'D BETTER GET A FRESH ONE.
OH!
FOOD
HUH?
HELLO.
WE SAW YOU TODAY IN THE PARK.
WE THOUGHT YOU WERE IN A HURRY, BUT I GUESS YOU WERE JUST GOING SHOPPING.
WELL, THAT WASN'T REALLY...
OH, HOW CUTE! HOW OLD?
UM...
SIX MONTHS.
YOUNGER THAN MINE. IS SHE A GIRL? WHAT'S HER NAME?
HE'S A BOY, ACTUALLY. HIS NAME IS HAYAMI.
WHAT A NICE NAME! THIS IS TAICHI. HE'S A BOY TOO. ♡
OH?
WAP
DAH
HEH

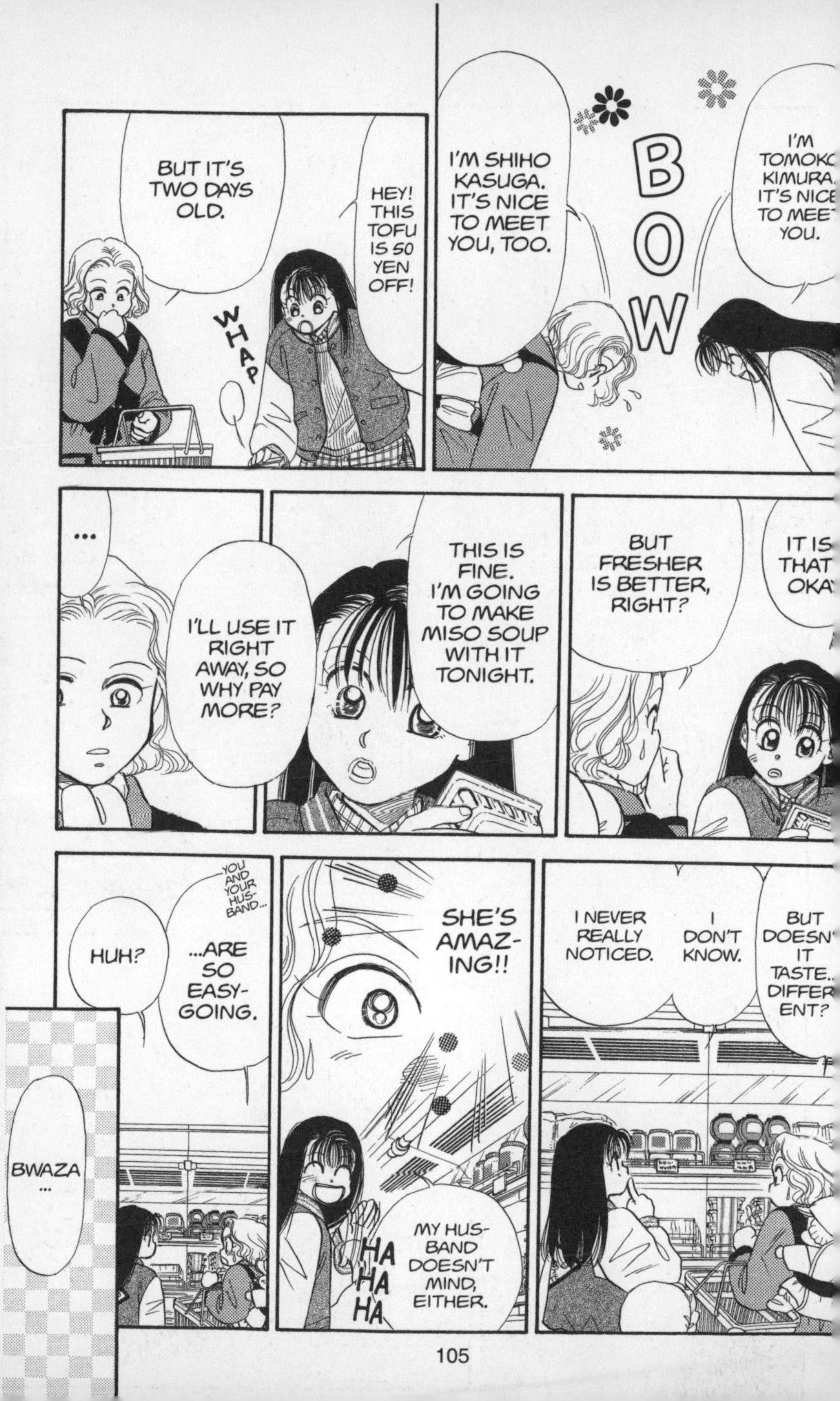
I'M TOMOKO KIMURA. IT'S NICE TO MEET YOU.
BOW
I'M SHIHO KASUGA. IT'S NICE TO MEET YOU, TOO.
HEY! THIS TOFU IS 50 YEN OFF!
WHAP
BUT IT'S TWO DAYS OLD.
IT IS THAT OKAY
BUT FRESHER IS BETTER, RIGHT?
THIS IS FINE. I'M GOING TO MAKE MISO SOUP WITH IT TONIGHT.
I'LL USE IT RIGHT AWAY, SO WHY PAY MORE?
...
BUT DOESN'T IT TASTE.. DIFFERENT?
I DON'T KNOW.
I NEVER REALLY NOTICED.
SHE'S AMAZ-ING!!
HA HA HA
MY HUS-BAND DOESN'T MIND, EITHER.
YOU AND YOUR HUS-BAND...
...ARE SO EASY-GOING.
HUH?
BWAZA ...

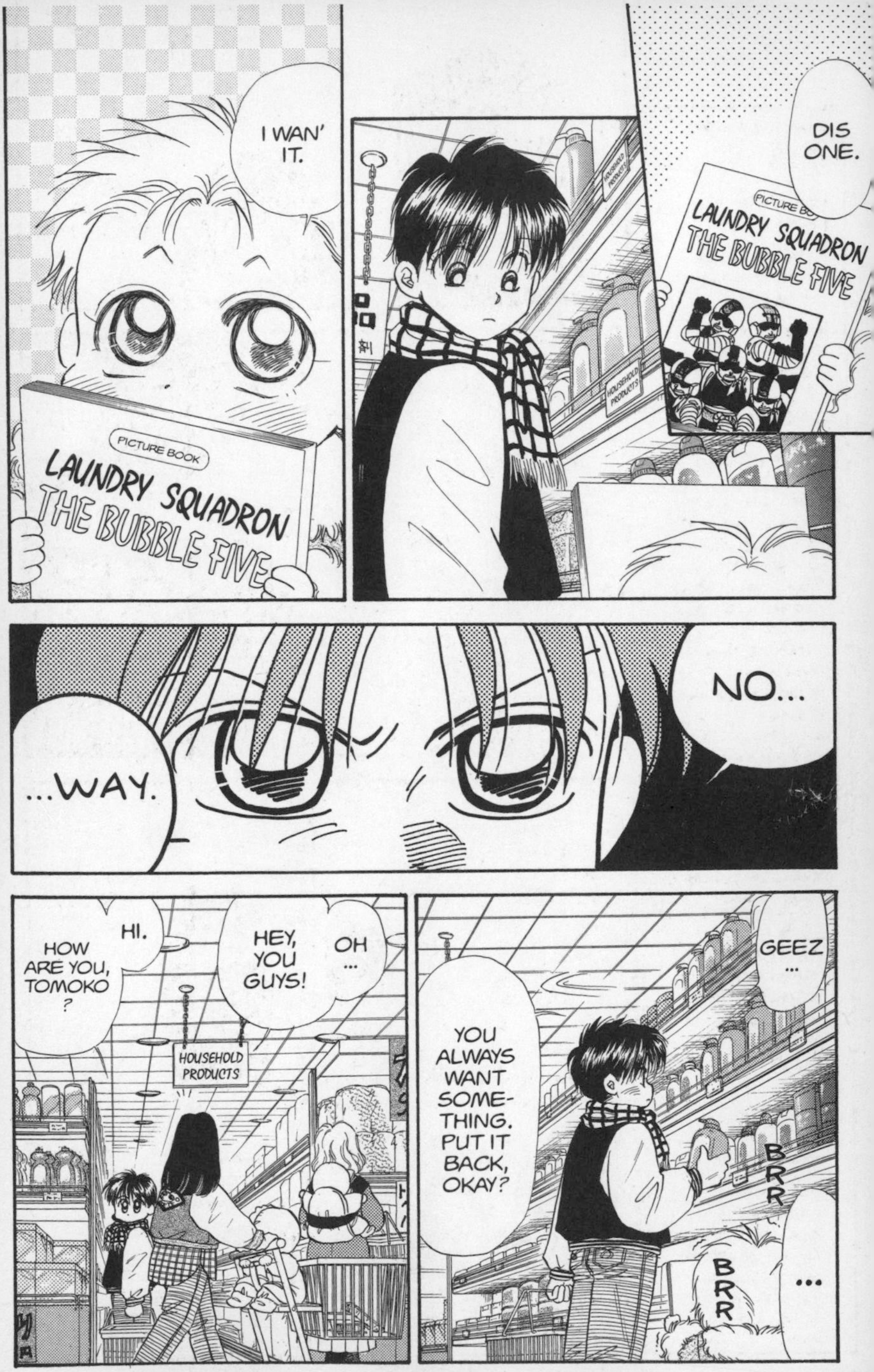
DIS ONE.
PICTURE BO
LAUNDRY SQUADRON THE BUBBLE FIVE
HOUSEHOLD PRODUCTS
HOUSEHOLD PRODUCTS
I WAN' IT.
PICTURE BOOK
LAUNDRY SQUADRON THE BUBBLE FIVE
NO...
...WAY.
GEEZ ...
YOU ALWAYS WANT SOME-THING. PUT IT BACK, OKAY?
BRR
BRR
...
OH ...
HEY, YOU GUYS!
HI.
HOW ARE YOU, TOMOKO?
HOUSEHOLD PRODUCTS

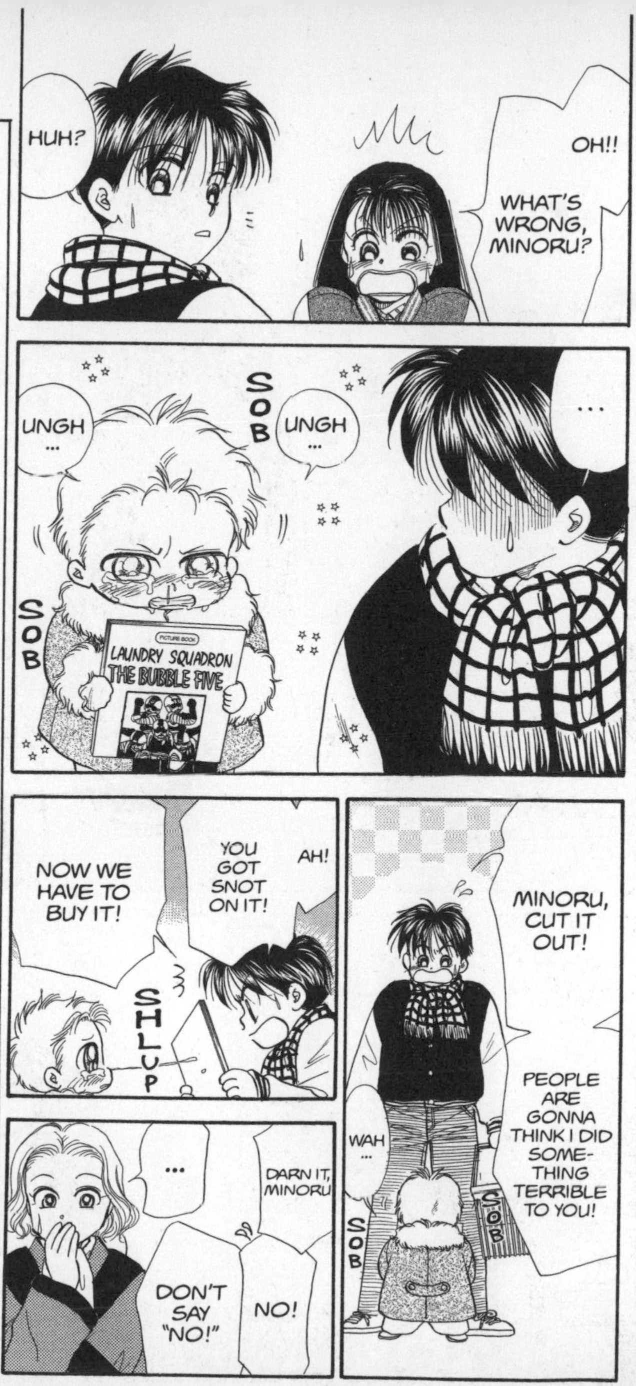
OH!!
WHAT'S WRONG, MINORU?
HUH?
...
UNGH ...
SOB
UNGH ...
SOB
PICTURE BOOK
LAUNDRY SQUADRON THE BUBBLE FIVE
MINORU, CUT IT OUT!
PEOPLE ARE GONNA THINK I DID SOME-THING TERRIBLE TO YOU!
SOB
WAH ...
SOB
AH!
YOU GOT SNOT ON IT!
NOW WE HAVE TO BUY IT!
SHLUP
DARN IT, MINORU
...
NO!
DON'T SAY "NO!"

Author's Note Part 4

Questions from My Readers:

Q: How long does it take you to finish a chapter?

A: I have a deadline every two weeks, so that's how long I spend on each chapter. I need a week or more to create a story-board with panels and rough sketches. It takes a couple of days to pencil it and about four days to ink it. I have assistants who help me with all this. But the truth is, even if I had a whole month to do the work, I'd probably still turn it in at the last minute.

Q: Did you use a colored pencil for the purple background behind Takuya on the back cover of Volume 11?

A: I used a crayon — an oil pastel, to be precise — which is for professional use and a little more expensive than children's crayons.

Q: What are the steps involved in creating manga?

A: Please refer to the Author's notes in volume 8. Do I go through these steps every time? Absolutely. It's the only way to create good stories.

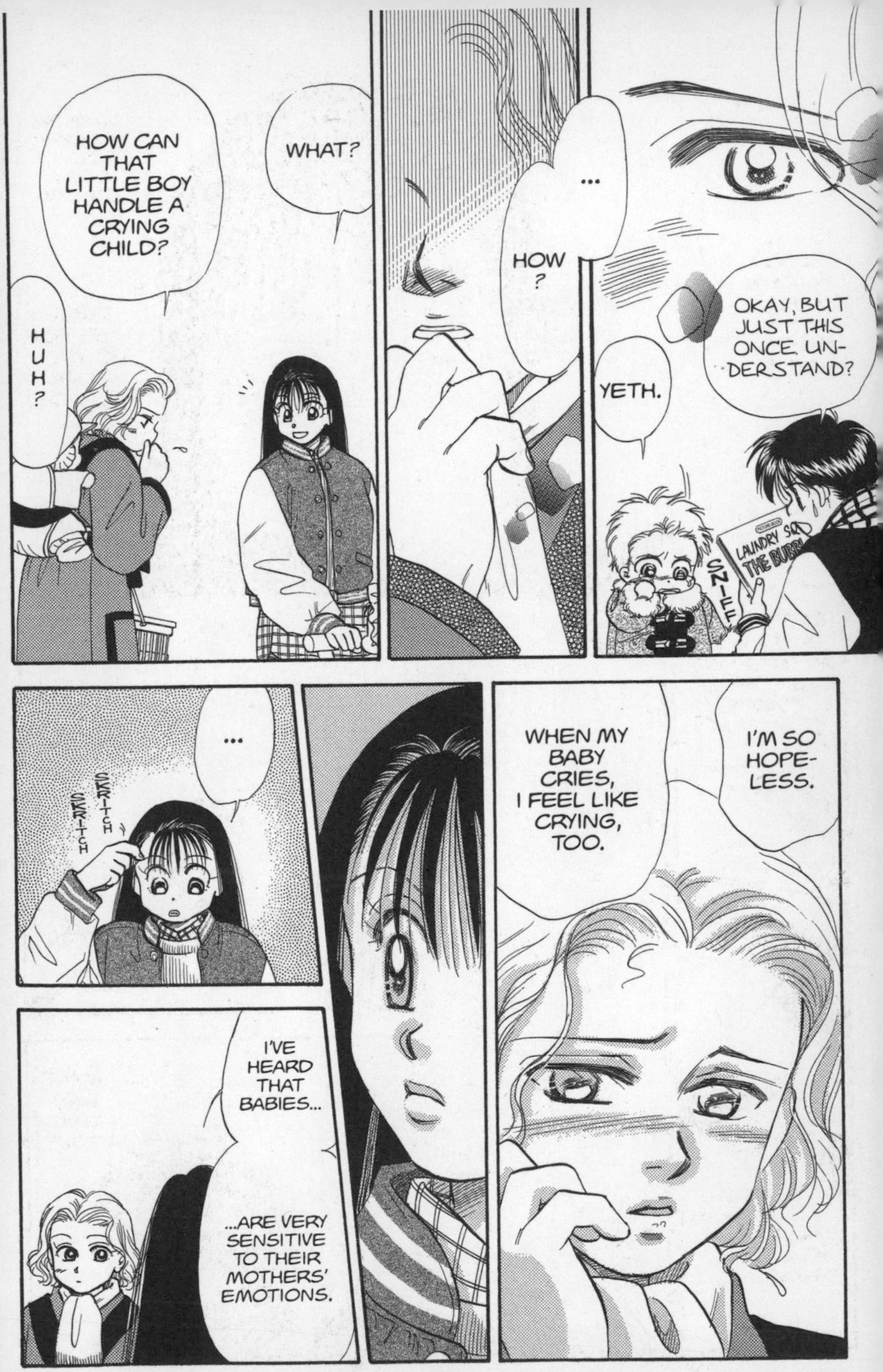
OKAY, BUT JUST THIS ONCE. UNDERSTAND?
YETH.
SNIFF
...
HOW?
WHAT?
HOW CAN THAT LITTLE BOY HANDLE A CRYING CHILD?
HUH?
I'M SO HOPELESS.
WHEN MY BABY CRIES, I FEEL LIKE CRYING, TOO.
...
SKRITCH
SKRITCH
I'VE HEARD THAT BABIES...
...ARE VERY SENSITIVE TO THEIR MOTHERS' EMOTIONS.

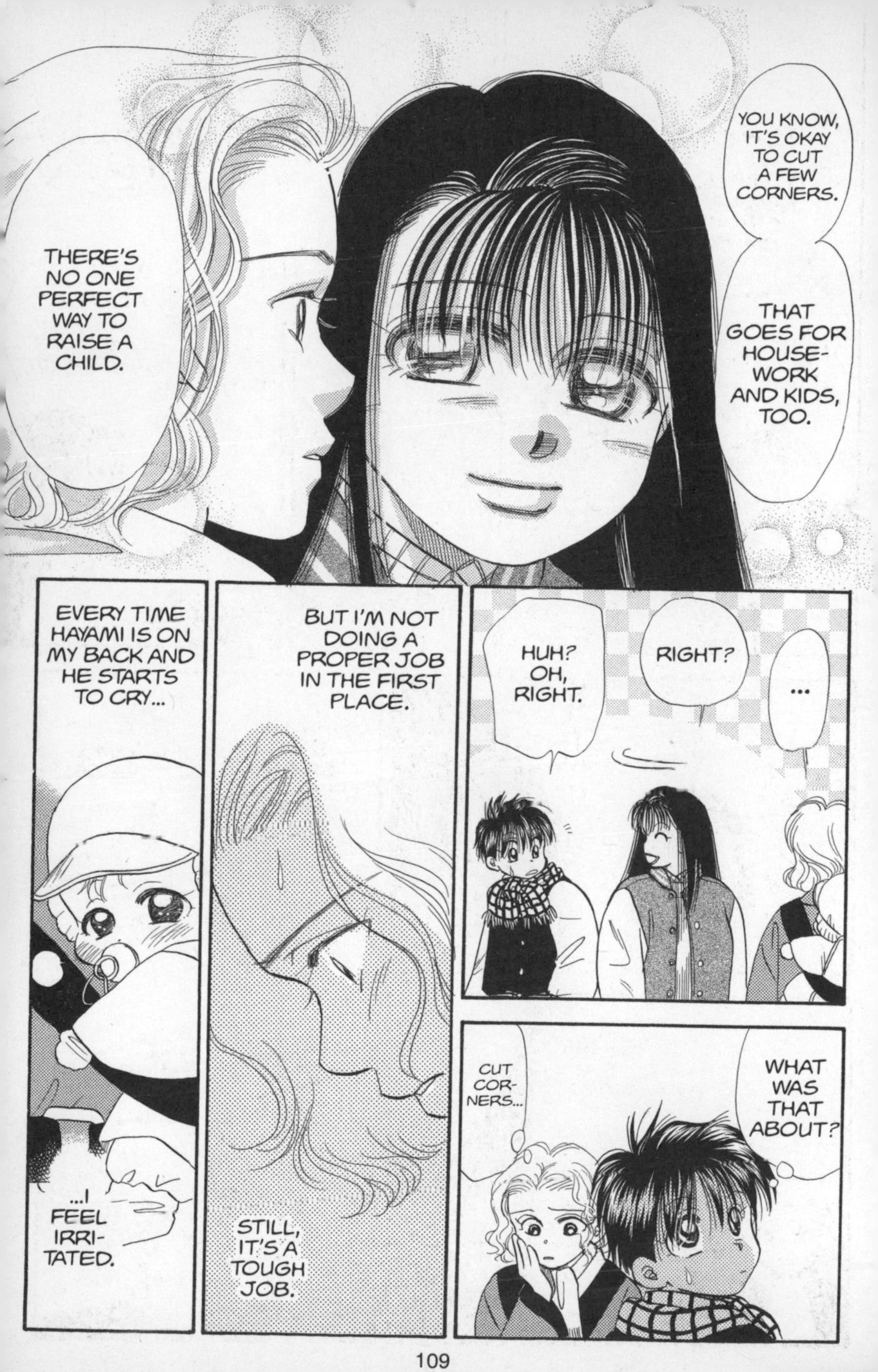
YOU KNOW, IT'S OKAY TO CUT A FEW CORNERS.
THAT GOES FOR HOUSE-WORK AND KIDS, TOO.
THERE'S NO ONE PERFECT WAY TO RAISE A CHILD.
...
RIGHT?
HUH? OH, RIGHT.
WHAT WAS THAT ABOUT?
CUT COR-NERS...
BUT I'M NOT DOING A PROPER JOB IN THE FIRST PLACE.
STILL, IT'S A TOUGH JOB.
EVERY TIME HAYAMI IS ON MY BACK AND HE STARTS TO CRY...
...I FEEL IRRI-TATED.

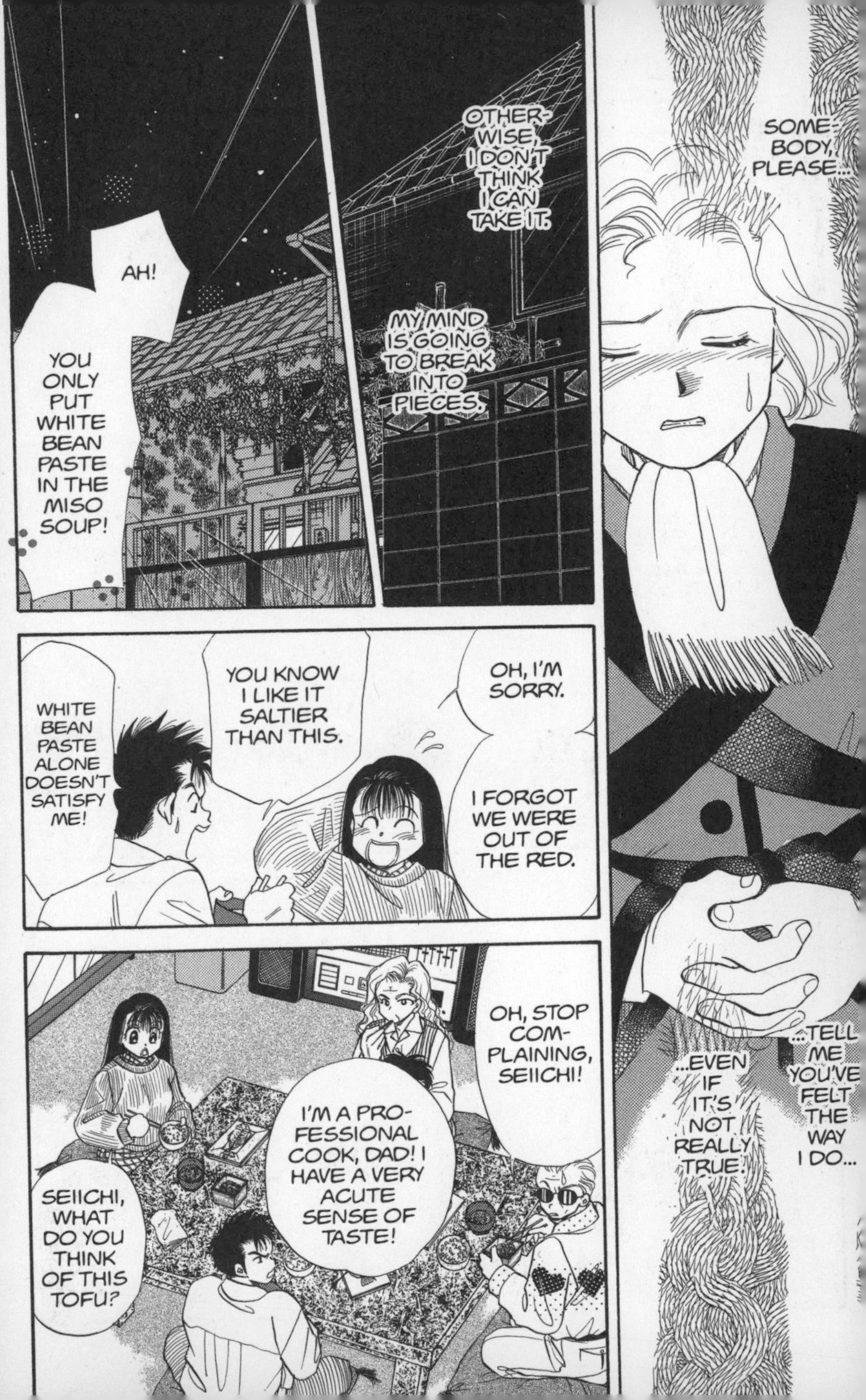
SOMEBODY, PLEASE...
...TELL ME YOU'VE FELT THE WAY I DO...
...EVEN IF IT'S NOT REALLY TRUE.
OTHERWISE, I DON'T THINK I CAN TAKE IT.
MY MIND IS GOING TO BREAK INTO PIECES.
AH!
YOU ONLY PUT WHITE BEAN PASTE IN THE MISO SOUP!
OH, I'M SORRY.
I FORGOT WE WERE OUT OF THE RED.
YOU KNOW I LIKE IT SALTIER THAN THIS.
WHITE BEAN PASTE ALONE DOESN'T SATISFY ME!
OH, STOP COMPLAINING, SEIICHI!
I'M A PROFESSIONAL COOK, DAD! I HAVE A VERY ACUTE SENSE OF TASTE!
SEIICHI, WHAT DO YOU THINK OF THIS TOFU?

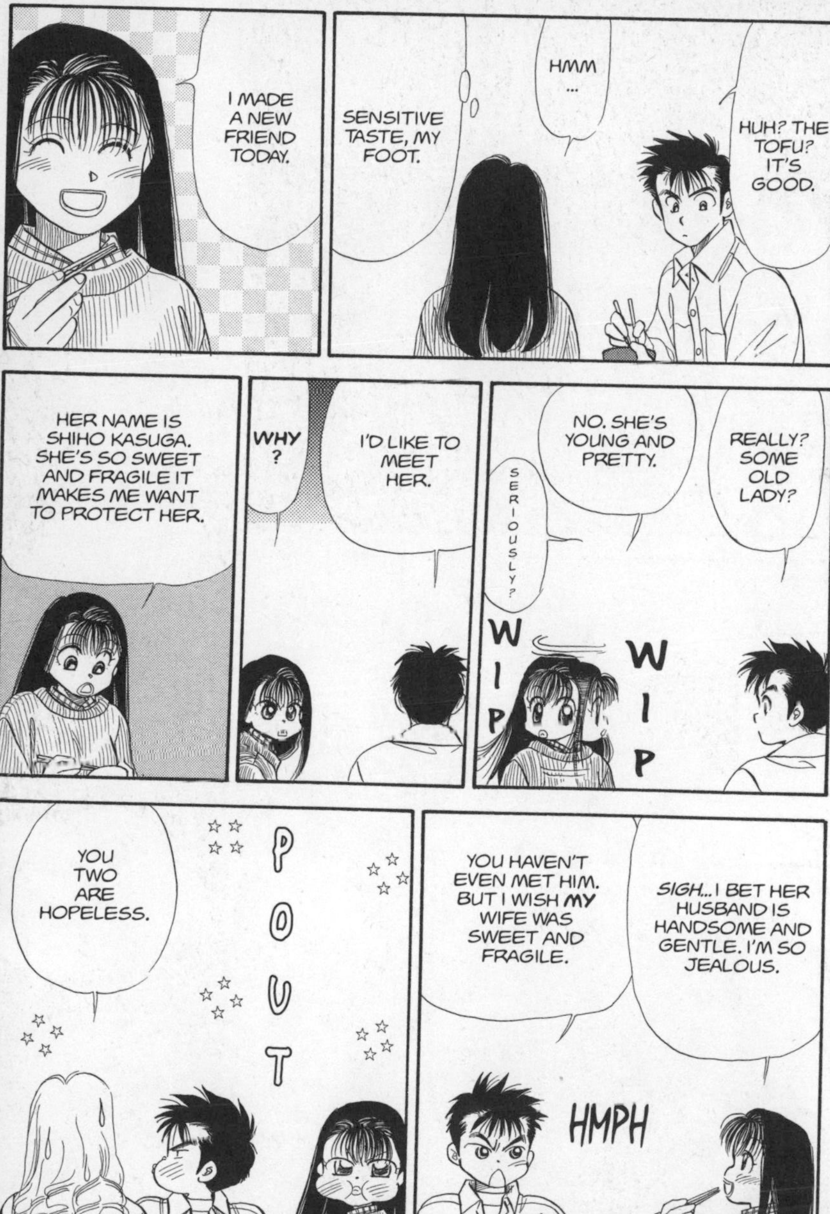
HUH? THE TOFU? IT'S GOOD.
HMM ...
SENSITIVE TASTE, MY FOOT.
I MADE A NEW FRIEND TODAY.
REALLY? SOME OLD LADY?
NO. SHE'S YOUNG AND PRETTY.
SERIOUSLY?
WIP
WIP
I'D LIKE TO MEET HER.
WHY?
HER NAME IS SHIHO KASUGA. SHE'S SO SWEET AND FRAGILE IT MAKES ME WANT TO PROTECT HER.
SIGH... I BET HER HUSBAND IS HANDSOME AND GENTLE. I'M SO JEALOUS.
YOU HAVEN'T EVEN MET HIM. BUT I WISH **MY** WIFE WAS SWEET AND FRAGILE.
HMPH
POUT
YOU TWO ARE HOPELESS.

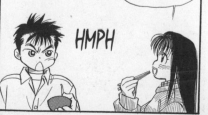

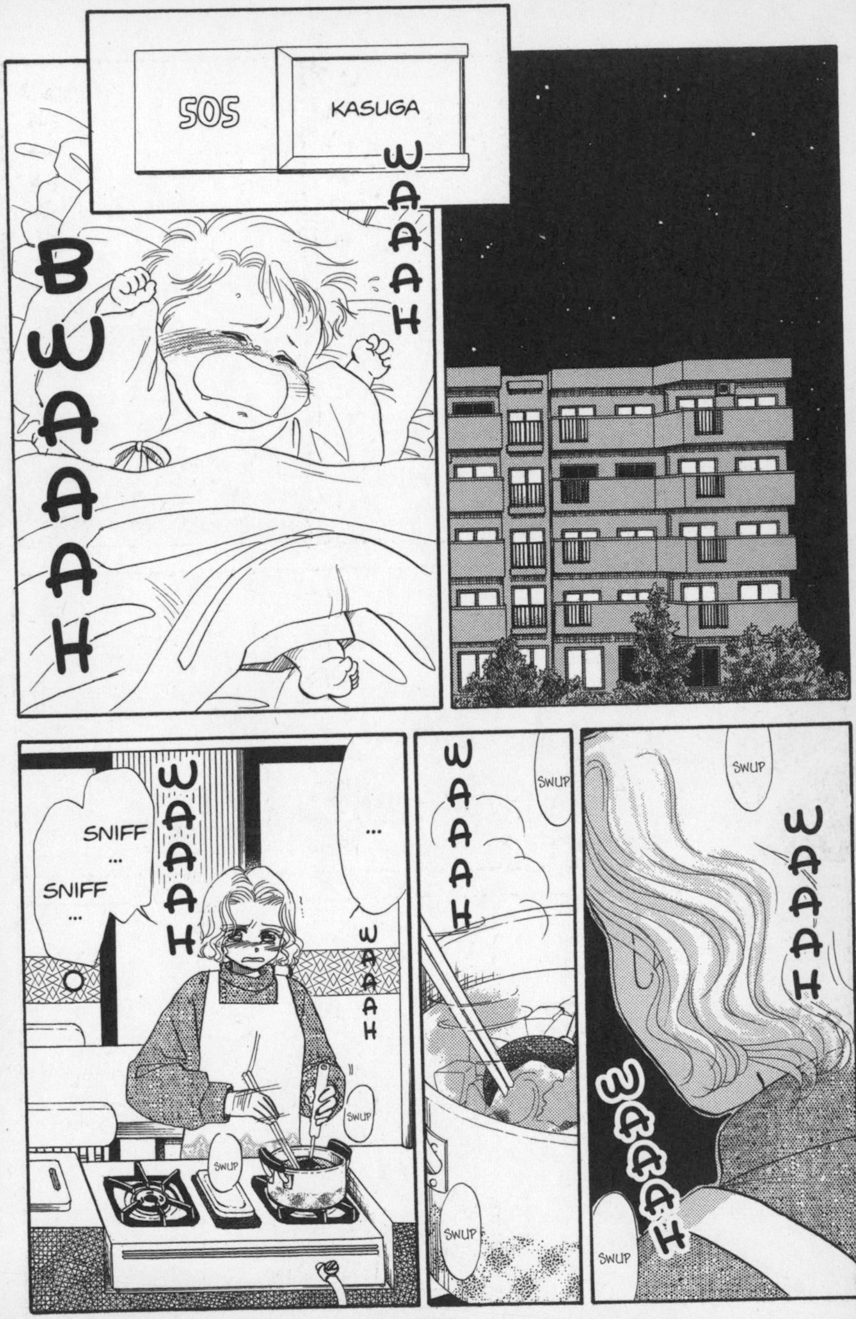
505
KASUGA
WAAAH
BWAAAH
SWUP
WAAAH
WAAAH
SWUP
SWUP
WAAAH
SWUP
...
WAAAH
SNIFF ... SNIFF ...
WAAAH
SWUP
SWUP

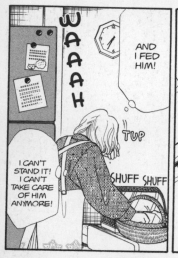

WAAAAAH
MY HEAD IS THROBBING.
SWUP
SWUP
WAAAAAH
WHY IS HE CRYING?
SOB SOB
I JUST CHANGED HIS DIAPER!
WAAAH
AND I FED HIM!
TUP
SHUFF SHUFF
I CAN'T STAND IT! I CAN'T TAKE CARE OF HIM ANYMORE!
EAR PLUGS
PLUNK
SKWIK
OOO
I JUST DON'T UNDERSTAND.
I WANTED A BABY SO BADLY.
TAK TAK TAK
I WANTED TO DO SO MANY THINGS FOR HAYAMI BEFORE HE WAS BORN.
SIGH

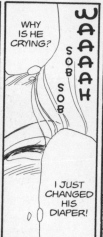

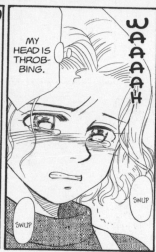

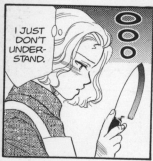

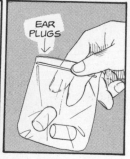

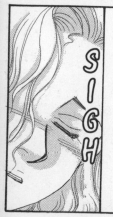

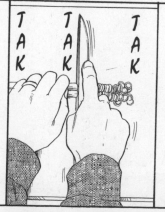

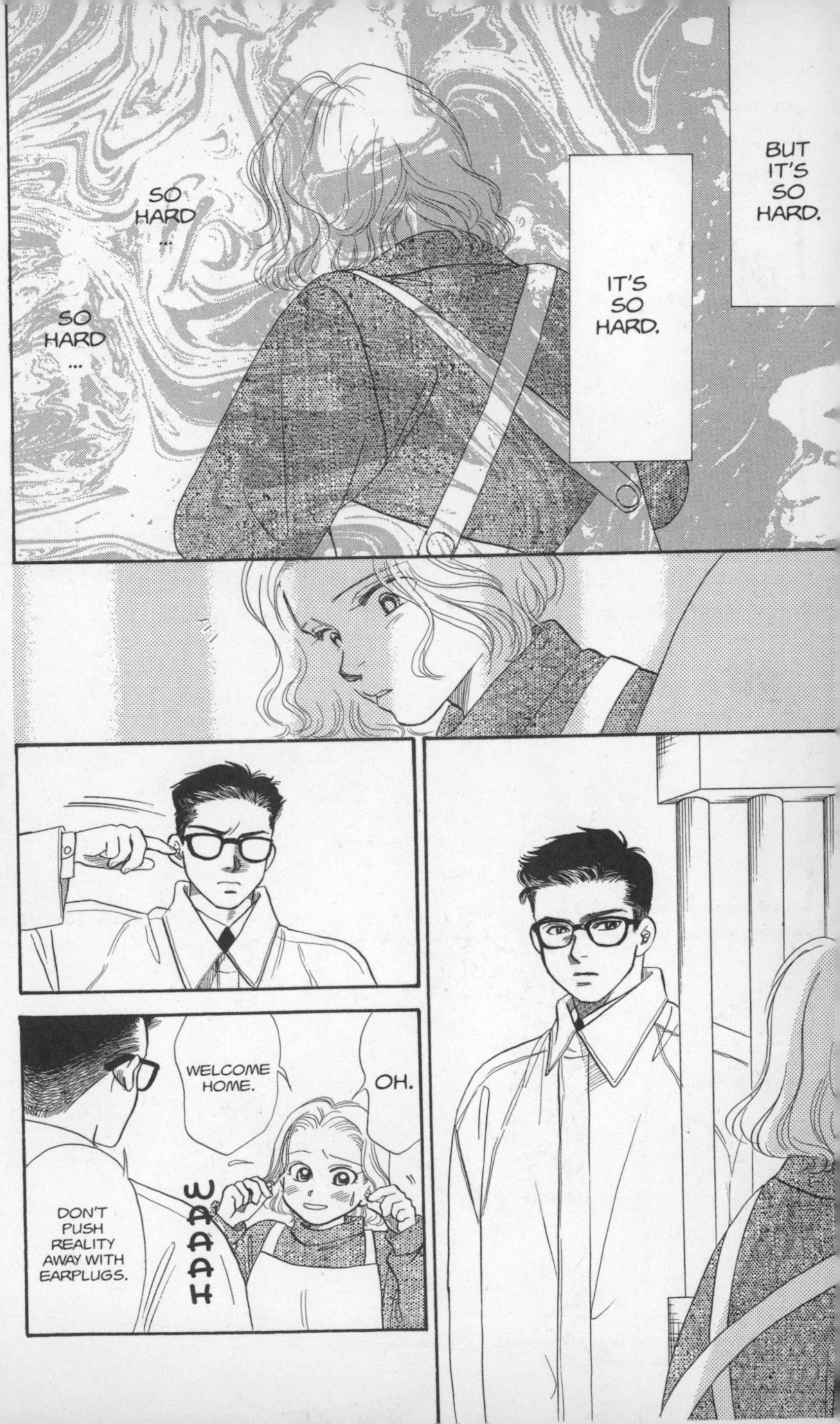

BUT IT'S SO HARD.
IT'S SO HARD.
SO HARD ...
SO HARD ...
OH.
WELCOME HOME.
WAAAH
DON'T PUSH REALITY AWAY WITH EARPLUGS.

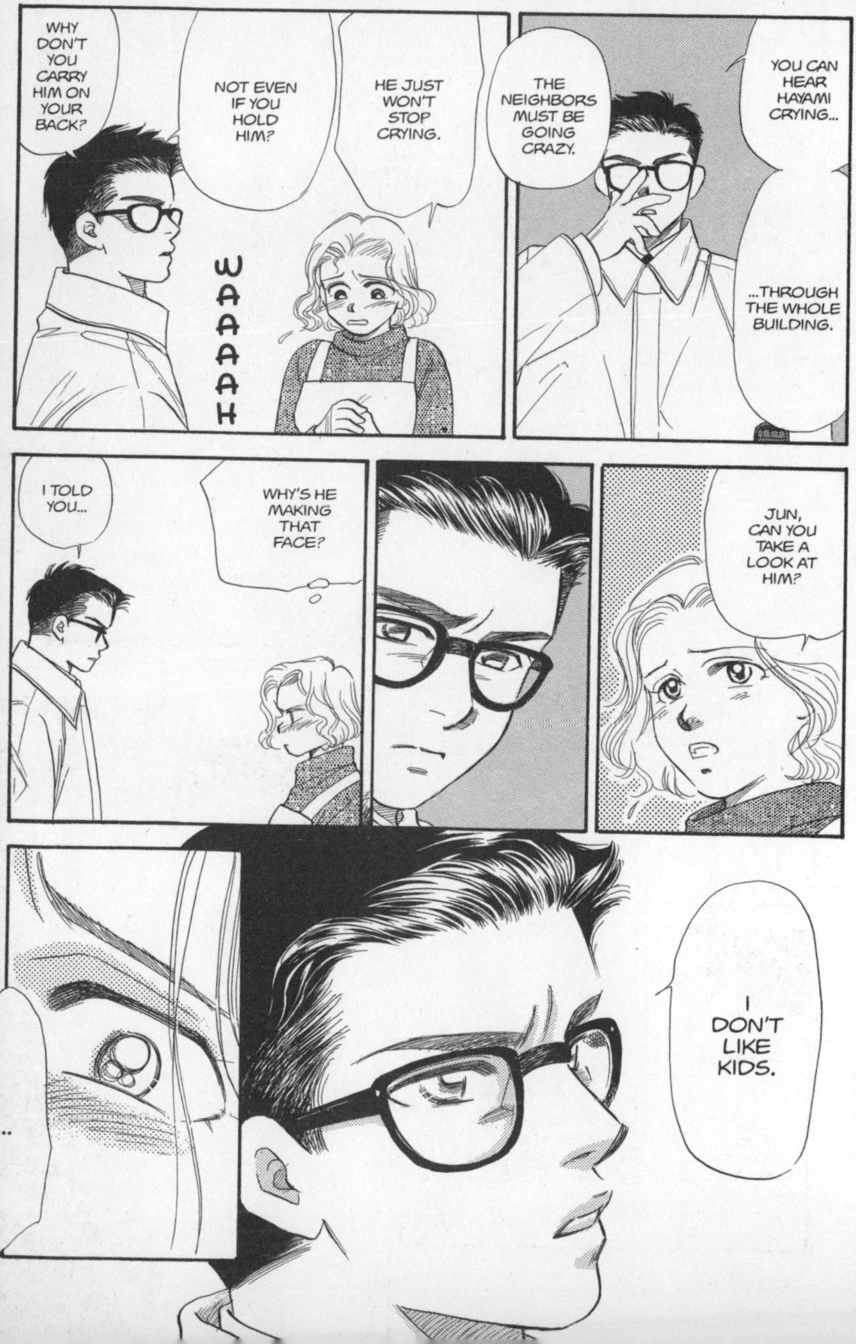
YOU CAN HEAR HAYAMI CRYING...
...THROUGH THE WHOLE BUILDING.
THE NEIGHBORS MUST BE GOING CRAZY.
HE JUST WON'T STOP CRYING.
NOT EVEN IF YOU HOLD HIM?
WHY DON'T YOU CARRY HIM ON YOUR BACK?
WAAAAAH
JUN, CAN YOU TAKE A LOOK AT HIM?
WHY'S HE MAKING THAT FACE?
I TOLD YOU...
I DON'T LIKE KIDS.
...

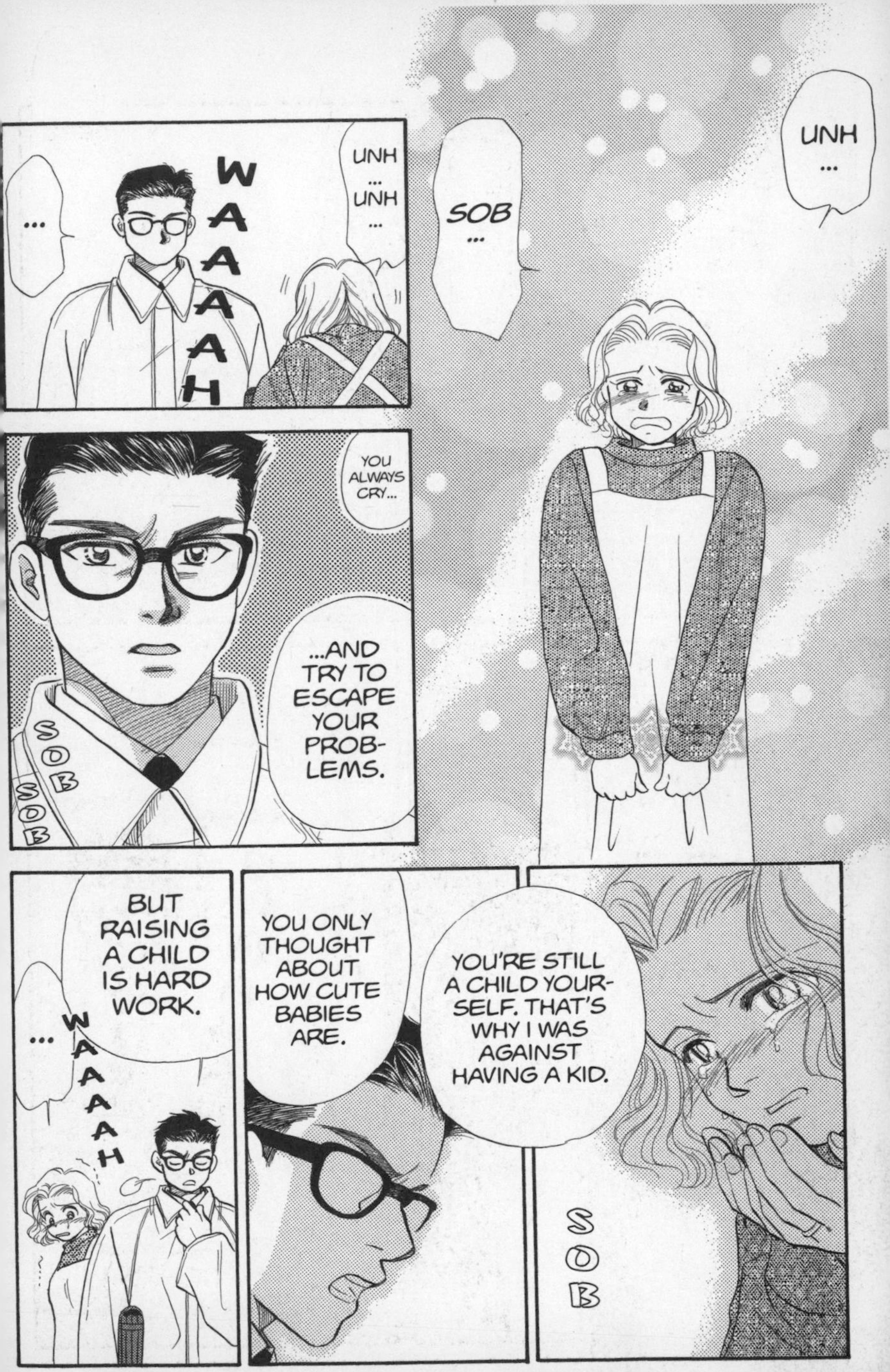
UNH ...
SOB ...
UNH ... UNH ...
WAAAAH
...
YOU ALWAYS CRY...
...AND TRY TO ESCAPE YOUR PROBLEMS.
SOB SOB
YOU'RE STILL A CHILD YOURSELF. THAT'S WHY I WAS AGAINST HAVING A KID.
SOB
YOU ONLY THOUGHT ABOUT HOW CUTE BABIES ARE.
BUT RAISING A CHILD IS HARD WORK.
...
WAAAAH

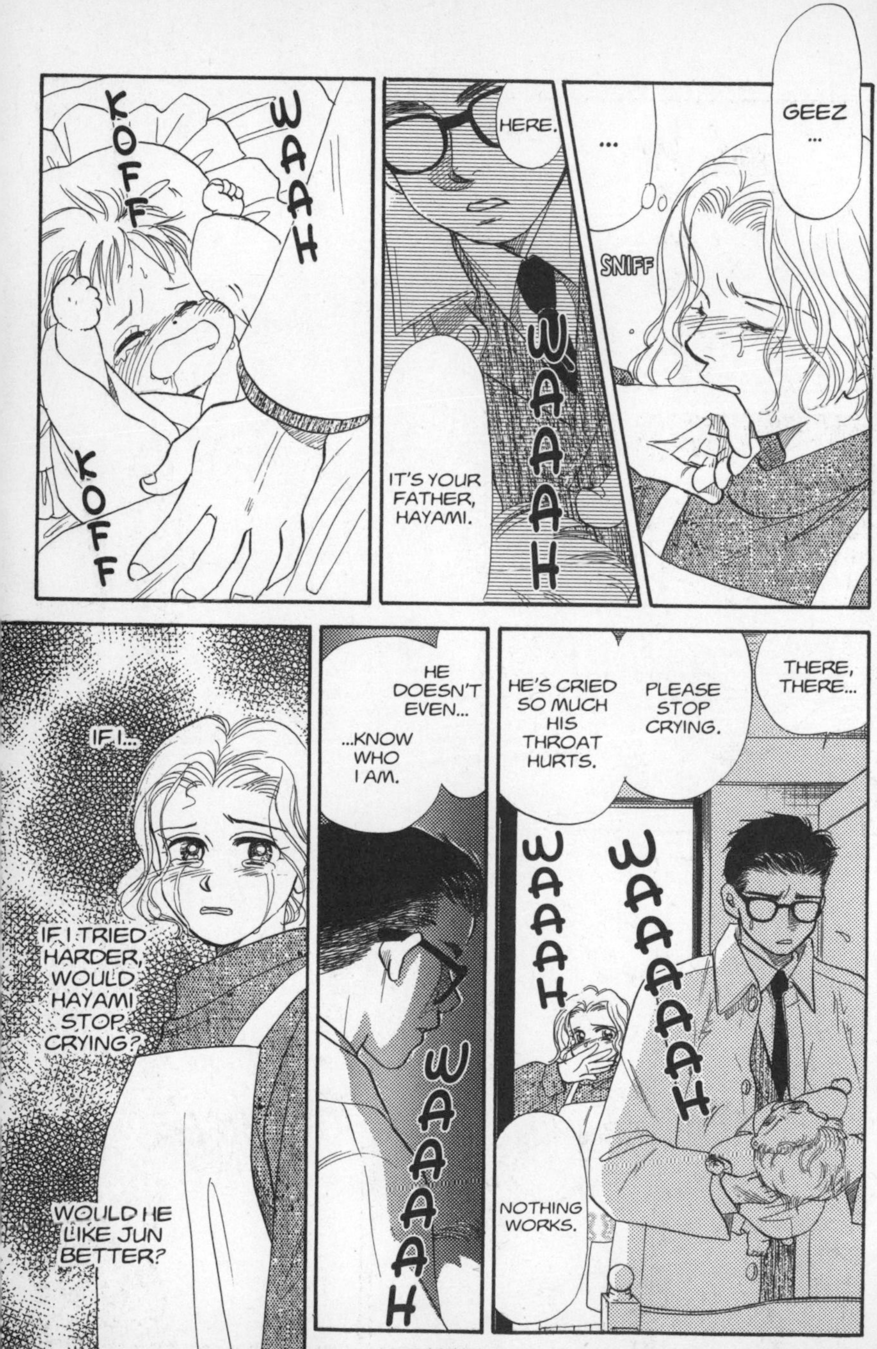
GEEZ ...
...
SNIFF
HERE.
WAAAAH
IT'S YOUR FATHER, HAYAMI.
KOFF
WAAH
KOFF
THERE, THERE...
PLEASE STOP CRYING.
HE'S CRIED SO MUCH HIS THROAT HURTS.
WAAAAAAH
WAAAAH
NOTHING WORKS.
HE DOESN'T EVEN...
...KNOW WHO I AM.
WAAAAAH
IF I...
IF I TRIED HARDER, WOULD HAYAMI STOP CRYING?
WOULD HE LIKE JUN BETTER?

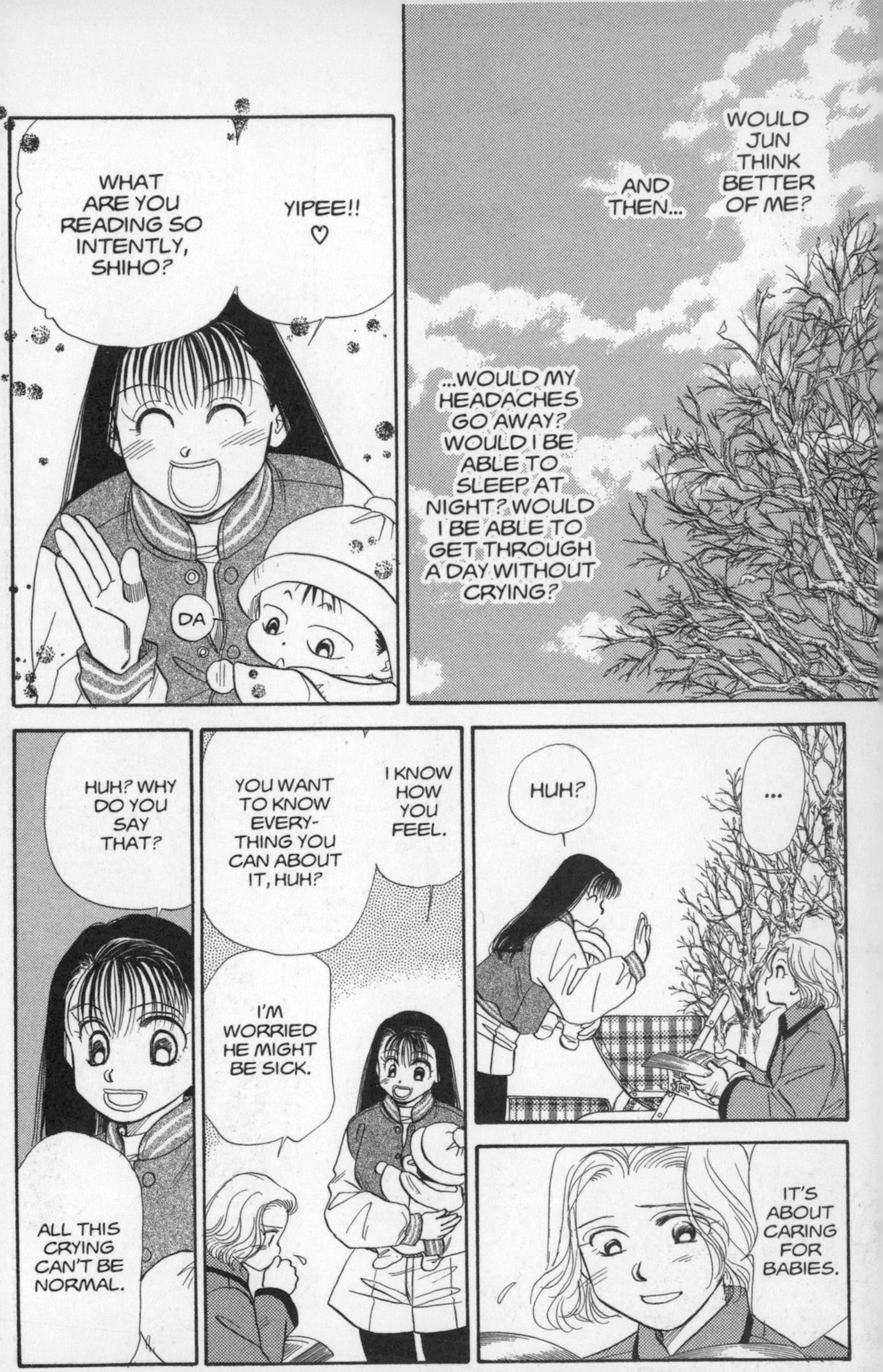
WOULD JUN THINK BETTER OF ME?
AND THEN...
...WOULD MY HEADACHES GO AWAY? WOULD I BE ABLE TO SLEEP AT NIGHT? WOULD I BE ABLE TO GET THROUGH A DAY WITHOUT CRYING?
YIPEE!! ♡
WHAT ARE YOU READING SO INTENTLY, SHIHO?
DA
...
HUH?
IT'S ABOUT CARING FOR BABIES.
I KNOW HOW YOU FEEL.
YOU WANT TO KNOW EVERY-THING YOU CAN ABOUT IT, HUH?
I'M WORRIED HE MIGHT BE SICK.
HUH? WHY DO YOU SAY THAT?
ALL THIS CRYING CAN'T BE NORMAL.

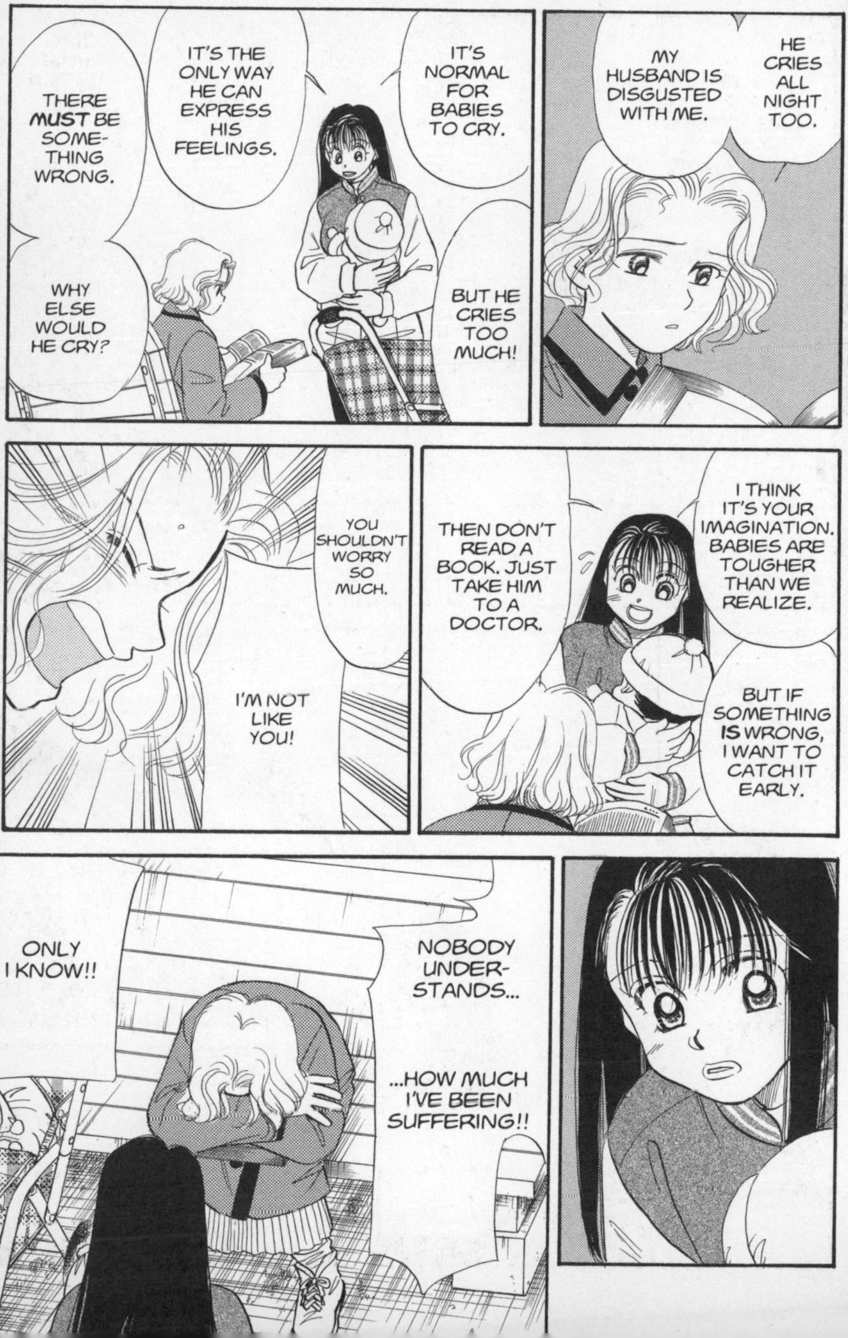
HE CRIES ALL NIGHT TOO.
MY HUSBAND IS DISGUSTED WITH ME.
IT'S NORMAL FOR BABIES TO CRY.
IT'S THE ONLY WAY HE CAN EXPRESS HIS FEELINGS.
BUT HE CRIES TOO MUCH!
THERE MUST BE SOMETHING WRONG.
WHY ELSE WOULD HE CRY?
I THINK IT'S YOUR IMAGINATION. BABIES ARE TOUGHER THAN WE REALIZE.
BUT IF SOMETHING IS WRONG, I WANT TO CATCH IT EARLY.
THEN DON'T READ A BOOK. JUST TAKE HIM TO A DOCTOR.
YOU SHOULDN'T WORRY SO MUCH.
I'M NOT LIKE YOU!
NOBODY UNDERSTANDS...
...HOW MUCH I'VE BEEN SUFFERING!!
ONLY I KNOW!!

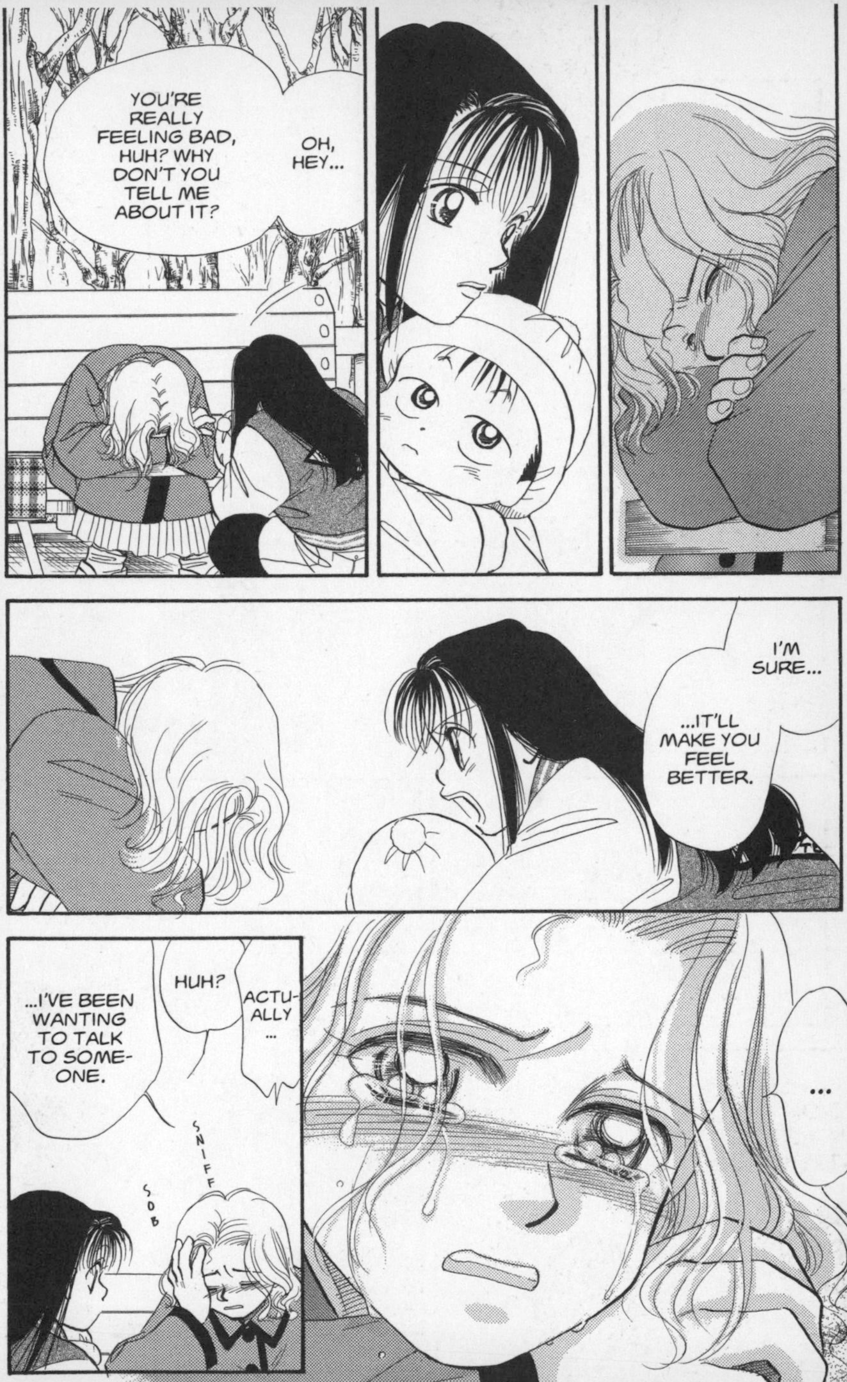
OH, HEY...
YOU'RE REALLY FEELING BAD, HUH? WHY DON'T YOU TELL ME ABOUT IT?
I'M SURE...
...IT'LL MAKE YOU FEEL BETTER.
...
ACTU-ALLY...
HUH?
...I'VE BEEN WANTING TO TALK TO SOME-ONE.
SNIFF
SOB

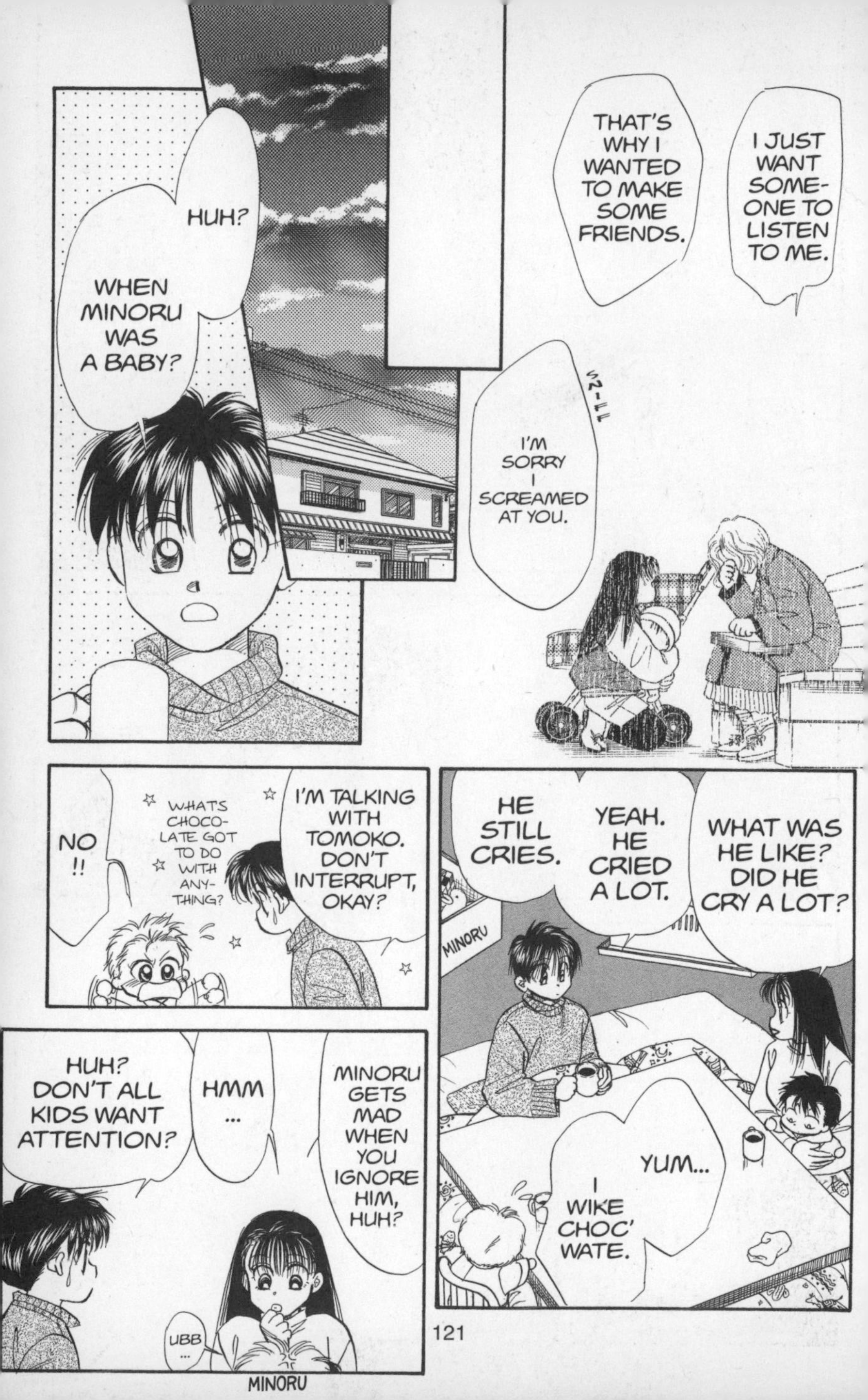
I JUST WANT SOME-ONE TO LISTEN TO ME.
THAT'S WHY I WANTED TO MAKE SOME FRIENDS.
SNIFF
I'M SORRY I SCREAMED AT YOU.
HUH?
WHEN MINORU WAS A BABY?
WHAT WAS HE LIKE? DID HE CRY A LOT?
YEAH. HE CRIED A LOT.
HE STILL CRIES.
MINORU
YUM...
I WIKE CHOC' WATE.
I'M TALKING WITH TOMOKO. DON'T INTERRUPT, OKAY?
WHATS CHOCO-LATE GOT TO DO WITH ANY-THING?
NO !!
MINORU GETS MAD WHEN YOU IGNORE HIM, HUH?
HMM ...
HUH? DON'T ALL KIDS WANT ATTENTION?
UBB ...
MINORU

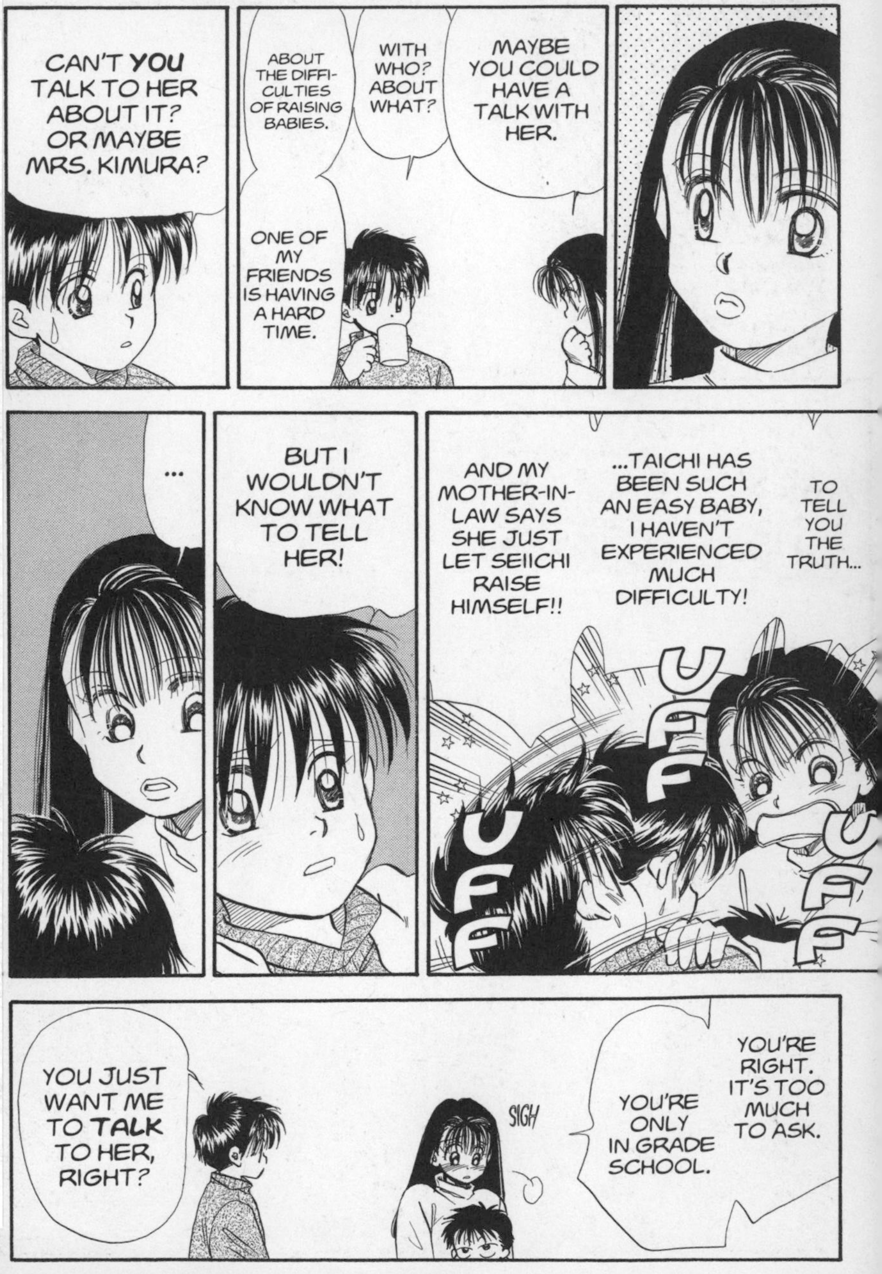
MAYBE YOU COULD HAVE A TALK WITH HER.
WITH WHO? ABOUT WHAT?
ABOUT THE DIFFICULTIES OF RAISING BABIES.
ONE OF MY FRIENDS IS HAVING A HARD TIME.
CAN'T **YOU** TALK TO HER ABOUT IT? OR MAYBE MRS. KIMURA?
TO TELL YOU THE TRUTH...
...TAICHI HAS BEEN SUCH AN EASY BABY, I HAVEN'T EXPERIENCED MUCH DIFFICULTY!
AND MY MOTHER-IN-LAW SAYS SHE JUST LET SEIICHI RAISE HIMSELF!!
UFF
UFF
UFF
UFF
BUT I WOULDN'T KNOW WHAT TO TELL HER!
...
YOU'RE RIGHT. IT'S TOO MUCH TO ASK.
YOU'RE ONLY IN GRADE SCHOOL.
SIGH
YOU JUST WANT ME TO **TALK** TO HER, RIGHT?

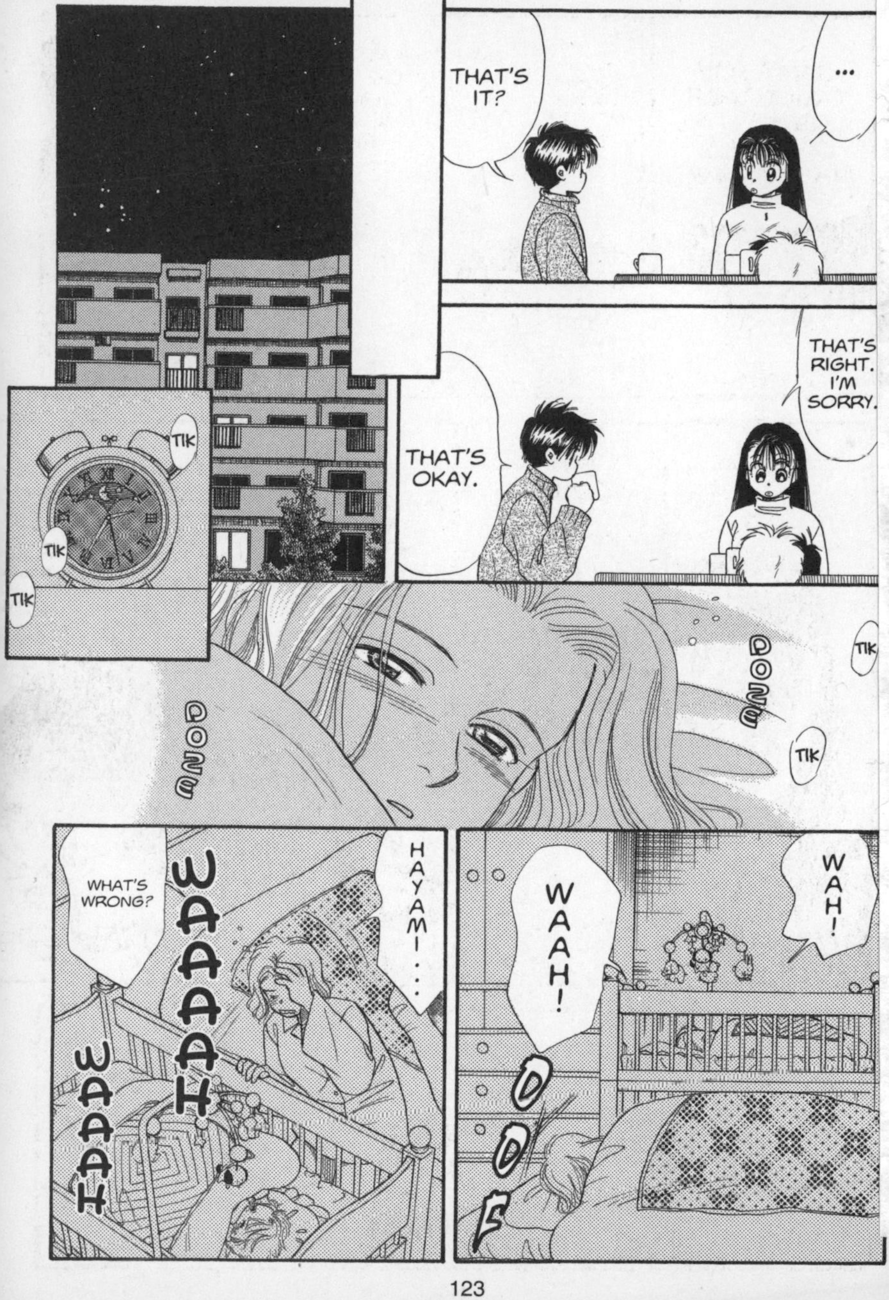
...
THAT'S IT?
THAT'S RIGHT. I'M SORRY.
THAT'S OKAY.
TIK
TIK
TIK
TIK
DOZE
TIK
DOZE
WAH!
WAAAH!
OOF
HAYAMI...
WHAT'S WRONG?
WAAAAAH
WAAAAH

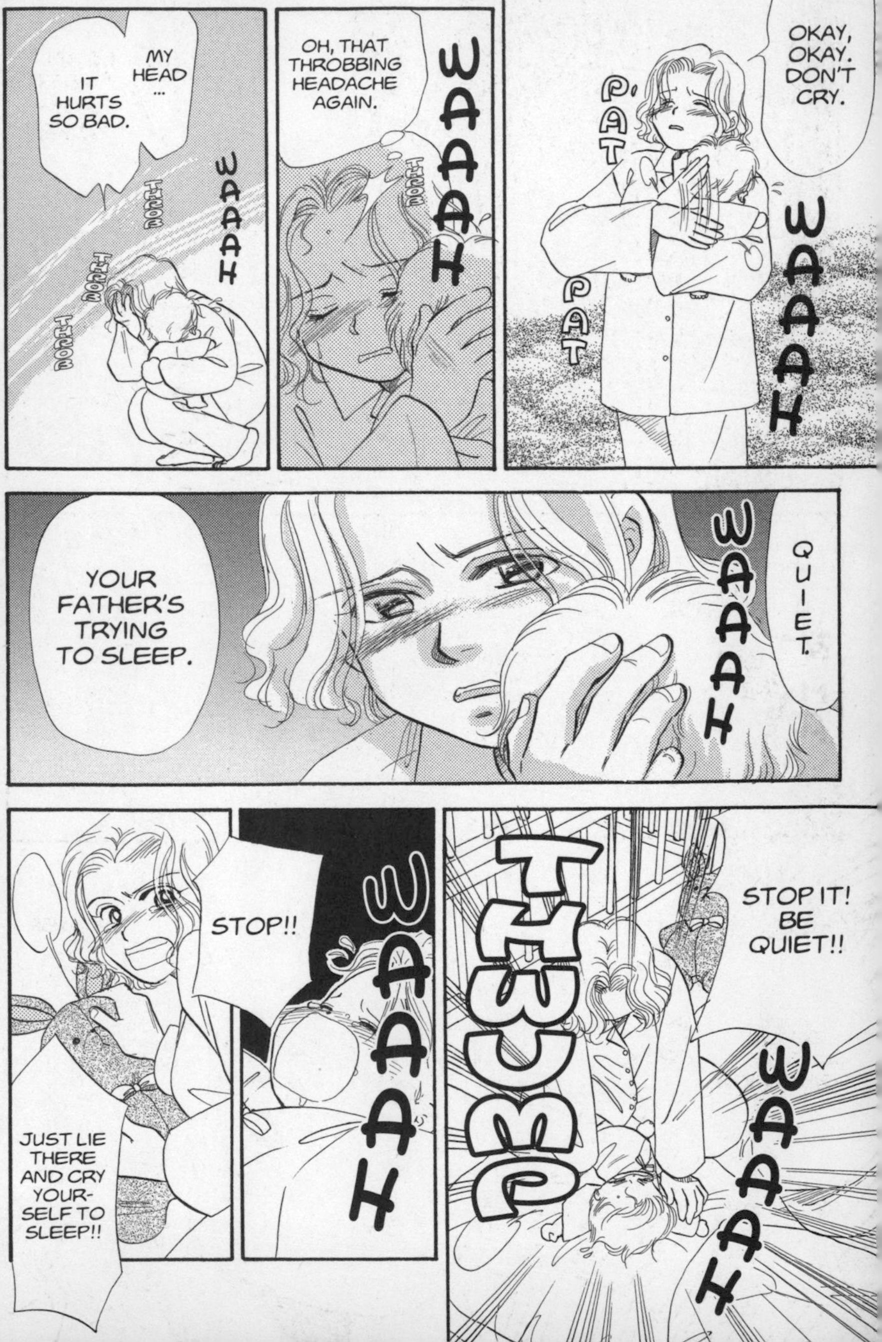
OKAY, OKAY. DON'T CRY.
PAT PAT
WAAAAH
OH, THAT THROBBING HEADACHE AGAIN.
WAAAAH
THROB
MY HEAD ...
IT HURTS SO BAD.
WAAAH
THROB
THROB
THROB
QUIET.
WAAAAAH
YOUR FATHER'S TRYING TO SLEEP.
STOP IT! BE QUIET!!
WAAAAH
THUMP
WAAAAH
STOP!!
JUST LIE THERE AND CRY YOURSELF TO SLEEP!!

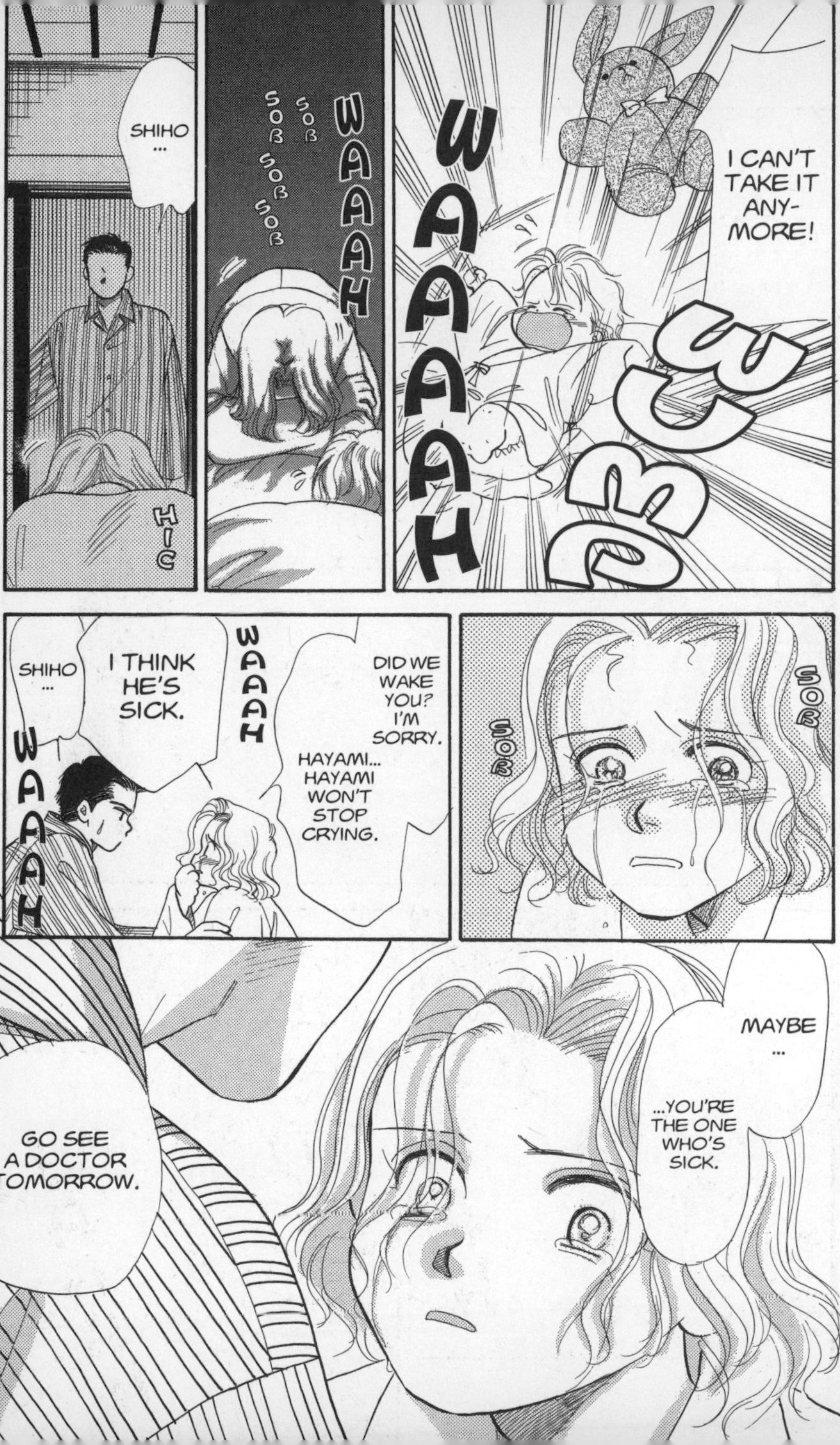
I CAN'T TAKE IT ANY-MORE!
WAAAAAH
WAAAAH
SOB SOB
SOB SOB SOB
SHIHO ...
HIC
SOB
SOB
DID WE WAKE YOU? I'M SORRY.
HAYAMI... HAYAMI WON'T STOP CRYING.
WAAAH
SHIHO ...
I THINK HE'S SICK.
WAAAH
MAYBE ...
...YOU'RE THE ONE WHO'S SICK.
GO SEE A DOCTOR TOMORROW.

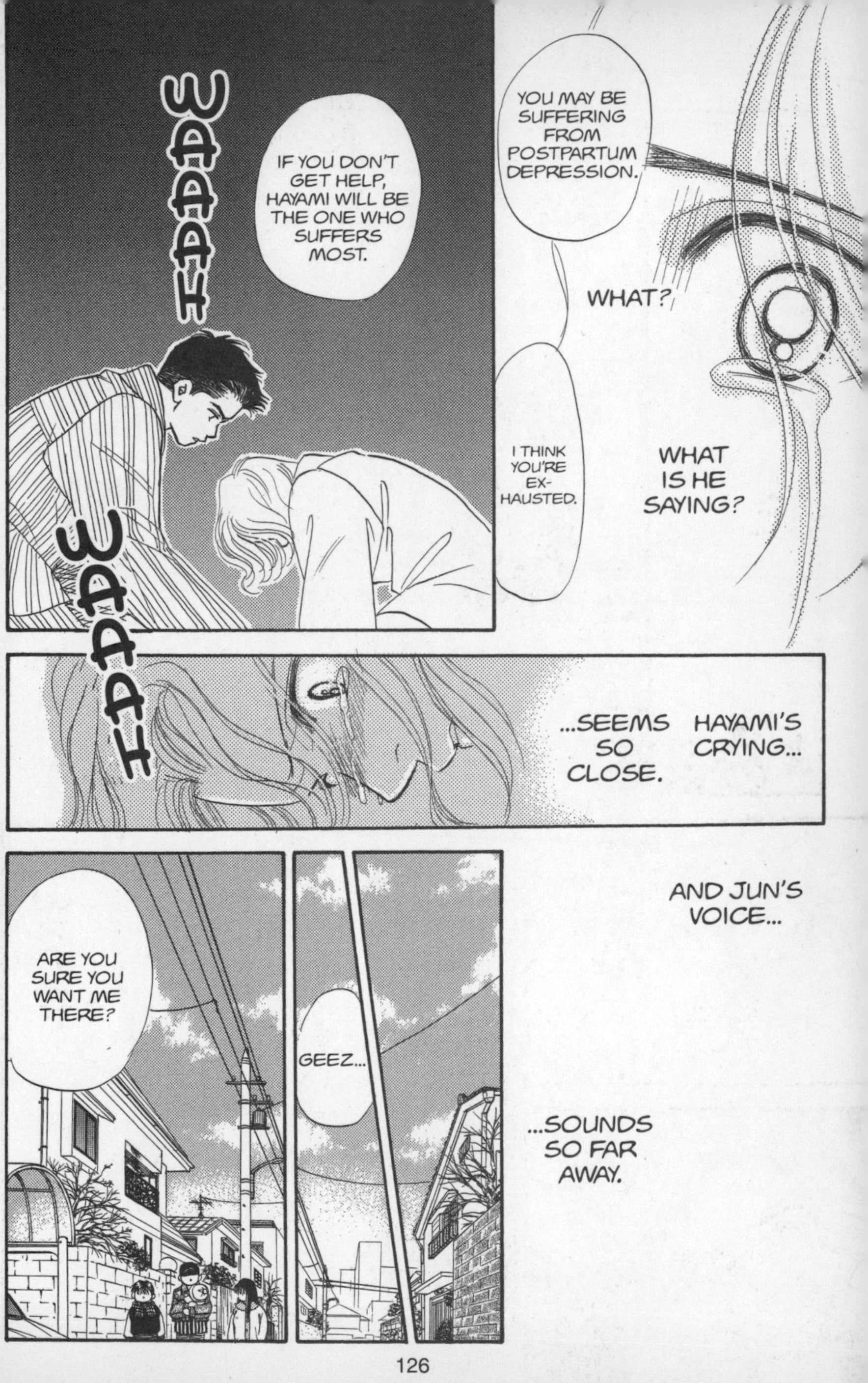
YOU MAY BE SUFFERING FROM POSTPARTUM DEPRESSION.
WHAT?
I THINK YOU'RE EX-HAUSTED.
WHAT IS HE SAYING?
IF YOU DON'T GET HELP, HAYAMI WILL BE THE ONE WHO SUFFERS MOST.
WAAAH
WAAAH
HAYAMI'S CRYING...
...SEEMS SO CLOSE.
AND JUN'S VOICE...
...SOUNDS SO FAR AWAY.
GEEZ...
ARE YOU SURE YOU WANT ME THERE?

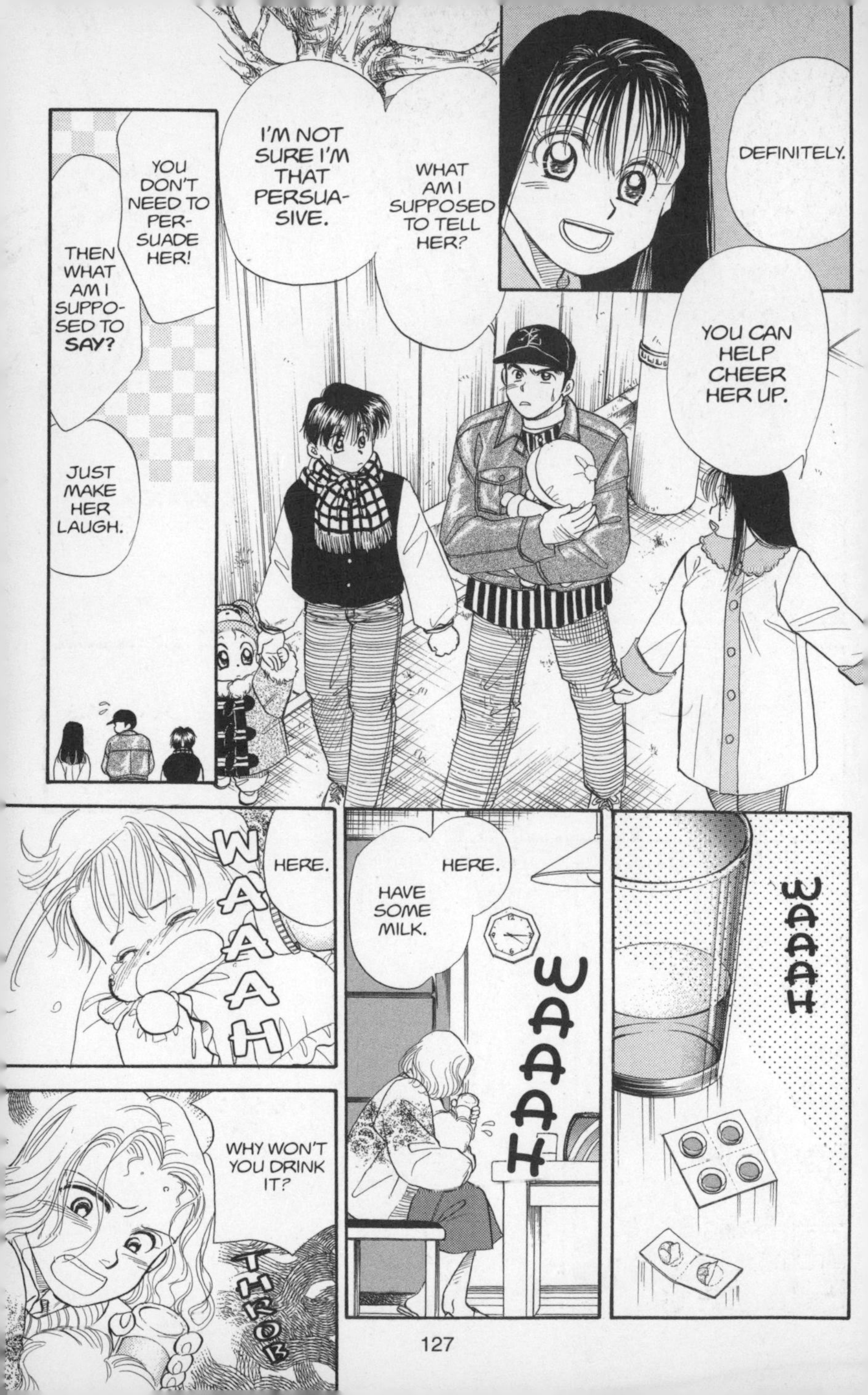
DEFINITELY.
YOU CAN HELP CHEER HER UP.
WHAT AM I SUPPOSED TO TELL HER?
I'M NOT SURE I'M THAT PERSUASIVE.
YOU DON'T NEED TO PERSUADE HER!
THEN WHAT AM I SUPPOSED TO SAY?
JUST MAKE HER LAUGH.
WAAAAH
HERE.
HAVE SOME MILK.
WAAAAH
HERE.
WAAAAH
WHY WON'T YOU DRINK IT?
THROB

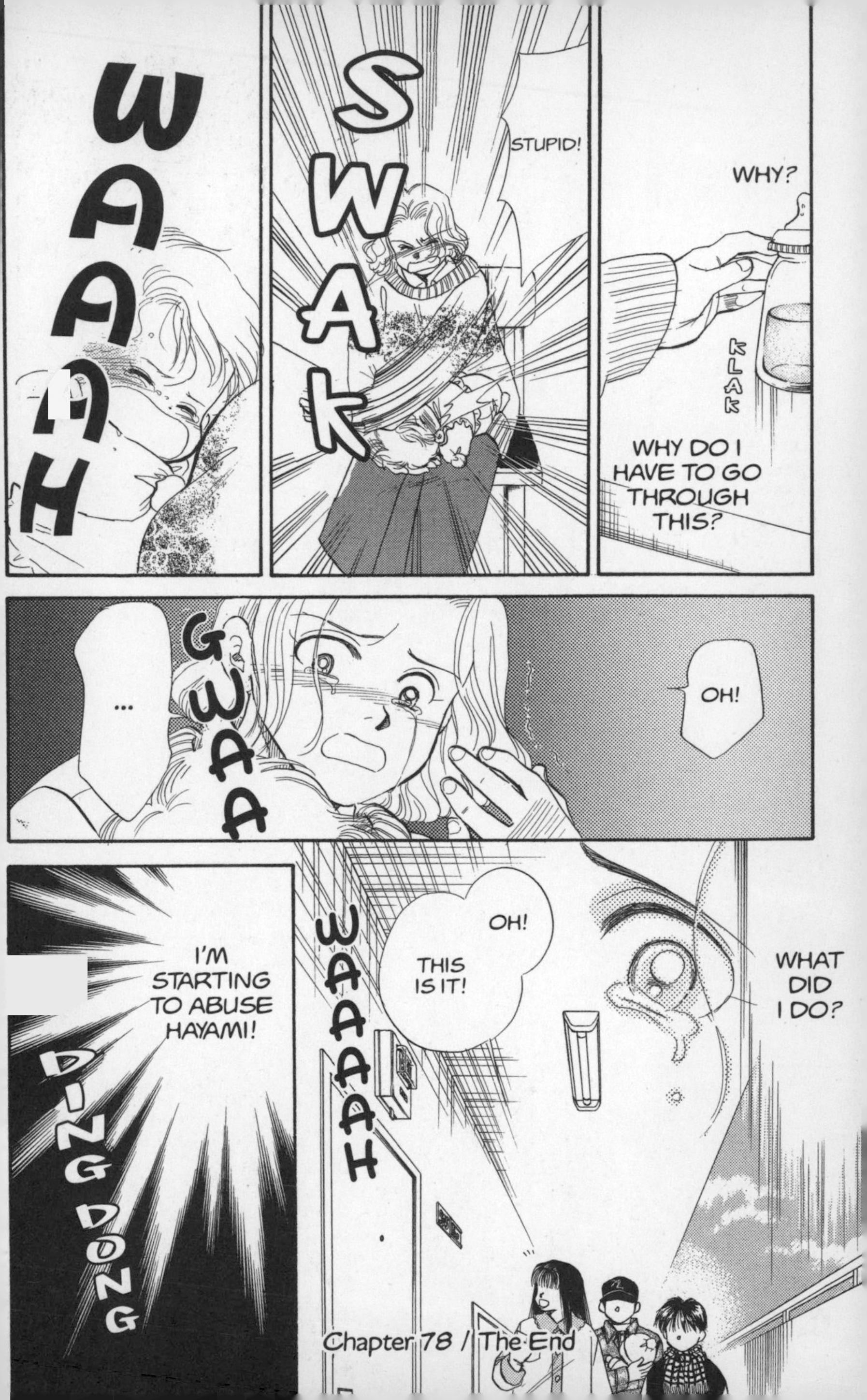
WHY?
KLAK
WHY DO I HAVE TO GO THROUGH THIS?
SWAK
STUPID!
WAAAH
OH!
GWAAA
...
WHAT DID I DO?
OH!
THIS IS IT!
WAAAAAH
I'M STARTING TO ABUSE HAYAMI!
DING DONG
Chapter 78 / The End

Chapter 79

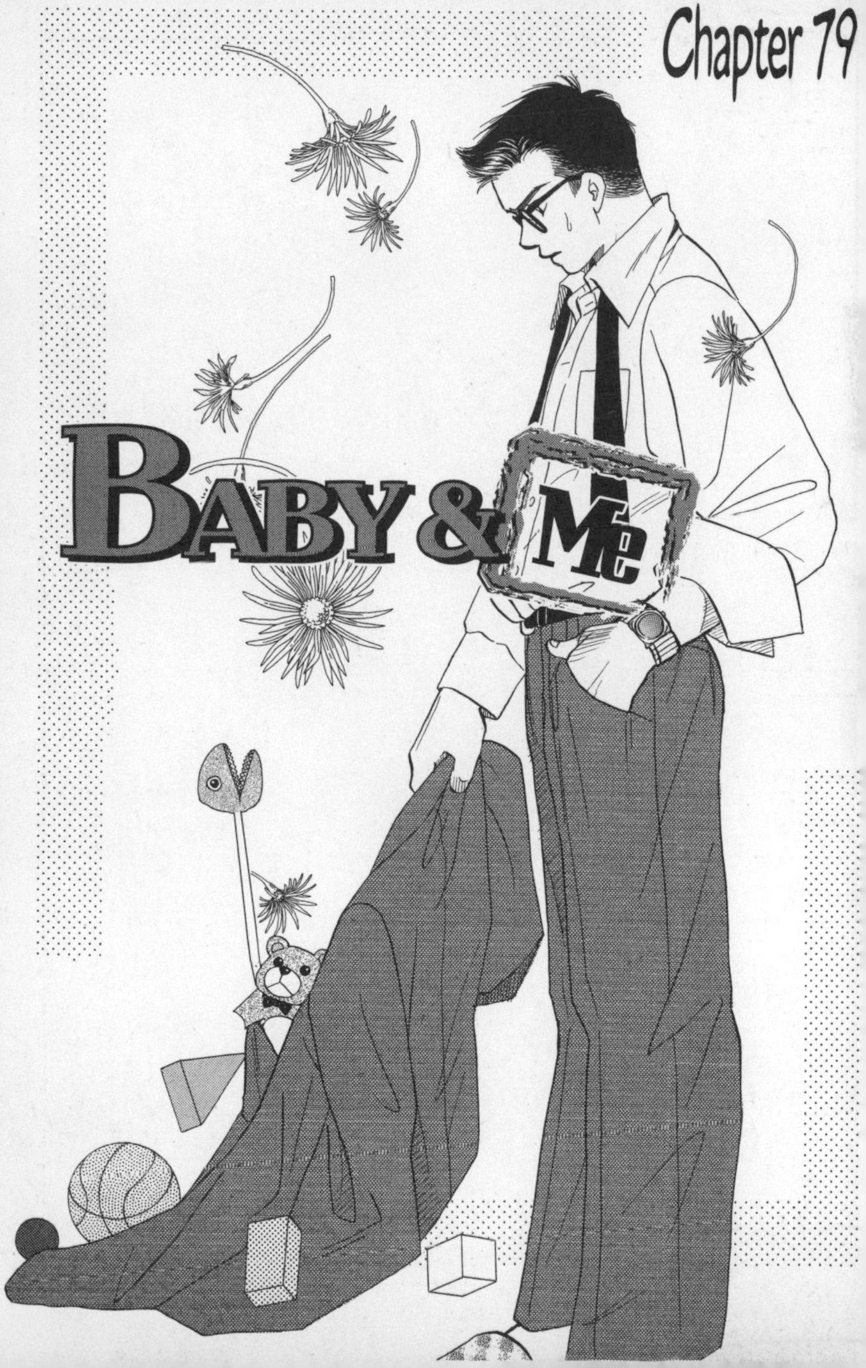
BABY & ME

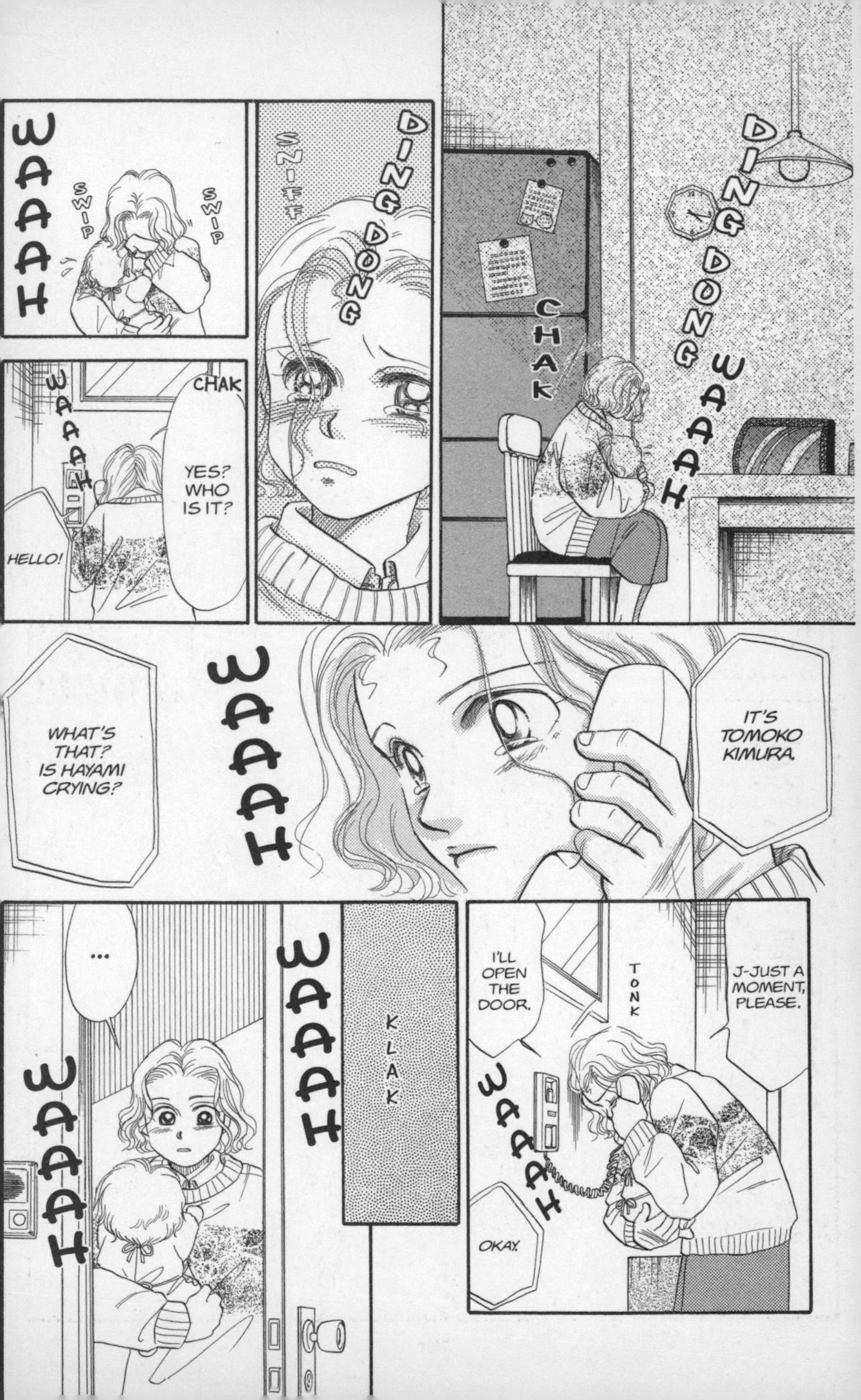
DING DONG
CHAK
WAAAAH
DING DONG
SNIFF
WAAAAH
SWIP
SWIP
CHAK
YES? WHO IS IT?
WAAAAH
HELLO!
IT'S TOMOKO KIMURA.
WAAAAH
WHAT'S THAT? IS HAYAMI CRYING?
J-JUST A MOMENT, PLEASE.
TONK
I'LL OPEN THE DOOR.
WAAAH
OKAY.
KLAK
WAAAAH
...
WAAAAH

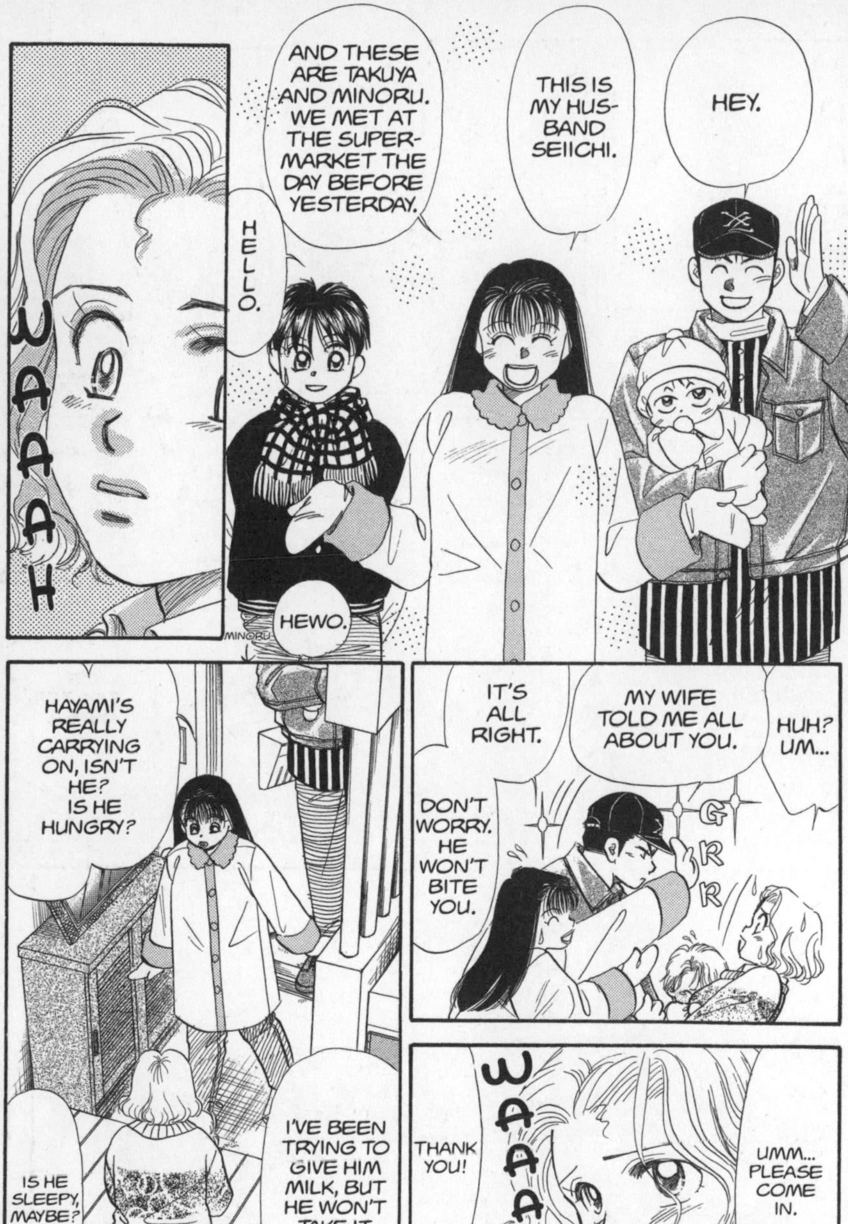
HEY.
THIS IS MY HUSBAND SEIICHI.
AND THESE ARE TAKUYA AND MINORU. WE MET AT THE SUPERMARKET THE DAY BEFORE YESTERDAY.
HELLO.
HEWO.
MINORU
WAAAH
HUH? UM...
MY WIFE TOLD ME ALL ABOUT YOU.
IT'S ALL RIGHT.
GRR
DON'T WORRY. HE WON'T BITE YOU.
UMM... PLEASE COME IN.
WAAAH
THANK YOU!
HAYAMI'S REALLY CARRYING ON, ISN'T HE? IS HE HUNGRY?
I'VE BEEN TRYING TO GIVE HIM MILK, BUT HE WON'T TAKE IT.
IS HE SLEEPY, MAYBE?

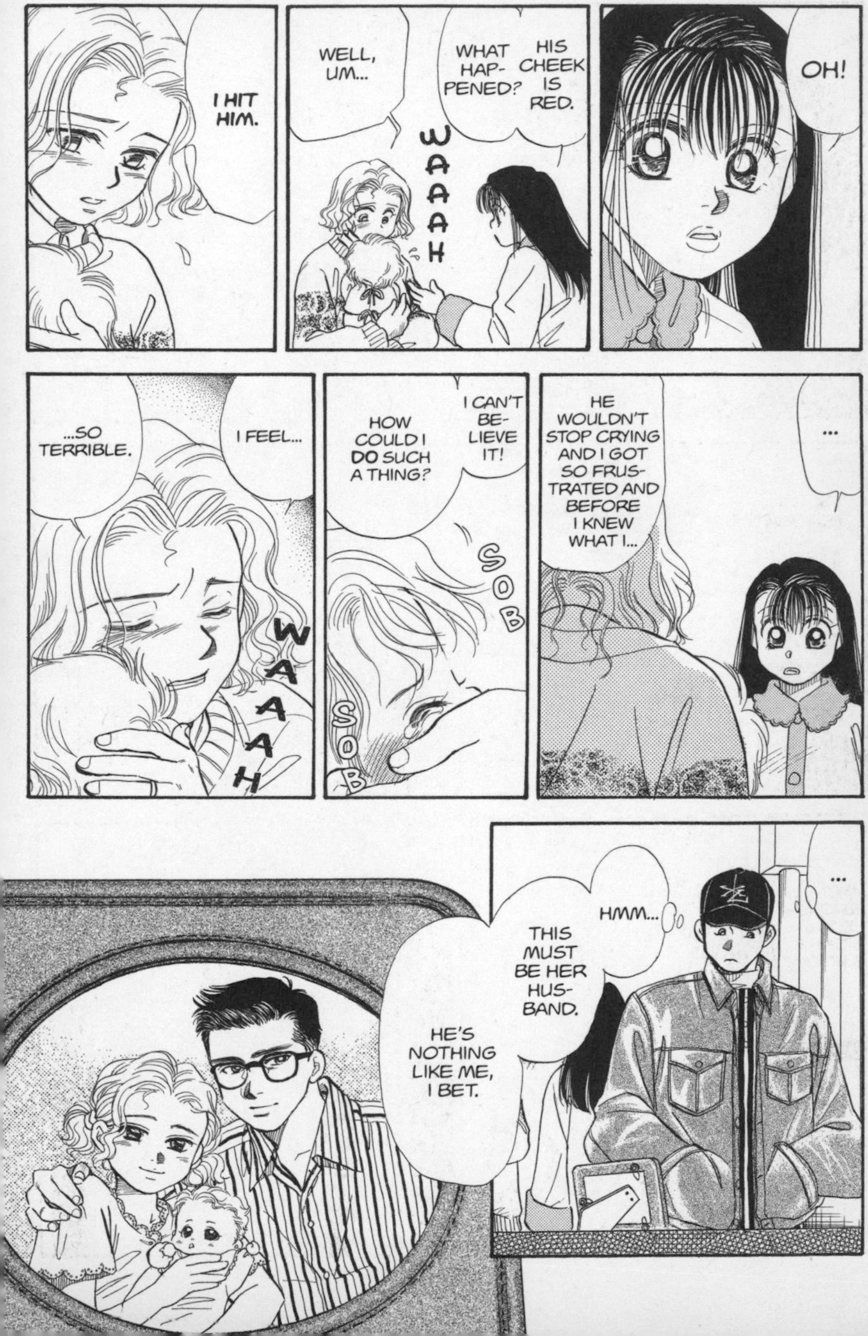
OH!
HIS CHEEK IS RED.
WHAT HAP-PENED?
WELL, UM...
WAAAH
I HIT HIM.
...
HE WOULDN'T STOP CRYING AND I GOT SO FRUS-TRATED AND BEFORE I KNEW WHAT I...
I CAN'T BE-LIEVE IT!
HOW COULD I **DO** SUCH A THING?
SOB
SOB
I FEEL...
...SO TERRIBLE.
WAAAH
...
HMM...
THIS MUST BE HER HUS-BAND.
HE'S NOTHING LIKE ME, I BET.

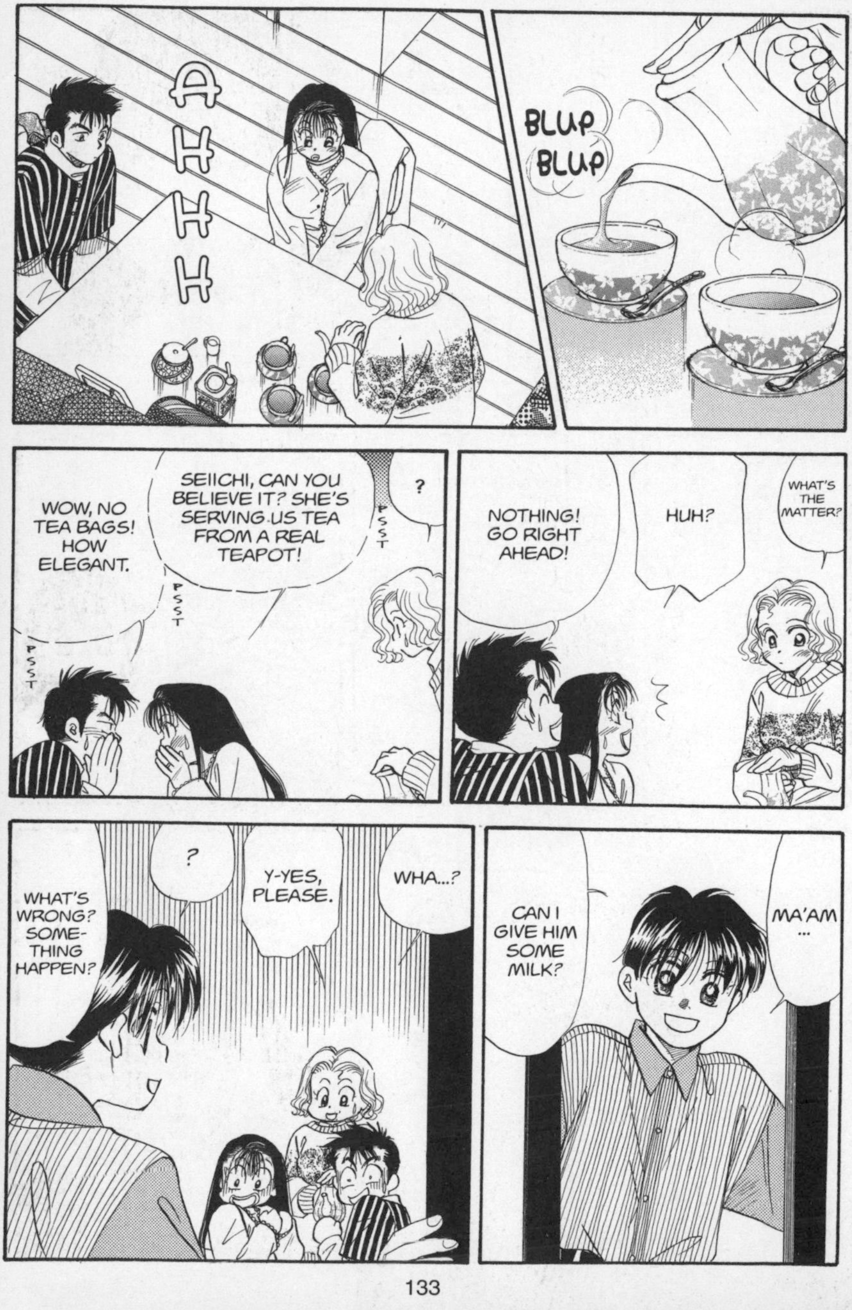
BLUP
BLUP
AHHH
?
PSST
SEIICHI, CAN YOU BELIEVE IT? SHE'S SERVING US TEA FROM A REAL TEAPOT!
PSST
WOW, NO TEA BAGS! HOW ELEGANT.
PSST
WHAT'S THE MATTER?
HUH?
NOTHING! GO RIGHT AHEAD!
MA'AM ...
CAN I GIVE HIM SOME MILK?
WHA...?
Y-YES, PLEASE.
?
WHAT'S WRONG? SOME-THING HAPPEN?

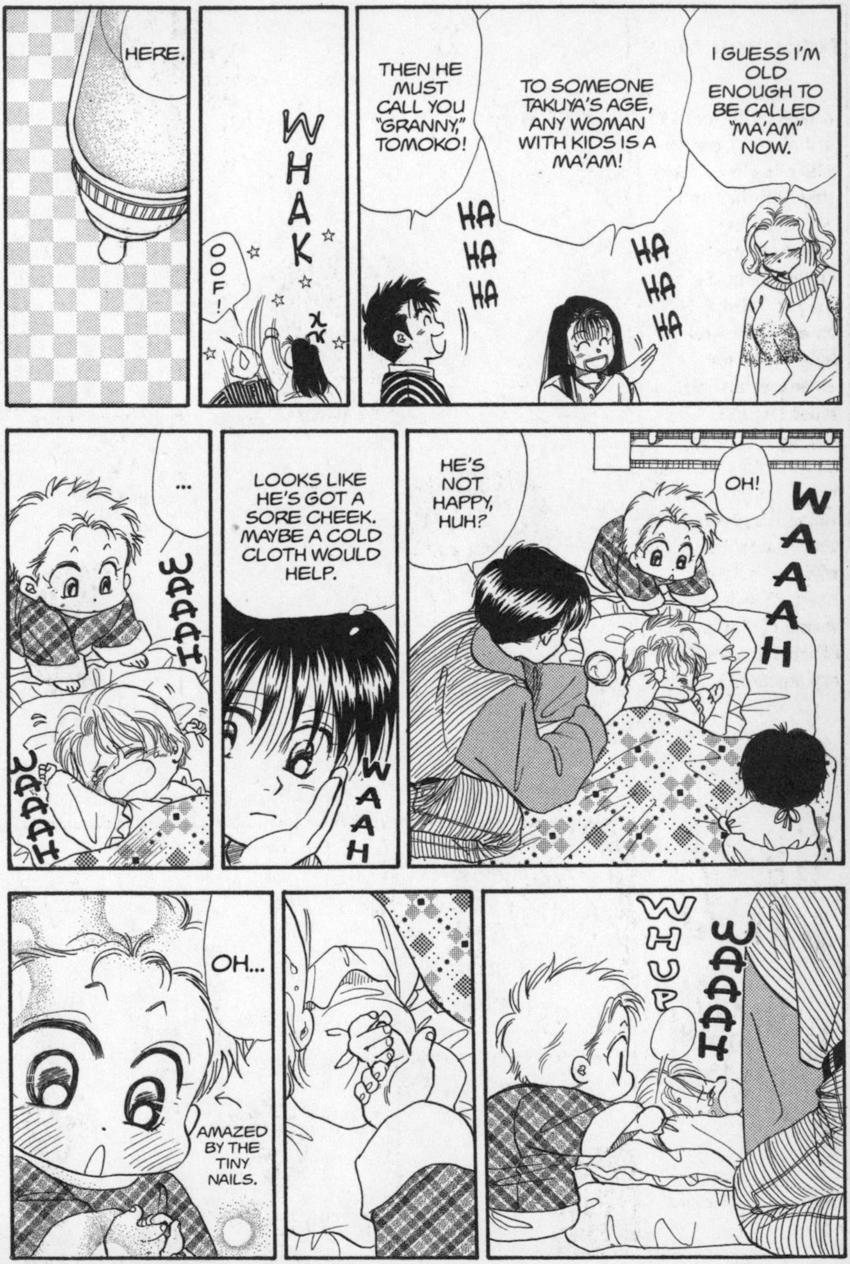
I GUESS I'M OLD ENOUGH TO BE CALLED "MA'AM" NOW.
TO SOMEONE TAKUYA'S AGE, ANY WOMAN WITH KIDS IS A MA'AM!
HA HA HA
THEN HE MUST CALL YOU "GRANNY," TOMOKO!
HA HA HA
WHAK
OOF!
HERE.
OH!
WAAAAH
HE'S NOT HAPPY, HUH?
LOOKS LIKE HE'S GOT A SORE CHEEK. MAYBE A COLD CLOTH WOULD HELP.
WAAH
...
WAAAAH
WAAAAH
WHUP
WAAAAH
OH...
AMAZED BY THE TINY NAILS.

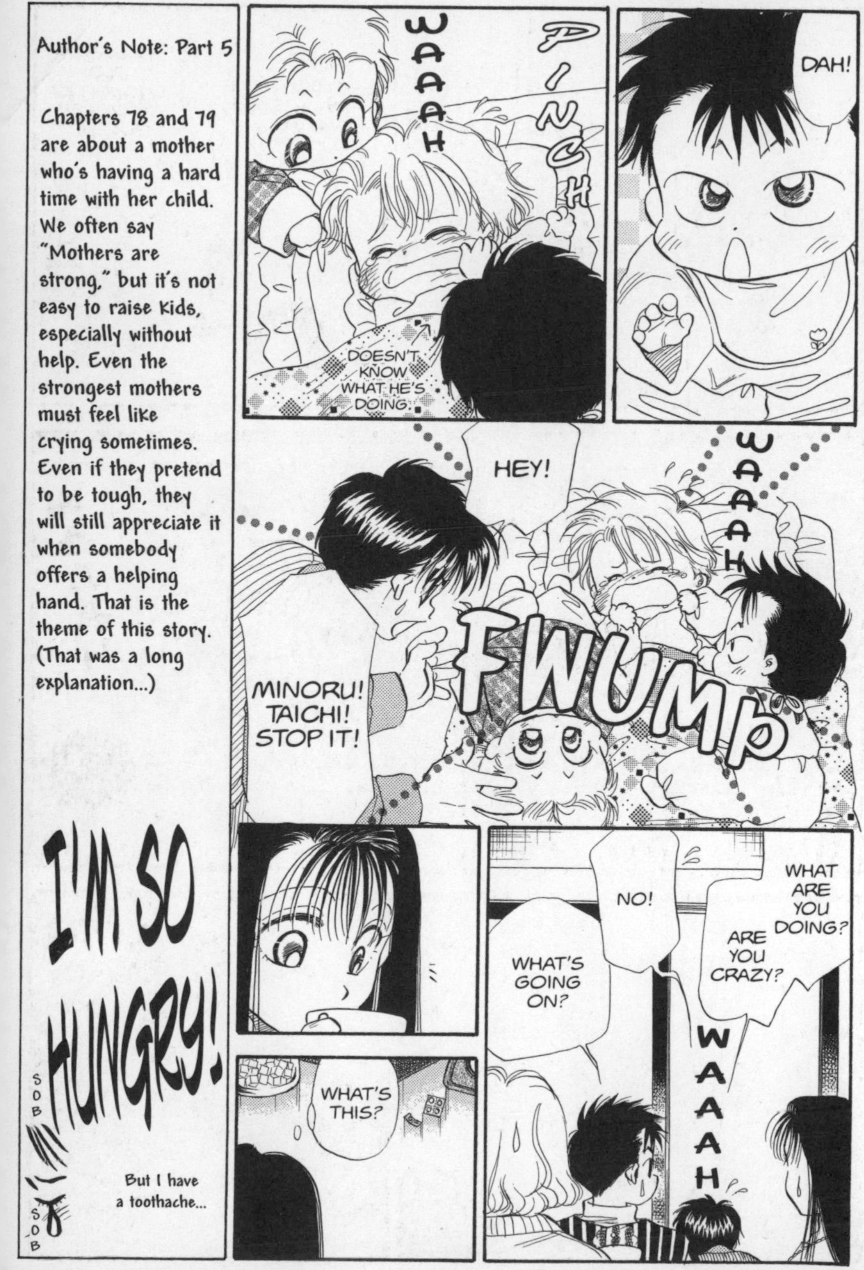
DAH!
PINCH
WAAAH
DOESN'T KNOW WHAT HE'S DOING
WAAAH
HEY!
FWUMP
MINORU! TAICHI! STOP IT!
WHAT ARE YOU DOING?
ARE YOU CRAZY?
NO!
WHAT'S GOING ON?
WAAAH
WHAT'S THIS?

Author's Note: Part 5

Chapters 78 and 79 are about a mother who's having a hard time with her child. We often say "Mothers are strong," but it's not easy to raise kids, especially without help. Even the strongest mothers must feel like crying sometimes. Even if they pretend to be tough, they will still appreciate it when somebody offers a helping hand. That is the theme of this story. (That was a long explanation...)

I'M SO HUNGRY!

SOB SOB

But I have a toothache...

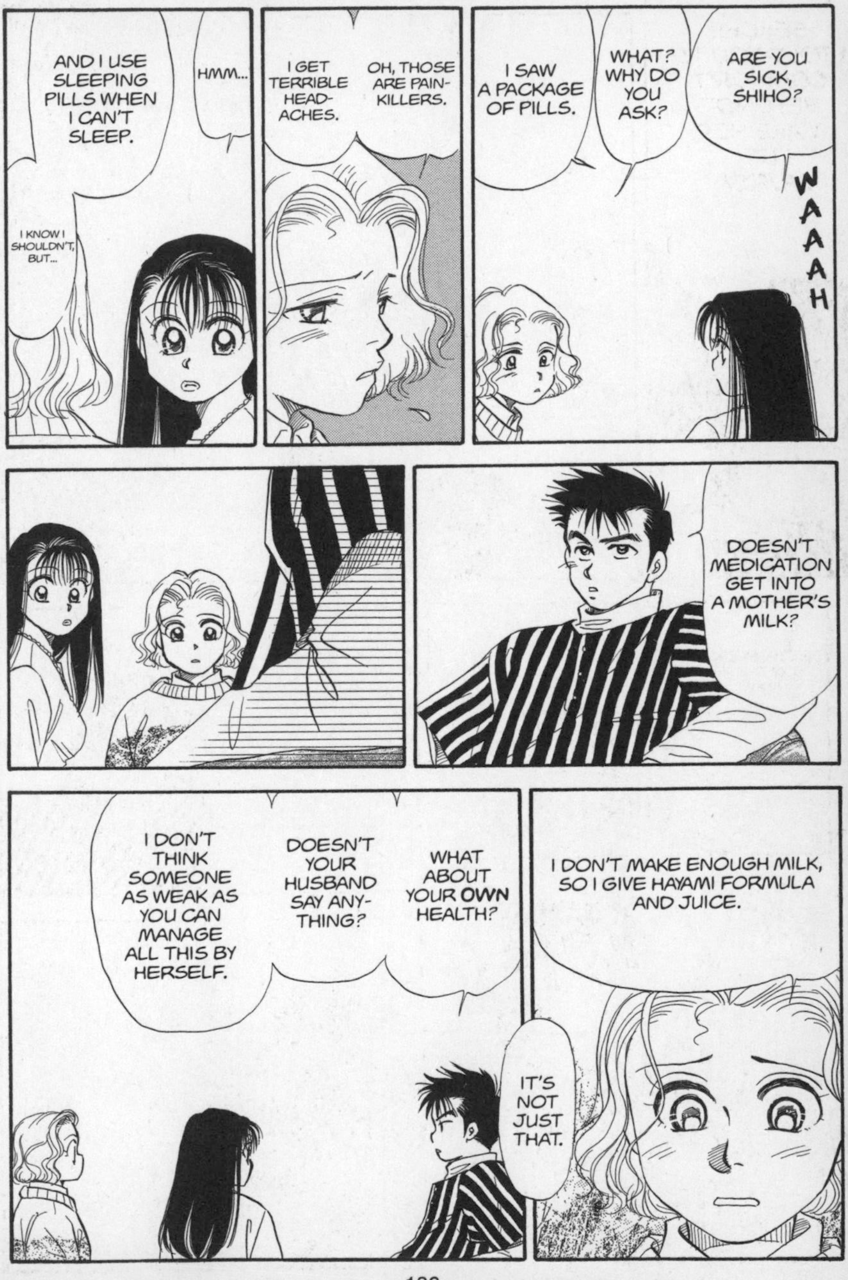
ARE YOU SICK, SHIHO?
WHAT? WHY DO YOU ASK?
I SAW A PACKAGE OF PILLS.
WAAAH
OH, THOSE ARE PAIN-KILLERS.
I GET TERRIBLE HEAD-ACHES.
HMM...
AND I USE SLEEPING PILLS WHEN I CAN'T SLEEP.
I KNOW I SHOULDN'T, BUT...
DOESN'T MEDICATION GET INTO A MOTHER'S MILK?
I DON'T MAKE ENOUGH MILK, SO I GIVE HAYAMI FORMULA AND JUICE.
IT'S NOT JUST THAT.
WHAT ABOUT YOUR OWN HEALTH?
DOESN'T YOUR HUSBAND SAY ANY-THING?
I DON'T THINK SOMEONE AS WEAK AS YOU CAN MANAGE ALL THIS BY HERSELF.

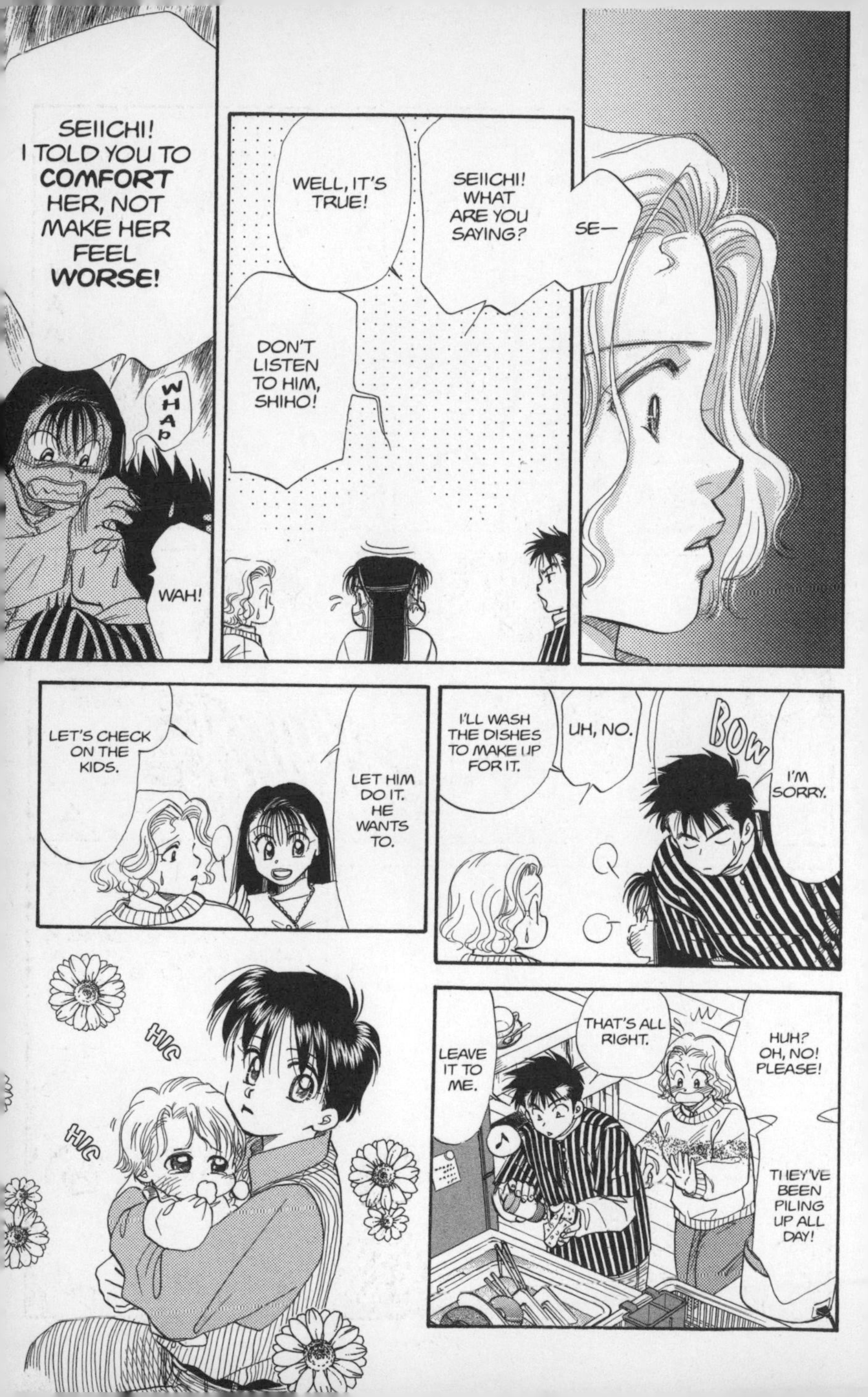
SE—
SEIICHI! WHAT ARE YOU SAYING?
WELL, IT'S TRUE!
DON'T LISTEN TO HIM, SHIHO!
SEIICHI! I TOLD YOU TO **COMFORT** HER, NOT MAKE HER FEEL **WORSE!**
WHAP
WAH!
BOW
I'M SORRY.
UH, NO.
I'LL WASH THE DISHES TO MAKE UP FOR IT.
LET HIM DO IT. HE WANTS TO.
LET'S CHECK ON THE KIDS.
HUH? OH, NO! PLEASE!
THAT'S ALL RIGHT.
LEAVE IT TO ME.
THEY'VE BEEN PILING UP ALL DAY!
HIC
HIC

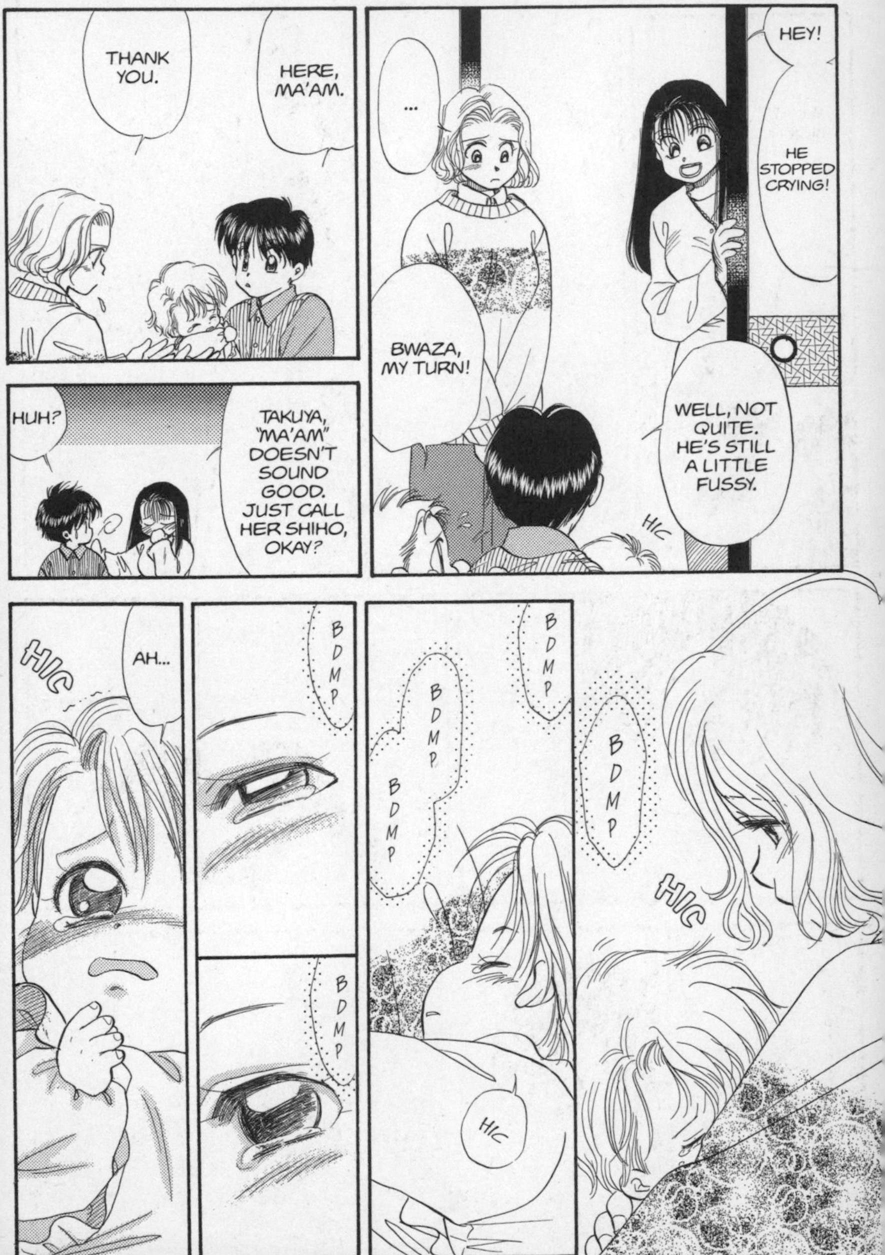
HEY! HE STOPPED CRYING!
...
WELL, NOT QUITE. HE'S STILL A LITTLE FUSSY.
HIC
BWAZA, MY TURN!
HERE, MA'AM.
THANK YOU.
TAKUYA, "MA'AM" DOESN'T SOUND GOOD. JUST CALL HER SHIHO, OKAY?
HUH?
BDMP
BDMP
HIC
BDMP
BDMP
HIC
BDMP
BDMP
AH...
HIC

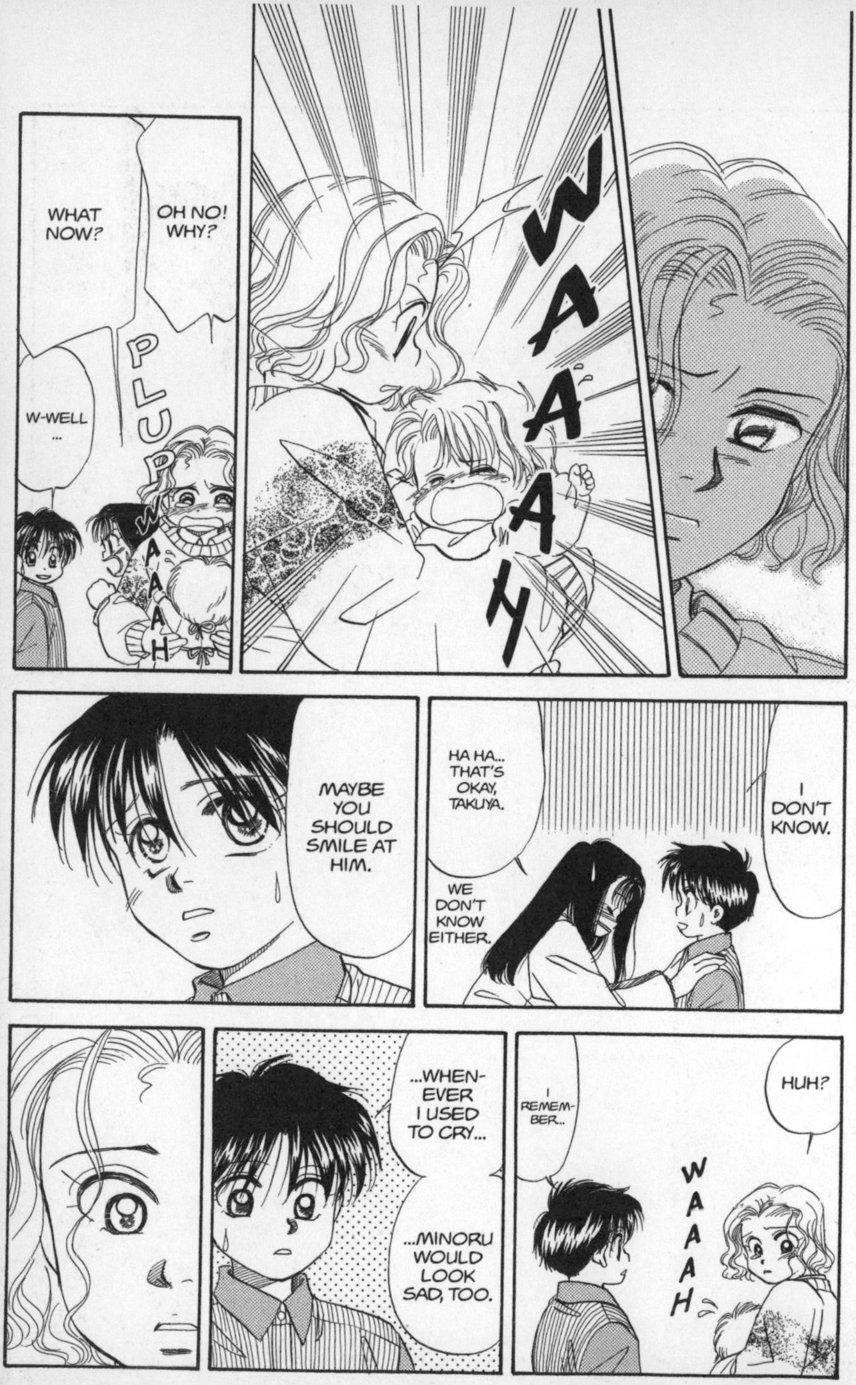
WAAAH
OH NO! WHY?
WHAT NOW?
PLUP
W-WELL ...
WAAAH
I DON'T KNOW.
HA HA... THAT'S OKAY, TAKUYA.
WE DON'T KNOW EITHER.
MAYBE YOU SHOULD SMILE AT HIM.
HUH?
WAAAH
I REMEMBER...
...WHENEVER I USED TO CRY...
...MINORU WOULD LOOK SAD, TOO.

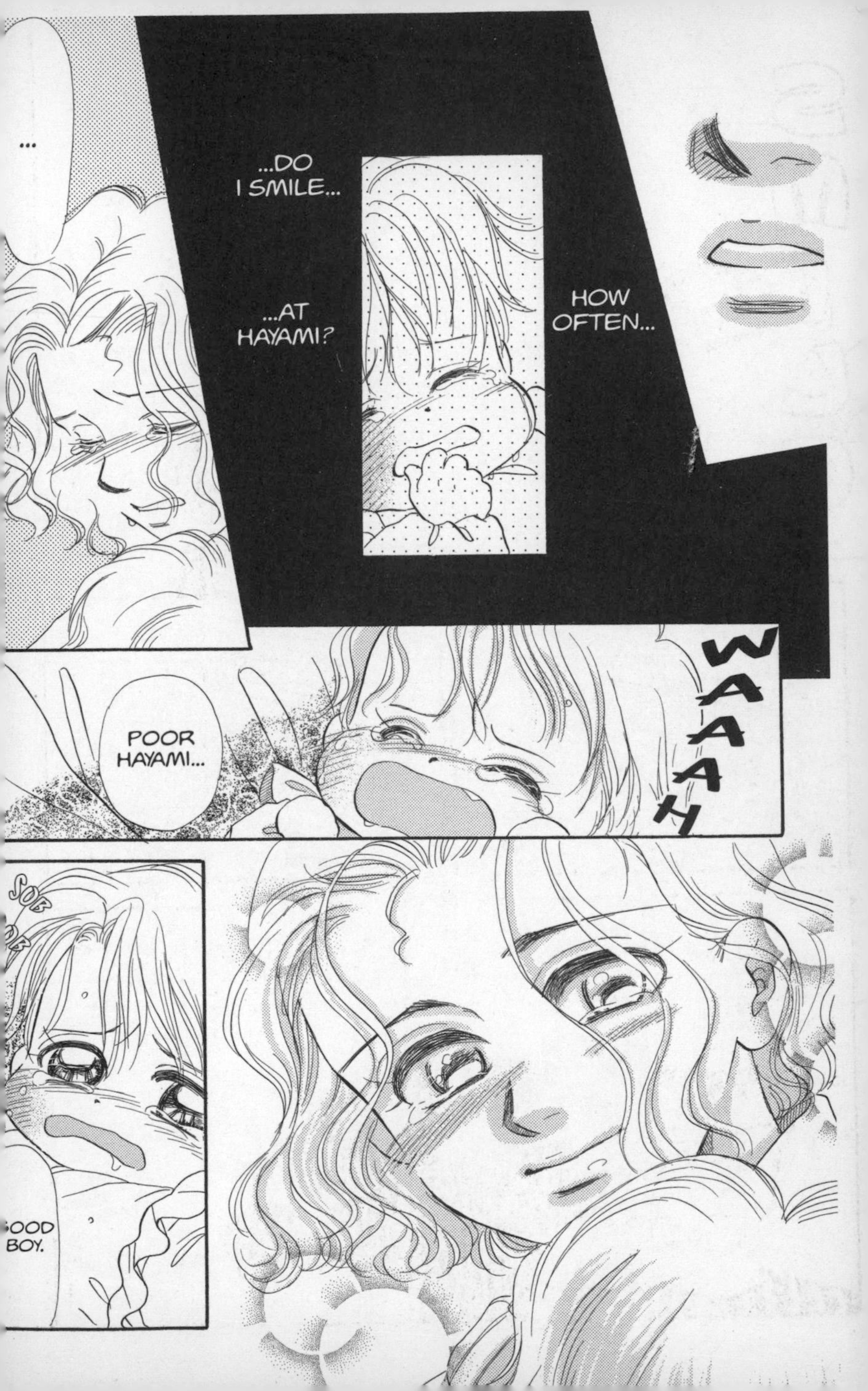
HOW OFTEN...
...DO I SMILE...
...AT HAYAMI?
...
WAAAAH
POOR HAYAMI...
SOB
GOOD BOY.

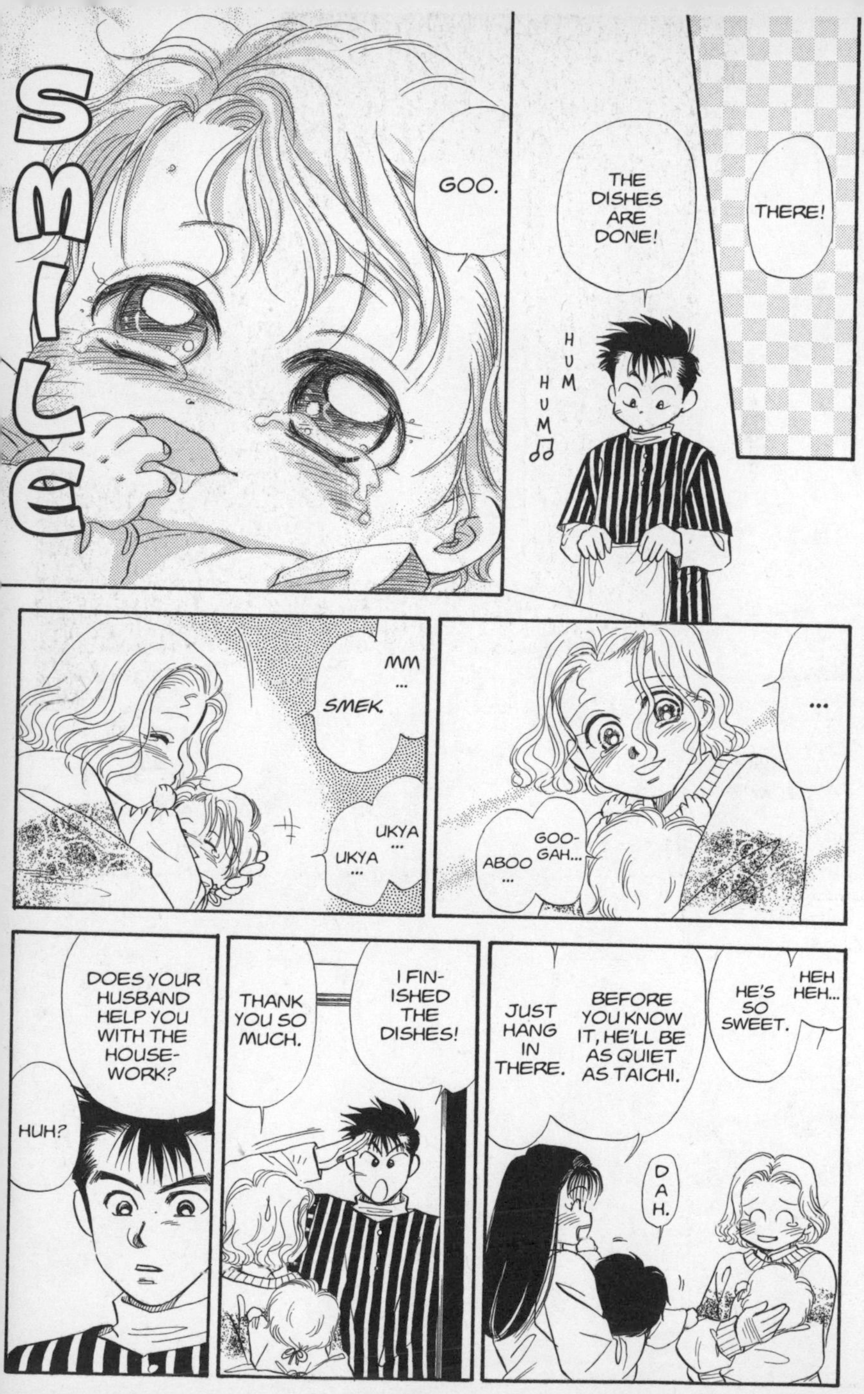
THERE!
THE DISHES ARE DONE!
HUM HUM HUM HUM ♫
GOO.
SMILE
...
GOO-GAH...
ABOO...
MM... SMEK.
UKYA... UKYA...
HEH HEH...
HE'S SO SWEET.
BEFORE YOU KNOW IT, HE'LL BE AS QUIET AS TAICHI.
JUST HANG IN THERE.
DAH.
I FIN-ISHED THE DISHES!
THANK YOU SO MUCH.
DOES YOUR HUSBAND HELP YOU WITH THE HOUSE-WORK?
HUH?

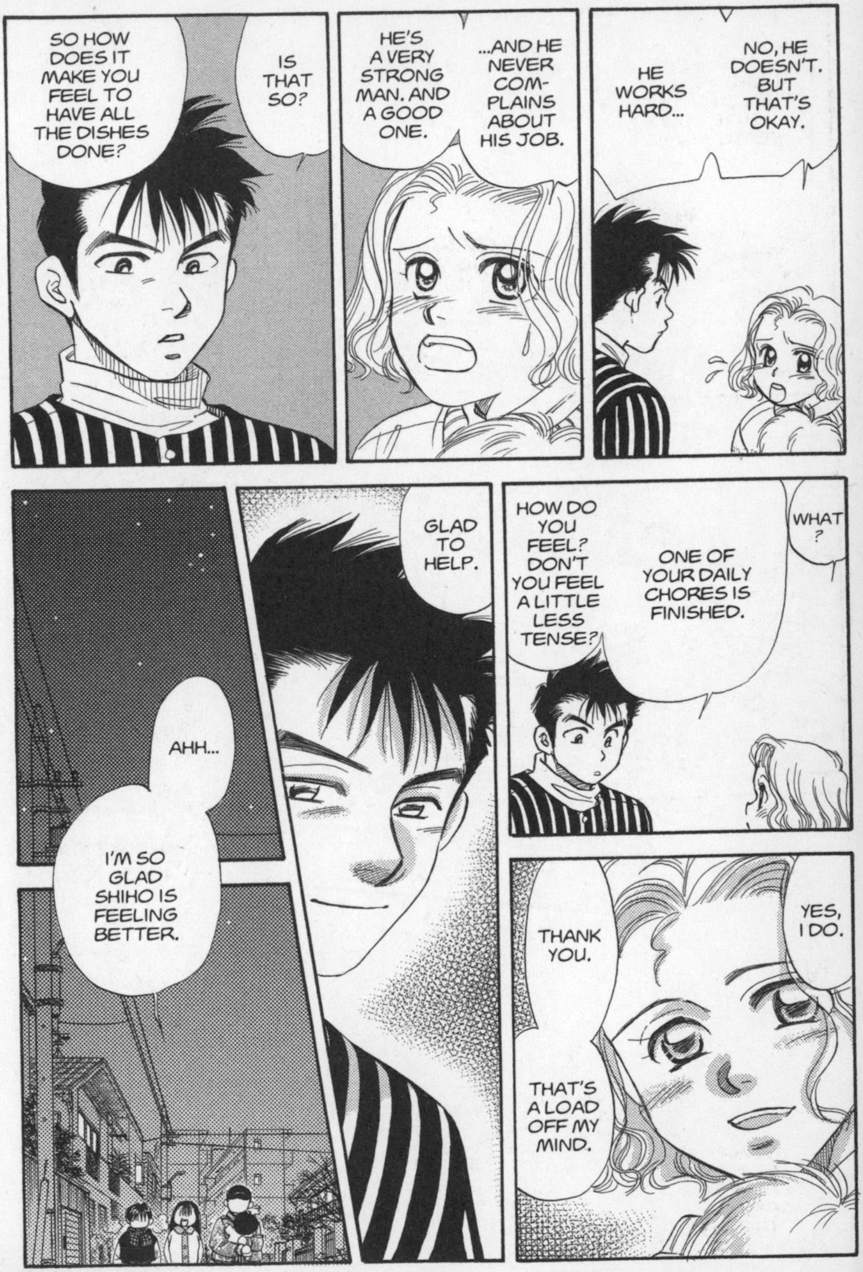
NO, HE DOESN'T. BUT THAT'S OKAY.
HE WORKS HARD...
...AND HE NEVER COM-PLAINS ABOUT HIS JOB.
HE'S A VERY STRONG MAN. AND A GOOD ONE.
IS THAT SO?
SO HOW DOES IT MAKE YOU FEEL TO HAVE ALL THE DISHES DONE?
WHAT?
ONE OF YOUR DAILY CHORES IS FINISHED.
HOW DO YOU FEEL? DON'T YOU FEEL A LITTLE LESS TENSE?
YES, I DO.
THANK YOU.
THAT'S A LOAD OFF MY MIND.
GLAD TO HELP.
AHH...
I'M SO GLAD SHIHO IS FEELING BETTER.

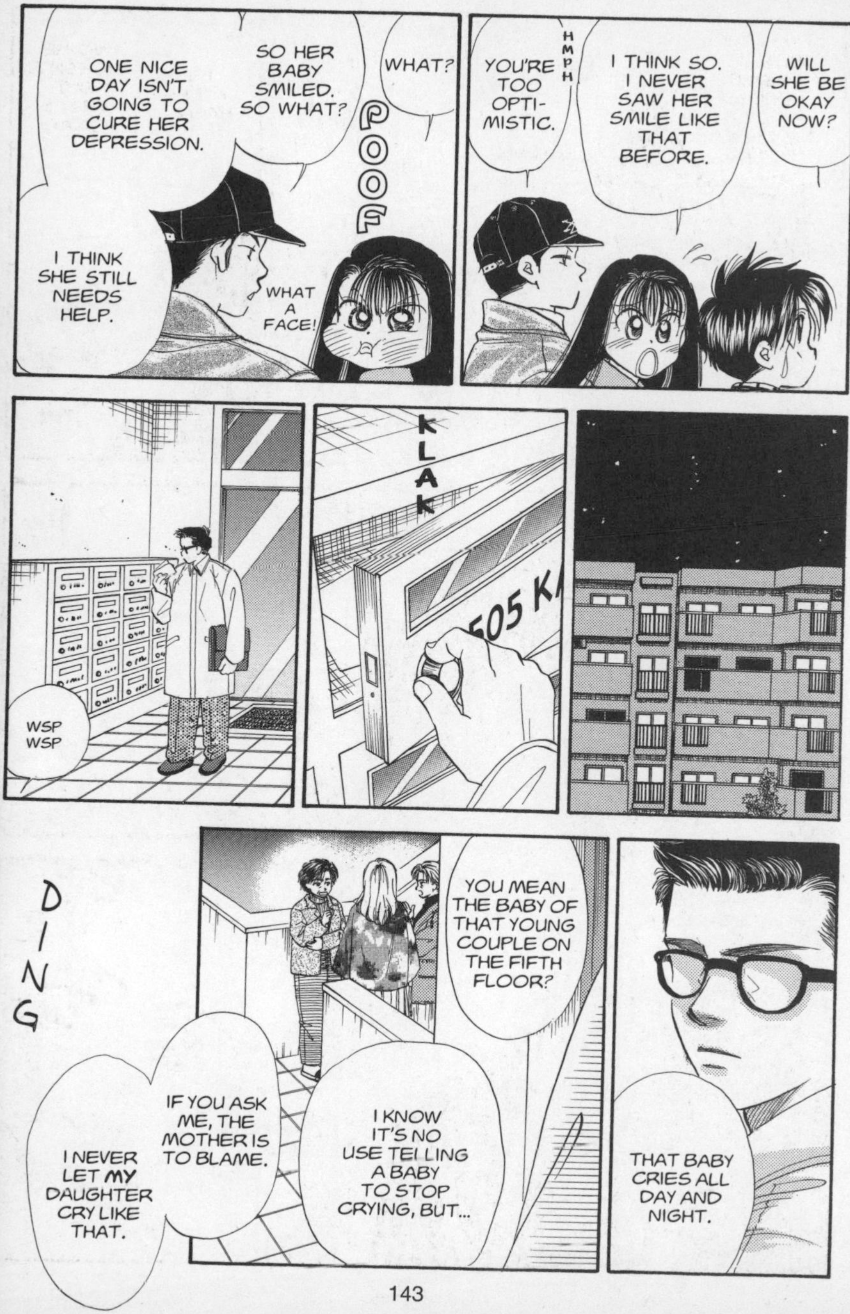
WILL SHE BE OKAY NOW?
I THINK SO. I NEVER SAW HER SMILE LIKE THAT BEFORE.
HMPH
YOU'RE TOO OPTI-MISTIC.
WHAT?
POOF
SO HER BABY SMILED. SO WHAT?
ONE NICE DAY ISN'T GOING TO CURE HER DEPRESSION.
WHAT A FACE!
I THINK SHE STILL NEEDS HELP.
KLAK
505 KA
WSP WSP
THAT BABY CRIES ALL DAY AND NIGHT.
YOU MEAN THE BABY OF THAT YOUNG COUPLE ON THE FIFTH FLOOR?
I KNOW IT'S NO USE TELLING A BABY TO STOP CRYING, BUT...
IF YOU ASK ME, THE MOTHER IS TO BLAME.
I NEVER LET MY DAUGHTER CRY LIKE THAT.
DING

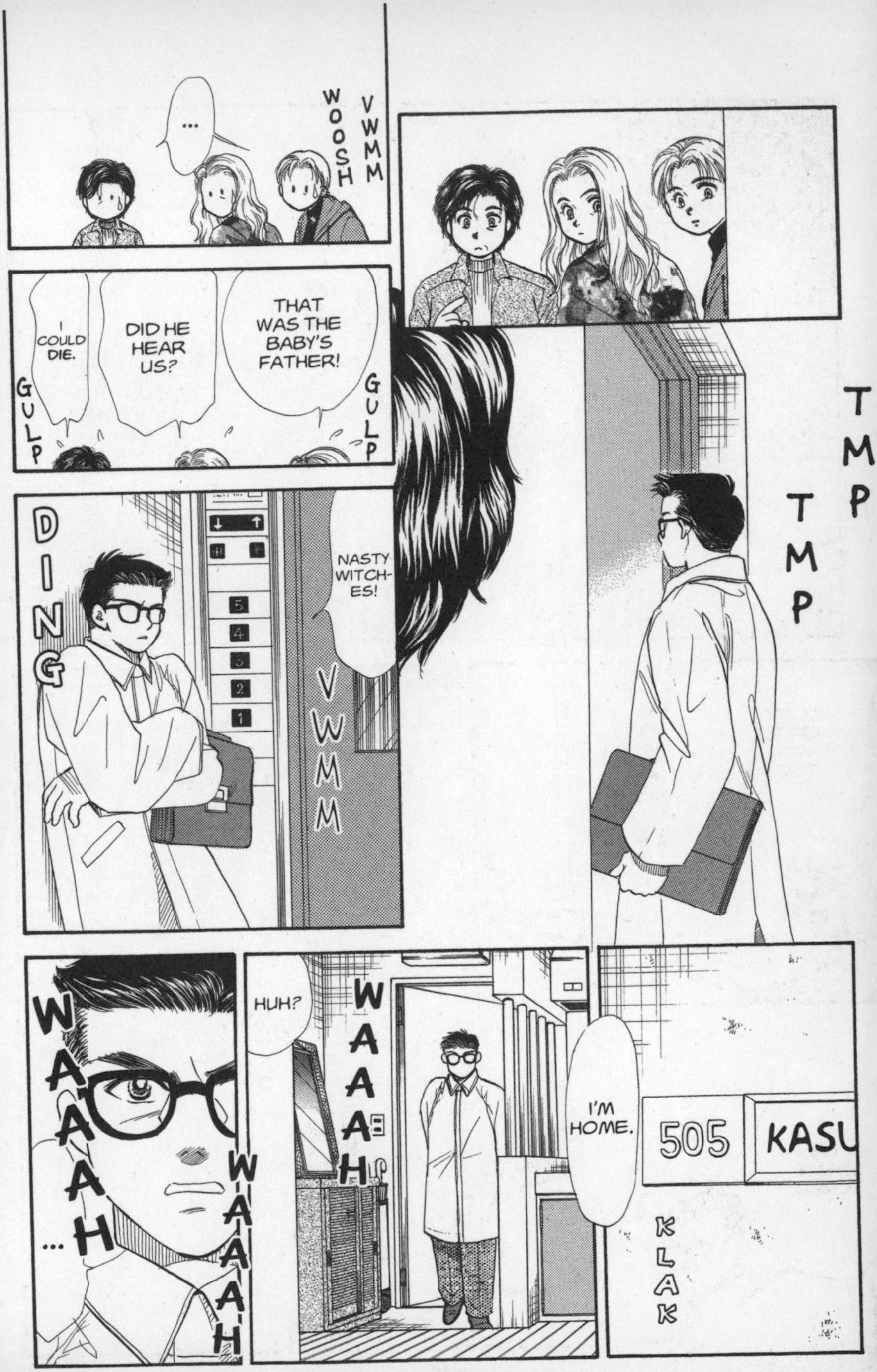

...
WOOSH
VWMM
THAT WAS THE BABY'S FATHER!
DID HE HEAR US?
I COULD DIE.
GULP
GULP
NASTY WITCH-ES!
VWMM
DING
TMP
TMP
505
KASU
I'M HOME.
KLAK
WAAAAH
HUH?
WAAAAAH
WAAAAH
...

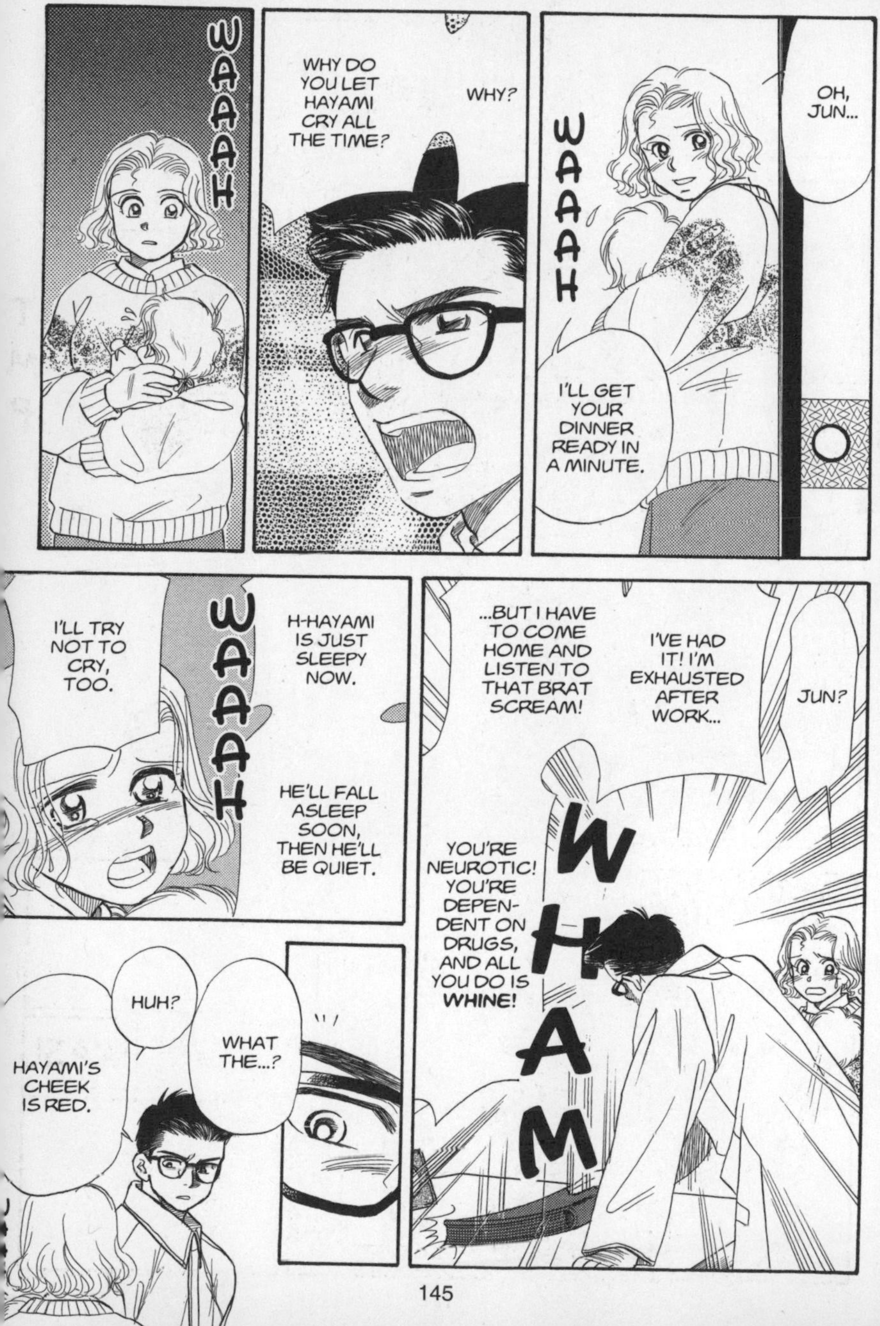
OH, JUN...
WAAAAH
I'LL GET YOUR DINNER READY IN A MINUTE.
WHY?
WHY DO YOU LET HAYAMI CRY ALL THE TIME?
WAAAAH
JUN?
I'VE HAD IT! I'M EXHAUSTED AFTER WORK...
...BUT I HAVE TO COME HOME AND LISTEN TO THAT BRAT SCREAM!
YOU'RE NEUROTIC! YOU'RE DEPEN-DENT ON DRUGS, AND ALL YOU DO IS **WHINE!**
WHAM
H-HAYAMI IS JUST SLEEPY NOW.
HE'LL FALL ASLEEP SOON, THEN HE'LL BE QUIET.
WAAAAH
I'LL TRY NOT TO CRY, TOO.
WHAT THE...?
HUH?
HAYAMI'S CHEEK IS RED.

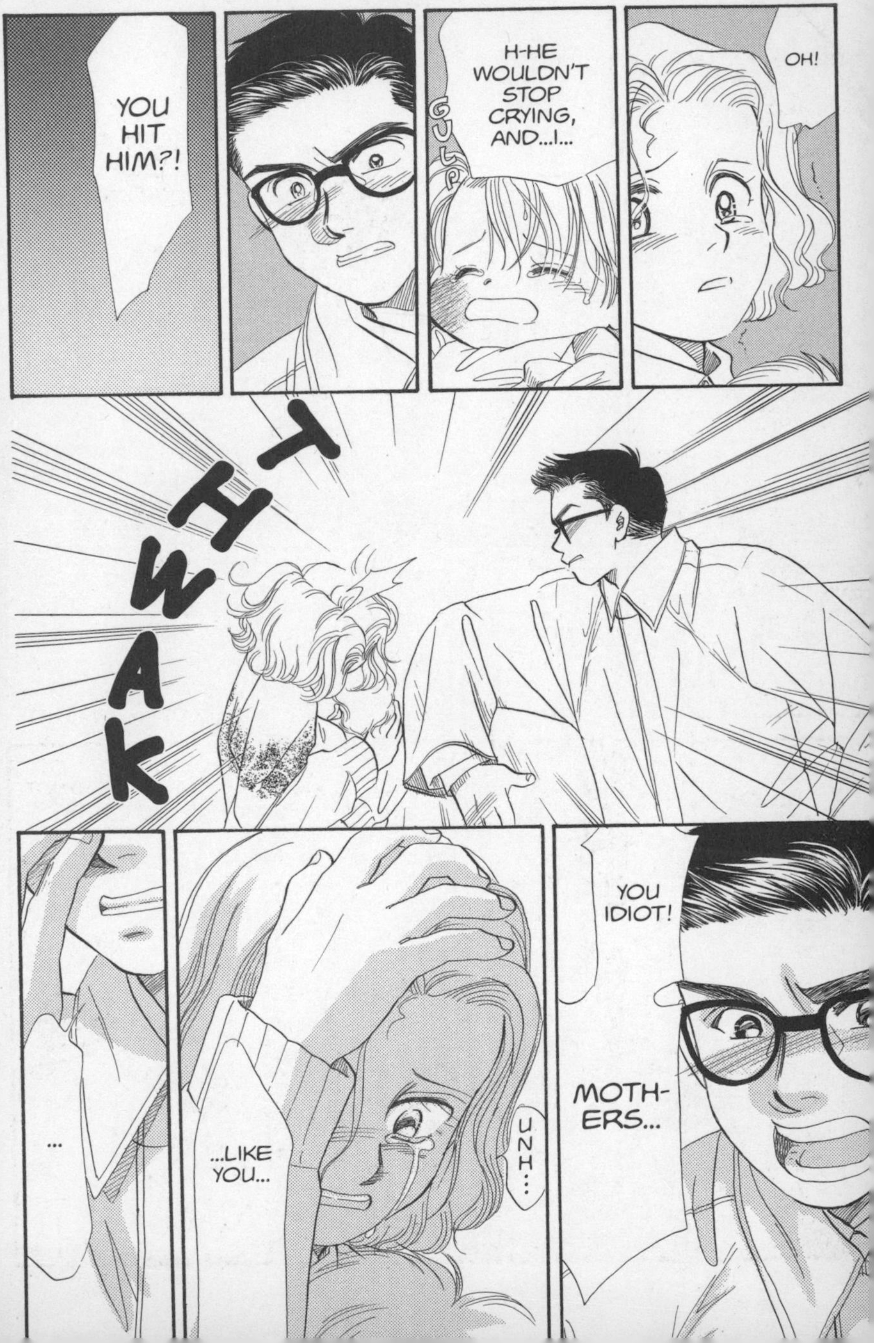
OH!
GULP
H-HE WOULDN'T STOP CRYING, AND...I...
YOU HIT HIM?!
THWAK
YOU IDIOT!
MOTHERS...
UNH...
...LIKE YOU...
...

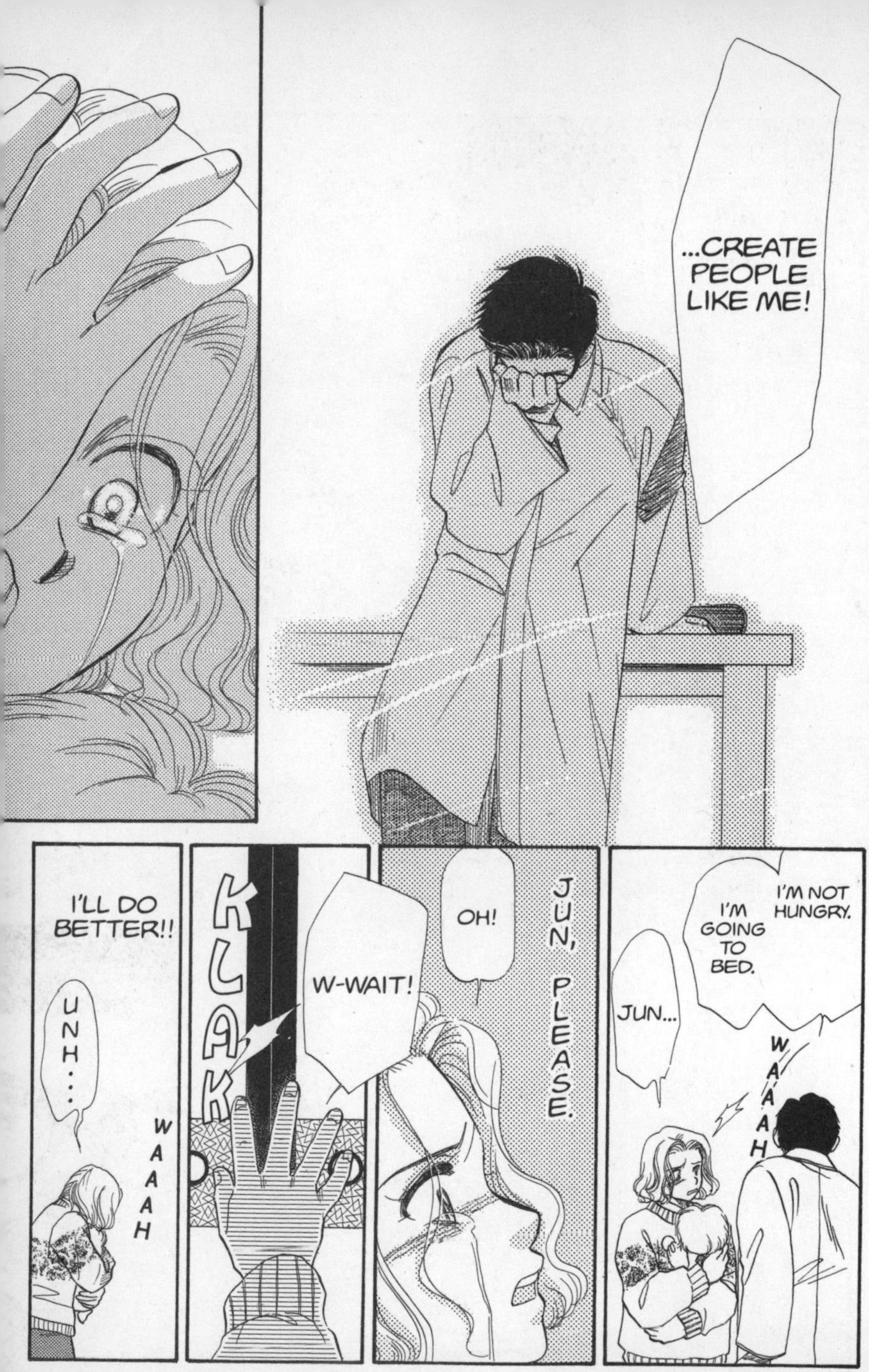
...CREATE PEOPLE LIKE ME!
I'M NOT HUNGRY. I'M GOING TO BED.
JUN...
WAAAH
JUN, PLEASE.
OH!
W-WAIT!
KLAK
I'LL DO BETTER!!
UNH...
WAAAH

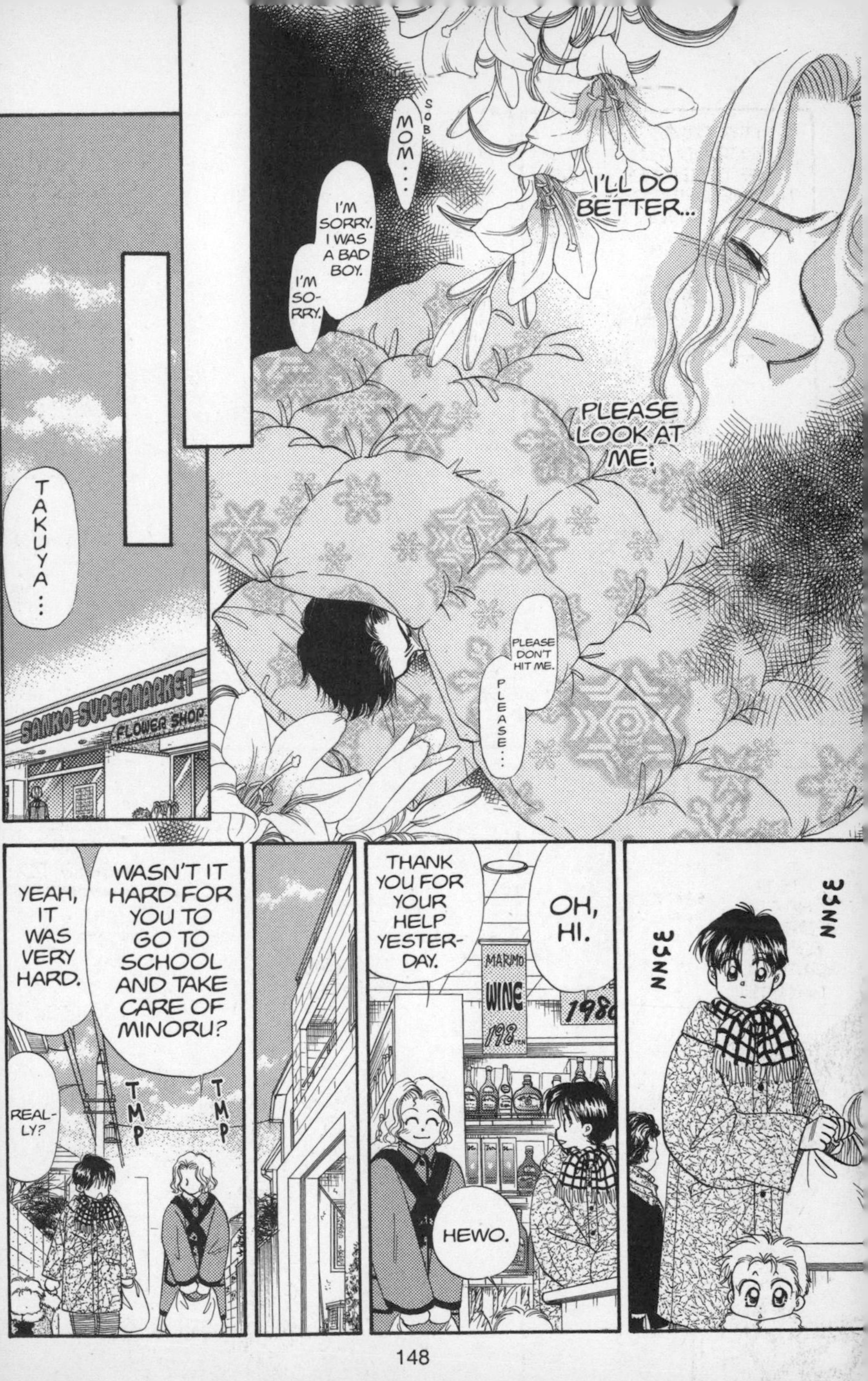
SOB
MOM...
I'M SORRY. I WAS A BAD BOY.
I'M SORRY.
I'LL DO BETTER...
PLEASE LOOK AT ME.
PLEASE DON'T HIT ME.
PLEASE...
TAKUYA...
SANKO SUPERMARKET
FLOWER SHOP
OH, HI.
THANK YOU FOR YOUR HELP YESTERDAY.
MARIMO
WINE
198 YEN
1980
HEWO.
WASN'T IT HARD FOR YOU TO GO TO SCHOOL AND TAKE CARE OF MINORU?
YEAH, IT WAS VERY HARD.
TMP
TMP
REALLY?

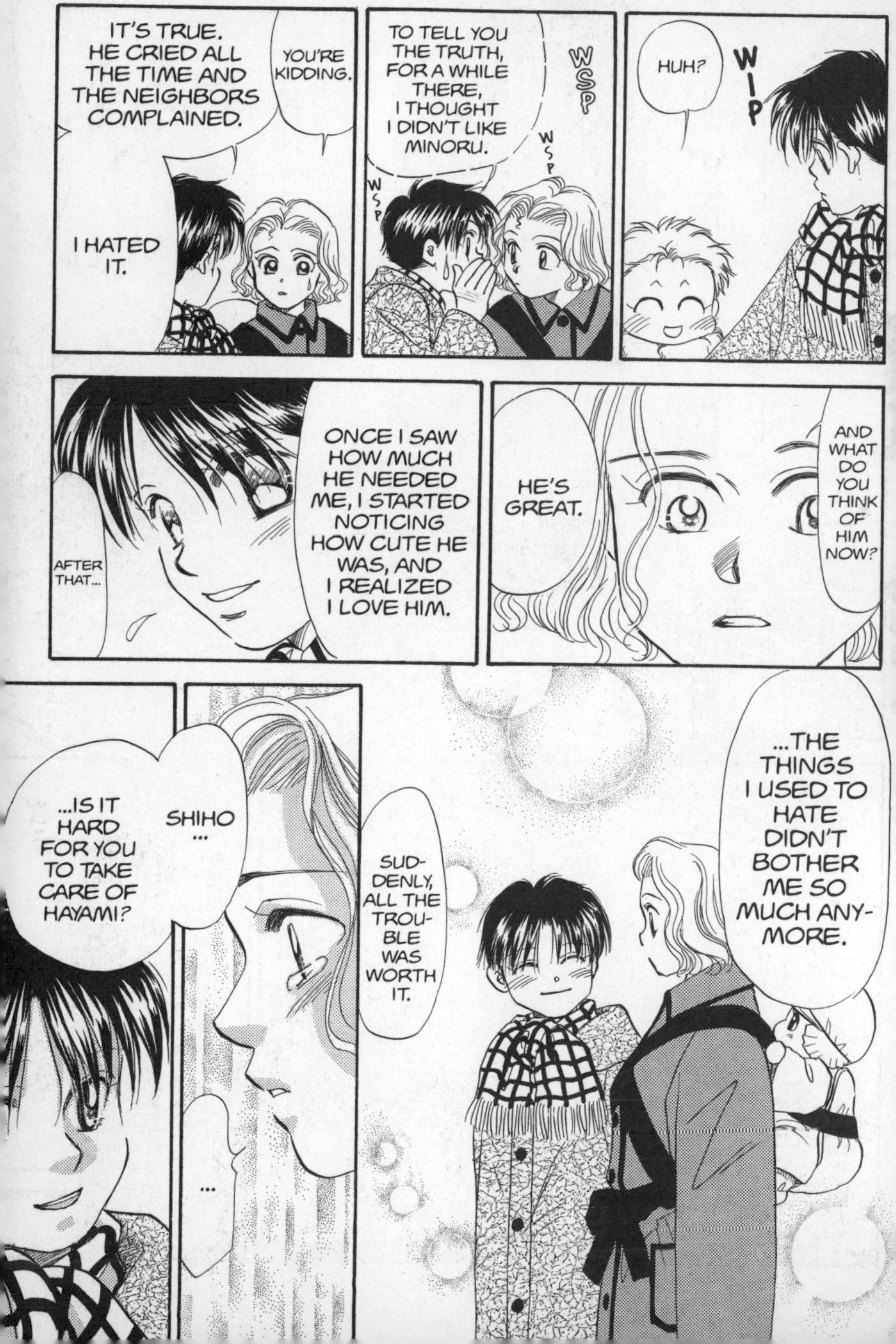
HUH?
WIP
TO TELL YOU THE TRUTH, FOR A WHILE THERE, I THOUGHT I DIDN'T LIKE MINORU.
WSP
WSP
WSP
YOU'RE KIDDING.
IT'S TRUE. HE CRIED ALL THE TIME AND THE NEIGHBORS COMPLAINED.
I HATED IT.
AND WHAT DO YOU THINK OF HIM NOW?
HE'S GREAT.
ONCE I SAW HOW MUCH HE NEEDED ME, I STARTED NOTICING HOW CUTE HE WAS, AND I REALIZED I LOVE HIM.
AFTER THAT...
...THE THINGS I USED TO HATE DIDN'T BOTHER ME SO MUCH ANYMORE.
SUDDENLY, ALL THE TROUBLE WAS WORTH IT.
SHIHO...
...
...IS IT HARD FOR YOU TO TAKE CARE OF HAYAMI?

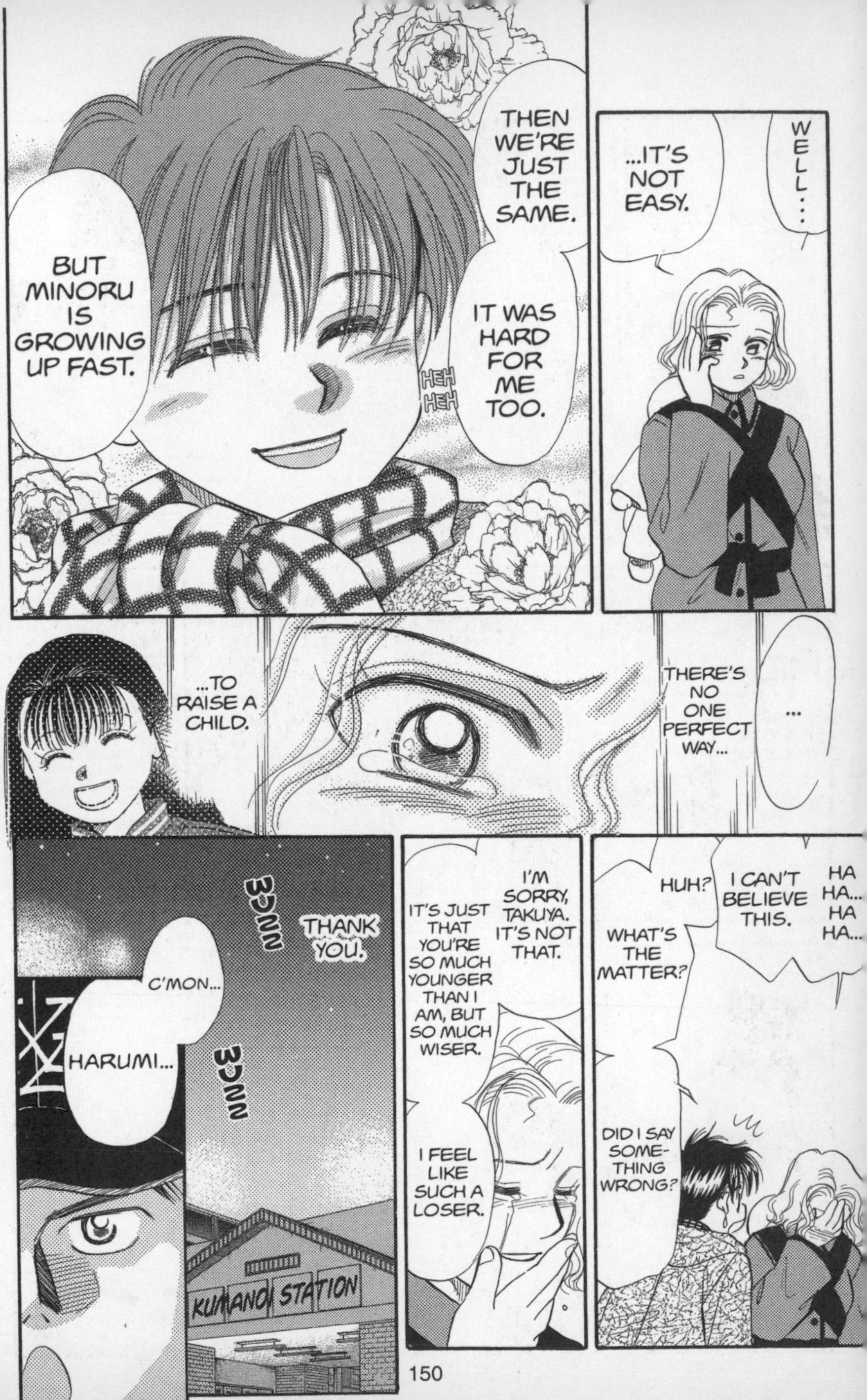
WELL...
...IT'S NOT EASY.
THEN WE'RE JUST THE SAME.
IT WAS HARD FOR ME TOO.
HEH HEH
BUT MINORU IS GROWING UP FAST.
...
THERE'S NO ONE PERFECT WAY...
...TO RAISE A CHILD.
HA HA... HA HA...
I CAN'T BELIEVE THIS.
HUH?
WHAT'S THE MATTER?
DID I SAY SOMETHING WRONG?
I'M SORRY, TAKUYA. IT'S NOT THAT.
IT'S JUST THAT YOU'RE SO MUCH YOUNGER THAN I AM, BUT SO MUCH WISER.
I FEEL LIKE SUCH A LOSER.
THANK YOU.
C'MON...
HARUMI...
KUMANOI STATION

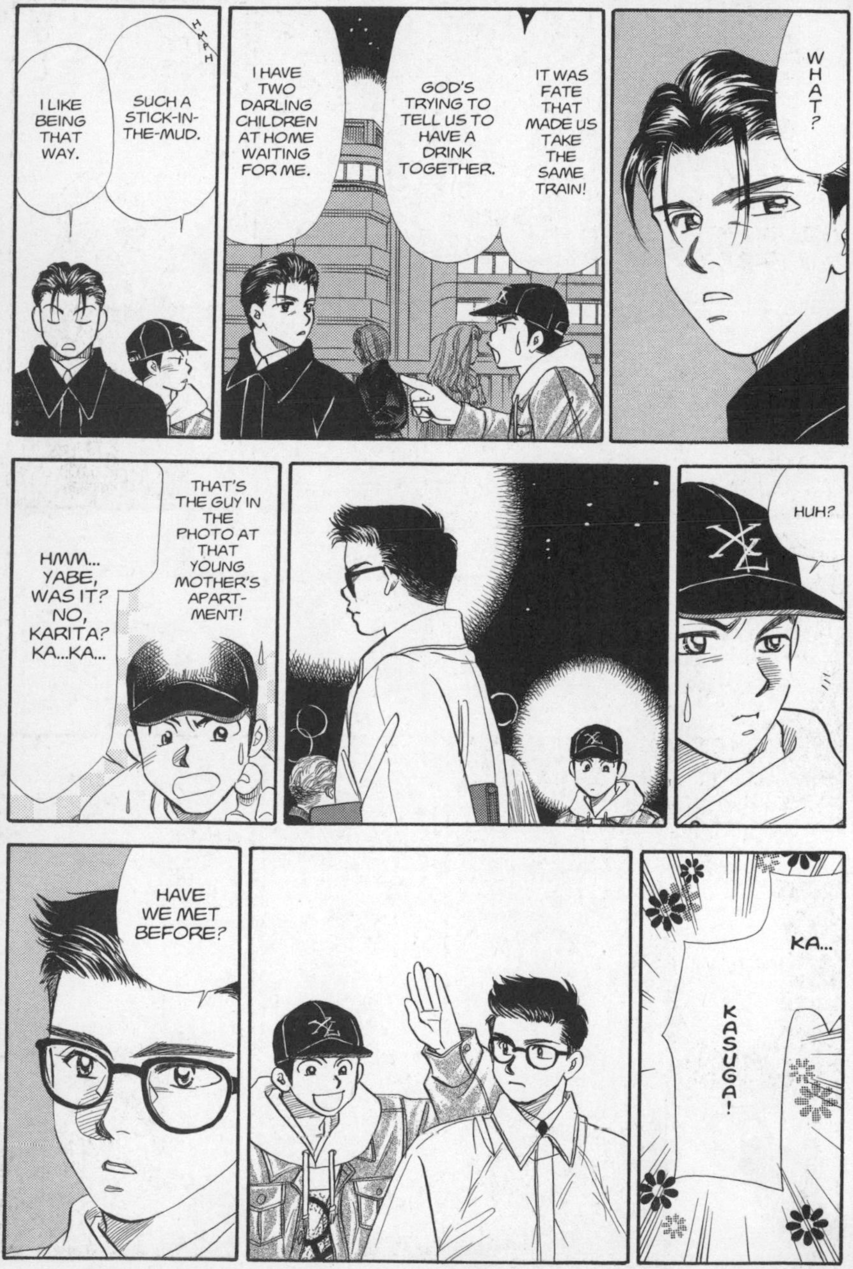
WHAT?
IT WAS FATE THAT MADE US TAKE THE SAME TRAIN!
GOD'S TRYING TO TELL US TO HAVE A DRINK TOGETHER.
I HAVE TWO DARLING CHILDREN AT HOME WAITING FOR ME.
HMPH
SUCH A STICK-IN-THE-MUD.
I LIKE BEING THAT WAY.
HUH?
THAT'S THE GUY IN THE PHOTO AT THAT YOUNG MOTHER'S APARTMENT!
HMM... YABE, WAS IT? NO, KARITA? KA...KA...
KA...
KASUGA!
HAVE WE MET BEFORE?

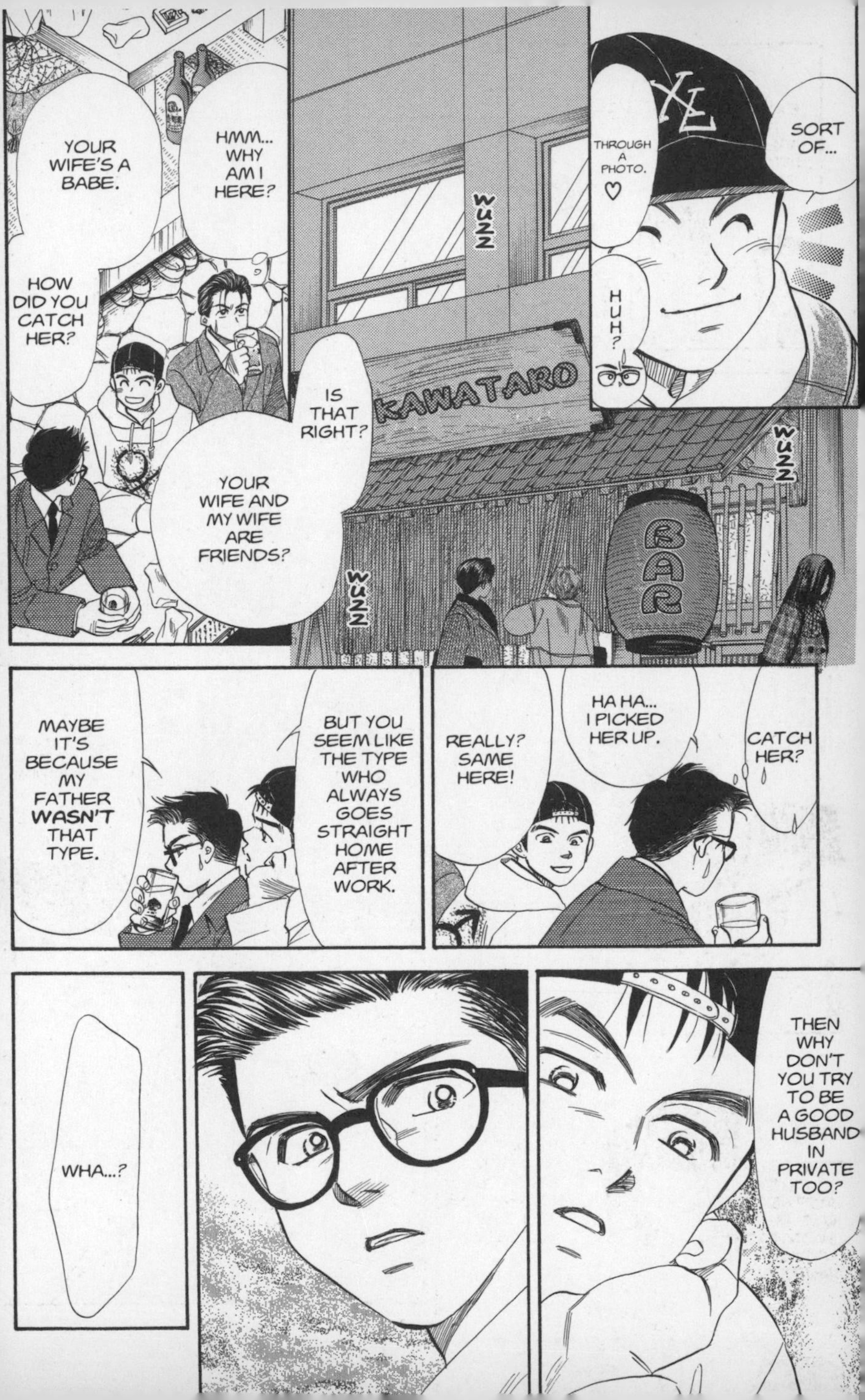

SORT OF...
THROUGH A PHOTO. ♡
HUH?
WUZZ
KAWATARO
IS THAT RIGHT?
YOUR WIFE AND MY WIFE ARE FRIENDS?
WUZZ
BAR
WUZZ
HMM... WHY AM I HERE?
YOUR WIFE'S A BABE.
HOW DID YOU CATCH HER?
CATCH HER?
HA HA... I PICKED HER UP.
REALLY? SAME HERE!
BUT YOU SEEM LIKE THE TYPE WHO ALWAYS GOES STRAIGHT HOME AFTER WORK.
MAYBE IT'S BECAUSE MY FATHER **WASN'T** THAT TYPE.
THEN WHY DON'T YOU TRY TO BE A GOOD HUSBAND IN PRIVATE TOO?
WHA...?

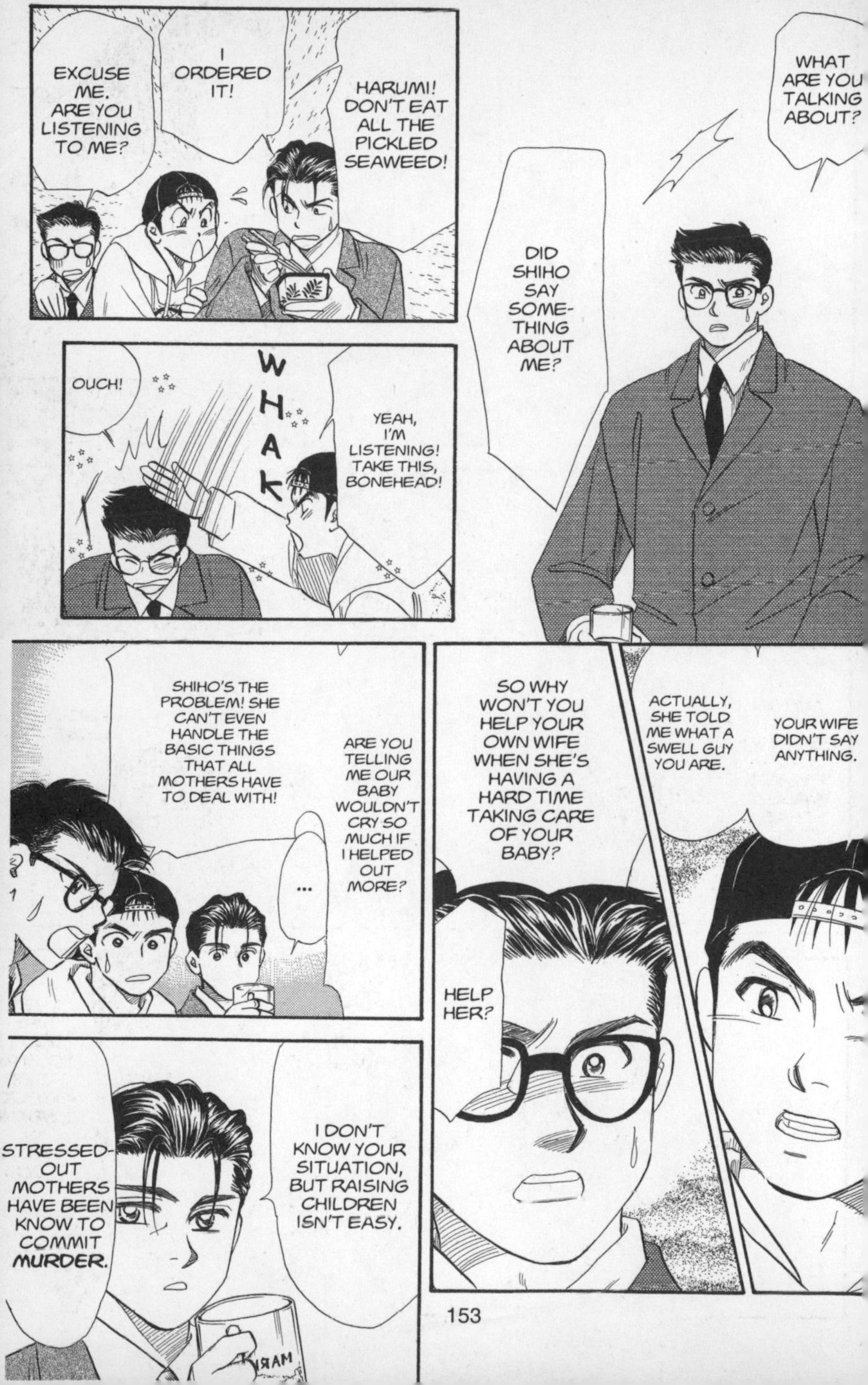
WHAT ARE YOU TALKING ABOUT?
DID SHIHO SAY SOME-THING ABOUT ME?
HARUMI! DON'T EAT ALL THE PICKLED SEAWEED!
I ORDERED IT!
EXCUSE ME. ARE YOU LISTENING TO ME?
YEAH, I'M LISTENING! TAKE THIS, BONEHEAD!
WHAK
OUCH!
YOUR WIFE DIDN'T SAY ANYTHING.
ACTUALLY, SHE TOLD ME WHAT A SWELL GUY YOU ARE.
SO WHY WON'T YOU HELP YOUR OWN WIFE WHEN SHE'S HAVING A HARD TIME TAKING CARE OF YOUR BABY?
HELP HER?
ARE YOU TELLING ME OUR BABY WOULDN'T CRY SO MUCH IF I HELPED OUT MORE?
SHIHO'S THE PROBLEM! SHE CAN'T EVEN HANDLE THE BASIC THINGS THAT ALL MOTHERS HAVE TO DEAL WITH!
...
I DON'T KNOW YOUR SITUATION, BUT RAISING CHILDREN ISN'T EASY.
STRESSED-OUT MOTHERS HAVE BEEN KNOW TO COMMIT **MURDER**.

I KNOW THAT. TOMOKO'S STRONG!

IS YOUR WIFE STRONG?

ONLY THE WEAK ONES.

DON'T YOU LOVE ME, DADDY?

KLAK

WHERE ARE YOU, DADDY?

WHY DON'T YOU STOP HER?

WHY DO PEOPLE HAVE KIDS IF THEY'RE NOT FIT TO RAISE THEM?

NO, MOMMY, IT HURTS!!

IT'S ALWAYS THE CHILDREN WHO SUFFER!

I'M SORRY. I'LL BE QUIET. PLEASE DON'T HIT ME.

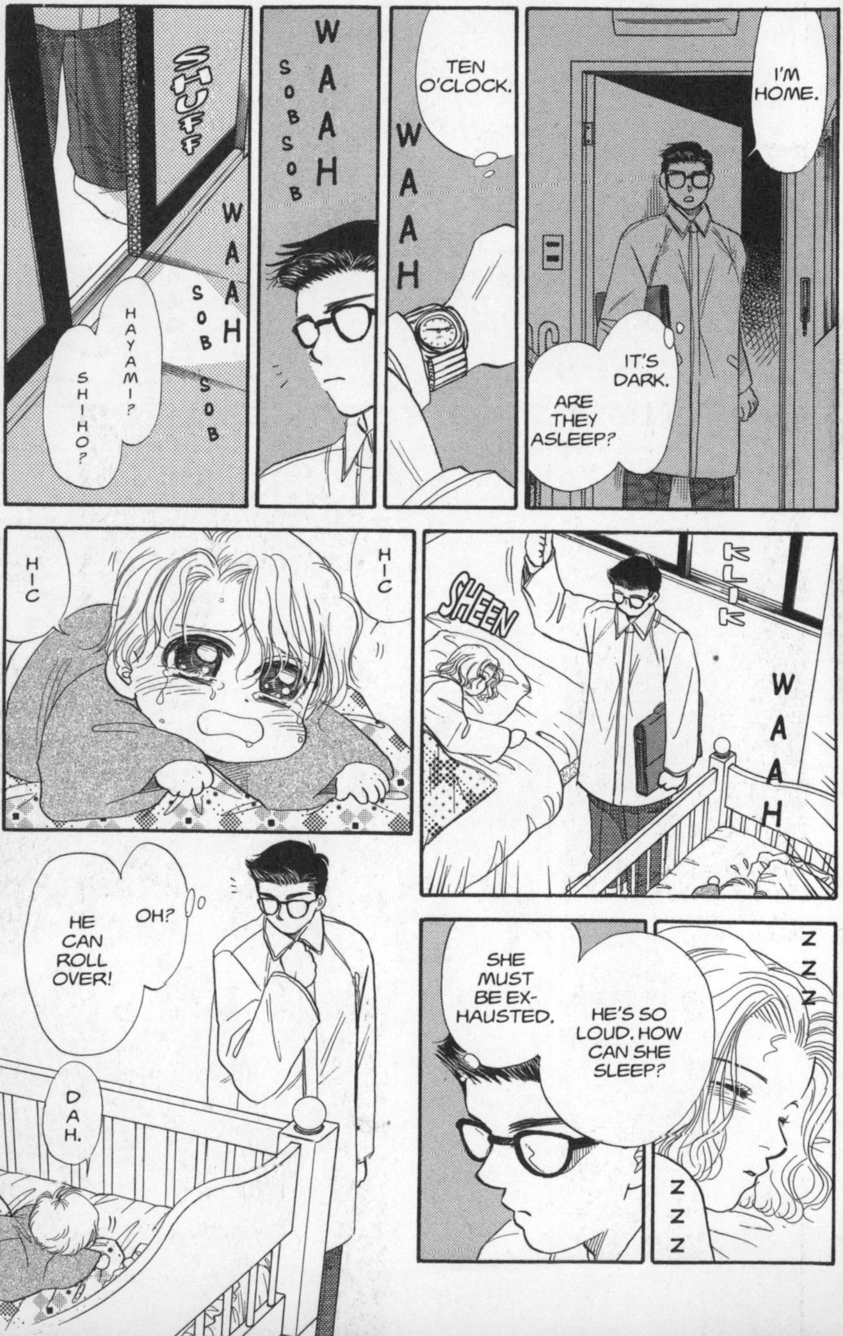
I'M HOME.
IT'S DARK.
ARE THEY ASLEEP?
TEN O'CLOCK.
WAAH
WAAH
SOBSOB
SHUFF
WAAH
SOB SOB
HAYAMI?
SHIHO?
KLIK
SHEEN
WAAH
HIC
HIC
ZZZ
HE'S SO LOUD. HOW CAN SHE SLEEP?
SHE MUST BE EX-HAUSTED.
ZZZ
OH?
HE CAN ROLL OVER!
DAH.

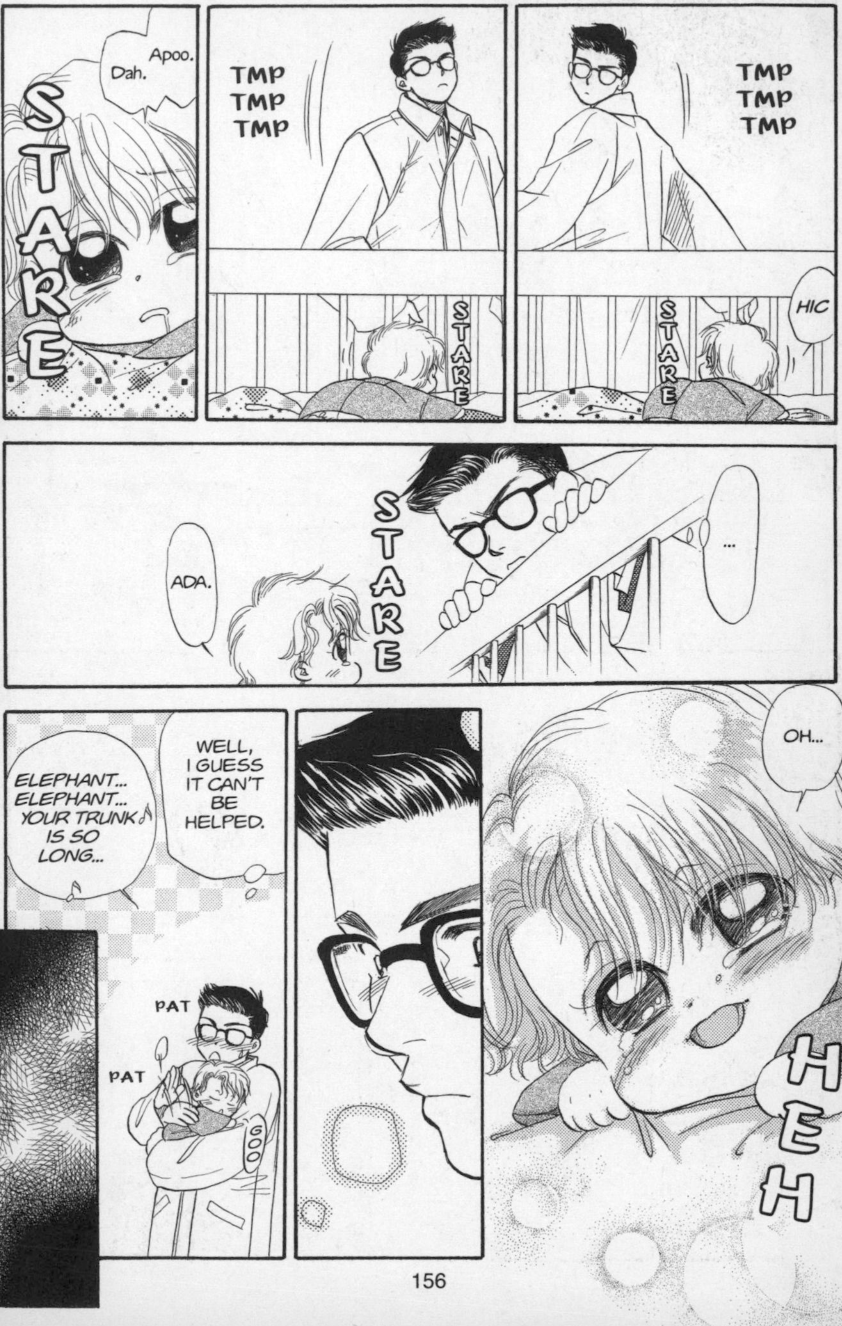
TMP
TMP
TMP
STARE
HIC
TMP
TMP
TMP
STARE
Apoo.
Dah.
STARE
...
STARE
ADA.
OH...
HEH
WELL, I GUESS IT CAN'T BE HELPED.
ELEPHANT... ELEPHANT... YOUR TRUNK IS SO LONG...
PAT
PAT
GOO

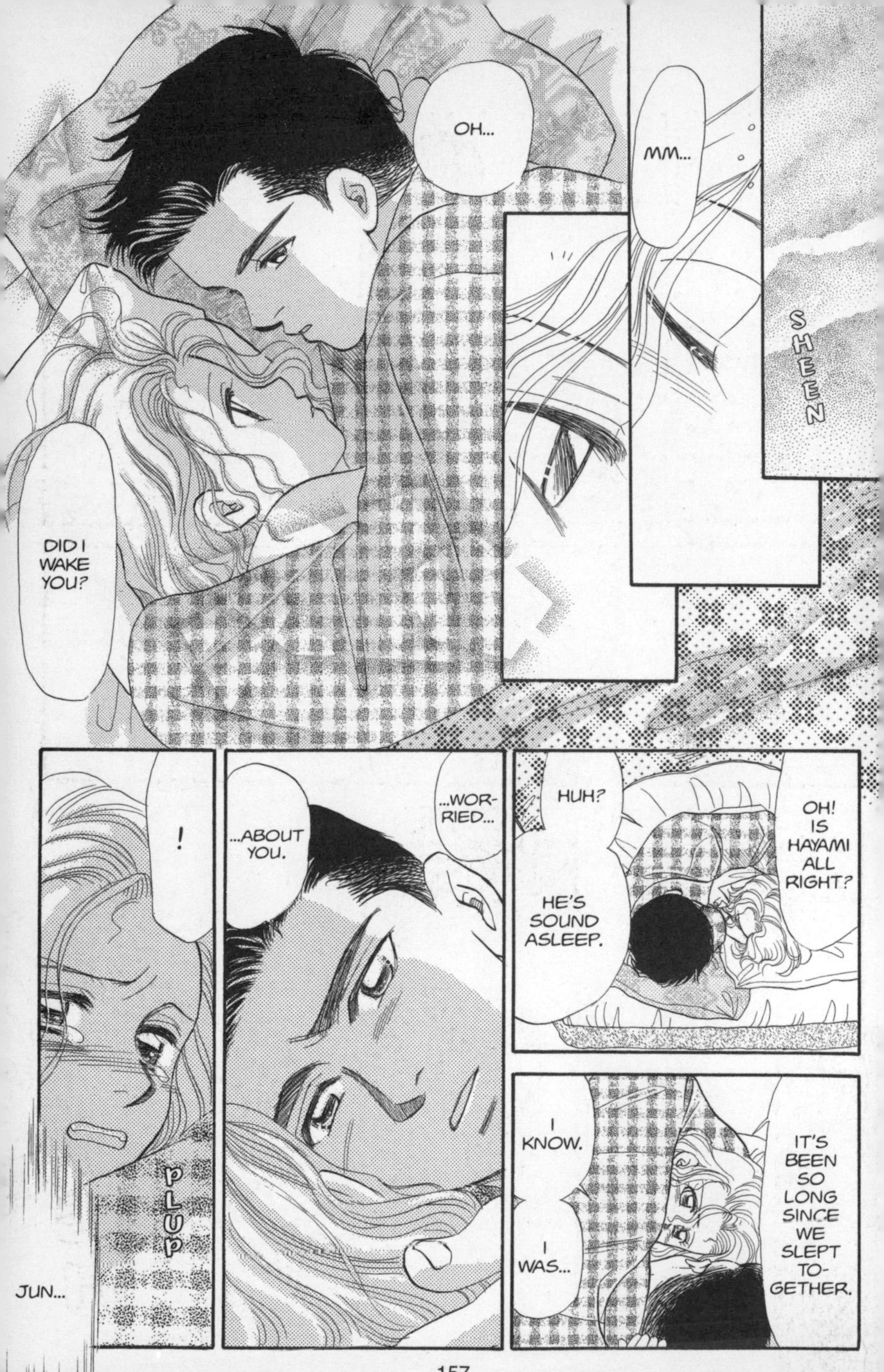
SHEEN
MM...
OH...
DID I WAKE YOU?
OH! IS HAYAMI ALL RIGHT?
HUH?
HE'S SOUND ASLEEP.
IT'S BEEN SO LONG SINCE WE SLEPT TO-GETHER.
I KNOW.
I WAS...
...WOR-RIED...
...ABOUT YOU.
!
PLUP
JUN...

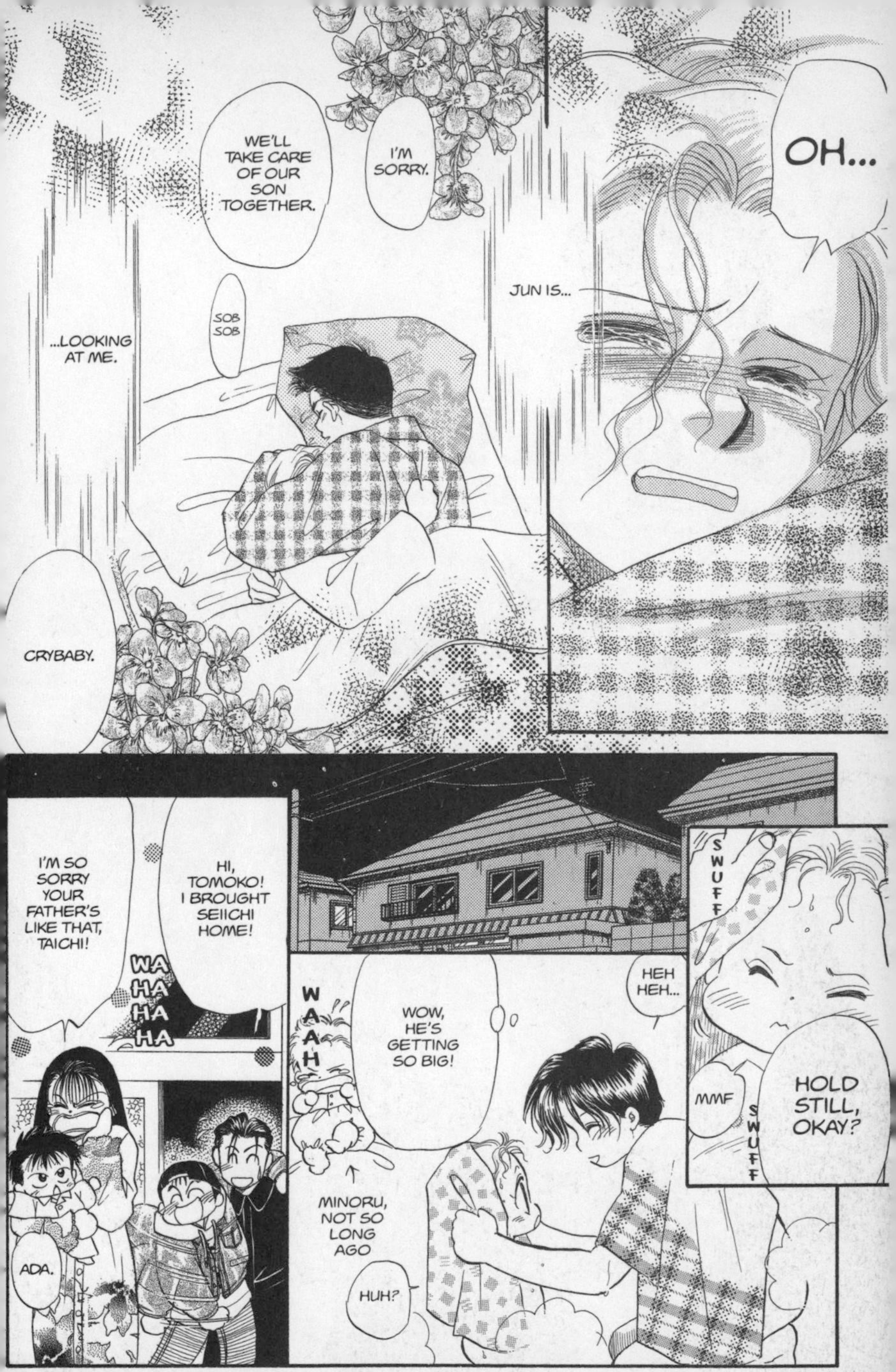
OH...
JUN IS...
I'M SORRY.
WE'LL TAKE CARE OF OUR SON TOGETHER.
SOB SOB
...LOOKING AT ME.
CRYBABY.
SWUFF
HOLD STILL, OKAY?
SWUFF
MMF
HEH HEH...
WOW, HE'S GETTING SO BIG!
WAAAH
MINORU, NOT SO LONG AGO
HUH?
HI, TOMOKO! I BROUGHT SEIICHI HOME!
I'M SO SORRY YOUR FATHER'S LIKE THAT, TAICHI!
WA HA HA HA
ADA.

Chapter 79 / The End

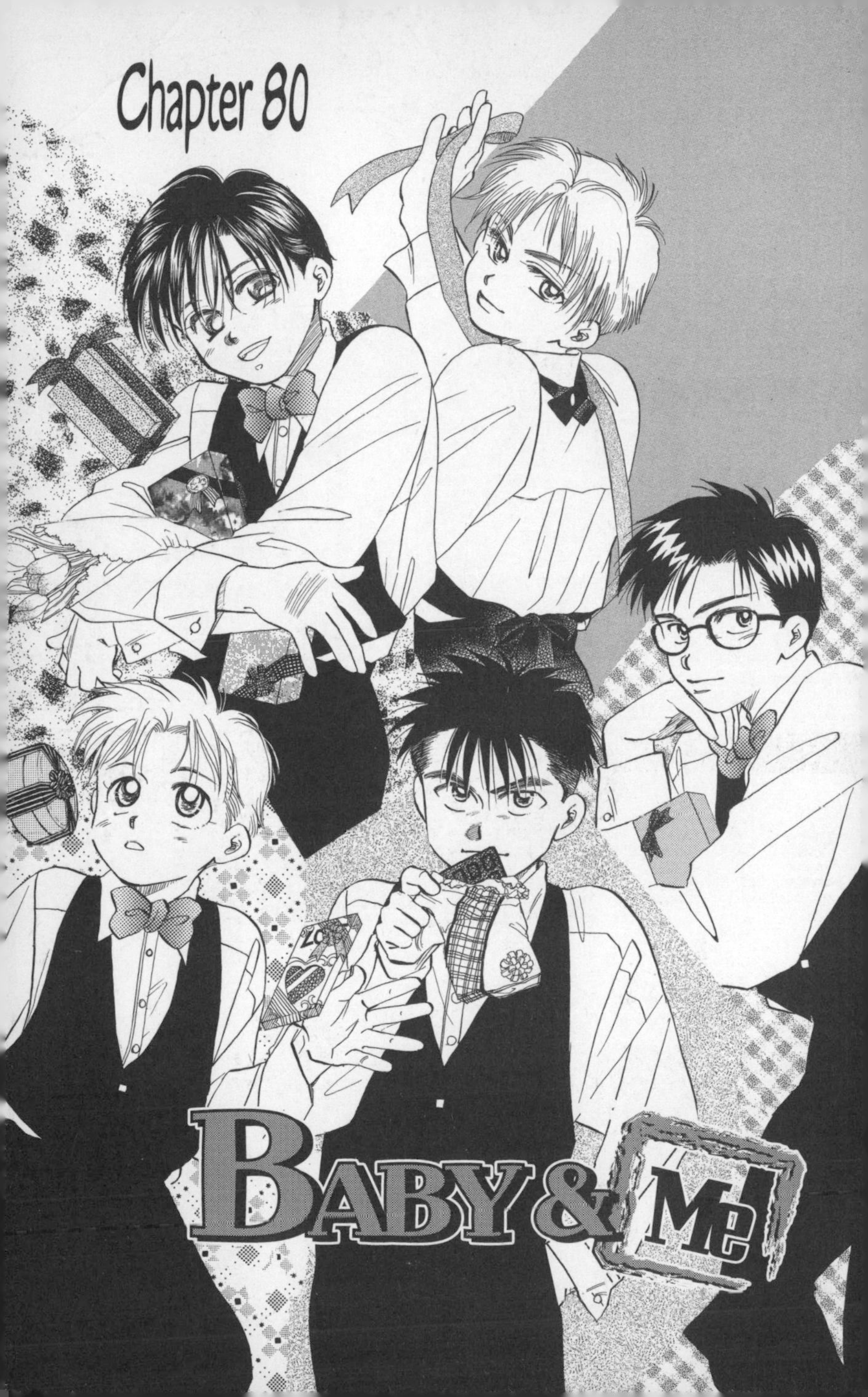
Chapter 80
BABY & ME

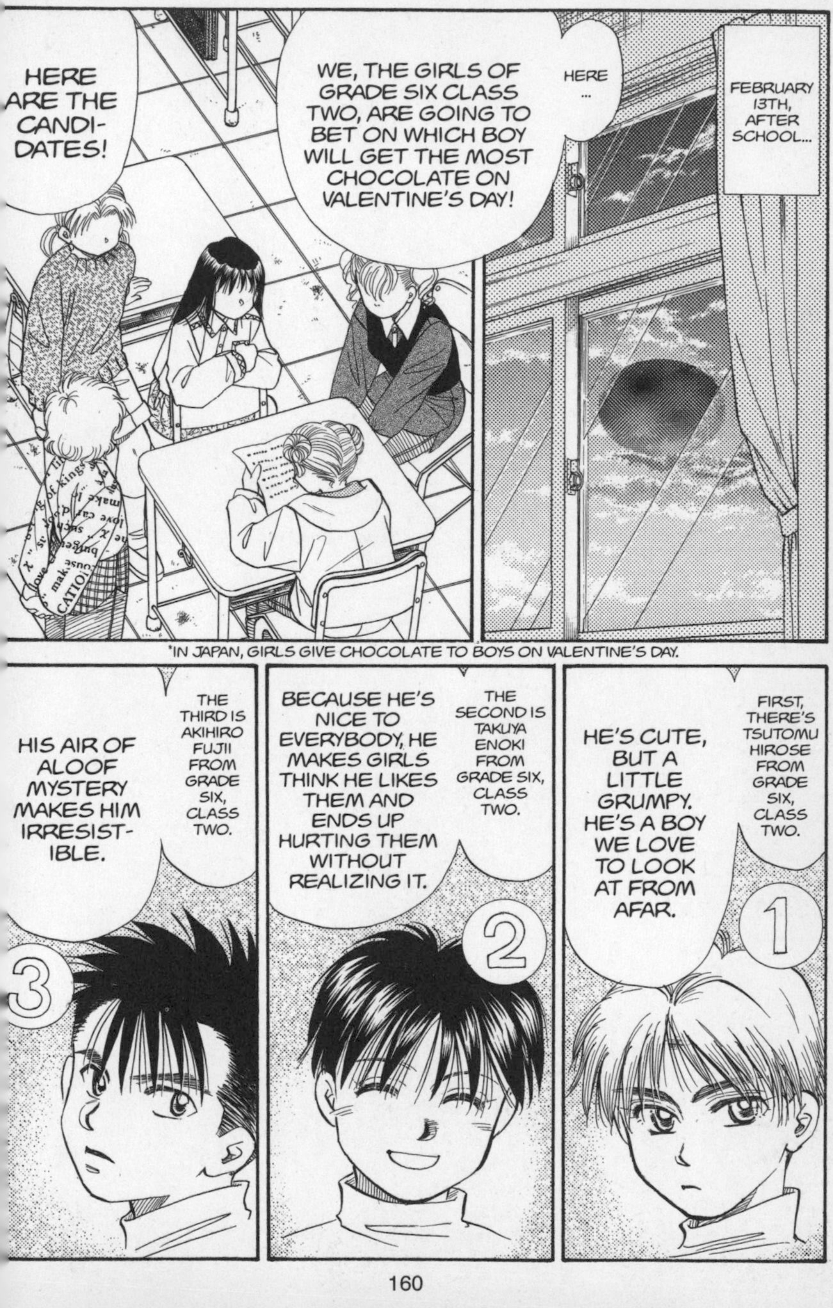
FEBRUARY 13TH, AFTER SCHOOL...
HERE ...
WE, THE GIRLS OF GRADE SIX CLASS TWO, ARE GOING TO BET ON WHICH BOY WILL GET THE MOST CHOCOLATE ON VALENTINE'S DAY!
HERE ARE THE CANDI-DATES!
*IN JAPAN, GIRLS GIVE CHOCOLATE TO BOYS ON VALENTINE'S DAY.
FIRST, THERE'S TSUTOMU HIROSE FROM GRADE SIX, CLASS TWO.
HE'S CUTE, BUT A LITTLE GRUMPY. HE'S A BOY WE LOVE TO LOOK AT FROM AFAR.
1
THE SECOND IS TAKUYA ENOKI FROM GRADE SIX, CLASS TWO.
BECAUSE HE'S NICE TO EVERYBODY, HE MAKES GIRLS THINK HE LIKES THEM AND ENDS UP HURTING THEM WITHOUT REALIZING IT.
2
THE THIRD IS AKIHIRO FUJII FROM GRADE SIX, CLASS TWO.
HIS AIR OF ALOOF MYSTERY MAKES HIM IRRESIST-IBLE.
3

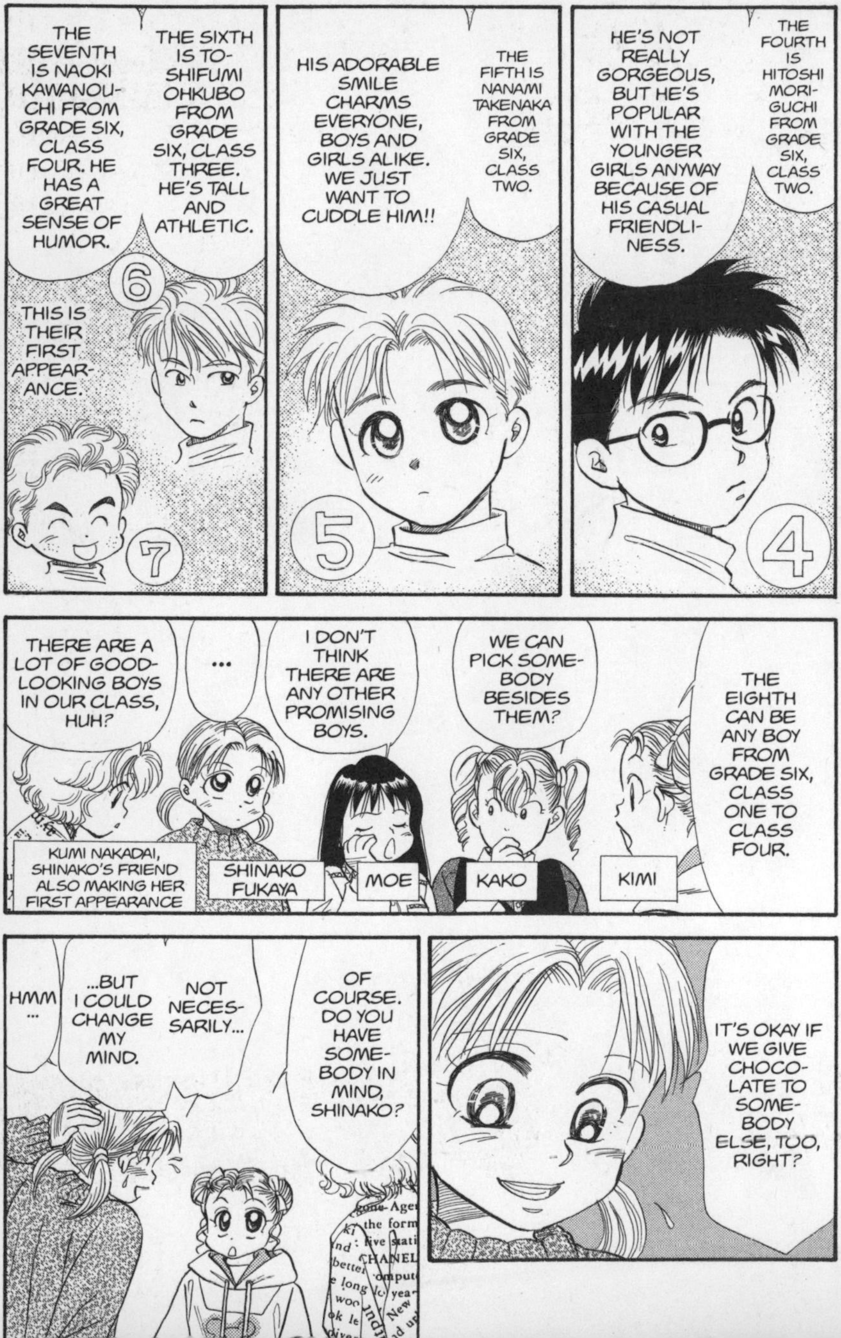
THE FOURTH IS HITOSHI MORIGUCHI FROM GRADE SIX, CLASS TWO.
HE'S NOT REALLY GORGEOUS, BUT HE'S POPULAR WITH THE YOUNGER GIRLS ANYWAY BECAUSE OF HIS CASUAL FRIENDLINESS.
4
THE FIFTH IS NANAMI TAKENAKA FROM GRADE SIX, CLASS TWO.
HIS ADORABLE SMILE CHARMS EVERYONE, BOYS AND GIRLS ALIKE. WE JUST WANT TO CUDDLE HIM!!
5
THE SIXTH IS TOSHIFUMI OHKUBO FROM GRADE SIX, CLASS THREE. HE'S TALL AND ATHLETIC.
THE SEVENTH IS NAOKI KAWANOUCHI FROM GRADE SIX, CLASS FOUR. HE HAS A GREAT SENSE OF HUMOR.
6
THIS IS THEIR FIRST APPEARANCE.
7
THE EIGHTH CAN BE ANY BOY FROM GRADE SIX, CLASS ONE TO CLASS FOUR.
KIMI
WE CAN PICK SOMEBODY BESIDES THEM?
KAKO
I DON'T THINK THERE ARE ANY OTHER PROMISING BOYS.
MOE
...
THERE ARE A LOT OF GOOD-LOOKING BOYS IN OUR CLASS, HUH?
SHINAKO FUKAYA
KUMI NAKADAI, SHINAKO'S FRIEND ALSO MAKING HER FIRST APPEARANCE
IT'S OKAY IF WE GIVE CHOCOLATE TO SOMEBODY ELSE, TOO, RIGHT?
OF COURSE. DO YOU HAVE SOMEBODY IN MIND, SHINAKO?
NOT NECESSARILY...
...BUT I COULD CHANGE MY MIND.
HMM ...

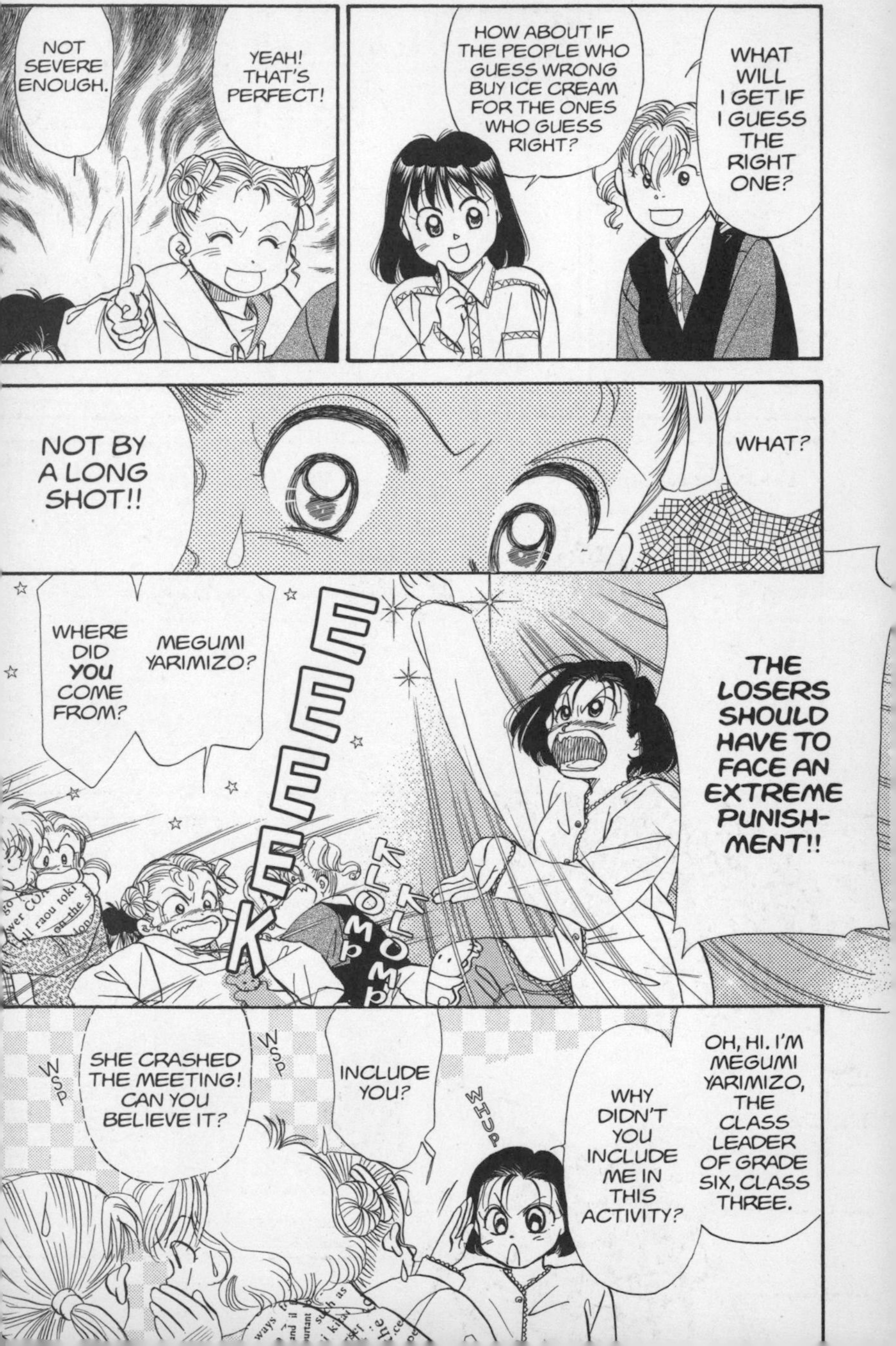
WHAT WILL I GET IF I GUESS THE RIGHT ONE?
HOW ABOUT IF THE PEOPLE WHO GUESS WRONG BUY ICE CREAM FOR THE ONES WHO GUESS RIGHT?
YEAH! THAT'S PERFECT!
NOT SEVERE ENOUGH.
WHAT?
NOT BY A LONG SHOT!!
THE LOSERS SHOULD HAVE TO FACE AN EXTREME PUNISH-MENT!!
KLOMP
KLOMP
EEEEEK
MEGUMI YARIMIZO?
WHERE DID YOU COME FROM?
OH, HI. I'M MEGUMI YARIMIZO, THE CLASS LEADER OF GRADE SIX, CLASS THREE.
WHY DIDN'T YOU INCLUDE ME IN THIS ACTIVITY?
WHUP
INCLUDE YOU?
WSP
SHE CRASHED THE MEETING! CAN YOU BELIEVE IT?
WSP

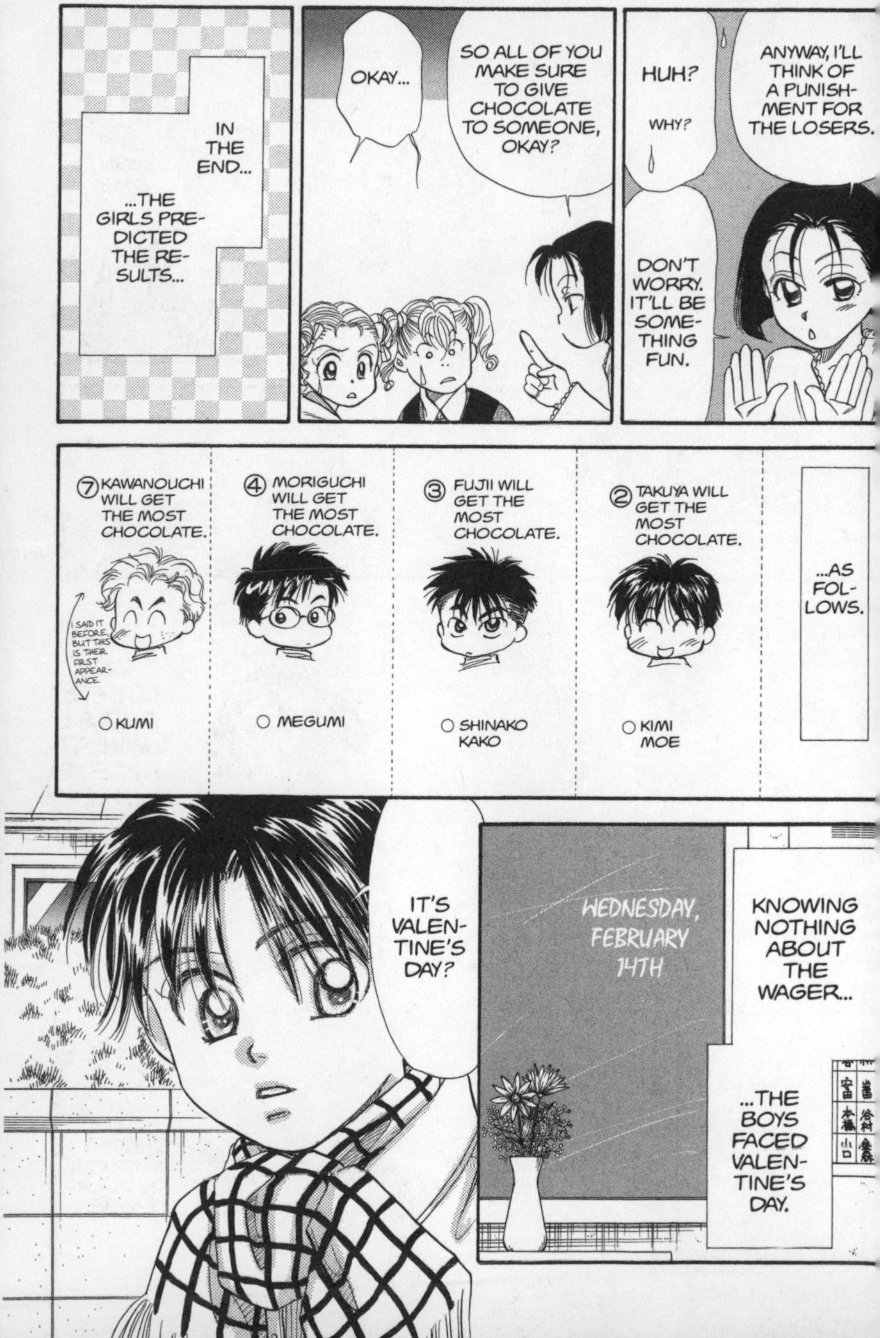
ANYWAY, I'LL THINK OF A PUNISHMENT FOR THE LOSERS.
HUH?
WHY?
DON'T WORRY. IT'LL BE SOMETHING FUN.
SO ALL OF YOU MAKE SURE TO GIVE CHOCOLATE TO SOMEONE, OKAY?
OKAY...
IN THE END...
...THE GIRLS PREDICTED THE RESULTS...
...AS FOLLOWS.
② TAKUYA WILL GET THE MOST CHOCOLATE.
○ KIMI
MOE
③ FUJII WILL GET THE MOST CHOCOLATE.
○ SHINAKO
KAKO
④ MORIGUCHI WILL GET THE MOST CHOCOLATE.
○ MEGUMI
⑦ KAWANOUCHI WILL GET THE MOST CHOCOLATE.
I SAID IT BEFORE, BUT THIS IS THEIR FIRST APPEARANCE.
○ KUMI
KNOWING NOTHING ABOUT THE WAGER...
WEDNESDAY, FEBRUARY 14TH
...THE BOYS FACED VALENTINE'S DAY.
IT'S VALENTINE'S DAY?

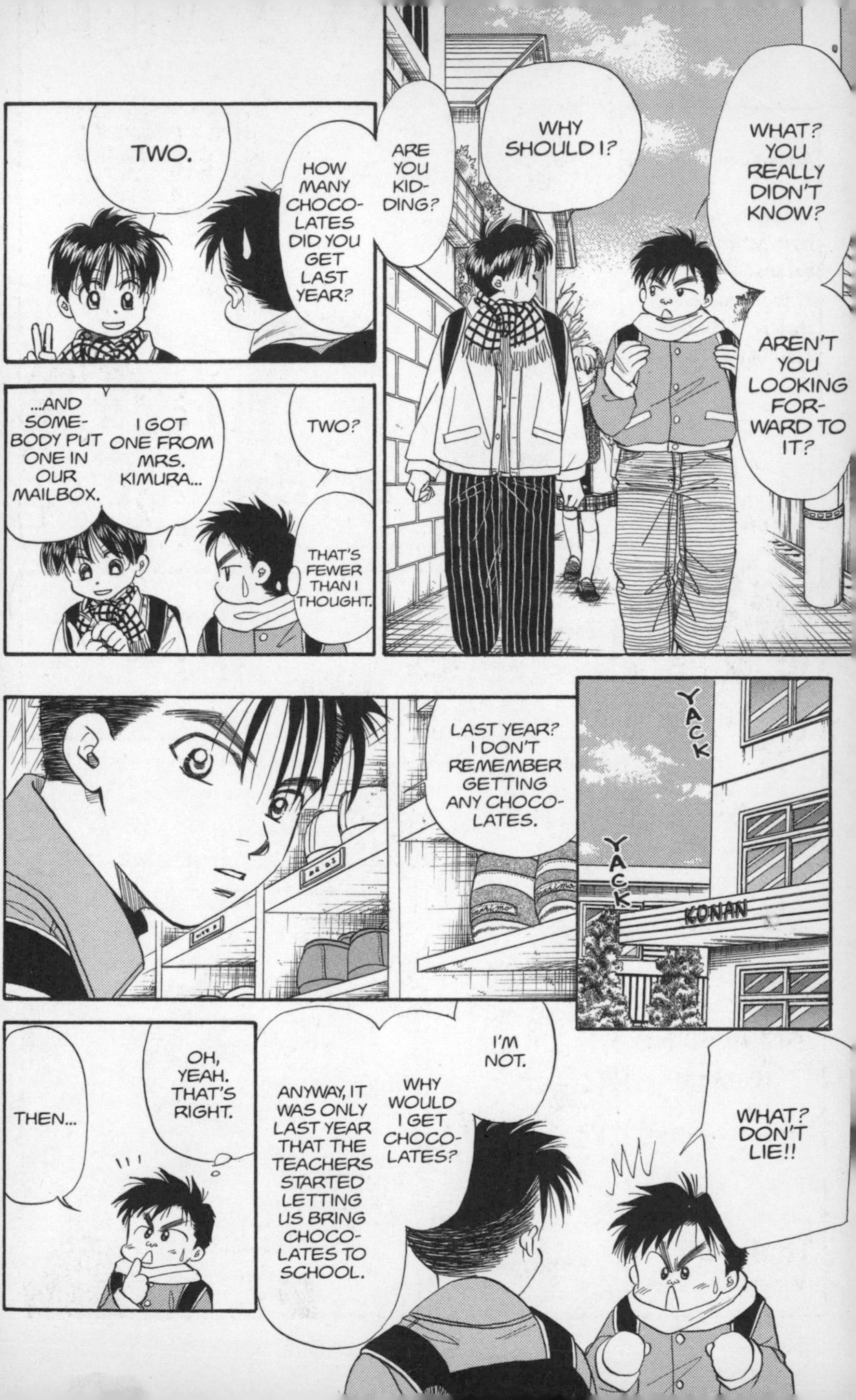
WHAT? YOU REALLY DIDN'T KNOW?
AREN'T YOU LOOKING FOR-WARD TO IT?
WHY SHOULD I?
ARE YOU KID-DING?
HOW MANY CHOCO-LATES DID YOU GET LAST YEAR?
TWO.
TWO?
THAT'S FEWER THAN I THOUGHT.
I GOT ONE FROM MRS. KIMURA...
...AND SOME-BODY PUT ONE IN OUR MAILBOX.
YACK
YACK
KONAN
LAST YEAR? I DON'T REMEMBER GETTING ANY CHOCO-LATES.
WHAT? DON'T LIE!!
I'M NOT.
WHY WOULD I GET CHOCO-LATES?
ANYWAY, IT WAS ONLY LAST YEAR THAT THE TEACHERS STARTED LETTING US BRING CHOCO-LATES TO SCHOOL.
OH, YEAH. THAT'S RIGHT.
THEN...

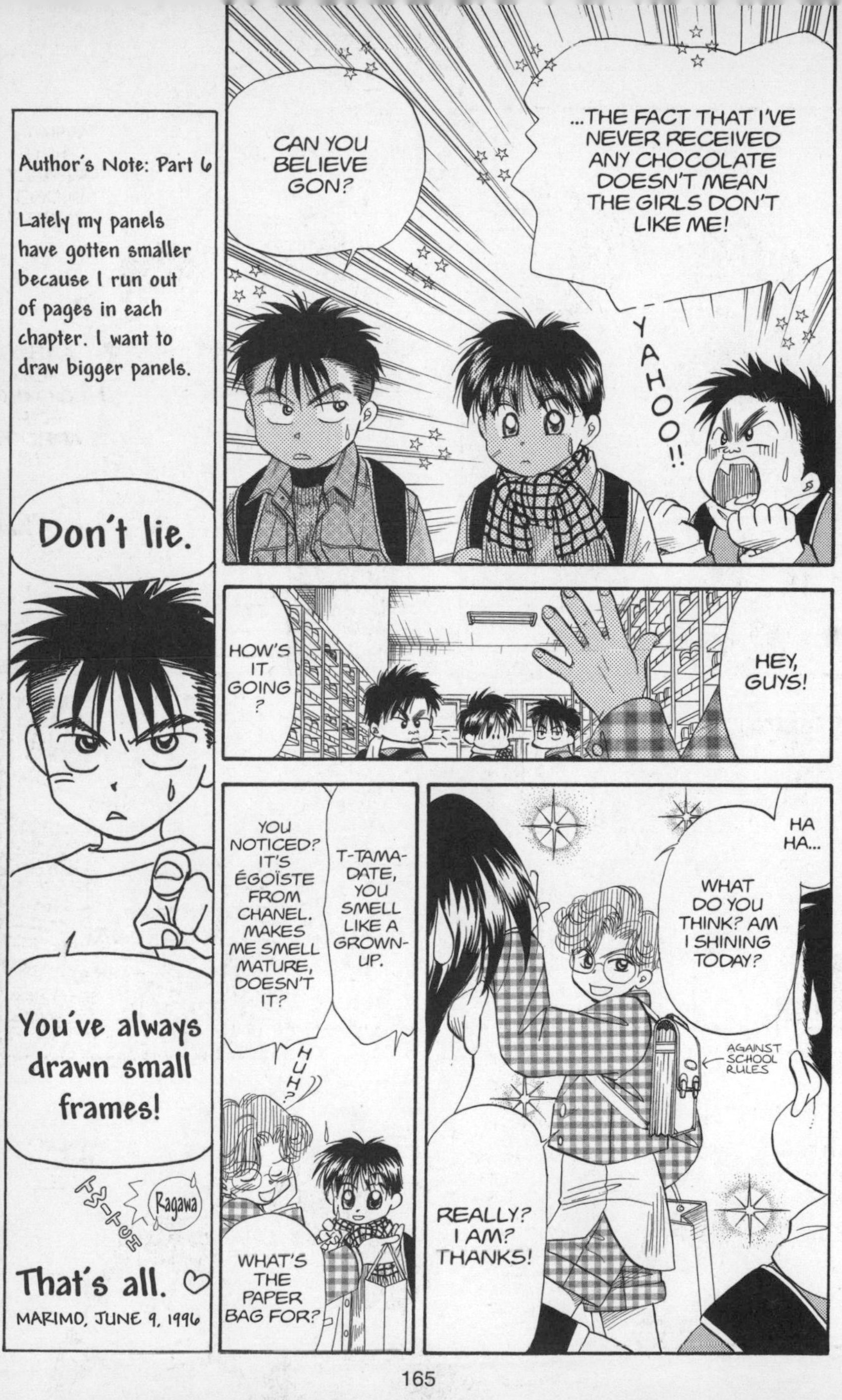
...THE FACT THAT I'VE NEVER RECEIVED ANY CHOCOLATE DOESN'T MEAN THE GIRLS DON'T LIKE ME!
YAHOO!!
CAN YOU BELIEVE GON?
HEY, GUYS!
HOW'S IT GOING?
HA HA...
WHAT DO YOU THINK? AM I SHINING TODAY?
AGAINST SCHOOL RULES
REALLY? I AM? THANKS!
T-TAMADATE, YOU SMELL LIKE A GROWN-UP.
YOU NOTICED? IT'S ÉGOÏSTE FROM CHANEL. MAKES ME SMELL MATURE, DOESN'T IT?
HUH?
WHAT'S THE PAPER BAG FOR?
Author's Note: Part 6
Lately my panels have gotten smaller because I run out of pages in each chapter. I want to draw bigger panels.
Don't lie.
You've always drawn small frames!
TWITCH
Ragawa
That's all. ♡
MARIMO, JUNE 9, 1996

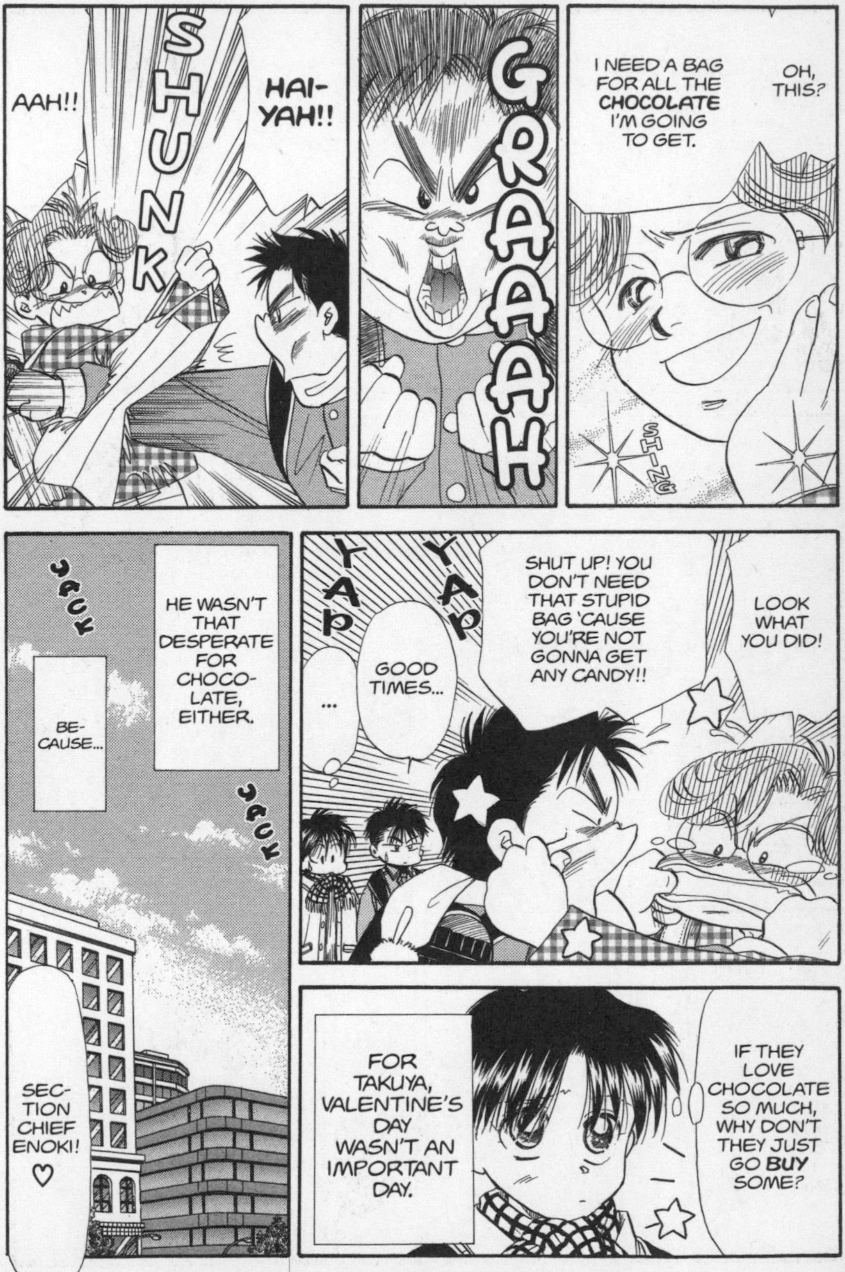
OH, THIS?
I NEED A BAG FOR ALL THE **CHOCOLATE** I'M GOING TO GET.
SHING
GRAAAAH
HAI-YAH!!
SHUNK
AAH!!
LOOK WHAT YOU DID!
SHUT UP! YOU DON'T NEED THAT STUPID BAG 'CAUSE YOU'RE NOT GONNA GET ANY CANDY!!
YAP YAP
GOOD TIMES...
...
IF THEY LOVE CHOCOLATE SO MUCH, WHY DON'T THEY JUST GO **BUY** SOME?
FOR TAKUYA, VALENTINE'S DAY WASN'T AN IMPORTANT DAY.
HE WASN'T THAT DESPERATE FOR CHOCO-LATE, EITHER.
YACK
BE-CAUSE...
YACK
SEC-TION CHIEF ENOKI! ♡

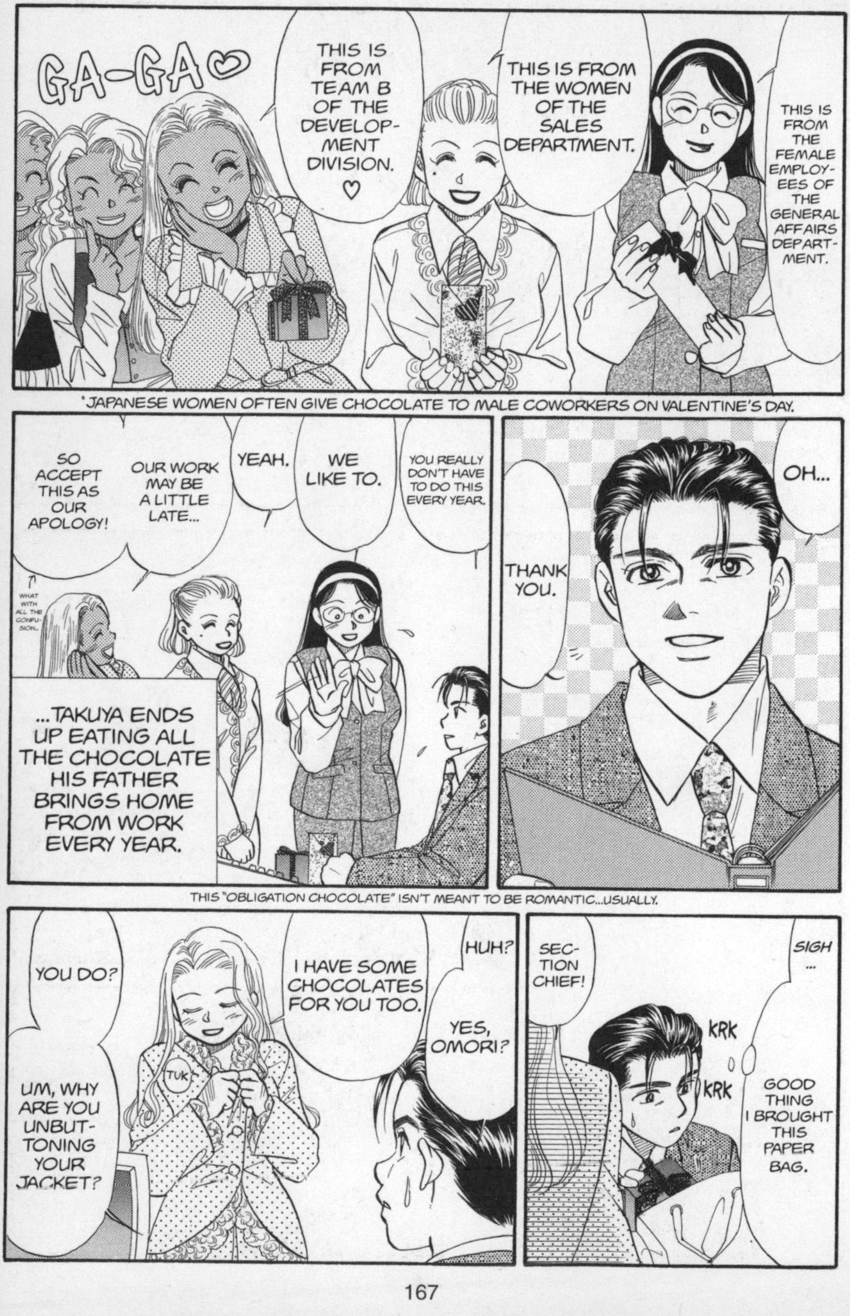
THIS IS FROM THE FEMALE EMPLOYEES OF THE GENERAL AFFAIRS DEPARTMENT.
THIS IS FROM THE WOMEN OF THE SALES DEPARTMENT.
THIS IS FROM TEAM B OF THE DEVELOPMENT DIVISION. ♡
GA-GA♡
*JAPANESE WOMEN OFTEN GIVE CHOCOLATE TO MALE COWORKERS ON VALENTINE'S DAY.
OH...
THANK YOU.
YOU REALLY DON'T HAVE TO DO THIS EVERY YEAR.
WE LIKE TO.
YEAH.
OUR WORK MAY BE A LITTLE LATE...
SO ACCEPT THIS AS OUR APOLOGY!
WHAT WITH ALL THE CONFUSION...
...TAKUYA ENDS UP EATING ALL THE CHOCOLATE HIS FATHER BRINGS HOME FROM WORK EVERY YEAR.
THIS "OBLIGATION CHOCOLATE" ISN'T MEANT TO BE ROMANTIC...USUALLY.
SIGH...
SECTION CHIEF!
KRK
KRK
GOOD THING I BROUGHT THIS PAPER BAG.
HUH?
YES, OMORI?
I HAVE SOME CHOCOLATES FOR YOU TOO.
YOU DO?
TUK
UM, WHY ARE YOU UNBUTTONING YOUR JACKET?

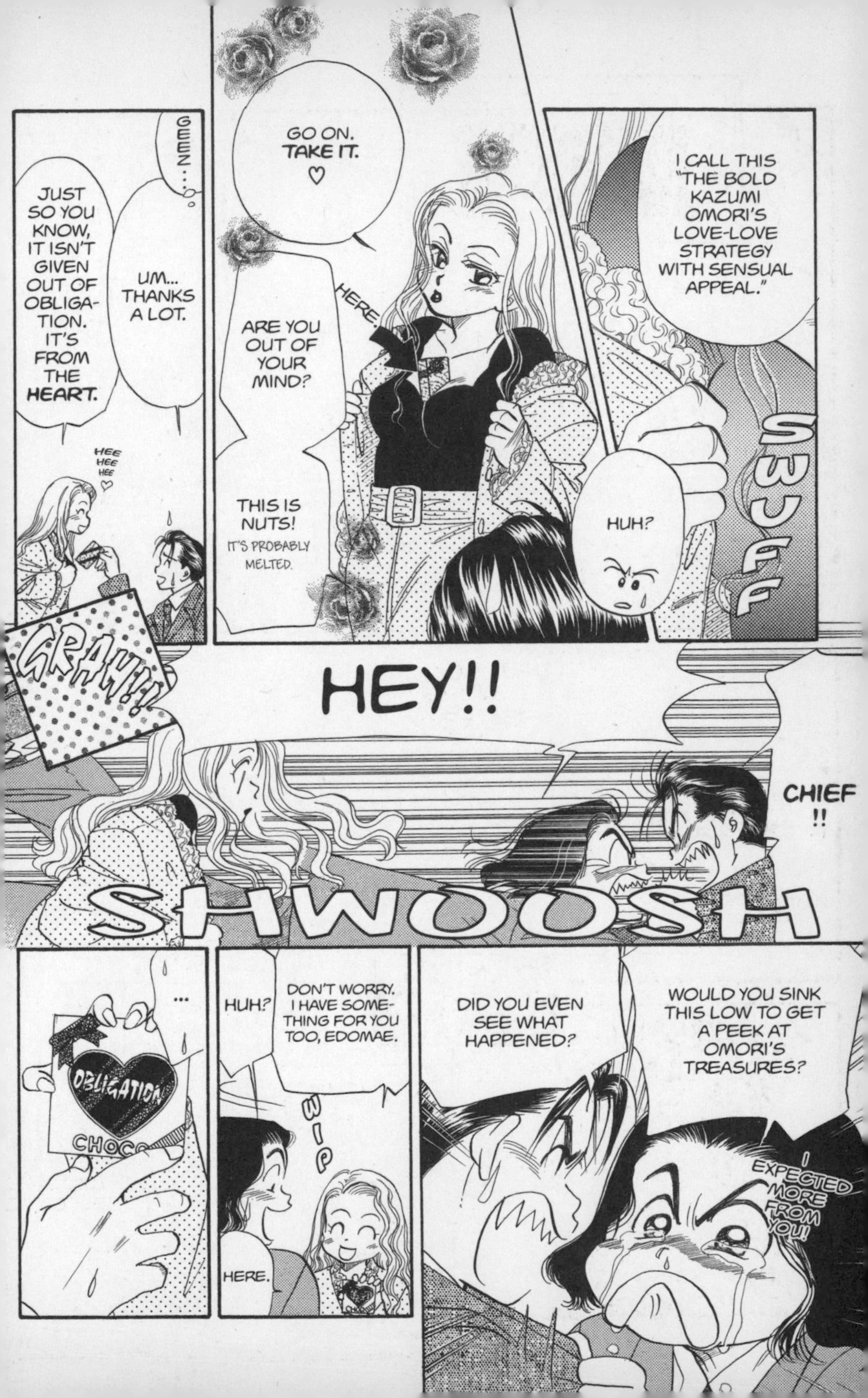
I CALL THIS "THE BOLD KAZUMI OMORI'S LOVE-LOVE STRATEGY WITH SENSUAL APPEAL."
SWUFF
HUH?
GO ON. TAKE IT. ♥
HERE.
ARE YOU OUT OF YOUR MIND?
THIS IS NUTS! IT'S PROBABLY MELTED.
GEEZ...
UM... THANKS A LOT.
JUST SO YOU KNOW, IT ISN'T GIVEN OUT OF OBLIGATION. IT'S FROM THE HEART.
HEE HEE HEE ♥
CHIEF!!
HEY!!
GRAAH!!
SHWOOSH
WOULD YOU SINK THIS LOW TO GET A PEEK AT OMORI'S TREASURES?
DID YOU EVEN SEE WHAT HAPPENED?
I EXPECTED MORE FROM YOU!
DON'T WORRY. I HAVE SOMETHING FOR YOU TOO, EDOMAE.
HUH?
WIP
HERE.
...
OBLIGATION
CHOCO

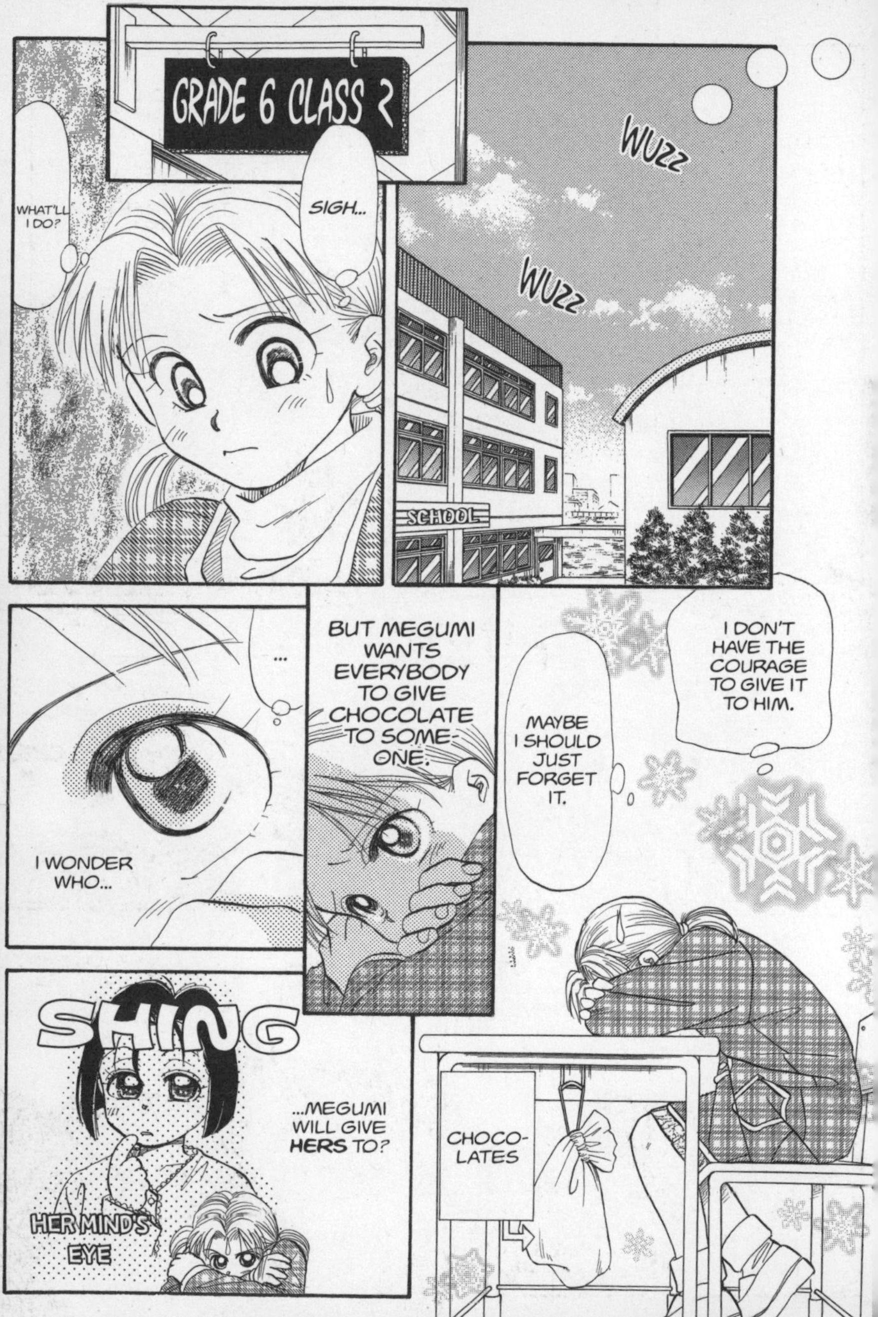
WUZZ
WUZZ
SCHOOL
GRADE 6 CLASS 2
SIGH...
WHAT'LL I DO?
I DON'T HAVE THE COURAGE TO GIVE IT TO HIM.
MAYBE I SHOULD JUST FORGET IT.
CHOCO-LATES
BUT MEGUMI WANTS EVERYBODY TO GIVE CHOCOLATE TO SOME-ONE.
...
I WONDER WHO...
...MEGUMI WILL GIVE **HERS** TO?
SHING
HER MIND'S EYE

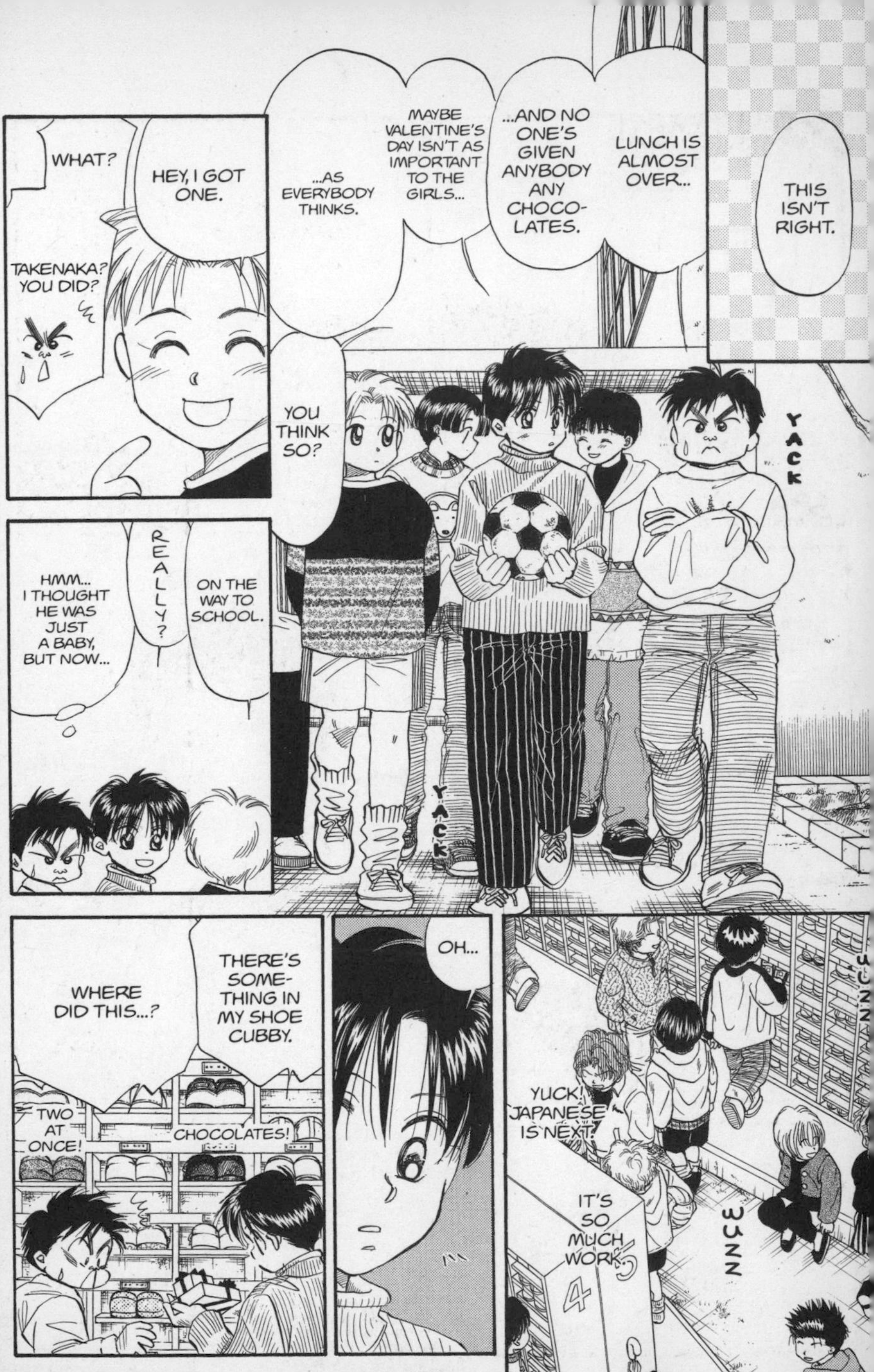
THIS ISN'T RIGHT.
LUNCH IS ALMOST OVER...
...AND NO ONE'S GIVEN ANYBODY ANY CHOCOLATES.
MAYBE VALENTINE'S DAY ISN'T AS IMPORTANT TO THE GIRLS...
...AS EVERYBODY THINKS.
YACK
YOU THINK SO?
YACK
HEY, I GOT ONE.
WHAT?
TAKENAKA? YOU DID?
ON THE WAY TO SCHOOL.
REALLY?
HMM... I THOUGHT HE WAS JUST A BABY, BUT NOW...
ZUNN
YUCK! JAPANESE IS NEXT.
IT'S SO MUCH WORK.
ZUNN
OH...
THERE'S SOMETHING IN MY SHOE CUBBY.
WHERE DID THIS...?
CHOCOLATES!
TWO AT ONCE!

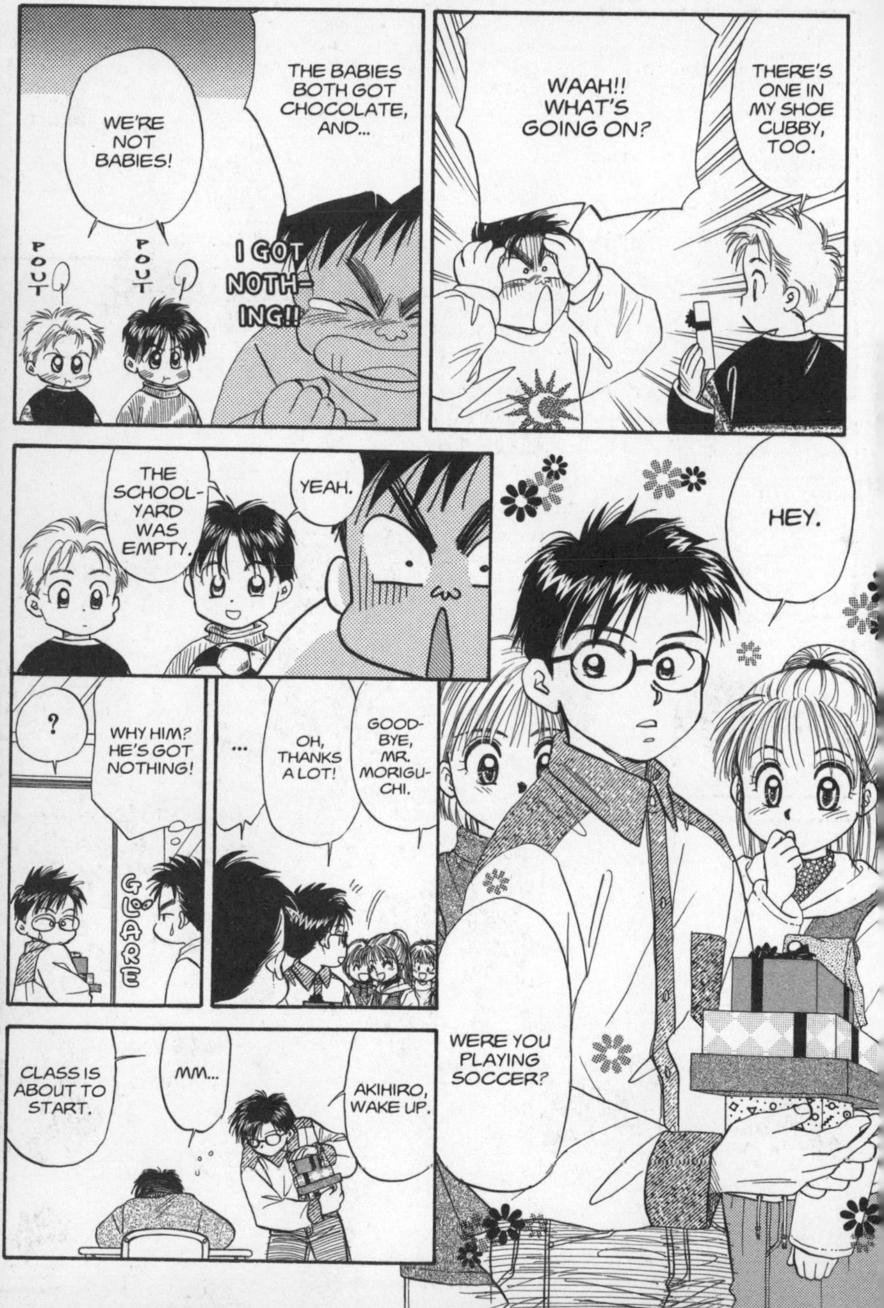
THERE'S ONE IN MY SHOE CUBBY, TOO.
WAAH!! WHAT'S GOING ON?
THE BABIES BOTH GOT CHOCOLATE, AND...
WE'RE NOT BABIES!
I GOT NOTHING!!
POUT
POUT
HEY.
WERE YOU PLAYING SOCCER?
YEAH.
THE SCHOOLYARD WAS EMPTY.
GOOD-BYE, MR. MORIGUCHI.
OH, THANKS A LOT!
...
WHY HIM? HE'S GOT NOTHING!
?
GLARE
AKIHIRO, WAKE UP.
MM...
CLASS IS ABOUT TO START.

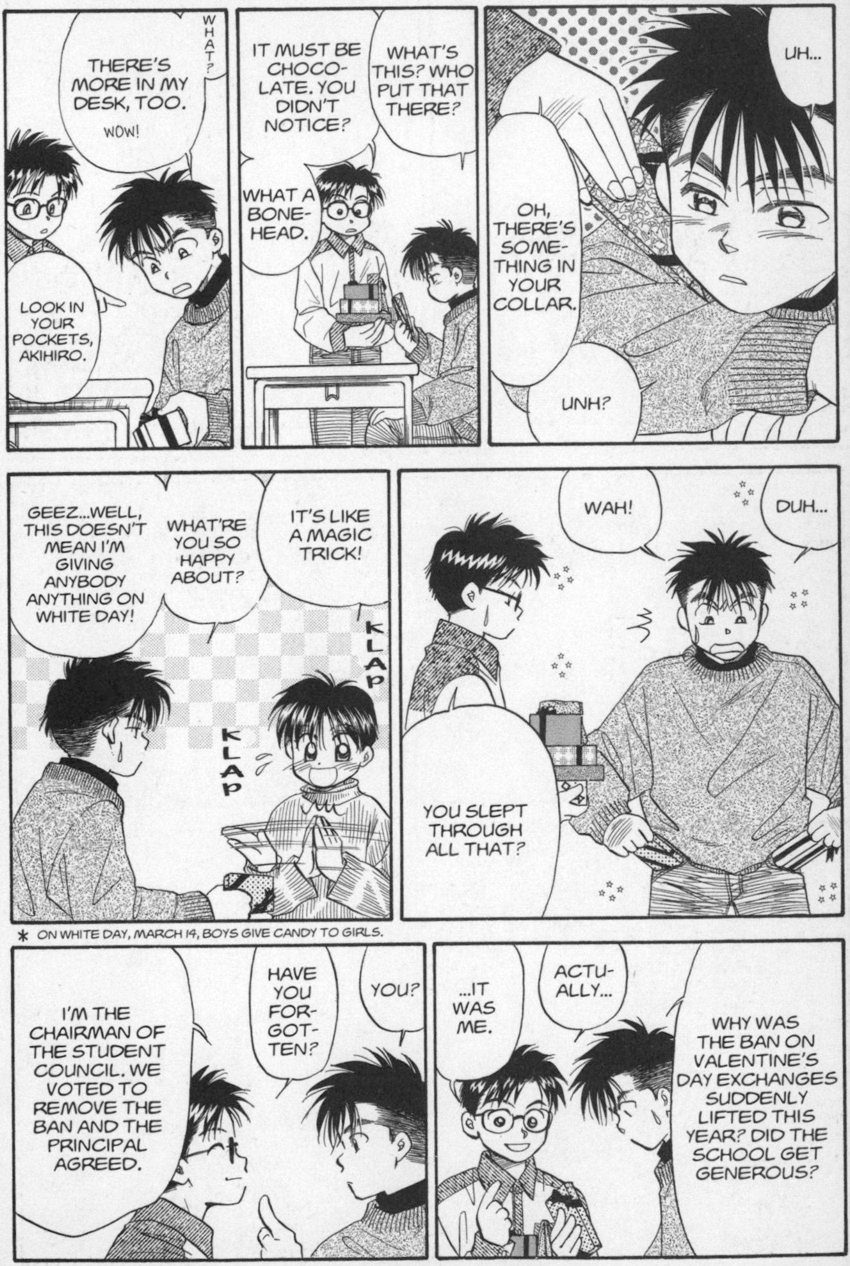
UH...
OH, THERE'S SOMETHING IN YOUR COLLAR.
UNH?
WHAT'S THIS? WHO PUT THAT THERE?
IT MUST BE CHOCOLATE. YOU DIDN'T NOTICE?
WHAT A BONEHEAD.
WHAT?
THERE'S MORE IN MY DESK, TOO.
WOW!
LOOK IN YOUR POCKETS, AKIHIRO.
DUH...
WAH!
YOU SLEPT THROUGH ALL THAT?
IT'S LIKE A MAGIC TRICK!
WHAT'RE YOU SO HAPPY ABOUT?
GEEZ...WELL, THIS DOESN'T MEAN I'M GIVING ANYBODY ANYTHING ON WHITE DAY!
KLAP
KLAP
WHY WAS THE BAN ON VALENTINE'S DAY EXCHANGES SUDDENLY LIFTED THIS YEAR? DID THE SCHOOL GET GENEROUS?
ACTUALLY...
...IT WAS ME.
YOU?
HAVE YOU FORGOTTEN?
I'M THE CHAIRMAN OF THE STUDENT COUNCIL. WE VOTED TO REMOVE THE BAN AND THE PRINCIPAL AGREED.

* ON WHITE DAY, MARCH 14, BOYS GIVE CANDY TO GIRLS.

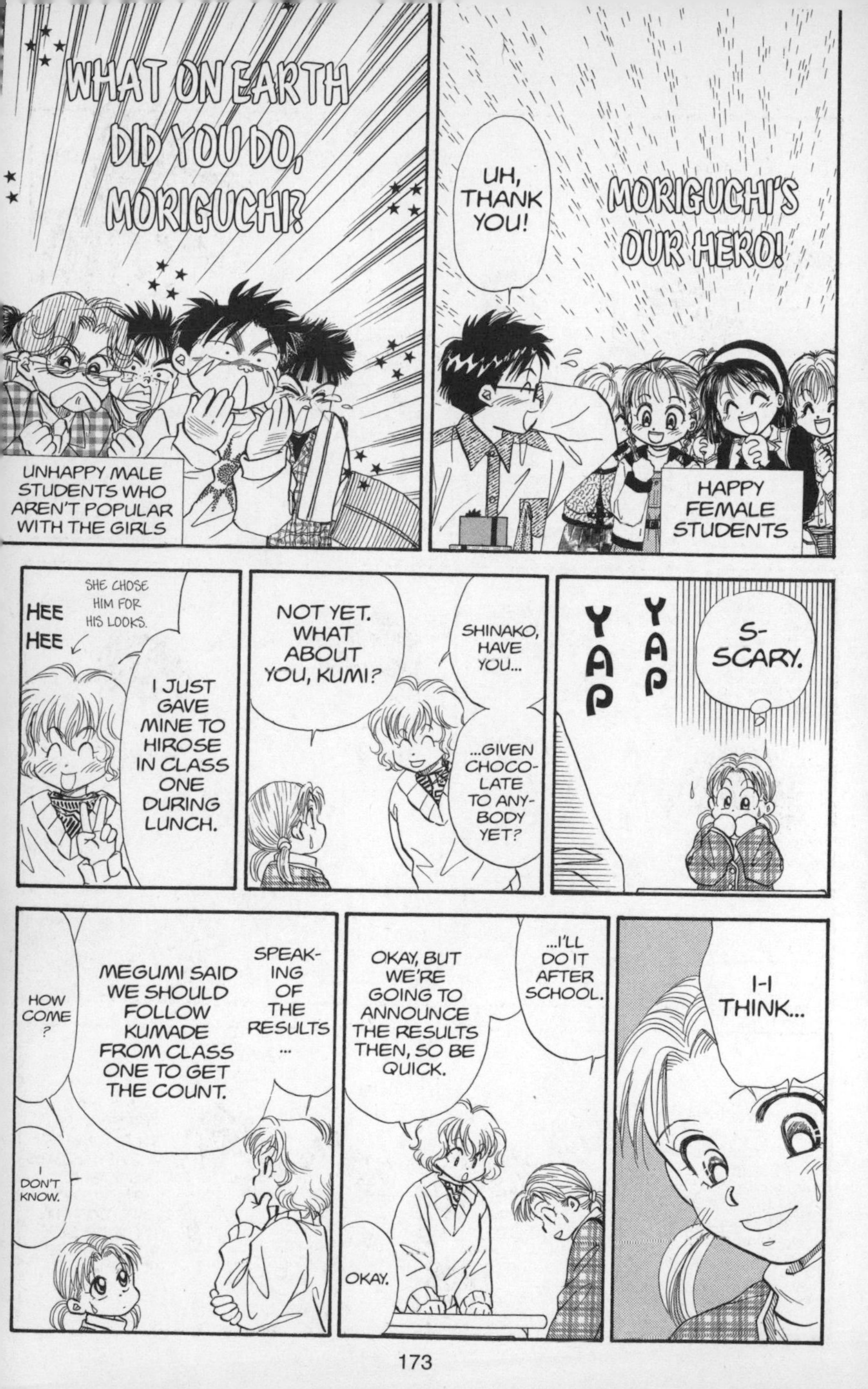
MORIGUCHI'S OUR HERO!
UH, THANK YOU!
HAPPY FEMALE STUDENTS
WHAT ON EARTH DID YOU DO, MORIGUCHI?
UNHAPPY MALE STUDENTS WHO AREN'T POPULAR WITH THE GIRLS
YAP YAP
S-SCARY.
SHINAKO, HAVE YOU...
...GIVEN CHOCOLATE TO ANYBODY YET?
NOT YET. WHAT ABOUT YOU, KUMI?
I JUST GAVE MINE TO HIROSE IN CLASS ONE DURING LUNCH.
SHE CHOSE HIM FOR HIS LOOKS.
HEE HEE
I-I THINK...
...I'LL DO IT AFTER SCHOOL.
OKAY, BUT WE'RE GOING TO ANNOUNCE THE RESULTS THEN, SO BE QUICK.
OKAY.
SPEAKING OF THE RESULTS...
MEGUMI SAID WE SHOULD FOLLOW KUMADE FROM CLASS ONE TO GET THE COUNT.
HOW COME?
I DON'T KNOW.

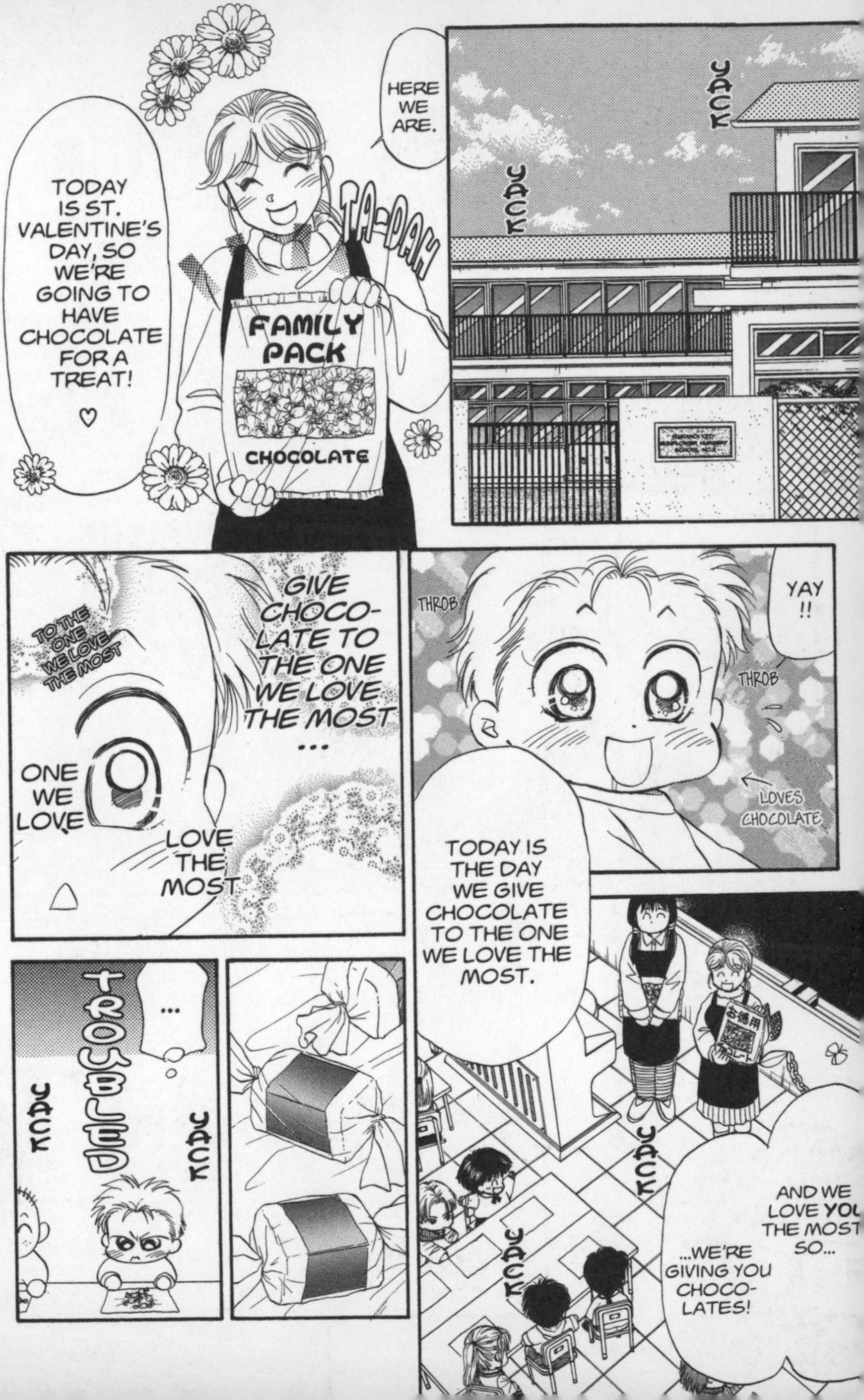
YACK
YACK
HERE WE ARE.
TA-DAH
TODAY IS ST. VALENTINE'S DAY, SO WE'RE GOING TO HAVE CHOCOLATE FOR A TREAT! ♡
FAMILY PACK CHOCOLATE
YAY!!
THROB
THROB
LOVES CHOCOLATE
GIVE CHOCOLATE TO THE ONE WE LOVE THE MOST...
TO THE ONE WE LOVE THE MOST
ONE WE LOVE
LOVE THE MOST
TODAY IS THE DAY WE GIVE CHOCOLATE TO THE ONE WE LOVE THE MOST.
AND WE LOVE YOU THE MOST SO...
...WE'RE GIVING YOU CHOCOLATES!
YACK
YACK
...
TROUBLED
YACK
YACK

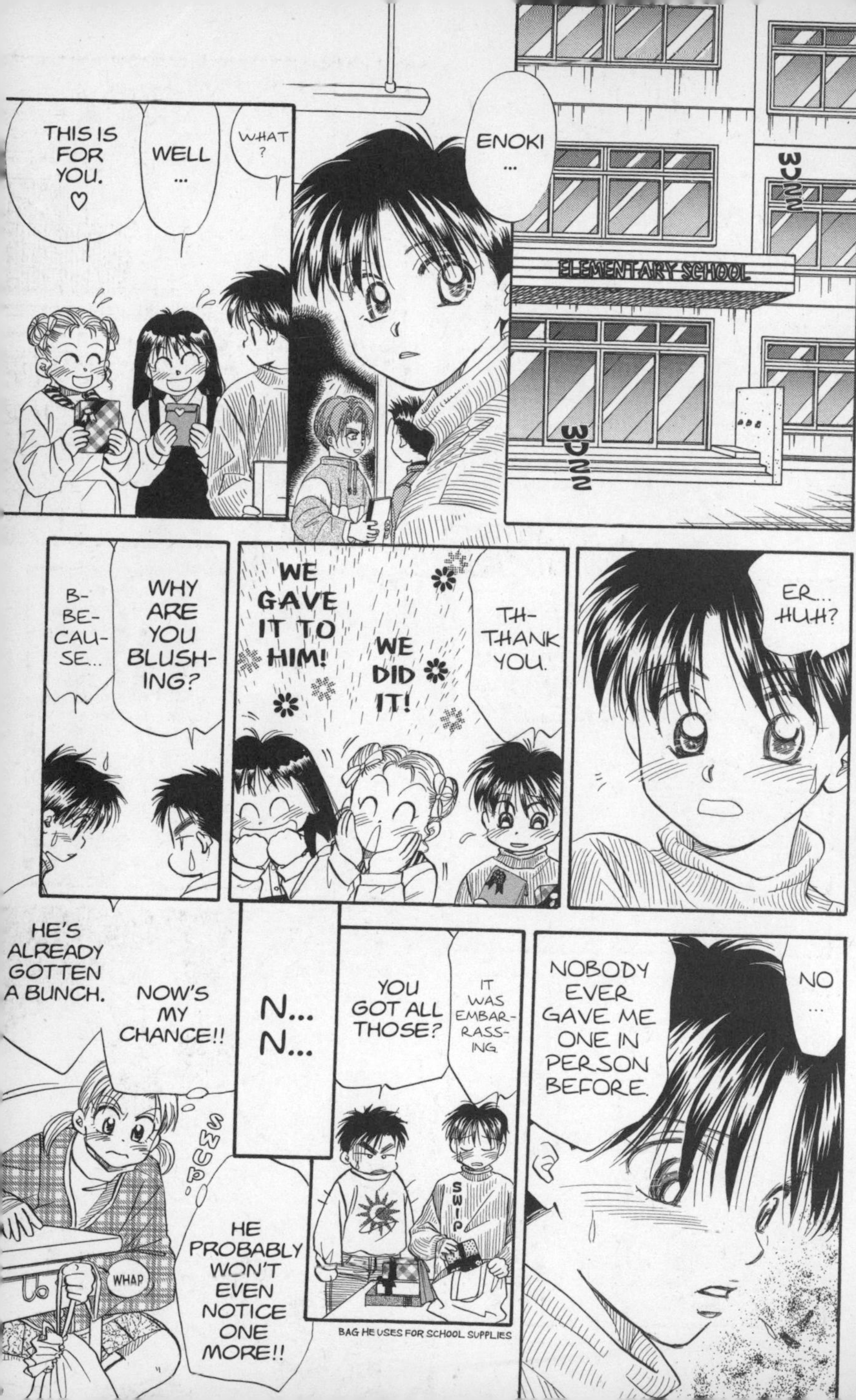
ELEMENTARY SCHOOL
ENOKI ...
WHAT ?
WELL ...
THIS IS FOR YOU. ♡
ER... HUH?
TH- THANK YOU.
WE GAVE IT TO HIM!
WE DID IT!
WHY ARE YOU BLUSH- ING?
B- BE- CAU- SE...
NO ...
NOBODY EVER GAVE ME ONE IN PERSON BEFORE.
IT WAS EMBAR- RASS- ING.
YOU GOT ALL THOSE?
SWIP
BAG HE USES FOR SCHOOL SUPPLIES
N... N...
HE'S ALREADY GOTTEN A BUNCH.
NOW'S MY CHANCE!!
SWUP!
HE PROBABLY WON'T EVEN NOTICE ONE MORE!!
WHAP

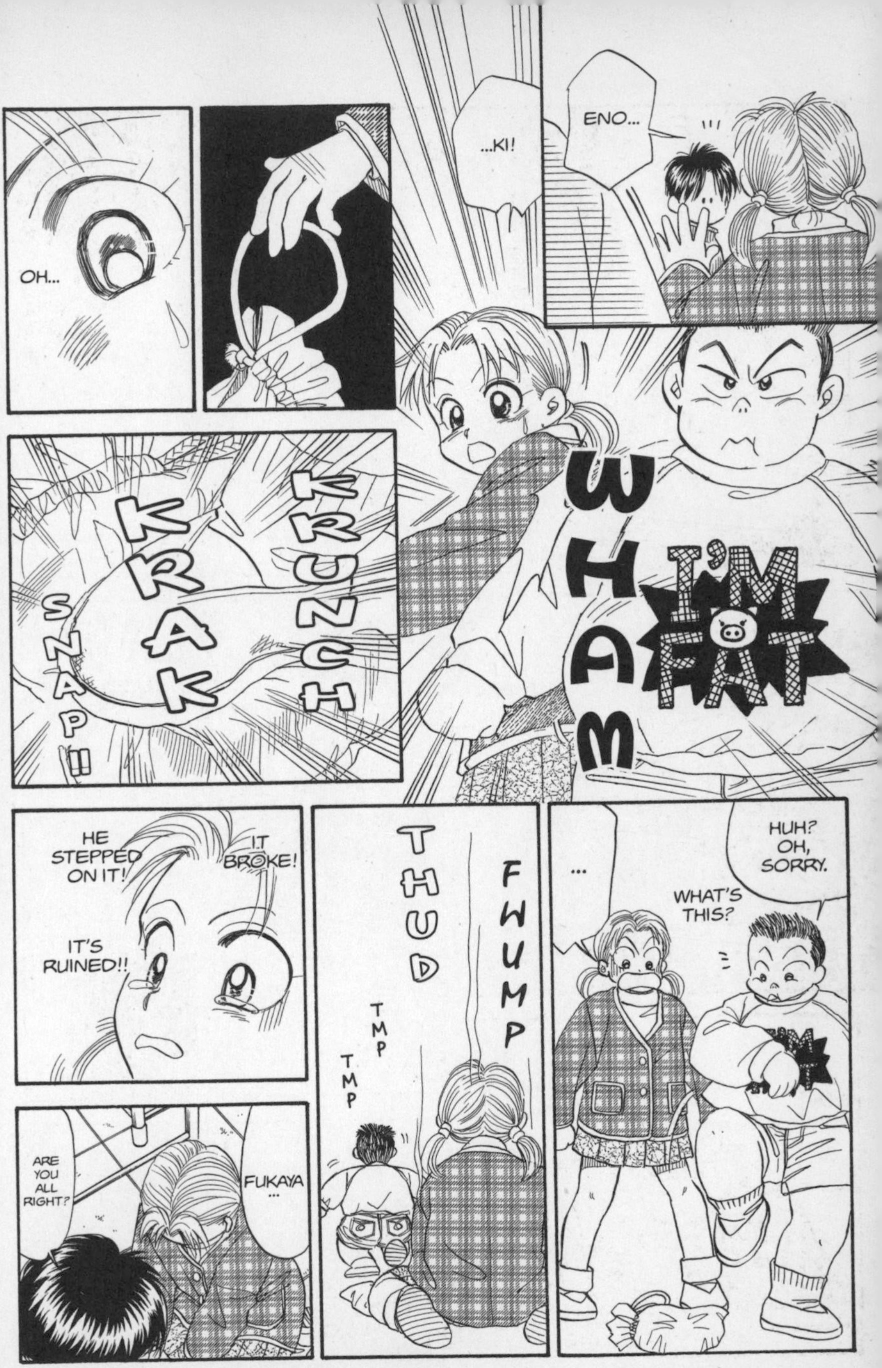
ENO...
...KI!
OH...
WHAM
I'M FAT
KRUNCH
KRAK
SNAP!!
HUH? OH, SORRY.
WHAT'S THIS?
...
THUD
FWUMP
TMP TMP
IT BROKE!
HE STEPPED ON IT!
IT'S RUINED!!
FUKAYA...
ARE YOU ALL RIGHT?

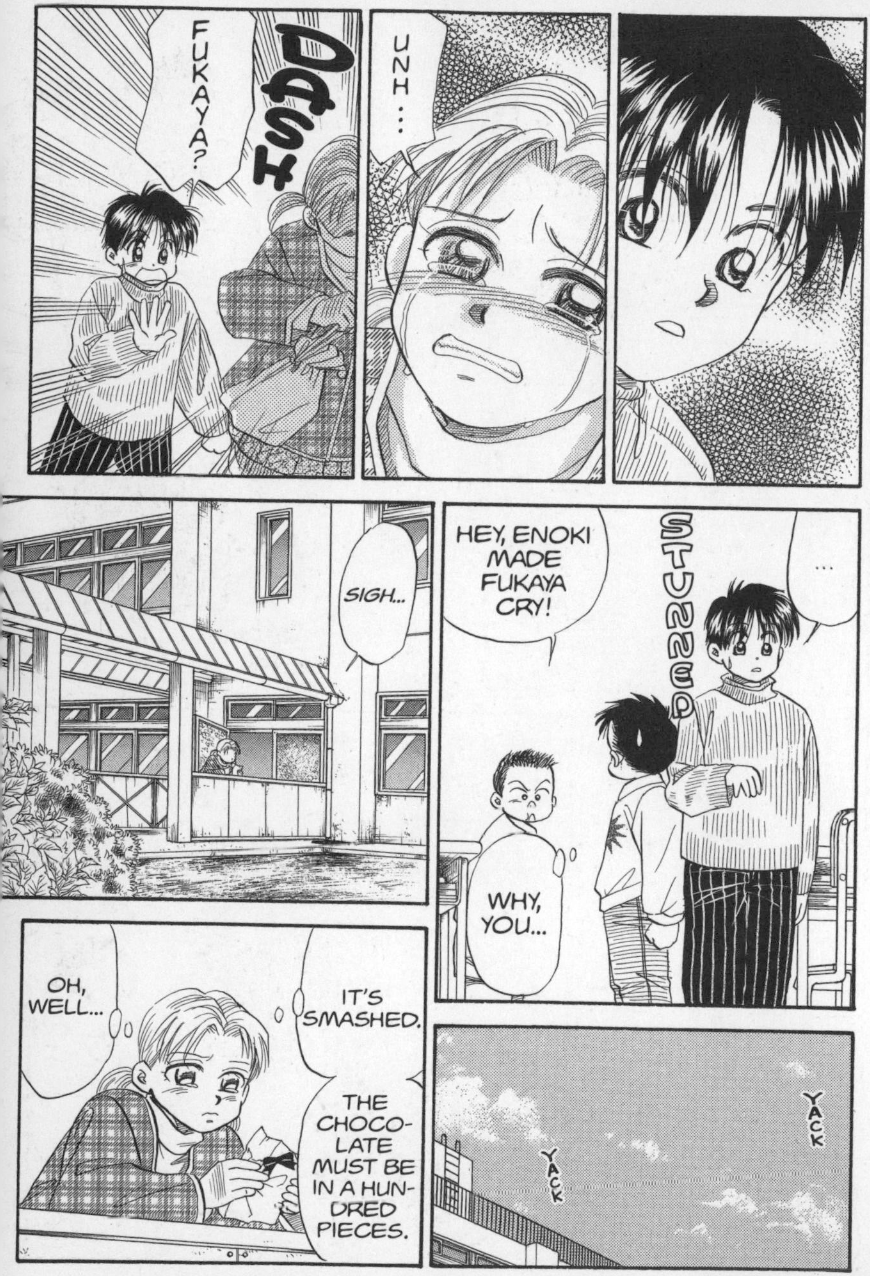
UNH...
DASH
FUKAYA?
...
STUNNED
HEY, ENOKI MADE FUKAYA CRY!
WHY, YOU...
SIGH...
YACK
YACK
IT'S SMASHED.
THE CHOCO-LATE MUST BE IN A HUN-DRED PIECES.
OH, WELL...

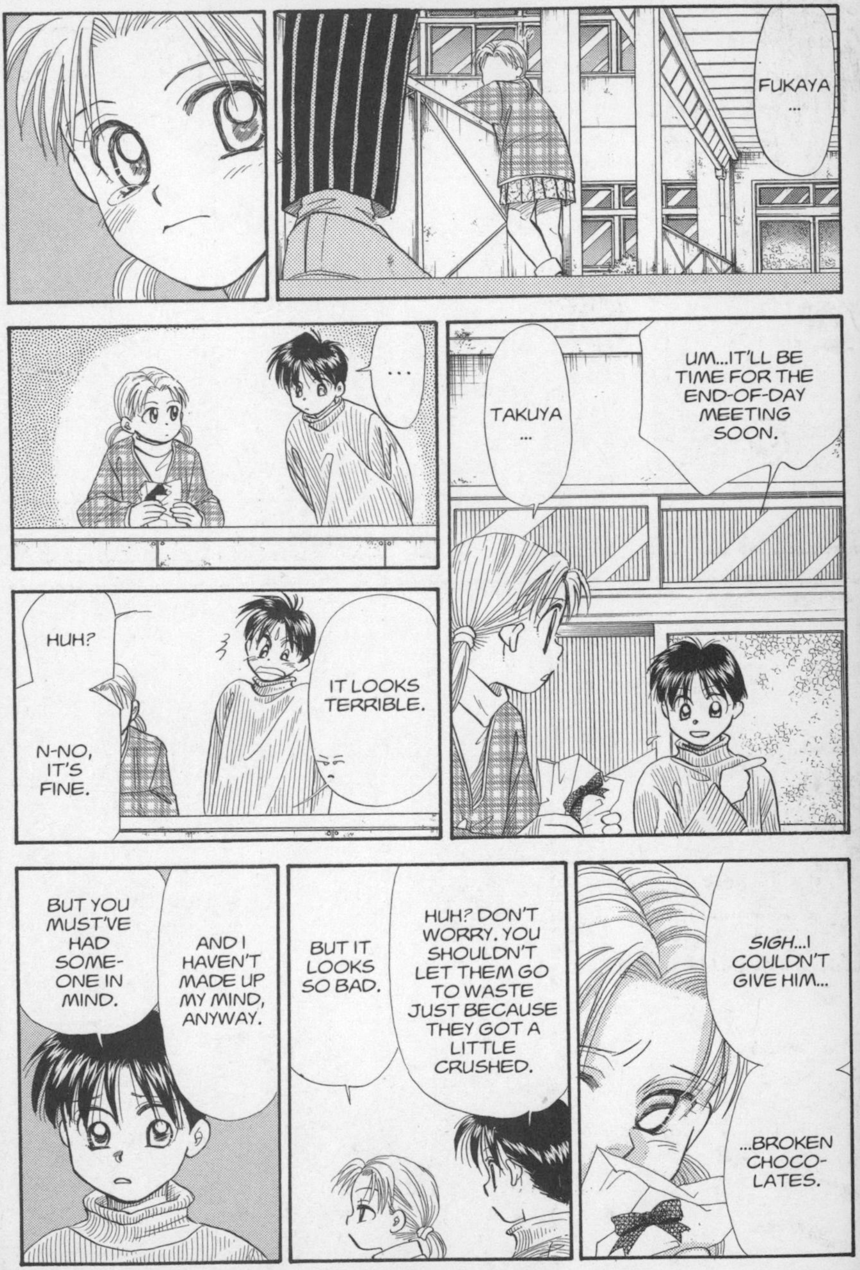
FUKAYA ...
UM...IT'LL BE TIME FOR THE END-OF-DAY MEETING SOON.
TAKUYA ...
...
IT LOOKS TERRIBLE.
HUH?
N-NO, IT'S FINE.
SIGH...I COULDN'T GIVE HIM...
...BROKEN CHOCOLATES.
HUH? DON'T WORRY. YOU SHOULDN'T LET THEM GO TO WASTE JUST BECAUSE THEY GOT A LITTLE CRUSHED.
BUT IT LOOKS SO BAD.
AND I HAVEN'T MADE UP MY MIND, ANYWAY.
BUT YOU MUST'VE HAD SOMEONE IN MIND.

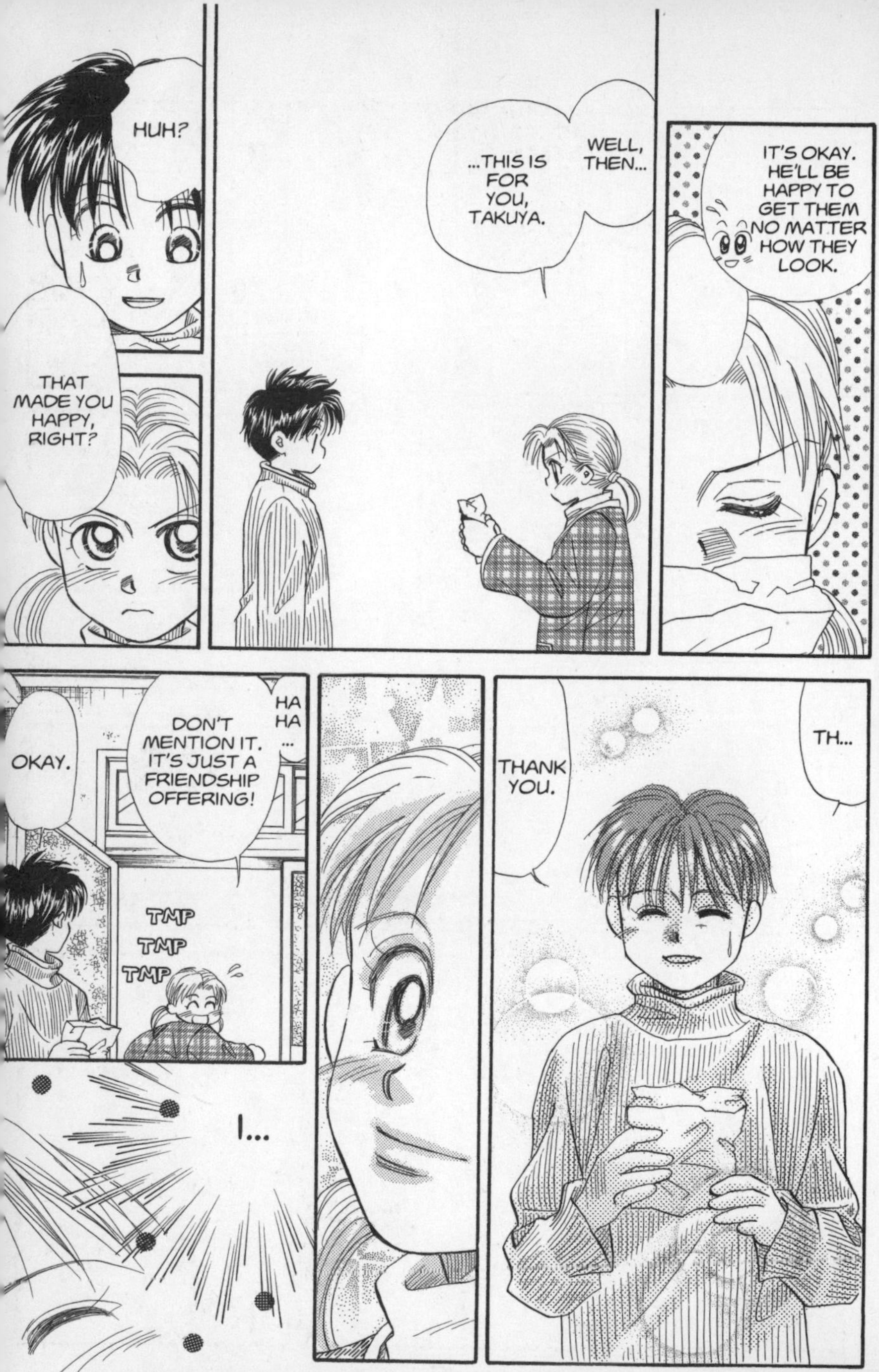
IT'S OKAY. HE'LL BE HAPPY TO GET THEM NO MATTER HOW THEY LOOK.
WELL, THEN...
...THIS IS FOR YOU, TAKUYA.
HUH?
THAT MADE YOU HAPPY, RIGHT?
TH...
THANK YOU.
HA HA ...
DON'T MENTION IT. IT'S JUST A FRIENDSHIP OFFERING!
OKAY.
TMP
TMP
TMP
I...

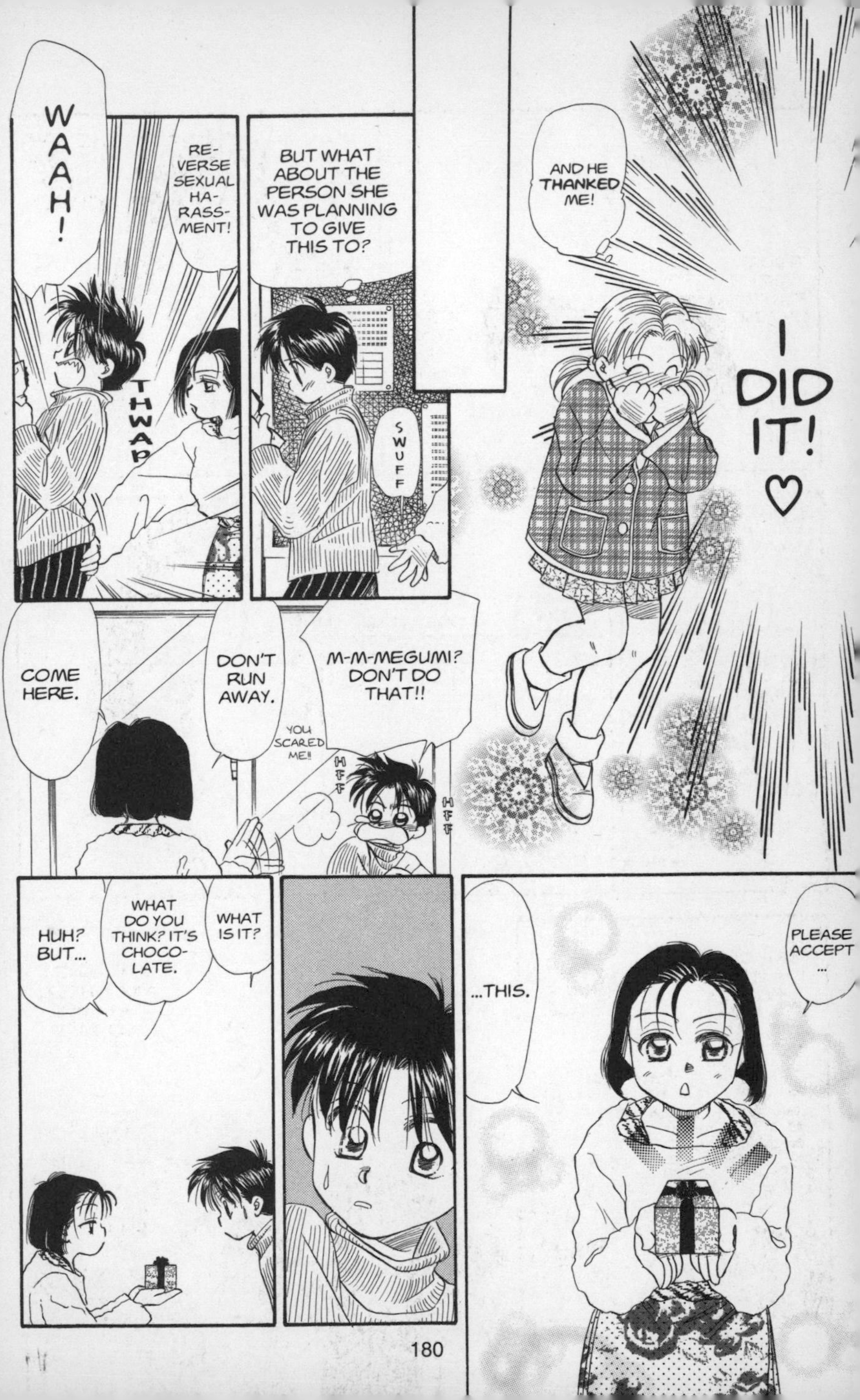
AND HE THANKED ME!
I DID IT! ♡
BUT WHAT ABOUT THE PERSON SHE WAS PLANNING TO GIVE THIS TO?
SWUFF
REVERSE SEXUAL HARASSMENT!
WAAH!
THWAP
M-M-MEGUMI? DON'T DO THAT!!
YOU SCARED ME!!
HFF
HFF
DON'T RUN AWAY.
COME HERE.
PLEASE ACCEPT ...
...THIS.
WHAT IS IT?
WHAT DO YOU THINK? IT'S CHOCOLATE.
HUH? BUT...

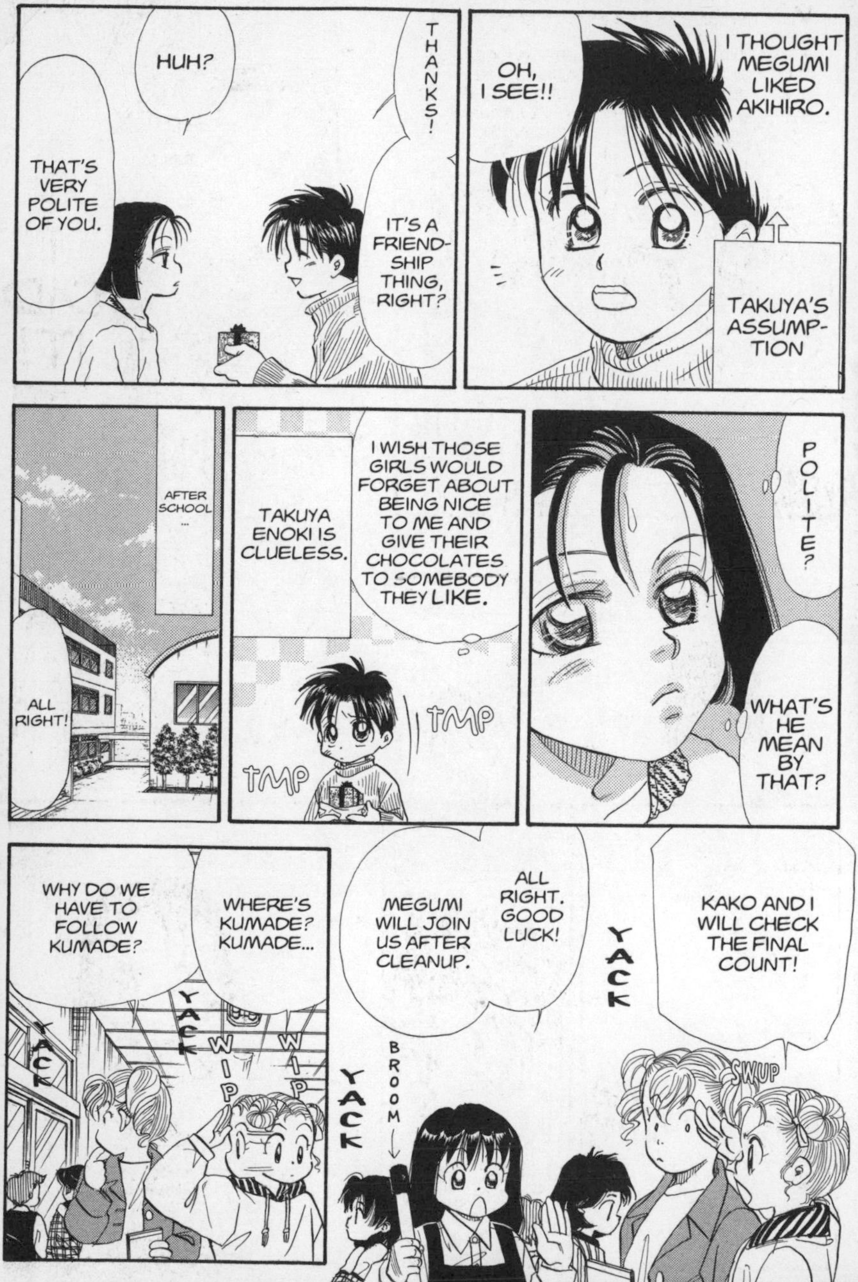
I THOUGHT MEGUMI LIKED AKIHIRO.
OH, I SEE!!
TAKUYA'S ASSUMPTION
THANKS!
HUH?
IT'S A FRIENDSHIP THING, RIGHT?
THAT'S VERY POLITE OF YOU.
POLITE?
WHAT'S HE MEAN BY THAT?
I WISH THOSE GIRLS WOULD FORGET ABOUT BEING NICE TO ME AND GIVE THEIR CHOCOLATES TO SOMEBODY THEY LIKE.
TAKUYA ENOKI IS CLUELESS.
TMP
TMP
AFTER SCHOOL...
ALL RIGHT!
KAKO AND I WILL CHECK THE FINAL COUNT!
SWUP
YACK
ALL RIGHT. GOOD LUCK!
MEGUMI WILL JOIN US AFTER CLEANUP.
BROOM
YACK
WHERE'S KUMADE? KUMADE...
WIP
WIP
YACK
WHY DO WE HAVE TO FOLLOW KUMADE?
YACK

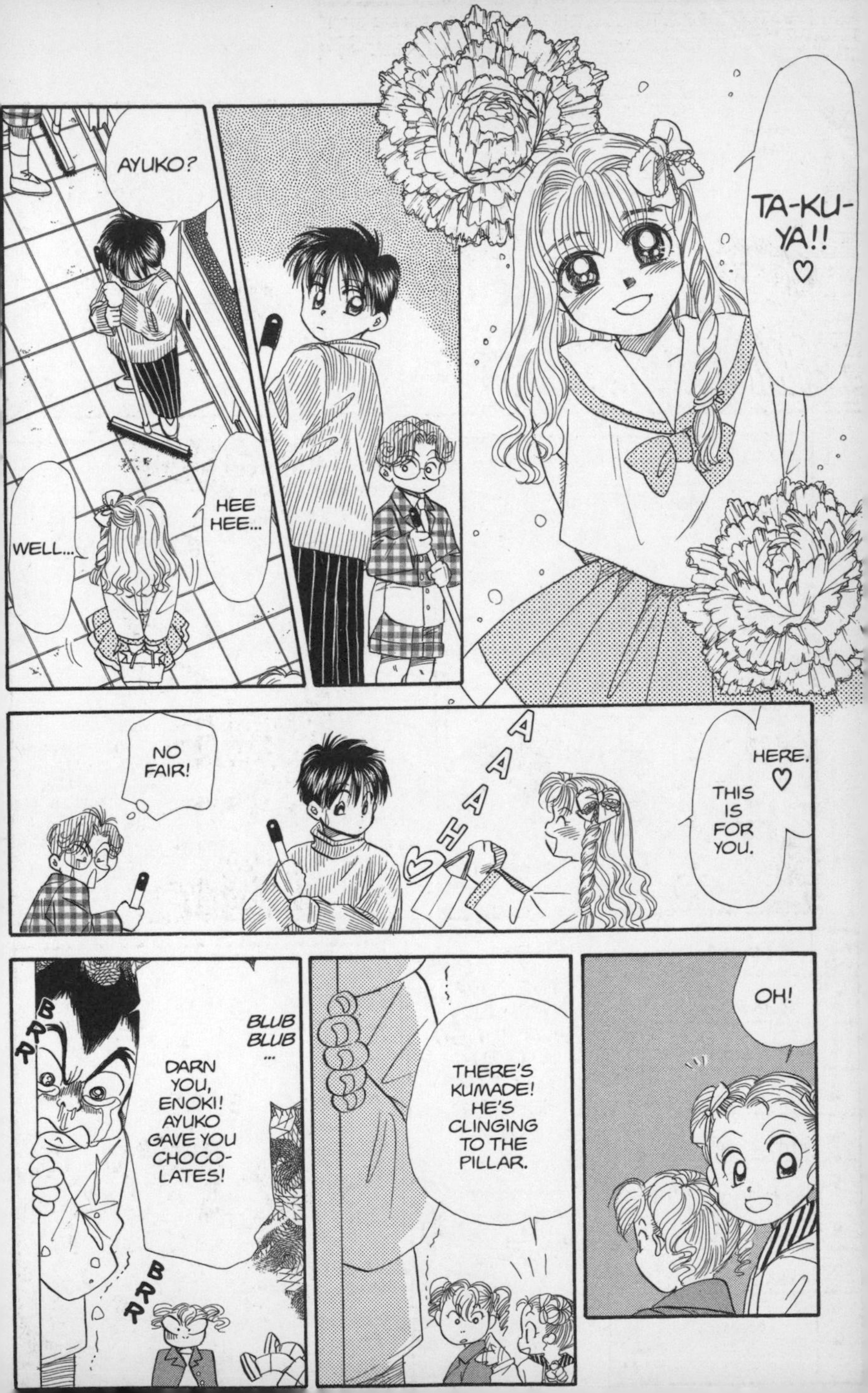
TA-KU-YA!! ♡
AYUKO?
HEE HEE...
WELL...
HERE. ♡ THIS IS FOR YOU.
HAAAA
NO FAIR!
OH!
THERE'S KUMADE! HE'S CLINGING TO THE PILLAR.
BLUB BLUB ...
DARN YOU, ENOKI! AYUKO GAVE YOU CHOCOLATES!
BRR
BRR

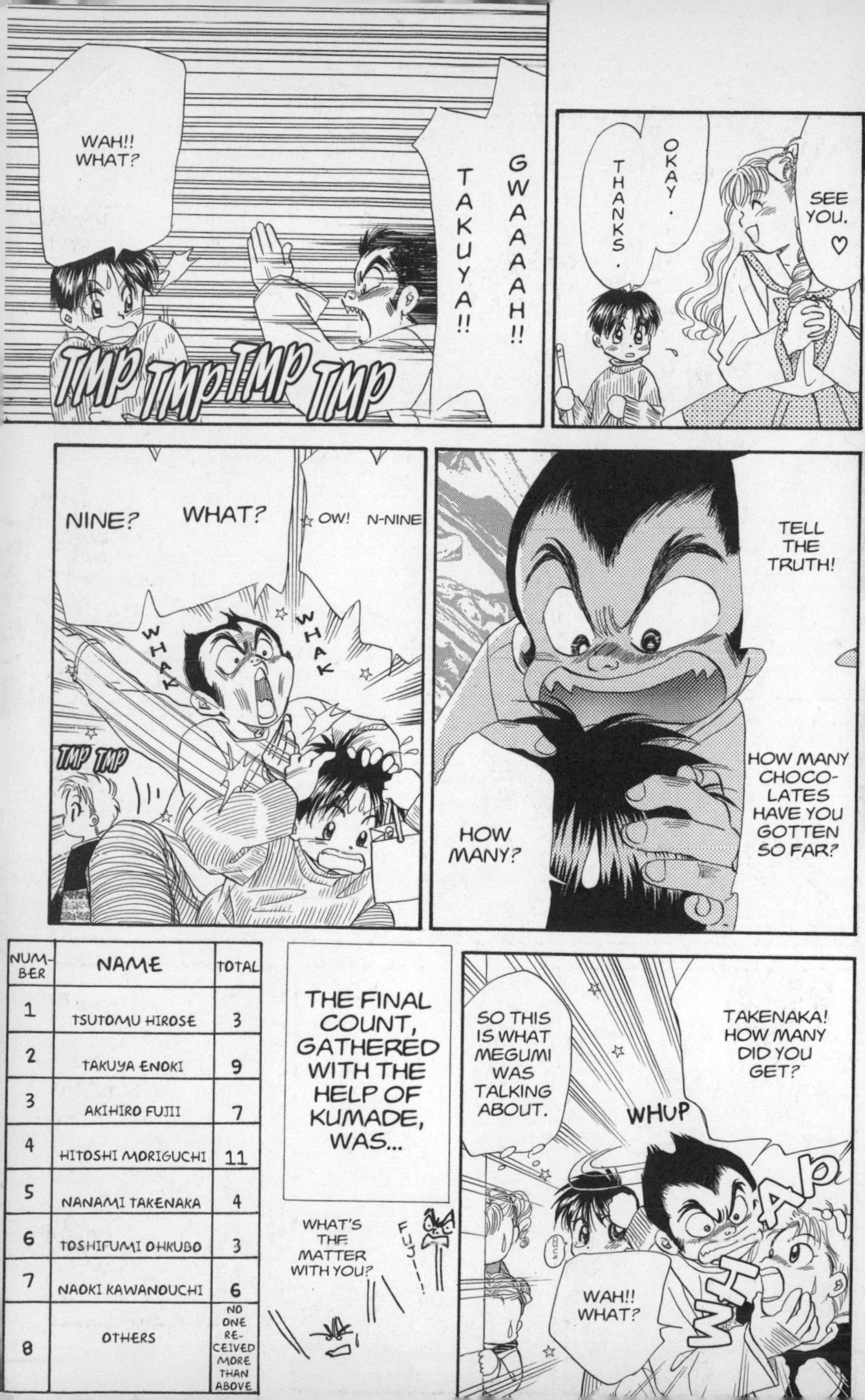
SEE YOU. ♥
OKAY. THANKS.
GWAAAAAH!!
TAKUYA!!
WAH!! WHAT?
TMP TMP TMP TMP
TELL THE TRUTH!
HOW MANY CHOCOLATES HAVE YOU GOTTEN SO FAR?
HOW MANY?
N-NINE
OW!
WHAT?
NINE?
WHAK WHAK
TMP TMP
TAKENAKA! HOW MANY DID YOU GET?
WHUP
SO THIS IS WHAT MEGUMI WAS TALKING ABOUT.
WHAP
WAH!! WHAT?
THE FINAL COUNT, GATHERED WITH THE HELP OF KUMADE, WAS...
FUJI--!
WHAT'S THE MATTER WITH YOU?

NUMBER	NAME	TOTAL
1	TSUTOMU HIROSE	3
2	TAKUYA ENOKI	9
3	AKIHIRO FUJII	7
4	HITOSHI MORIGUCHI	11
5	NANAMI TAKENAKA	4
6	TOSHIFUMI OHKUBO	3
7	NAOKI KAWANOUCHI	6
8	OTHERS	NO ONE RECEIVED MORE THAN ABOVE

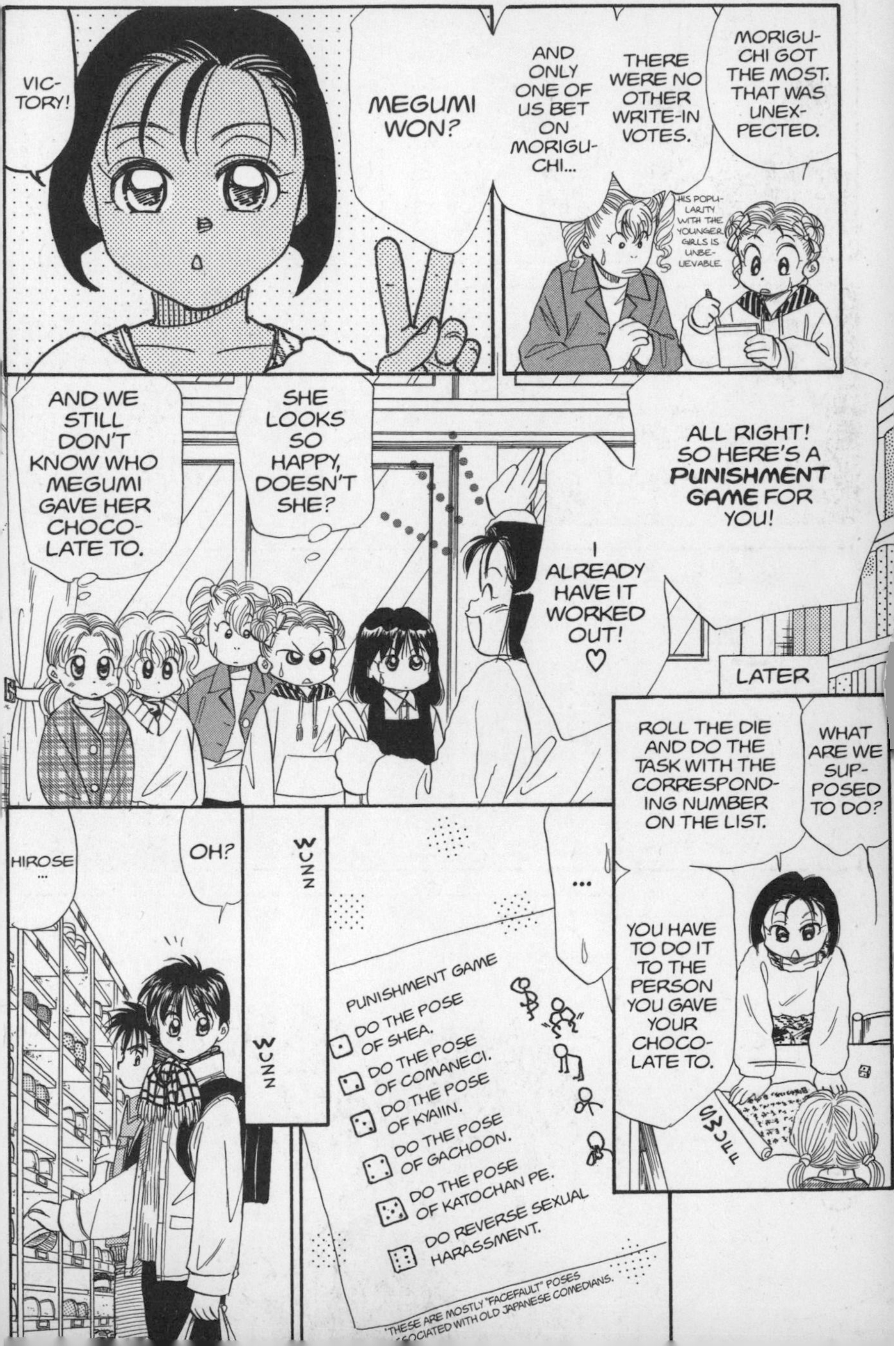
MORIGUCHI GOT THE MOST. THAT WAS UNEXPECTED.
THERE WERE NO OTHER WRITE-IN VOTES.
AND ONLY ONE OF US BET ON MORIGUCHI...
HIS POPULARITY WITH THE YOUNGER GIRLS IS UNBELIEVABLE.
MEGUMI WON?
VICTORY!
ALL RIGHT! SO HERE'S A **PUNISHMENT GAME** FOR YOU!
I ALREADY HAVE IT WORKED OUT! ♡
SHE LOOKS SO HAPPY, DOESN'T SHE?
AND WE STILL DON'T KNOW WHO MEGUMI GAVE HER CHOCOLATE TO.
LATER
WHAT ARE WE SUPPOSED TO DO?
ROLL THE DIE AND DO THE TASK WITH THE CORRESPONDING NUMBER ON THE LIST.
YOU HAVE TO DO IT TO THE PERSON YOU GAVE YOUR CHOCOLATE TO.
...
PUNISHMENT GAME
DO THE POSE OF SHEA.
DO THE POSE OF COMANECI.
DO THE POSE OF KYAIIN.
DO THE POSE OF GACHOON.
DO THE POSE OF KATOCHAN PE.
DO REVERSE SEXUAL HARASSMENT.
*THESE ARE MOSTLY "FACEFAULT" POSES ASSOCIATED WITH OLD JAPANESE COMEDIANS.
WUZZ
WUZZ
OH?
HIROSE...

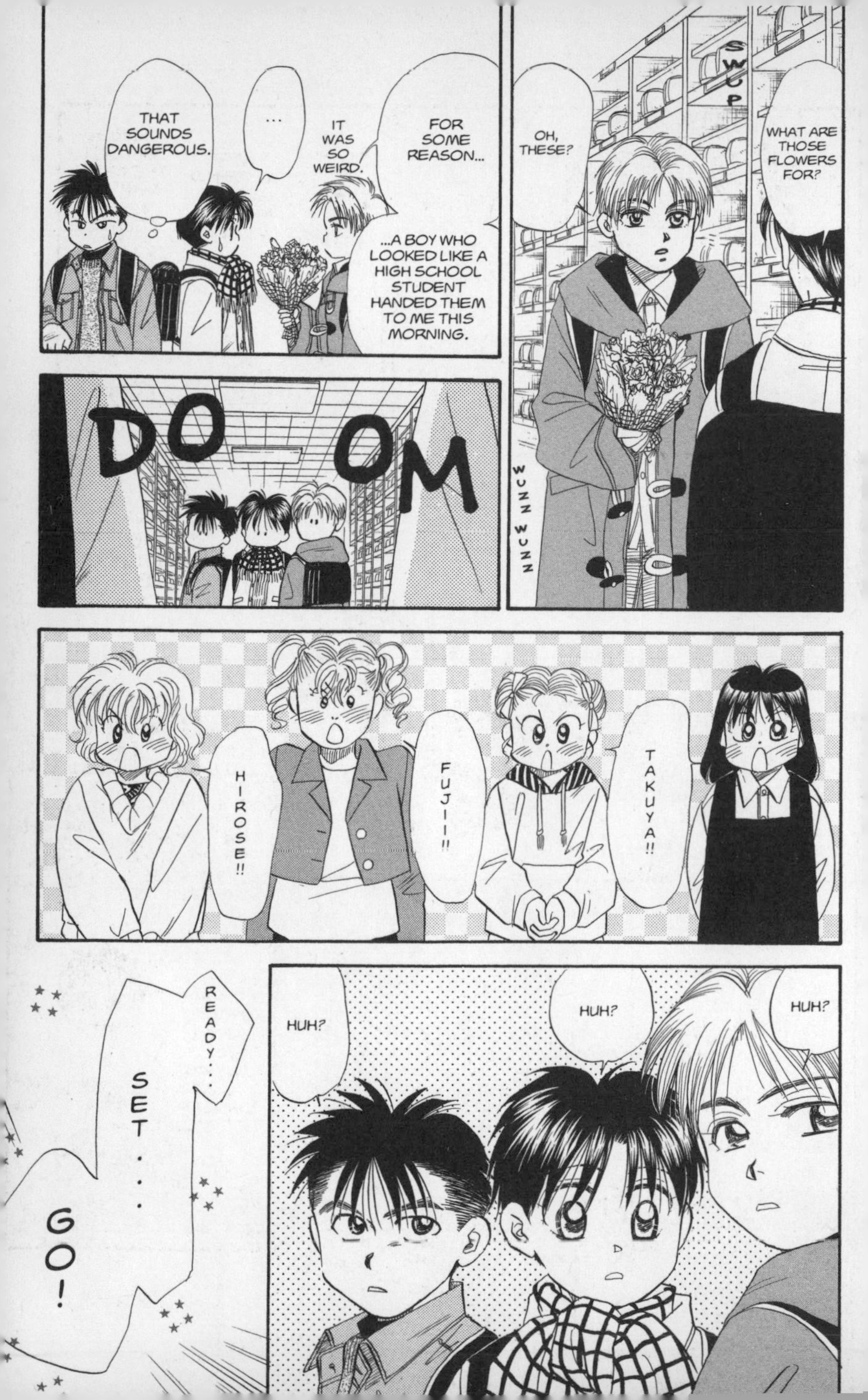
SWUP
WHAT ARE THOSE FLOWERS FOR?
OH, THESE?
WUNZ WUNZ
FOR SOME REASON...
...A BOY WHO LOOKED LIKE A HIGH SCHOOL STUDENT HANDED THEM TO ME THIS MORNING.
IT WAS SO WEIRD.
...
THAT SOUNDS DANGEROUS.
DO OM
TAKUYA!!
FUJI!!
HIROSE!!
HUH?
HUH?
HUH?
READY...
SET...
GO!

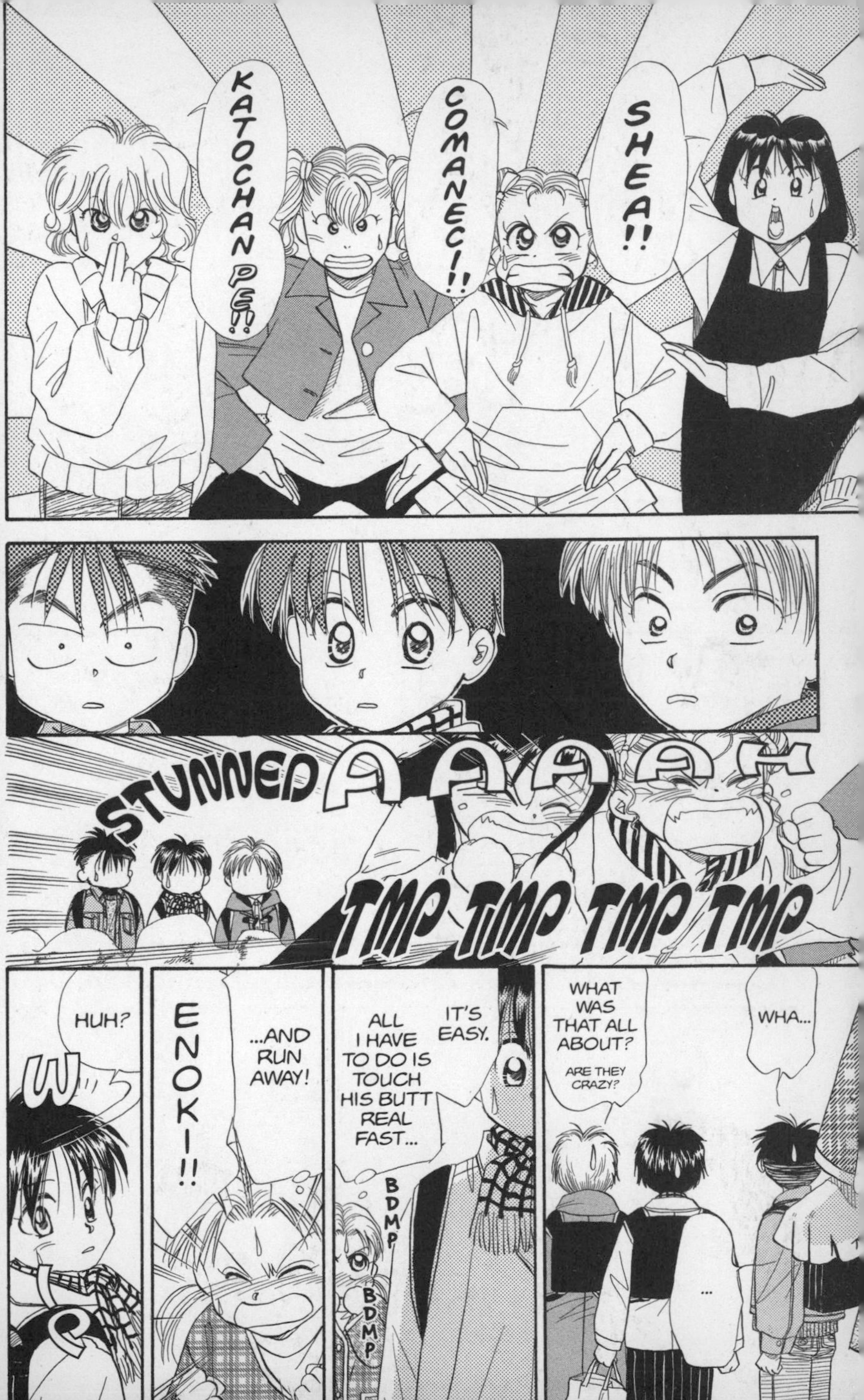
SHEA!!
COMANECI!!
KATOCHANPE!!
AAAAH
TMP TMP TMP TMP
STUNNED
WHA...
WHAT WAS THAT ALL ABOUT?
ARE THEY CRAZY?
...
IT'S EASY.
ALL I HAVE TO DO IS TOUCH HIS BUTT REAL FAST...
BDMP
BDMP
...AND RUN AWAY!
ENOKI!!
HUH?

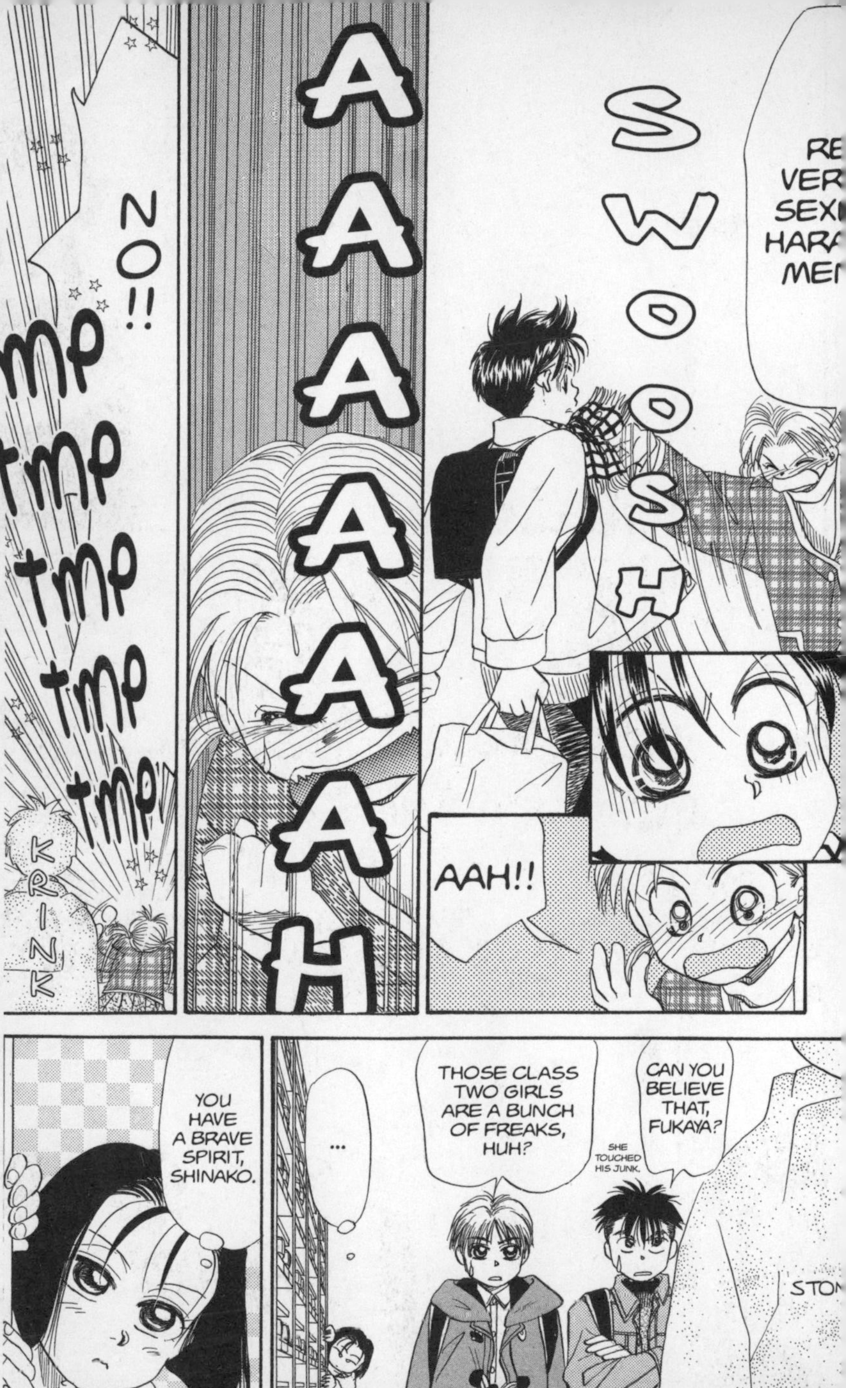
RE
VER
SEX
HARA
MEN
SWOOSH
AAH!!
AAAAAAH
NO!!
tmp tmp tmp tmp tmp
KRINK
STON
CAN YOU BELIEVE THAT, FUKAYA?
SHE TOUCHED HIS JUNK.
THOSE CLASS TWO GIRLS ARE A BUNCH OF FREAKS, HUH?
...
YOU HAVE A BRAVE SPIRIT, SHINAKO.

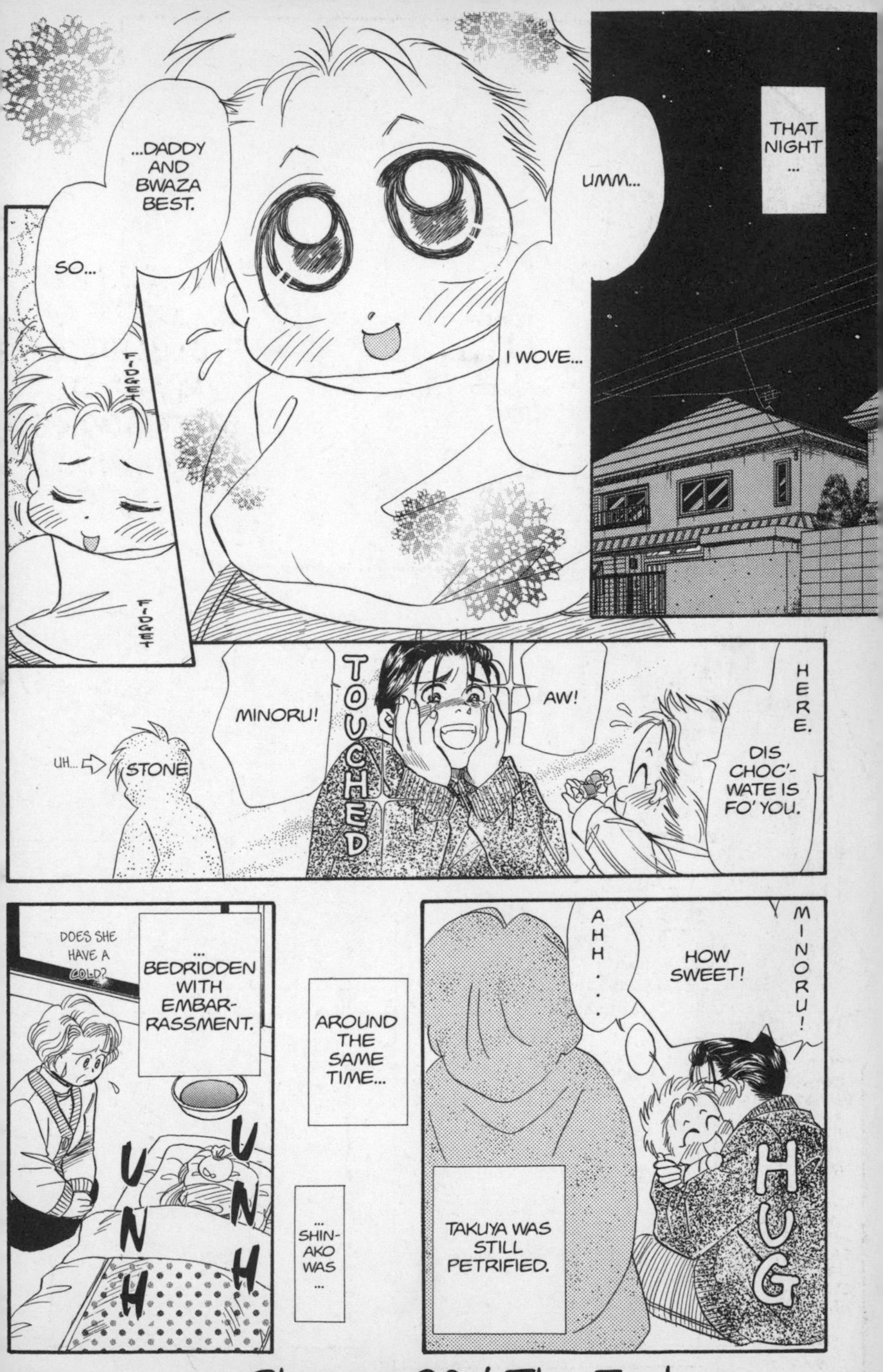
THAT NIGHT ...
UMM...
...DADDY AND BWAZA BEST.
I WOVE...
SO...
FIDGET
FIDGET
HERE. DIS CHOC'WATE IS FO' YOU.
AW!
TOUCHED
MINORU!
UH...
STONE
MINORU!
HOW SWEET!
AHH...
HUG
TAKUYA WAS STILL PETRIFIED.
AROUND THE SAME TIME...
...SHIN-AKO WAS ...
...BEDRIDDEN WITH EMBAR-RASSMENT.
DOES SHE HAVE A COLD?
UNH
UNH

Chapter 80 / The End

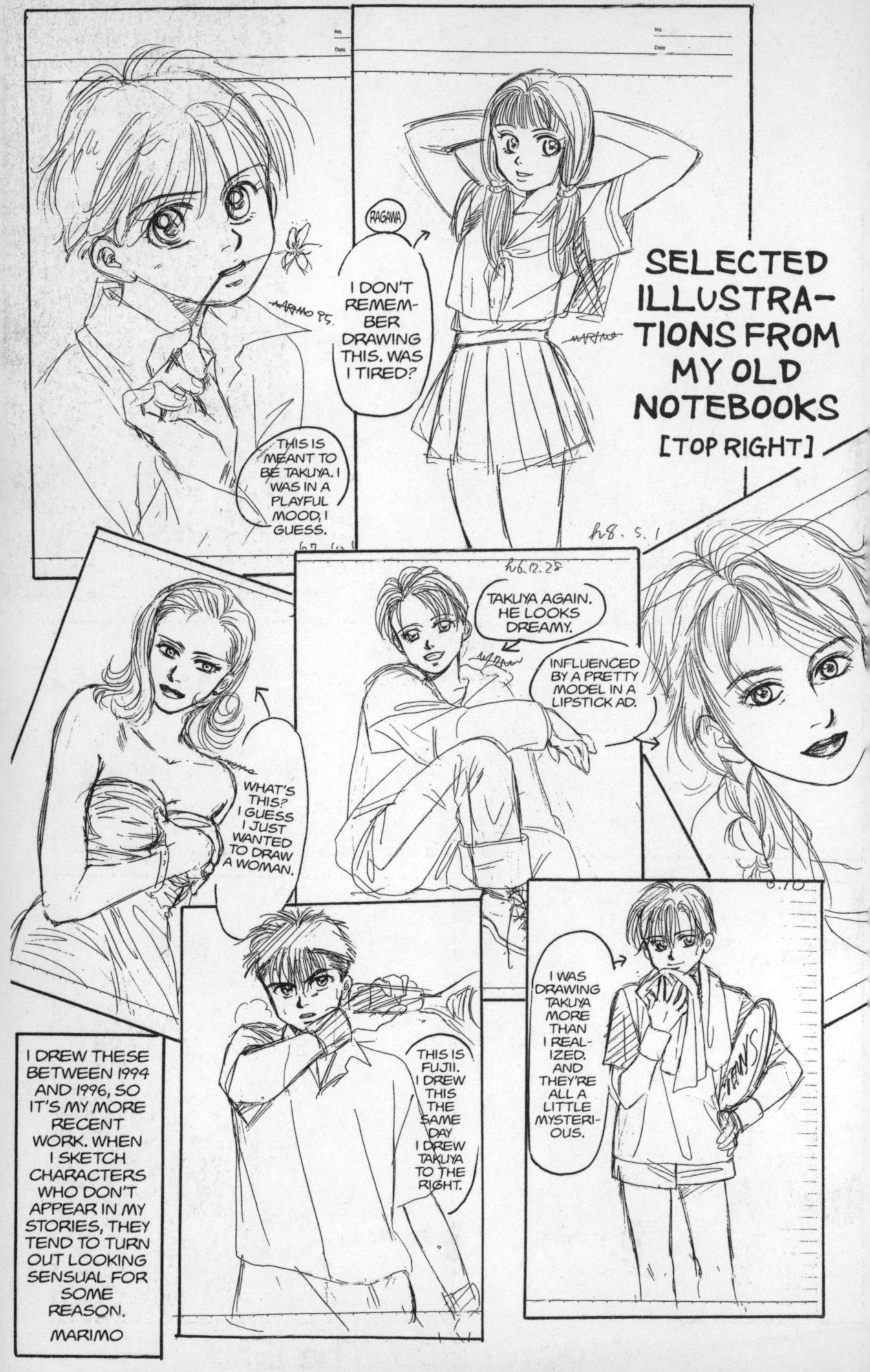

SELECTED ILLUSTRATIONS FROM MY OLD NOTEBOOKS
[TOP RIGHT]
RAGAWA
I DON'T REMEMBER DRAWING THIS. WAS I TIRED?
THIS IS MEANT TO BE TAKUYA. I WAS IN A PLAYFUL MOOD, I GUESS.
INFLUENCED BY A PRETTY MODEL IN A LIPSTICK AD.
TAKUYA AGAIN. HE LOOKS DREAMY.
WHAT'S THIS? I GUESS I JUST WANTED TO DRAW A WOMAN.
I WAS DRAWING TAKUYA MORE THAN I REALIZED. AND THEY'RE ALL A LITTLE MYSTERIOUS.
THIS IS FUJII. I DREW THIS THE SAME DAY I DREW TAKUYA TO THE RIGHT.
I DREW THESE BETWEEN 1994 AND 1996, SO IT'S MY MORE RECENT WORK. WHEN I SKETCH CHARACTERS WHO DON'T APPEAR IN MY STORIES, THEY TEND TO TURN OUT LOOKING SENSUAL FOR SOME REASON.
MARIMO

————AS YOU MAY KNOW...

LET'S CELEBRATE!

...*BABY & ME* IS GOING TO BE AN ANIME!

BY THE TIME THIS VOLUME COMES OUT, THE SHOW WILL ALREADY BE ON THE AIR. BEST OF LUCK TO ALL THE CREW AND THE VOICE ACTORS! BUTTER THEM UP, TAKUYA!

I'D LIKE TO THANK EVERYONE IN ADVANCE!

PLEASE ACCEPT THIS SMALL GIFT AS A TOKEN OF MY APPRECIATION.

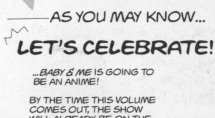

NMM

A SMALL GIFT

TOTALLY UNCON-CERNED

SWUP

WELL, THEN... SEE YOU IN VOLUME 15! MARIMO, ~~NE~~ 9, 1996

3 1901 05270 7371